Shifting Grounds

Shifting Grounds

The Social Origins of Territorial Conflict

Burak Kadercan

OXFORD
UNIVERSITY PRESS

Oxford University Press is a department of the University of Oxford. It furthers the University's objective of excellence in research, scholarship, and education by publishing worldwide. Oxford is a registered trade mark of Oxford University Press in the UK and certain other countries.

Published in the United States of America by Oxford University Press 198 Madison Avenue, New York, NY 10016, United States of America.

© Oxford University Press 2023

All rights reserved. No part of this publication may be reproduced, stored in a retrieval system, or transmitted, in any form or by any means, without the prior permission in writing of Oxford University Press, or as expressly permitted by law, by license, or under terms agreed with the appropriate reproduction rights organization. Inquiries concerning reproduction outside the scope of the above should be sent to the Rights Department, Oxford University Press, at the address above.

You must not circulate this work in any other form and you must impose this same condition on any acquirer.

Library of Congress Cataloging-in-Publication Data
Names: Kadercan, Burak, author.
Title: Shifting grounds : the social origins of territorial conflict / Burak Kadercan.
Description: New York, NY : Oxford University Press, [2023] |
Includes bibliographical references and index.
Identifiers: LCCN 2023011916 (print) | LCCN 2023011917 (ebook) |
ISBN 9780197686690 (hardback) | ISBN 9780197686713 | ISBN 9780197686706 (epub) |
ISBN 9780197686720
Subjects: LCSH: Territory, National. | Boundaries. | War—Causes. |
Geopolitics. | Nationalism. | Political geography.
Classification: LCC JZ3675 .K34 2023 (print) | LCC JZ3675 (ebook) |
DDC 320.1/2—dc23/eng/20230411
LC record available at https://lccn.loc.gov/2023011916
LC ebook record available at https://lccn.loc.gov/2023011917

DOI: 10.1093/oso/9780197686690.001.0001

Printed by Integrated Books International, United States of America

For Batu

Contents

Acknowledgments	ix

1. Introduction: A Tale of Two Countries	1

PART I. CONCEPTUAL AND THEORETICAL FRAMEWORK

2. Territory, War, and the "Territorial Trap"	23
3. Territorial Orders and War	43

PART II. HOW TERRITORIAL IDEAS AFFECT WARS

4. Rigid Borders, Spasmodic Wars: Mosaic and Monolithic Territorial Orders	67
5. Fluid Frontiers and Forever War I: Amorphous Territorial Orders	108
6. Fluid Frontiers and Forever War II: Virulent Territorial Orders	140

PART III. HOW WARS AFFECT TERRITORIAL IDEAS

7. Systemic Wars and the Evolution of Territorial Orders	175
8. Conclusion: Territory and Territoriality in the Twenty-First Century	229

References	265
Index	295

Acknowledgments

Every book tells a story, just like every book has its own story. The story behind *Shifting Grounds* involves many individuals who have helped me in many different ways, in different times, in different geographies. Without those individuals, this book would not be possible in the first place; in more ways than I can count, I owe this book to them. I apologize in advance to those I may have missed, since the list is rather long, but a chronological approach can hopefully help me invoke as many of those individuals as I possibly can.

This book began as a dissertation at the Department of Political Science at the University of Chicago. Even though the book evolved into something else entirely, it was at the University of Chicago where I first began to experiment with ideas about the nature, or the meaning, of territory in international politics. Therefore, my first debt of gratitude is to my dissertation committee, comprising Duncan Snidal, John Mearsheimer, and Charles Lipson. Charles was instrumental in forcing me to think "historically"; his uncanny mastery of the history of the modern state system, not to mention keen eye for *seemingly* small details, inspired me greatly.

John Mearsheimer, in many ways, was my rock and has been so throughout my career. John never wore kid gloves when it came to criticism, but he was always there for me whenever I needed his good advice. I learned tremendously from John, but probably the most valuable lesson involved his openness and penchant for new, *big* ideas, even, or especially, when those ideas challenged his own. I went to Chicago as a young, aspiring graduate student to work with John Mearsheimer, to become a "neorealist." I ended up building much of my career on criticizing neorealism, but John couldn't care less. He did not care if I was a realist or this and that. He pushed me to think "big," or think like an IR theorist as he would say, regardless of where those thoughts took me. In that, he was a great mentor. Furthermore, this entire project was inspired by a certain course that John has been teaching at Chicago, *for decades*: War and the Nation-State. I still remember the time, as a young teaching assistant for the course, when I began thinking about where territory and territoriality stood in terms of the relationship between armed conflict and the so-called modern states.

x Acknowledgments

Duncan Snidal was probably my ultimate linchpin at the University of Chicago. His open-mindedness, impeccable logic, supernatural work ethic, and soft-spoken but razor-sharp attitude have all set the bar for me as a scholar. To be precise, it was, and still remains, a very high bar; yet, to this day, Duncan serves as an "aspirational model" for me. Duncan's natural ability to sift through and combine a diverse array of disciplines, methods, and approaches was probably what inspired me most. From him I learned the invaluable lesson of *not* confining oneself to a certain discipline, certain method, or a certain school of thought. A graduate student cannot ask for a better chair or a better mentor.

I'd also like to thank my fellow graduate students at Chicago, who have helped me grow as a thinker and a scholar. I do not remember a single day in campus that went without some heated debate about IR theories or foreign affairs. Every single one of these debates helped me learn how to better formulate my ideas, receive criticism with grace, and offer constructive criticism in return. Of my fellow graduate students, I'd like to thank especially Ahsan Butt. Over the years, we remained in touch, both personally and academically, and I benefited greatly from his wise advice, especially with respect to *Shifting Grounds*. Ahsan read multiple versions of multiple chapters over the years, and, as he used to do when we were both at Chicago as graduate students, he helped me to formulate my arguments.

In 2011, I took my first assistant professor position at Institut Barcelona d'Estudis Internacionals (IBEI). Trained in the so-called American IR, my time in Barcelona was an eye-opener; I was exposed to a wide variety of approaches and ideas, which forced me to rethink how I approached what I was studying. It was during my time at IBEI that I began to think of "territory" in a more sophisticated way. Fellow scholars such as Fulya Apaydın and Matthias vom Hau, and the excellent research seminars held at IBEI, made my stay in Barcelona an intellectually enriching experience. In 2013, I moved to the University of Reading. In the UK, I became even more appreciative of the constructivist and critical approaches to IR, and benefited greatly from interacting with scholars like Patrick Porter and Tarak Barkawi.

I finally moved to the US Naval War College, my current institution, in 2014. My time here has been exceptionally rewarding. In my department, Strategy and Policy, I ended up not only teaching, but also coteaching with, countless military officers. Of those, Commander Rob Krivacs (retired) deserves special credit. Rob has not only been an amazing friend, but also a sanity check of some sort. Whenever I needed an additional pair of eyes for my obscure, half-cooked manuscripts, he was always there. His sharp mind, unworldly attention to detail, and unyielding penchant for helping me write better and clearer proved invaluable. I can only hope that he can one day forgive me for the hundreds of semifinished pages I made him read; I don't think I can ever repay my debt. At the college, I was also blessed with extremely smart and accommodating colleagues. Dave Stone and Kevin McCraine, as department chairs, have always been extremely helpful; with their support, I was able to secure research grants to travel to the Library of Congress and take my research to numerous conferences and workshops. I also would like to thank the US Naval War College and its support; the college also granted me a sabbatical during parts of 2017–18 that allowed me to formulate the very ideas that eventually paved the way for *Shifting Grounds*. My colleague Michael Dennis has always been first to volunteer to offer comments for various segments of the broader research project. Dave Stone was kind enough to provide very valuable comments for the segment on the Russo-Ukrainian War.

I also would like to thank a certain individual, John Agnew. For me, John has been an inspiration in more than one way. *Before* I met him in person, he served as a key inspiration, if only via his scholarly contribution to the study of territory. In fact, John's research was *the* portal through which I was able to glance at the incredibly rich literature in political geography. For someone like me, who was trained as a political scientist at the University of Chicago, who worked with John Mearsheimer (the realist) and Duncan Snidal (the rational choice theorist), Agnew's writings were like a bucket of ice thrown right at my face; they acted as true eye-openers. I realized that even though I had long believed that I was studying "territorial conflicts" from a macrohistorical perspective, like many IR scholars, I did not have a good understanding of the term "territory" itself. Once I saw what Agnew meant by the "territorial trap," I could not *unsee* it. I had only two options: ignore political geography (as many in IR scholarship do) or train myself to better understand it. Taking Agnew's writings as my cue, I eventually got myself into what looked like a rabbit hole at the time, but still decided to move toward an interdisciplinary approach that brought together insights from both IR and political geography. It was quite a journey, and it was quite a challenge. I spent a couple of years trying to teach myself "how to read political geography" as if I were learning a new language, and a couple of more years on top of that to synthesize ideas that would be amenable to both IR scholars and political geographers. I eventually learned, loud and clear, that while interdisciplinary research is an ever-popular catchphrase, it also comes with the risk of being seen as "too IR" (or "not enough IR") or "too political geography" (or "not enough political geography") by many. It was xii Acknowledgments

at this juncture, when I was having second thoughts about interdisciplinary research, that I met John Agnew in person, I believe around 2015. John is a *mensch*. When we met, in fact even before we met, he began to generously support my project, offering me sage advice, always helping me better understand the literature in political geography. Over the years, he has become a mentor, in fact, *the* mentor for this book. He's read an earlier version of the manuscript, not to mention numerous segments of the broader project, always offering extremely valuable comments. It is safe to say that without John's unyielding support and encouragement, this book would not have been possible in the first place.

During the interdisciplinary journey that birthed this book, I also came across numerous scholars from whom I benefited greatly. Boaz Atzili is probably at the top of that list. Somewhere down the line, we discovered that we were both interested in the possibility of direct interaction between IR scholars and political geographers. Boaz and I eventually spearheaded and coedited a special issue for *Territory, Politics, Governance* (which was later picked up as a book by Routledge), built around what we dubbed as territorial designs, that brought together IR scholars like Jordan Branch and Harris Mylonas and political geographers like Gerry Kearns. Boaz also read a good portion of an earlier manuscript, and offered laser-sharp comments that helped me clarify my arguments. I have never met Gerard Toal in person, but have been impressed by his unparalleled generosity; Gerard actually did read almost the entire manuscript (an older version) and offered not only great comments, but also great encouragement. Over the years, Sinem Arslan provided excellent comments on the project. I also would like to thank Alex Wendt and the editorial team (and reviewers) for *International Theory*; back in 2015, Alex and the editorial team went to great lengths to offer incredibly constructive feedback for my very first article on the possibility of interdisciplinary dialogues between IR and political geography.

Beyond the institutions where I have taught, the Fletcher School's Center for Strategic Studies (CSS) at Tufts University played a crucial role in finalizing this book. I spent my sabbatical there during parts of 2017–18, as an inaugural fellow. I couldn't ask for a better environment to sort out the conceptual and analytical framework that lies at the heart of this book. Monica Toft, Kerim El Kady, Thomas Cavanna, and Rita Konaev, among other CSS fellows, provided exceptionally helpful feedback on various segments of the book. Rita, in particular, pushed me to think more like a "simplifier" and less like a "complexifier." I also had the good fortune of being able to present my research in numerous outlets, including but not limited to the Belfer Center at Harvard Kennedy School, political science departments at Ohio State University and

University of Central Florida, School of International Service at American University, and the Department of Geography at UCLA. The Department of Geography at UCLA deserves special credit; the comments I received from geographers were instrumental in reshaping my ideas about territoriality. I also benefited greatly from the reviewers' and editors' comments at *Territory, Politics, Governance* and *Cambridge Review of International Affairs*, where some of the arguments in the book previously appeared (reprinted with permission from Burak Kadercan, "Territorial Logic of the Islamic State: An Interdisciplinary Approach," *Territory, Politics, Governance* 9 [1] , Winter 2021; "Territorial Design and Grand Strategy in the Ottoman Empire," *Territory, Politics, Governance* 5 [2], Spring 2017; "Nationalism and War for Territory: From 'Divisible' Territories to Inviolable Homelands," *Cambridge Review of International Affairs* 30 [4], Summer 2017). At Oxford University Press, Dave McBride made the process as smooth as is humanly possible. Two anonymous reviewers, in my book (pun intended), are nothing but stars; their comments were not always easy to address, *but they were great comments* that helped me improve the final product in ways that I had not thought about before.

Finally, I owe a great debt to two special individuals who have helped me make it through the entire process. I dedicate this book to my son, Batu. Ever since he entered my life, he has been my beacon of hope, my ultimate motivator, my North Star when I felt like I was perhaps drifting away from whatever I was trying to accomplish. When I finally decided to turn my collection of ideas on territory into a book project some six years ago, Batu and I were mostly talking about dinosaurs, sharks, and the like. Our conversations these days are mostly about the intricacies of world history and Metallica (to be honest, probably more about the latter, especially about how to play Metallica songs together). In a way, as I was working on the book, I was also watching him grow. So this book means much more to me than just *a* book; it is also the story of me watching my son grow while writing my first book. Batu was also watching me as I was writing the book; as a thirteen-year-old who has always been exceptionally curious about history and geography, he can now easily deliver the "elevator pitch" for the book, probably far better than I ever can. Last but not least, I owe an unparalleled gratitude to my wife, my "good news," Müjde. Her unflinching support and faith in me kept me going through thick and thin; more precisely, it was her unflinching support and faith in me that kept me going. She is a computer scientist by training and trade, far removed from what I study, but that didn't stop her from listening to and reading almost every revision that I came up with over the years. She *always* offered sage, practical, and actionable advice. When I look at the cover of the finished

xiv Acknowledgments

manuscript, I see my son's face; when I peruse the individual pages, I see Müjde's patience, her analytical mind, and our, daily, never-ending "book talks" on our porch. I feel blessed to have such a loving and supportive family. They say writing a book is often a thankless job. It may be so; but when I was writing *this* book, I had these two wonderful people in my life, and their love kept me grounded, and kept me going, *every single day*. For that, I remain eternally thankful to Batu and Müjde.

Shifting Grounds

1

Introduction

A Tale of Two Countries

> Germany, but where does it lie? [I] do not know how to find the country.
> —**Johann Wolfgang von Goethe and Friedrich Schiller**[1]

> We are not here today [in this battle] to defend a line, we are here to defend a territory. And that territory is the whole of the homeland.
> —**Mustafa Kemal Atatürk, during the Turkish War of Independence (1919–23)**[2]

In September 2015, German chancellor Angela Merkel declared that she was "happy that Germany has become a country that many people abroad associate with hope."[3] Merkel was setting the grounds for the decision to welcome undocumented asylum seekers from the Middle East and beyond to Germany. This was a momentous decision: as of 2022, the number of refugees in Germany was around 1.2 million, up from 240,000 in 2014. The ways in which Merkel framed the new German policy over refugees and asylum seekers in 2015 was particularly informative: the German chancellor highlighted that this decision was "something very valuable, especially in view of our history."[4]

Merkel's emphasis on "our history" had a lot to do with Germany's horrendous actions during World War II. This reference to Germany's less-than-ideal past was not one-off. For example, in May 2015, Merkel went on the record to suggest that "we Germans have a special responsibility to be alert, sensitive and aware of what we did during the Nazi era and about lasting damage caused

---

[1] Quoted in Smith 2020, xvi.
[2] Quoted in Ronart 1937, 127. The author's own translation.
[3] Mihret Yohannes, "Angela Merkel Welcomes Refugees to Germany Despite Rising Anti-immigrant Movement," *Washington Times*, September 10, 2015, https://www.washingtontimes.com/news/2015/sep/10/angela-merkel-welcomes-refugees-to-germany-despite/.
[4] Yohannes, "Angela Merkel Welcomes Refugees."

Shifting Grounds. Burak Kadercan, Oxford University Press. © Oxford University Press 2023.
DOI: 10.1093/oso/9780197686690.003.0001

2 Shifting Grounds

in other countries."[5] In this master narrative, Germany, a country once closely associated with the horrors of World War II, was finally becoming a land of hope for the dispossessed and the oppressed across the globe. Not surprisingly, Merkel's decision over refugees and asylum seekers triggered a backlash from the right-wing parties, who made the case that opening the borders to refugees in such a drastic way was anathema to the very principles that made Germany what it was for centuries, an ethnically homogeneous nation-state exclusively for Germans.[6]

The question then becomes, what *is* Germany? On the one hand, Germany is a sovereign nation-state that is also a leading participant in the boldest supranational experiment in the modern age, the European Union (EU). Germany no longer has its own national currency, a hallmark of many nation-states, but instead uses the euro, just like most EU countries. Unlike most nation-states, Germany's borders are essentially permeable if mainly by the citizens and residents of other EU member states. While its pre-1945 history was marked by numerous wars, Germany is also a peaceful nation-state that has not directly participated in a major conflict since.

On the other hand, Germany is also a territory, defined by a certain set of discrete borders and its own unique societal arrangements. Of course, the Germany-as-territory interpretation begs a question: where is Germany? At face value, this is an easy question to answer. The German territory can be easily defined in terms of its geographical coordinates on a map. Merkel's statements, however, involved a stark comparison between the present and the past. In such a setting, perhaps the biggest challenge is answering dual questions: What was Germany, and where was Germany?

Just as is the case for practically all modern nation-states, Germany-as-territory is, and always has been, a social and political construct. We may think of territory as an "object" and equate it with the basic tenets of physical geography (e.g., defined in terms of geographical coordinates or geographical markers such as rivers and mountains), but that approach is misleading. For territories to exist in any meaningful sense, human groups need to think of them in the first place, and then act upon these thoughts. Put bluntly, *territory is what states and societies make of it*. Take Germany. As an ideational and political construct, Germany-as-territory has undergone some extreme transformations in the last half millennium. In other words, in history, there existed a wide variety of different ideas about what constituted "Germany."

---

[5] Reuters, "Germans Must Be 'Sensitive' to What Nazis Did to Other Countries, Merkel Says," *Haaretz*, May 2, 2015, https://www.haaretz.com/2015-05-02/ty-article/germans-cannot-turn-backs-on-nazi-past-merkel-says/0000017f-db56-df62-a9ff-dfd7a7790000.

[6] Dostal 2017.

These *territorial ideas* neither were limited to Germany, nor merely existed on the margins of the society, only to be discussed by philosophers. To the contrary, these ideas were essentially internalized en masse and usually taken for granted, just as we have internalized the dominant territorial ideas of our times and usually take them for granted. As is the case today, in the past these ideas, as aspirational as they were, affected how state elites and societies conceived the space-society-politics nexus.

This observation has a direct implication for the study of war, broadly defined. Research on armed conflict points toward a distinct trend: of all issues that are associated with war, territorial issues stand out. Put differently, from a macrohistorical perspective, territory, broadly defined, has always played a key, or perhaps *the* key, role in the causes, conduct, and consequences of armed conflict. Therein lies the aforementioned implication: if territory meant different things to different societies across time and space, then these different ideas attributed to territories must have affected the ways in which states and societies approached armed conflict. To a large extent, *war is what states and societies make of territory.* The relationship between territory and armed conflict is not unidirectional; just as different territorial ideas affect wars in different ways, wars themselves can also shape and transform the dominant territorial ideas in a given geography. In this context, the German case is illustrative for two reasons. First, as highlighted above, the question of what and where Germany was has varied over time. Second, the emergence of Germany as we know it today is most essentially a story embedded with armed conflict; Germany (as a geographical expression) witnessed countless wars, and some of these wars categorically transformed what and where Germany was.

So, what and where was Germany? Up until the turn of the sixteenth century, no one really had a clear idea about where Germany began and where it ended. Maps of the time had yet to portray Germany as a distinct territorial unit with distinguishable borders and scope.[7] Of course, the concept of *Germania*, the Latin designation for the area north of the Danube and east of the Rhine, was used as early as the first century BC.[8] However, German cartographer and cosmographer Martin Waldseemüller's map, *Germania*, dated 1513, was probably the first two-dimensional representation of Germany. Even then, the boundaries and scope of this Germany was a far cry from our present-day understanding; for example, the map treated Prussia not as a part of Germany, but as a distinct nation of its own.[9]

---

[7] Smith 2020, 3.
[8] Smith 2020, 12.
[9] Smith 2020, 30.

4 Shifting Grounds

Beyond cartographic representations, the territorial structure of Germany during the sixteenth century was exceptionally complex, even for the time. The Holy Roman Empire, independent cities and city leagues, numerous proto-states like the Electorate of Saxony, and ecclesial arrangements all coexisted in an array of fluid boundaries and overlapping jurisdictions.[10] That being said, until 1517, when Martin Luther ignited the Reformation, Christianity unified Germany at some level. Christianity, however, did not necessarily distinguish Germany per se from other territories inhabited mainly by Christians; they were all parts of the greater Christian lands. The Reformation effectively created a confessional chasm between the Catholics and the Protestants within these Christian lands, especially in Germany as a geographical expression, eventually paving the way for the Thirty Years' War (1618–48). The war was also a civil war of some sorts for the German-speaking populations. Especially the Catholic princes and the Emperor tried to impose their religion within and beyond their domains. In other words, the competing factions sought to impose what we can refer to as *sociospatial homogenization*, so that both the [Germanic] lands and people would be defined in terms of a singular, confessional identity.

The Thirty Years' War and the postwar settlements, exemplified by the Peace of Westphalia (1648), not only redrew the existing boundaries, but also tilted the balance in favor of a territorial model that already existed, if only as an aspirational principle. Let's call this aspirational model *mosaic territoriality*. In its simplest form, mosaic territoriality is built on two tenets. First, unlike fluid, ambiguous, and overlapping boundaries and frontiers, it privileges clearly demarcated borders. Second, mosaic territoriality is not about standardizing or homogenizing the ways in which the society defines its attachment to state territories. In this context, the German rulers no longer aimed to "purify" their domains in terms of religious affiliations; instead, there existed a preference for (or at least institutionalized tolerance of) *sociospatial heterogeneity*. Mosaic territoriality was closely associated with a certain way of fighting over territory: state elites could approach their territories as divisible goods (partially because the society, on average, did not have an emotive attachment to the entirety of the state territory), a dynamic that paradoxically rendered wars for territory ubiquitous in Europe, while also preventing them from becoming extremely costly "people's wars."[11]

Of course, mosaic territoriality did not take over Europe overnight. In fact, Germany as a geographical expression lagged behind some leading polities

---

[10] Kratochwil 1986 and Ruggie 1993.
[11] Clausewitz [1832] 1976.

of the time, such as France. This is hardly surprising. Even after Westphalia, Germany as a geographical expression remained politically and culturally fragmented. The idea of Germany as territory, a contained, sociospatial unit exclusively for Germans, had yet to capture the imagination of the masses. In the meantime, a number of German dynasties were on their way to establishing what we can refer to as proto-modern states. Of these, a latecomer, Prussia, would eventually rise as a major, if not great, power in the so-called European state system through the course of the eighteenth century.

For Germany as a geographical expression, the eighteenth century was tumultuous. War for territory remained ubiquitous. Considering the dynastic nature of European politics at the time, not to mention the principle of primogeniture, the death or even illness of a monarch was one of the best predictors of armed conflict. At the societal level, people might or might not have an affinity for their respective rulers, but such affinities rarely extended to the entirety of the state territories, which, to an extent, were still considered dynastic possessions. As Goethe once alluded to, the inhabitants of Prussia did care about Frederick the Great (r. 1740–86), but their affection for "Prussia" (as territory) was questionable.[12] Under such circumstances, neither the masses nor the rulers prioritized the idea of (greater) Germany-as-territory.[13]

The French Revolution of 1789 posed an unprecedented challenge to the monarchical-dynastic nature of territorial arrangements all across Europe. More specifically, the Revolution paved the way for the rise of cosmopolitan republicanism and, eventually, nationalism as vibrant political ideologies that threatened the old regime in its entirety. The subsequent Revolutionary and Napoleonic Wars (1792–1815), in turn, practically remade Germany (as a geographical expression). In the conventional wisdom, the story of this great transformation is rather linear, and occurs in three main acts. In the first act, the German dynasties, especially the Hohenzollerns of Prussia, are consumed with their hubris and inability to comprehend the potential might of nationalistic energies that first revealed themselves in France, a tendency that leads to Prussia's humiliating defeat at the hands of Napoleon in 1806 at the Battle of Jena. In the second act, this humiliation and the risk of further French expansion fuel German nationalism and a penchant for defending (or "saving") the German homeland.

The third act is all about triumph: in the historic Battle of Leipzig (1813), also known as the Battle of *Nations*, Germans rose as one nation and played a key role in the defeat of Napoleon. This is a particularly convenient story about

[12] Quoted in Morgenthau 1949, 118.
[13] Smith 2020, 96.

6 Shifting Grounds

the rise of German nationalism and Germany (broadly defined)—perhaps a little too convenient. In reality, in 1813 the "new nationalism remained largely a Prussian phenomenon."[14] Furthermore, Germans did not join the Battle of Nations as one nation; many Germans and numerous Germanic states, such as Saxony, Baden, and Württemberg, fought *for* Napoleon, against an alliance that included other Germans. If so, why does this interpretation still persist? The German nationalists' efforts to construct a consistent, all-German history during the century that followed the Battle of Leipzig most certainly played a role. In addition, our tendency to see the past through the lenses of our present-day territorial ideas often "traps" us inside analytical blindfolds that obscure or oversimplify the past.[15] German nationalism was most certainly on the rise, but the process was neither imminent nor linear.

From 1815 onward, the story of Germany becomes a story of nation-building. It is, however, hardly the story of a German nation that magically woke up from its a thousand-year sleep to rediscover its national identity and homeland. The story is one of political turmoil, numerous uprisings, the revolutions of 1848, fierce geopolitical competition, and, once again, war. The Prussian state, now accepted by many in Europe as a great power, spearheaded the emergence of the first German nation-state in history through a combination of cunning diplomacy and multiple wars, some of which were fought against Germans.[16] The Prussian efforts culminated in the Franco-Prussian War (1870–71). That war then served as the backdrop for the creation of the German Empire.

The idea of a German nation-state entailed a radical departure from the territorial ideas and practices of the previous centuries. In essence, nationalism is not merely about the people, it is also about the *relationship between the people and a specific territory*, often designated as a homeland. Recall that we can refer to the dominant territorial model of the previous centuries as mosaic territoriality, with its emphasis on fixed borders and heterogeneous populations. The idea(l) of the nation-state, or nationalism, cannot be portrayed through mosaic territoriality, for a simple reason: nationalism entails the idea(l) of a socially homogeneous group with an undeniable attachment to its own discrete homeland. Let's call this aspirational model *monolithic territoriality*.

The distinction between mosaic and monolithic territoriality may appear epiphenomenal, but it is far from it. Most scholars and spectators usually define the present-day global territorial arrangements in terms of the so-called

---

[14] Smith 2020, 187.
[15] See Agnew 1994.
[16] While imperial Germany's constitution did not define the empire as a nation-state, it paved the way for its emergence. See Smith 2020, 259.

Westphalian territoriality. In this context, some commentators suggest that the rise of globalization will eventually lead to a post-Westphalian world order. A closer look at the societal components of territories, however, suggests that we are already living in a post-Westphalian territorial arrangement: while the original Westphalian arrangement entailed strict borders and a heterogeneous society (mosaic territoriality), the age of the nation-states involves a penchant for strict borders and a homogeneous society (monolithic territoriality). In this sense, the creation of the German Empire was closely associated with the rise of a new territorial template, that is, monolithic territoriality. In fact, it is only at this stage in our story where we can use "Germany" without a qualifier. From 1871 onward, in the English-speaking world to be sure, the term "Germany" became a synonym for both Germany as nation-state and Germany as territory.

So how does the idea of a territorially defined nation, or monolithic territoriality, affect state elites' and societies' approach to war? Simply put, state territories are now portrayed as indivisible, or inviolable, homelands. Under such circumstances, wars, when they involve a territorial component, can easily become a people's war, which may drive up the severity of the conflict, increase the risk of civilian victimization, and make it extremely difficult to terminate the war. The expected costs of war raise the bar for decisions over the war's initiation, limiting the frequency of war without eliminating the risk of war. Germany's experience during World War I directly speaks to this dynamic. Following an almost half a century of peace, Germany plunged into the Great War and imposed as well as suffered an enormous cost in blood and treasure, mostly portrayed as a "sacrifice" in the name of the fatherland, or Germany as territory.[17]

At this juncture, an important digression is in order. It is true that Germany (as a nation-state) was increasingly professing monolithic territoriality from 1871 onward, but imperial Germany's territorial ideas and practices were not limited to Europe. The German Empire was also a colonial power, that is, until it lost its colonial possessions as a result of World War I. Before the war, the German Empire ruled over more than ten million people and an impressive collection of territories, mostly in Africa, almost four times the size of Germany. Similar to other colonizing European powers, Germany professed an entirely different set of territorial ideas and practices in its colonies. Germany-in-Europe existed in a regional system of sovereign territorial states, and behaved accordingly. Germany-in-Africa, by contrast, considered the targeted territories "open" and "inferior" places, waiting for a European

---

[17] Smith 2020, 308–320.

8 Shifting Grounds

colonizer to pacify and tame them. The former set of territorial ideas also had significant consequences for how Germany utilized organized violence for the purpose of territorial expansion and control beyond Europe.

Most notably, imperial Germany launched two brutal military campaigns in the context of the Maji Maji Rebellion (1905–7) in German East Africa and the Herero Wars (1904–8) in German Southwest Africa. German battle-field deaths amounted to less than a thousand, but Germany ended up killing almost a quarter million Africans, including civilians.[18] During the early twentieth century, it was virtually unthinkable for German state elites and so-ciety to launch such brutal campaigns into the territories of their European neighbors. From the late 1930s onward, however, what had been unthinkable for most Germans only a few decades ago came to be seen as not only accept-able, but perhaps even a natural right: During the course of World War II, Nazi Germany would end up killing millions, including civilians in Europe and Eurasia, in just a matter of years. So the question becomes, how did Germany get there?

Of course, it would be misleading to try to "explain Nazi Germany" through a single, territorial, perspective. However, it would also be misleading to ig-nore the role that territorial ideas played in the onslaught that Nazi Germany unleashed in Europe. Most commentators portray Nazi Germany as a polity with too much nationalism. This may be true, but the territorial ideas that motivated Adolf Hitler and Nazi Germany did not necessarily follow the basic tenets of territorially defined nationalism; they were something else. Hitler adhered to the (social Darwinism-inspired) geopolitik school of thought of the time, which portrayed the (German) state as the core of a racially defined, territorial organism that needed to grow or perish.[19] Consequently, Nazi Germany sought to create a greater Lebensraum for what Hitler perceived to be the Aryan race, which included but was not limited to Germans. This as-pirational territorial model went beyond the basic tenets of both mosaic and monolithic territoriality. If that's the case, how should we classify territorial models like the one professed by Nazi Germany?

Perhaps, *virulent territoriality* would be an apt phrase. This vision conceptualizes the state space as if it is a virus that needs to constantly grow and remake anything and everything on its way in its own image. Virulent territoriality recognizes no strict boundaries, as it seeks to expand almost in-definitely. In addition, and most importantly, this aspirational model seeks to "purify" the lands within and beyond its territorial core in social, political,

[18] Smith 2020, 287.
[19] Smith 2020, 366.

economic, and cultural terms. In other words, it entails *radical homogenization of the sociospatial arrangements* in areas where it is dominant. Following the basic tenets of this territorial model, Nazi Germany violently pursued policies to purify the lands it controlled, within and beyond Germany, while also seeking to expand indefinitely. Jews, the Romani people, political dissidents, and even the disabled were deemed "impure" parasites that simply needed to be wiped off the Lebensraum, as if they were stains on a white countertop. In this imagery, other inferior races, such as the Slavs, were seen as (barely) tolerable social groups; if they were lucky enough to escape extermination, they would be allowed to take on the role of slaves, who would then attend to the needs of their Aryan masters in the territories that should have belonged to the Aryan race in the first place. Nazi Germany's purification efforts also extended to the territories it occupied in Western Europe, where the agents of the Third Reich and their local collaborators (most of whom were deemed Aryans) strove to homogenize the sociospatial arrangements and remake them in the image of Nazi Germany, supposedly the apex of the Aryan race.

World War II ended up destroying not only Nazi Germany, but also the Germany-as-territory that had existed in Europe since 1871. Germany lost considerable territories in the east, more than fifteen million Germans were expelled from what they had considered their homeland for generations, and what was left of Germany was formally divided in two in 1949. For the next forty years, there would be not one, but two Germanies: the Federal Republic of Germany (FRG) in the west, and the German Democratic Republic in the east, each with its own territory, individual seat at the United Nations (as of 1973), and flag to be flown in the Olympics. Under the close supervision of the Allied powers, the inhabitants of West Germany reimagined their territory as a peaceful land, where the idea of territorial expansion via military force eventually became virtually unthinkable.[20] Under Soviet tutelage East Germany was reimagined as a garrison or police state that was a natural extension of the Communist bloc.

As the Cold War was coming to an end, the two Germanies finally united, or more precisely, five federal states in East Germany joined the FRG. One can imagine the collective confusion that took hold among many Germans in the immediate aftermath of the unification. Where is, what is Germany *now*? How will we ever reconcile what Germany as territory has been with what Germany will become in the future? These were questions that troubled many Germans (due to the weight of a complex territorial history), while exciting

---

[20] Smith 2020, 425.

others (since the unification meant the possibility of an entirely new beginning for the *whole* of Germany).

Fast-forward to the present day: Germany is still trying to find answers to the questions, where is Germany and what is Germany? Chancellor Merkel's controversial decision in 2015 to accommodate large numbers of refugees can be seen as one attempt to redefine what Germany as territory and Germany as nation-state would be in the twenty-first century. Merkel's decision in 2015 also dovetails with the radical policy reversal of 2000, which redefined the criteria for acquiring German citizenship: while German citizenship, since 1913, had been based on the principle of *jus sanguinis* (the right of blood, or heritage), the reversal of 2000 institutionalized *jus soli* (the right of soil).[21] Consequently, immigrants can now become citizens much more easily, and their children who are born in German territory can automatically become German citizens, or *just Germans*, if we are to employ a civic (as opposed to ethnic) interpretation of nationalism and nationhood. Most notably, these policies mean much more in present-day Germany, where more than 10% of the population are immigrants, as opposed to the immediate aftermath of World War II, when non-Germans (defined in terms of ethnicity) constituted less than 1% of the population. The future, of course, is uncertain. The aforementioned policies are already creating a backlash, as right-wing political parties such as Alternative für Deutschland (AfD) are increasingly pushing forward the argument that Germany as territory is primarily for ethnic Germans to live in, invoking the ethnicity-based homogeneity that defined what kind of territory Germany was for a long time.

So what is the moral of this story? It is more about the relationship between the socially constructed nature of territories and armed conflict than it is about Germany per se, and can be expressed in three points. First, territories are essentially social and political constructs, the meaning of which can show great variation across time. Second, different territorial ideas are associated with different ways to fight over territory. Third, wars themselves can also exert a transformative effect on the dominant territorial ideas in a given geography, sometimes reshaping them in radical ways.

Of course, Germany is one case among many others. It is also an essentially European case. While we may be living in a world that is guided by European/Western ideas and principles about territory and territoriality—such as the notion of Westphalian sovereignty and the nation-state ideal—the "European" (or "Western") is not a synonym for the "international." Some commentators conceive the evolution of the present-day global order in terms

---

[21] Smith 2020, 462.

of a linear narrative, where Europeans first create an "international society" among themselves, which eventually (and almost effortlessly) "expands" to include non-Western geographies.[22] This perspective not only is a product of a Eurocentric vision of world politics, but also ossifies a deterministic understanding of the evolution of the global territorial arrangement that treats non-Western experiences as if they are minor footnotes. To understand the aforementioned evolution, we most certainly need to move beyond such narratives that conflate particular "European" experiences with the story of how the "international" came to emerge.

Of numerous non-Western examples, Turkey stands out as an intriguing case, partially because "What and where was Turkey?" is a challenging question to address. On paper, Turkey is quintessentially a unitary nation-state, established in 1923 on the ashes of the Ottoman Empire. So where *is* Turkey? The answer depends on the intention behind the question. If the intention is to parse out Turkey's geographical location, Turkey's geographical coordinates and its position vis-à-vis its neighbors may suffice. However, if the intention is to parse out Turkey's territorial influence and even control, the answer is more complicated: Turkey has military bases in Somalia and Qatar, has been a major player in the civil war in Libya, and effectively controls and governs substantial chunks of territory in northern Syria.

Turkey's "territorial past" is far more complicated. Turkey, or *Türkiye* in its Turkish designation, simply means the "land of the Turks." Two historical factors complicate this designation. First, ethnic Turks arrived in large numbers where modern Turkey is located only in the late eleventh century. Accordingly, at least until the late nineteenth century, Asia Minor was home to a diverse set of ethnic and religious groups, including but not limited to ethnic Turks. Second, more interestingly, up until the late nineteenth century, "Turkey" was not a widely used geographical designator in the lands now we refer to as Turkey, with a twist: while Europeans often referred to the Ottomans as the "Turks" and the Ottoman territories as "Turkey" at least from the fifteenth century onward, neither the Ottoman rulers nor the inhabitants of their territories prioritized these identity- and territory-based designators. A comparison with Germany helps drive home the point. If we could travel back in time, say, to the eighteenth century, we could observe that the term "Germany" (at least as a geographical expression) was known to many Germans and Europeans, even though there existed disagreements over where exactly Germany really was. During the same century, the term "Turkey" would mean little to the rulers and inhabitants of the Ottoman Empire. Paradoxically, the

---

[22] Bull 1977.

12 Shifting Grounds

term "Turkey" would mean something for Europeans, since Europeans had traditionally preferred to refer to the Ottoman territories as such.

The conventional wisdom on "Turkey," either as a state or territory, "fixes" the relevant conceptual tensions through a simple approach: Turkey is often imagined as a smaller Ottoman Empire, an assumption that ends up portraying the Ottomans as a larger Turkey. In reality, Turkey is not a smaller Ottoman Empire, just as the Ottoman Empire was anything but a larger Turkey. The dominant territorial ideas of our times, which trap us in analytical blindfolds of some sorts,[23] further ossify this interpretation: in the present day, we see Turkey, and when we're thinking about the past, we almost automatically project our understanding of today's Turkey into a past where it does not belong.

More specifically, the roots of the term "Turkey" are not in present-day Turkey, but can be traced all the way to Central Asia, where Turkic peoples and the Turkish language originate. To be precise, Turkic peoples who live in Central Asia actually do share certain cultural characteristics with modern-day Turks, broadly defined, especially in terms of traditions and linguistics similarities. So, how did we get here, that is, to modern-day Turkey? In the first millennium AD, Turkic peoples of Central Asia were, to a large extent, nomadic. A series of environmental crises such as droughts prompted some of the Turkic tribes, who began to convert to Islam in large numbers from the eight century onward, to migrate westward. These tribes' nearly unparalleled ability to fight on horseback and impressive (collective) mobility on the battlefield, a product of their nomadic lifestyle, rendered them sought-after military assets, especially in the territories controlled by the Islamic empires of the day. Some of these Turkic tribes first served as slave soldiers in the Islamic armies and some, by the mid-eleventh century, established their own empire, the Seljuks.

It was in fact during the Seljuk dynasty (1037–1194) that the Turkic tribes asserted themselves in Asia Minor, which had been controlled, to an extent, by the Byzantine Empire. The twelfth and thirteenth centuries witnessed an influx of Turkic tribes into Asia Minor. At the time, there existed little reason to refer to the area controlled by the Seljuks as "Turkey"; Asia Minor was a societal mosaic and hosted numerous Christian communities, from Greeks to Armenians, not to mention other Muslim ethnic groups like the Kurds. In the meantime, an increasing number of Turkic tribes began to turn to a sedentary lifestyle, making Asia Minor their adopted home. After the fall of the Seljuks by the end of the twelfth century, Asia Minor hosted numerous

---

[23] See Agnew 1994.

Turkish *beyliks*, or emirates. Osman Ghazi (Os̱mān Ġāzī), the leader of one of these emirates, established the House of Osman in northwestern Asia Minor by the turn of the fourteenth century. A common mispronunciation of Osman's name established the dynasty as the "Ottomans" in the eyes of the European/Christian world.[24] The Turkish designation of the term, to be precise, is *Osmanlı*, which roughly means "those who belong with the House of Osman." This clarification is of importance not merely for the sake of etymology. The term "Ottoman" (or *Osmanlı*) did not refer to a certain territory or a country (as, say, France does even to this day); it referred to a specific dynasty and the associated state apparatus.

The House of Osman amounted to little more than a minor emirate by 1300; by 1453, it was already a transcontinental empire that called Constantinople, one of the most important historical cities in Christendom, its capital. The sixteenth century witnessed the zenith of the Ottomans' politico-military might. The Ottomans conquered large swaths of territory in Europe, even laying siege to Vienna in 1529. In 1517, the Ottomans made significant advances into the Middle East, and eventually assumed the title of caliphs, a title now reserved for the Ottoman sultans. The Ottomans' territorial expansion halted around the late seventeenth century, and by the nineteenth century, the imminent territorial dissolution of the empire earned the Ottomans the moniker "the sick man of Europe." World War I served as the final nail in the Ottomans' coffin. The question then becomes, where is *Turkey* (as a distinct territory) in this story? The short answer is that it did not exist, simply because the Ottoman rulers and society en masse had not yet imagined it to exist.

The Ottomans' territorial ideas were built on two principles: a strong preference for fluid, contingent, ever-changing frontiers, and an emphasis on *societal heterogeneity*. The Ottomans aimed to expand indefinitely and did not try to unify the society they ruled over around a certain, singular territorial identity. There never was a distinct "Ottoman homeland," partially because the Ottomans were not interested in creating one, and partially because the Ottomans were, in the end, a dynasty (similarly, we usually do not talk about a specific Romanov or Bourbon [national] homeland). Instead, the Ottomans ruled through the principle of fluid frontiers and indirect rule for centuries. An illustration may clarify this point. Most historical-political maps would depict the Ottoman Empire as a territorial unit with a single color, capped by clear-cut, discrete borders. In reality, the administrative and societal dynamics

---

[24] To be precise, Osman's real name is controversial. Some argue that it was the Europeans who got his name right (Utman or Ataman), not the other way around. For the debate, see Gedikli 2021.

14 Shifting Grounds

of the Ottoman state space would be better defined in terms of a hodgepodge of different colors, surrounded by hazy frontiers.

We can refer to this territorial model as *amorphous territoriality*. In the presence of such aspirational territorial models, war over territory is usually seen as a continuous enterprise, which can be carried out through not only set-piece battles, but also incessant raids and other, unconventional, forms of gradual expansion. This is a major divergence from the ways in which European states, especially from the seventeenth century onward, conceived armed conflict over territory. For the Europeans of the time, and for us today, war is usually seen as a discrete event with a clear beginning and a clear end; for the Ottomans, the struggle for territorial expansion (or defense) was an omnipresent process. Amorphous territoriality also does not entail intention and dedicated effort to homogenize the societies in target areas around a certain identity. The Ottomans' meteoric territorial expansion during the empire's early centuries was partially a result of the ways in which they thought of territory and acted upon those thoughts; these ideas and associated practices helped the Ottomans expand rapidly and rule on the cheap. Chapter 5 will examine the relationship between amorphous territoriality and the Ottoman expansion in detail, but a crucial point about the Ottomans' territorial ideas needs to be highlighted: amorphous territoriality was not specific to the Ottomans. To the contrary, from a macrohistorical perspective, amorphous territoriality was not the exception, but the rule for countless geographies and societies. In fact, the mosaic and monolithic territorial orders that emerged in Europe were the exceptions to this rule.

So what about the relationship between the Ottomans' territorial ideas and the chronic absence of robust and systematic references to "Turkey," that is, until the end of the nineteenth century? Simply put, the Ottomans considered themselves rulers of a transnational, multiethnic *Islamic* empire. Most notably, the Ottoman focus was on the *ummah*, a Muslim collective. Islamic political thought of the time was essentially incompatible with the practice of prioritizing a national or ethnic group at the expense of others. If any identity was to be prioritized, that identity would be, and was, defined in terms of religious affiliations. Furthermore, the Ottomans, even if they had wanted to (and they did not), could not afford to emphasize their Turkishness and impose a Turkish identity on a collection of territorial units that were defined by a multitude of non-Turkish (and non-Muslim) societal groups. In such a landscape, the Ottomans refrained from (or did not even consider) defining their territorial possessions as the "land of the Turks."

The Ottomans did not exist in an ideational vacuum. Especially from the nineteenth century onward, the idea of national homelands, or monolithic territoriality, was beginning to gain traction in the Ottomans' European territories. The Greeks, Bulgarians, and Serbians, among others, eventually rose against their imperial overlords, seeking their own sovereign, socially homogeneous homelands. The Ottomans' amorphous territoriality, which helped the empire expand and rule on the cheap for centuries, was inherently incompatible with the rise of monolithic territoriality. In the past, their reliance on indirect rule shielded the Ottomans from large-scale (nationalistic or even religious) insurgencies. In the age of nationalistic aspirations, co-optation of the local rulers or temporary appeasement of the masses would no longer do the trick.

So what about nationalism within the Ottomans' core territories in Asia Minor? For the Ottoman rulers, the idea of nationalism, *even Turkish nationalism*, was an anathema. Instead, to prevent the dissolution of the empire, the Ottoman sultans experimented with an openly Islamist ideology that would emphasize the role of the sultan as the caliph, and what is sometimes referred to as Ottomanism, which was an attempt to emphasize the transnational character of the societies living in the Ottoman lands to unify them. Not surprisingly, these attempts to circumvent nationalism and its territorial underpinnings did not pay off. At the same time, the late nineteenth century also witnessed the rise of a younger generation of military officers and bureaucrats, who were well versed in Western ideologies and institutions. This was hardly a composite collective. Some believed that, with reforms, the empire could be salvaged as a transnational entity. Others favored so-called *Turanism*, the idea that all Turkic peoples in Asia Minor, the Caucasus, and beyond should join together to establish their own state. Yet others, including Turkey's founder, Mustafa Kemal Atatürk, believed that the empire was beyond saving and Turanism barely amounted to more than a fantasy; the only solution was the creation of a Turkish nation-state in Asia Minor and eastern Thrace. Furthermore, the idea of a Turkish homeland, or *vatan*, was becoming more pronounced in the decades leading up to World War I;[25] however, its rise to prominence was far from a foregone conclusion.

The Ottomans entered World War I on the side of the Axis powers. When the Great War ended, the Ottomans faced the risk of a draconian punishment at the hands of the Allied powers. According to the Treaty of Sèvres (1920), the Ottoman lands would be confined to north central Asia Minor, a fraction of the present-day Turkey. Even Istanbul (or Constantinople), the Ottoman capital since 1453, would lie outside of the Ottomans' direct jurisdiction. Furthermore, in May 1919, the Greek army, backed by Britain, landed

---

[25] Özkan 2012.

16 Shifting Grounds

in Izmir, present-day Turkey's third biggest city and a major trading port in the Aegean, effectively setting the stage for the Greek invasion of Asia Minor. In other words, as of 1919–20, the Ottomans were allowed to exist, but in a truncated territory and most likely as a quasi-colonial dependency. When combined, these developments and the Ottoman sultans' tacit acquiescence eventually triggered the Turkish War of Independence (1919–23), fought against not only the Greek army and (to a lesser extent, and often indirectly) other European states like Britain and France, but also the Ottoman sultan. If not for this war, we might still have ended up with Turkey as a state and a territory of some sorts, but that Turkey would most certainly not resemble present-day Turkey.

In particular, World War I tilted the balance in favor of those who championed the ideal of "Turkey" (as a nation-state and territory) in two ways. The first is straightforward: post–World War I settlements almost turned Asia Minor into a collection of colonial territories and dependencies, and the Ottoman sultan could not, or did not, step up to resist. Atatürk, a highly acclaimed general in the Gallipoli Campaign (1915–16), lit the nationalistic fire, and the Republic of Turkey was eventually established as a unitary nation-state. This outcome was not a foregone conclusion. Turkey could have been established as a federation, or perhaps a constitutional monarchy. The founding fathers of modern Turkey, however, had a strict preference for a unitary nation-state and its territorial underpinnings. Furthermore, Ataturk envisioned Turkey as a secular (or secularized) territory, where Islam would play only a tertiary role in politics and society. In addition, the founding fathers envisioned Turkey as a distinct territorial entity, that is, distinct (and distanced) from the broader Middle Eastern geographies in terms of culture and identity.

The second factor was the ideational trends in the post–World War I environment. Simply put, the postwar settlements established a stark paradox for non-Western geographies: while the principle of "self-determination" was continuously emphasized, it was also categorically denied to non-European societies. The rationale for such denial reflected what can be referred to as geographical racism, a centuries-long tradition among European colonial powers: the aforementioned non-European geographies, so the argument went, were not yet mature and civilized enough to host nation-states, so these territories essentially needed Western guidance, supervision, and tutelage for some time to come. In such a landscape, arguably, the founding fathers were further incentivized to establish Turkey as a West-compatible, unitary nation-state, so that Turkey could escape the wrath of Western colonialism, paradoxically, by becoming more like the Western states of the time. On the one hand, they succeeded; Turkey was one of the very few non-Western polities that entered the club of sovereign nation-states without having to go through an episode of Western colonialism. On the other hand, founding fathers' attempts also failed, as the efforts to construct a homogeneous and secular nation-state on the ashes of an Islamic empire that hosted a multitude of ethnic and religious groups met with fierce societal resistance.

In this sense, modern Turkey was not a smaller Ottoman Empire; it was in fact imagined by its founders as a partial, but radical, refutation of the core territorial principles that made the Ottoman Empire what it was. The young republic ruled out any irredentist claims and went to lengths to sacralize the newly established borders through nationalistic discourses that boil down to the popular phrase "Turkey belongs to the Turks." The caliphate, an institution that represented both the transnational nature of the Ottoman Empire and the religious conservatism of the majority of the population, was abolished in 1924. The Turkish state also attempted to create a new, all-Turkish historiography that painted the timeless Turkish nation as a beacon of pride and glory. These new narratives made selective use of the Ottoman past; great sultans such as Mehmed (II) the Conqueror (r. 1444–46, 1451–81) and Süleyman (I) the Magnificent (r. 1520–66) were applauded for their accomplishments, but the final centuries of the empire were often depicted in terms of institutional decay, scientific backwardness (a byproduct of religious bigotry), and incompetent leadership. Even the alphabet was not spared. In 1928, Ataturk replaced the Arabic alphabet that the Ottomans used for centuries with a newly created, Latin-based Turkish alphabet. From 1932 onward, the newly established Turkish Language Association made an effort to jettison Farsi and Arabic words and phrases from written Turkish, literally replacing some of them with newly formulated[26] Turkish terms. The intention behind these measures was straightforward: to create a secular, West-compatible, unitary nation-state where a singular Turkish identity was defined vis-à-vis a unique Turkish homeland, and vice versa.

The remainder of the twentieth century was marked by successive attempts to establish a compact and secular nation-state. Population exchanges (with Greece), the atrocities and traumas of World War I,[27] systemic economic discrimination, and societal pressures (such as the pogroms of September 6–7, 1955) eventually drove away the overwhelming majority of the Christian and Jewish communities, reducing them to a collection of minuscule religious

---

[26] To be precise, the grammatical structure of the Turkish language allows for formulating new words by building on existing ones.

[27] Suny 2017.

18 Shifting Grounds

minorities. The main challenge for the nationalizing elites of the Turkish state was in fact the assimilation of the Muslim, non-Turkish minorities. In some cases, like the refugees from the Balkans and the Caucasus (and their descendants), the relevant efforts, if arguably, succeeded. The state-led assimilation efforts, however, not only failed but also backfired vis-à-vis the Kurds. Successive Turkish governments attempted to "solve" the so-called Kurdish question through harsh assimilation methods and an institutionalized denial of the Kurdish identity. One consequence was the rise of the Kurdish Workers' Party (PKK) by the early 1980s; the conflict that ensued between the PKK and the Turkish state has so far claimed some fifty thousand lives. The conflict was a testimony to the salience of monolithic territoriality as an aspirational model in the twentieth century: the PKK sought independence and/or autonomy for what it considered to be the Kurdish homeland. This demand was the one thing that a unitary nation-state like Turkey, where the Turkish territory (or homeland) is sacralized and deemed inviolable, could not grant. The result was an intractable conflict, which eventually spread to Iraq and, later, Syria.

In sum, Turkey (as a territory) has been a much newer social and political construct than is usually assumed. This construct became possible only as a result of World War I, and it was then forged in the Turkish War of Independence. Successive governments went to great lengths to ossify the idea of a unitary, secular, socially homogeneous nation-state with a singular territorial identity, with mixed results.

Fast forward to 2022, and the story of the evolution of territorial ideas in (or about) Turkey becomes even more complicated. Obviously, the Kurdish question remains unsolved to this day. In addition, the nationalizing elites also failed to construct Turkey as an essentially secular territory. A majority of the population remained conservative Muslims, and some considered Ankara's attempts to secularize the Turkish territory to be direct assault on their traditional way of life. Most notably, in 2002, Turkey's controversial president Recep Tayyip Erdoğan and his newly established party, the Adalet ve Kalkınma Partisi (AKP), came to power. Erdoğan never hid his credentials and background as a conservative Muslim; in fact, his discourses, even to this day, are built on a specific narrative of victimhood, where the conservative Muslims, the majority of the population, had to live under the yoke of what Erdoğan branded the "White Turks," or the secular and secularizing minority, for almost a century.

In full control of state institutions and mainstream media, Erdoğan and the AKP have so far spent two decades trying to reconstruct, or recalibrate, what and where Turkey (both as a nation-state and as a territory) really is, or should be. Doing so, the AKP draws heavily on a glorified and sacralized interpretation of the Ottoman Empire. According to this territorial vision, sometimes referred to as neo-Ottomanism,[28] Turkey is not, or should not be, conceived as a secular, or secularized, territory. In the age of the Ottomans, Turkey, or the specific geographical area we now call Turkey, was essentially a Muslim territory; so what needs to be done is to simply go back to the (territorial) principles that made the Ottomans great in the first place. This set of territorial ideas has remarkable implications for Turkey's societal dynamics. Recall that the founding fathers strove to distance Turkey from the broader Middle Eastern cultures and societies. The AKP virtually reversed this approach, systematically making the case that Turkey has always been a central part of Middle Eastern geography, history, and culture. Under the AKP rule, for example, Turkey has become exponentially more welcoming to refugees from the Middle East. In the span of the last decade, in a country that officially had only eighteen thousand refugees in 2009, the number of dislocated civilians,[29] especially from Syria, and illegal immigrants (from countries like Afghanistan) has reached an estimated five million, roughly 6% of the population.[30] Such a policy would have been unimaginable, say, during the course of 1990s, when the nationalist-secular state elites were in control of the state institutions.

The AKP's new set of territorial ideas also has important implications for Turkey's behavior in the international arena. For decades, the AKP argued that Turkey, as a direct heir to the Ottomans, had a historical responsibility to lead, if not rule over, the Muslim-majority (or Sunni-majority) societies in its multiregional geopolitical environment. This is not a hyperbolic statement, but instead follows directly from Erdoğan's discourses and foreign policy preferences. For example, Erdoğan and the AKP continuously make the case that Turkey is in fact far greater than its borders. Even Erdoğan's electoral victories in Turkey are often portrayed as victories not only for Turkey, but also for "Sarajevo, Beirut, Damascus, Ramallah, Nablus, Jenin, West Bank, Jerusalem, and Gaza Strip."[31] Furthermore, in a radical break with the past Turkish foreign policy posture, Erdoğan's Turkey became heavily involved in the Palestinian issue (which soured Turkish-Israeli relations) and threw its

---

[28] See Özkan 2014.

[29] Turkish law does not recognize dislocated civilians that come to Turkey from the Middle East countries as refugees. Therefore, even to this day, the Syrian refugees in Turkey are not legally refugees; they have a special legal status, which can be defined as dislocated civilians under (Turkish) protection.

[30] The debate on actual numbers is divided; while some claim that the number is around four million, others claim it is closer to eight million, if not more.

[31] Taner Akcam, "Türkiye'nin İnsan Hakları İki Yüzlülüğü," https://www.nytimes.com/2012/07/20/opinion/turkiyenin-insan-haklar-iki-yuzlulugu.html, *New York Times*, 19 July 2012.

weight behind a transnational entity, the Muslim Brotherhood, a policy that can help explain Turkey's involvement in numerous regional crisis, ranging from those in Syria to Libya and even Egypt. Put bluntly, Erdoğan's rule in Turkey paved the way for the rise of a new set of territorial ideas in Turkey, which exert a real impact on Turkey's foreign policy initiatives and priorities.

The moral of this story, once again, is more about the socially constructed nature of territories than it is about Turkey per se. We often think of territory as a self-obvious term or a mute, physical object. When we think of state territories, more precisely, we usually focus on the location of borders, or the "lines" in our political maps. However, territory is far more than just lines on a map. Territories, especially the lines on the maps, are social and political constructs, fueled by particular ideas about the relationship between the society, space, and politics. These ideas are reified by institutional practices. The direct implication is clear: territory is, and has always been, what states and societies make of it. Furthermore, these territorial ideas exert important influence on the ways in which states and societies conceive war. Considering that territorial issues, broadly defined, have been a key component of armed conflict, this observation suggests that while human societies have fought over territory since time immemorial, they have not necessarily been fighting over the same thing, simply because territory meant different things to different societies. Last, the relationship between territorial ideas and armed conflict is not unidirectional; just as territorial ideas affect wars, wars themselves can transform and shape the dominant territorial ideas in a geography.

The remainder of this study develops the aforementioned claims in four steps. The first part first offers an overview of the existing literature, and then presents a novel conceptual-analytical framework to examine the two-way relationship between territorial ideas and armed conflict. Part II includes a wide variety of case studies that range from revolutionary France to the Islamic State (ISIS), and from the Ottomans to the British colonial incursions into South Asia. These cases help illuminate how different territorial ideas, or "territorial orders," affect the ways in which states fight over territory in different ways. In Part III, I deal with how wars, more precisely what international relations (IR) scholars call "systemic wars," affect the transformation of the aforementioned territorial orders. This part goes beyond the typical approaches on the subject, and deals with the consequences of these systemic wars not only in Europe and the Western world, but also in non-Western geographies, or the Global South. The conclusion elaborates on some of the implications of the broader arguments for the present day, and deals with topics that include, but are not limited to, the legacies of geographical racism in IR as well as international politics and the Russo-Ukrainian War.

PART I
CONCEPTUAL AND THEORETICAL FRAMEWORK

2
Territory, War, and the "Territorial Trap"

> It is truly astonishing that the concept of territoriality had been so little studied by students of international politics; its neglect is akin to never looking at the ground that one is walking on.
>
> —John Gerard Ruggie[1]

Territory lies at the heart of both practice and theory of international politics. The so-called Westphalian state, on which modern diplomacy and the discipline of international relations (IR) are built, is defined in terms of its distinctive quality: territorial sovereignty. Research on armed conflict has also revealed that territory, broadly defined, has constituted the single most salient issue in interstate wars and disputes for the last half a millennium.[2] Ever since they existed, well before the rise of the Westphalian system, states made war with each other, and most of these wars had territorial causes as well as consequences.

Most notably, wars of territorial conquest have radically declined after World War II.[3] The end of the Cold War and rise of globalization also triggered what can be called "territorial optimism," the idea that territory has now lost its salience and will eventually cease to act as a source of conflict.[4] However, territorial issues remain a salient component of interstate disputes. Pakistan and India, for example, have been locked in a territorial dispute over Jammu and Kashmir for more than seventy years, just as Azerbaijan and Armenia have over Nagorno-Karabagh for the past three decades. The Syrian Civil War,

---

[1] Ruggie 1993, 174.

[2] Diehl and Goertz 2002, 2; Kahler and Walter 2006; Lake and O'Mahony 2006, 153. According to Toft (2014, 186), "Armed disputes over territory are a major source of the global distribution of violence and destruction, and this trend appears to be increasing over time. Indeed, when states fight, they often tend to fight over territory. Territorial disputes produced some 65% of the dyadic wars fought from 1816 to 1945 and produced an even higher percentage—72%—in the post-1945 period." In addition, "Civil wars are also frequently fought over territory" (Toft 2014, 187).

[3] As Michael Mann (2018) highlights, interstate wars might have declined, but broader war—organized violence—does not seem to go away. Instead it occurs in different paces and patterns across time and space.

[4] Sassen 1996, 1998; Strange 1998; Friedman 2000, 2007; Greig 2002; Ohmae 1999. Mary Kaldor (1999) noted that "new wars" in the post–Cold War era are typically not fought over territory.

Shifting Grounds. Burak Kadercan, Oxford University Press. © Oxford University Press 2023.
DOI: 10.1093/oso/9780197686690.003.0002

24 Conceptual and Theoretical Framework

in turn, evolved into a conflict where numerous states and nonstate actors are competing with each other in order to exert territorial control in the country. China's efforts to create artificial islands in the South China Sea also suggest that great powers are still interested in and capable of expanding their spatial reach, sometimes through unconventional measures. The case of the self-proclaimed Islamic State (ISIS), in turn, has prompted scholars and analysts to question the scope of variation in territorial practices in the twenty-first century.[5] More recently, Russia invaded Ukraine, paving the way for the first large-scale interstate war over territory in Europe since the end of World War II. In other words, while many cheered for the "end of geography"[6] and the birth of a networked and aterritorial world in the aftermath of the Cold War, "territory retains its allure."[7] The longevity of territory's allure, in turn, renders exploring the relationship between territory and armed conflict important not only for making sense of the past but also for analyzing the present trends as well as thinking about the future of world politics.

The literature of territorial conflict in IR is vast. An overwhelming majority of the research conducted on the subject, in turn, deals with the "material" (and, more often than not, quantifiable) aspects of territory, such as resources, location of borders, contiguity, distance, and topography. However, the relevant studies tend to bypass or downplay territory's (or territories') contingent and ideational characteristics. As political geographers have long recognized, "territorial ideas" have displayed considerable variation across time and space. Acknowledging and then scrutinizing this dynamic is crucial for establishing a more comprehensive understanding of the origins, conduct, and consequences of armed conflict over territory both in the past and present.

Malcolm Anderson, in his 1996-dated monograph *Frontiers*, offers a most valuable insight on the relationship between territorial ideas and conflict. Anderson draws attention to the role that "territorial ideologies" play in driving the patterns in territorial conflict. According to Anderson, both scholars and policymakers have underestimated the importance of these ideologies for making sense of—and even resolving—territorial disputes and conflicts.[8] For Anderson, "Some kind of territorial ideology—namely, a set of beliefs about the relationship of the population to the area which it inhabits—is a necessary part of the basis for any political order," and "Their content is a crucial factor in initiating and sustaining a struggle for territory."[9] More

---

[5] Kadercan 2019.
[6] Graham 1998.
[7] Murphy 2013, 1214. Also see Newman 2010, 775; Agnew 2009; Walter 2006, 288.
[8] Anderson 1996, 34. On the concept of "territorial ideology," also see Murphy 2005.
[9] Anderson 1996, 34, 36.

specifically, territorial ideologies may emanate from "religious dominion, notions of homelands, historical myths, living spaces, natural frontiers, civilizing missions, ethnicity, human biology, claims of natural rights, and the optimal use of space."[10] Regardless of their origin, these ideologies have "motivated people to fight and die."[11] Overall, Anderson identifies the relationship between territorial ideas (or ideologies) and war but does not develop a systematic analysis of this relationship.

This study takes up where Anderson left off and examines the interactive relationship between territory and war from conceptual, theoretical, and historical standpoints by building on a simple observation that lies at the heart of the relevant research in political geography: territory is what states and societies make of it. In other words, territory can hardly be seen as a synonym for physical space but is in fact a social and political construct.[12] More specifically, states and societies across time and space have adhered to different forms of territoriality, and territory as well as territorial control implied different ideas and practices in different time periods and regions.[13]

In this context, *Shifting Grounds* addresses two questions: First, how exactly do different territorial ideas affect the ways in which states fight their wars? Second, *what specific roles* have wars played in the evolution of the dominant territorial ideas in world politics? This study addresses both questions through the prism of what I refer to as "territorial orders,"[14] or the set of institutionalized ideas (and associated practices) that aim to regulate the ways in which states demarcate the spatial extent of their political authority and organize the relationship between space and society. This framework identifies four territorial orders—*mosaic, monolithic, amorphous*, and *virulent*—each of which points toward different geopolitical objectives, military strategies, and patterns in war.

The relationship between territorial orders and wars is not unidirectional: just as territorial orders can affect how states approach wars, wars themselves can have an impact on the transformation of territorial orders. In particular, I examine the impacts of four "systemic wars" on this transformation: The Thirty Years' War, the Revolutionary and Napoleonic Wars, World War I, and World War II. *Shifting Grounds* makes two claims about the impact of wars on the evolution of the present-day global territorial arrangement.

---

[10] Anderson 1996, 186.

[11] Anderson 1996, 186.

[12] As will be discussed in detail in Chapter 3, "territory" does not merely follow from ideas per se, but also entails a "physical" component.

[13] Gottmann 1975, 29; Buzan and Lawson 2015, 5; Osiander 2007. This study does not deal with etymology or the historical roots of the word "territory." For such an approach, see Elden 2013.

[14] Kratochwil (1986) first used the term "territorial orders."

26 Conceptual and Theoretical Framework

First, the so-called systemic wars played an essential and nonlinear role in the transformation of territorial ideas. More specifically, how these wars were fought as well as postwar settlements triggered categorical shifts in how state elites, and eventually societies, envisioned the "appropriate" demarcation as well as organization principles.[15]

The second claim is that the impacts of these systemic wars varied in the "West" and the "Rest."[16] In the Western world, the mechanism through which systemic wars led to the transformation of territorial orders often entailed "problem-solving." The participants in the postwar settlements attempted to address the perceived problems that led to war in the first place by setting a new ideational gold standard over the question of how to demarcate space and organize space-society association, usually with unintended consequences. In the non-Western geographies, the transformation of territorial orders took place in the presence of imperialism-induced hierarchies and ethnocentric biases. Especially World War I and World War II disrupted, if temporarily, the hierarchical relationship between the Western states and local populations, creating opportunities for the local elites to challenge these hierarchies, with varying degrees of success. Therefore, the evolution of the so-called modern state system entails a far more nonlinear and far less "egalitarian" narrative than usually acknowledged in mainstream IR.

The remainder of this chapter unfolds in three sections. First, I briefly overview the relevant literature in IR and make a case for an interdisciplinary approach that brings together insights from IR and political geography. In the second section, I elaborate on the research methodology. The third section highlights the contributions of the preceding discussion.

Background: Toward an Interdisciplinary Approach

The salience of territorial issues in interstate and intrastate conflicts is well established in IR literature.[17] This has not always been the case. Until the end of the Cold War, with few notable exceptions, IR scholarship paid little attention to territory.[18] From the early-1990s onward, the empirical and theoretical

---

[15] Examining the interactive relationship between nationalism and war from a macrohistorical perspective, Hutchinson (2017, 19) also emphasizes the importance of these four systemic wars for understanding the evolution of the present-day world politics. For a more detailed discussion, see Chapter 7.

[16] In this study, recognizing the relevant nuances, I use the terms "non-Western" and "Global South," as well as "Western" and "Global North," interchangeably, *when doing so is applicable*.

[17] Reviewing twenty-one leading journals in IR, Toft (2014, 185) finds that in the last fifty-five years, 198 articles on territory and war were published, with a trend that significantly increased in 1990s and peaked by mid-2000s.

[18] Herz 1957; Luard 1987; Kratochwil 1986.

Territory, War, and the "Territorial Trap"   **27**

inquiries into the relationship between territory and conflict have grown into a robust research program.[19] Overall, the perspectives on the relationship between war and territory can be examined in terms of three categories that are not mutually exclusive:[20] evolutionary, materialistic, and constructivist.

In IR, the evolutionary perspective is as almost as old as the surge of interest in territory.[21] In his pathbreaking 1993 book, *The War Puzzle*, Vasquez examined the existing data sets on war and came to the conclusion that "territorial issues" constitute the most salient set of (independent) variables that can help explain the outbreak of interstate wars.[22] To explain why territory, of all possible issues, stands out, Vasquez then invoked an evolutionary interpretation of human territoriality. This perspective portrays human territoriality as a reflection of a "biological drive or aggressive instinct, a genetically transmitted behavioral trait which humans share with many other animal species."[23] While this idea has long been in circulation,[24] it was developed into a full-fledged theory only recently by Johnson and Toft.[25] For Johnson and Toft, "Humans have a built-in propensity . . . to privilege territory as all-important and indivisible,"[26] and this propensity can help explain the trends in conflict over territory, presumably from the dawn of humankind to the present day.

However, while the evolutionary perspective's interpretation of human territoriality is a constant, the patterns in frequency and severity of territorial conflict show significant variation across time and space; a constant can hardly explain a variable. The application of the evolutionary logic to the modern era also comes with temporal and scalar problems. For example, Johnson and Toft draw upon contemporary examples such as territorial disputes between Ethiopia and Eritrea, Chechnya as well as Ukraine and Russia, and the Abkhaz and Georgians—*which are inextricably associated with nationalistic discourses*—to provide anecdotal evidence for human territoriality.[27] From a temporal point of view, while the roots of human territoriality presumably go back to the dawn of the humankind, nationalism is a relatively new phenomenon by world-historical standards.[28] The evolutionary approach does not

[19] For example, Goertz and Diehl 1992; Vasquez 1993; Ruggie 1993; Huth 1996; Starr 2005; Wright and Diehl 2016.

[20] For research that explicitly combines different approaches, see Shelef 2016; Hensel and Mitchell 2005; Dzurek 2005; O'Lear et al. 2005.

[21] Note that in political geography, the view that "human territoriality is a natural, instinctive phenomenon" has been largely discredited (Penrose 2002, 279). Also see Newman 2006a, 108; Vollaard 2009, 690; Sack 1986; Storey 2012, 20; Paasi 2003, 111.

[22] Vasquez 1993.

[23] Johnston 1995, 213. Also see Ardrey 1969. For a critical perspective, see Malešević 2010, 54.

[24] For example, Tir 2010, 416.

[25] Johnson and Toft 2014.

[26] Johnson and Toft 2014, 15.

[27] Johnson and Toft 2014, 7.

[28] Anderson 1996, 63. Also see Malešević 2013.

28   Conceptual and Theoretical Framework

offer a compelling argument for why and how the aforementioned human territoriality "reawakened" only in the last couple of centuries, after thousands of years of dormancy. The application of the evolutionary logic to the present day is also misleading in terms of "scale."[29] According to the logic of the evolutionary approach, humans are "soft-wired"[30] to be sensitive toward their immediate habitat. Modern-day nationalism dictates that people (should) care about the (national) homeland, the scale of which goes far beyond an individual's habitat.[31] Even by the standards of its own logic, the evolutionary perspective cannot explain why people in the modern age care deeply about places that they may never even visit. In sum, the evolutionary approach to territory is rife with analytical problems.[32]

The overwhelming majority of IR researchers explicitly adhere to the materialistic interpretation of the relationship between territory and armed conflict, and usually emphasize one or more of three factors: physical geography, resources that territory hosts, and tangible (or quantifiable) factors associated with (Westphalian) borders. The relationship between physical geography and war plays out through environmental factors such as (rough) terrain, oceans, mountains, rivers, and other topographical elements. In relation, the relevant research also highlights the impacts of technological innovations (e.g., railways, steamboats, aircraft, the advent of the internet) or human-made changes to physical geography (e.g., the Suez Canal) on patterns in armed conflict and great power competition.[33] Historically speaking, emphasis on physical geography gained prominence with the study of [classical] geopolitics of the late nineteenth and early twentieth centuries,[34] which sought to uncover the "geographical causation in universal history."[35] In recent times,

[29] In political geography, scale usually refers to "the nested hierarchy of bounded spaces of differing size, such as the local, regional, national and global" (Delaney and Leitner 1997, 93).

[30] Johnson and Toft 2014.

[31] For a similar point, see Etherington 2010, 324. In relation, the evolutionary approach offers an explanation for why humans (in general) might be "soft-wired" for territorial affinity, but it is the state elites who decide when, how, and how hard to fight over territory. On the relevant concept of "microfoundations," see Little 1991; Schelling 1978. Lopez (2016, 105) argues that, even from an evolutionary approach, "individual-level aggression is fundamentally different from (although related to) coalitional-level aggression." In Malešević's (2010, 56) words, the relevant perspectives on human violence ignore "the unintended products of human action such as social structure, culture and ideology but also institutions and social organizations, which have acquired a substantial autonomy and are able to generate new social dynamics."

[32] Antonsich 2015. Edward Soja (1971) also warns against direct comparisons between human territoriality and animal territoriality.

[33] On relevant debates, see Porter 2015. Donnelly (2012, 619) refers to this dynamic as "geotechnics," or "the material dimension of social positions and relations, conceptualized in terms of geography and technology."

[34] According to Hudson (1977, 147) the three classics of deterministic geography are Friedrich Ratzel's *Anthropogeographie* (1899), Ellen Churchill Semple's *Influences of Geographic Environment* ([1911] 1968), and Ellsworth Huntington's Civilization and Climate (1915).

[35] Mackinder 1943, 596; 1904; Kearns 2009, 6; 2004, 344; 2010, 187; Blouet 2004. Also see Mahan 1890; Hudson 1977, 149. As is well known, the notion of environmental or geographic determinism as well as Mackinder's ideas about a "land-based global empire" were used as an "ideological buttress for imperialism

the proponents of the so-called neoclassical geopolitics adhere to this perspective, making the case for the centrality of the "dictates of geography" for understanding contemporary world politics.[36]

Physical geography can help explain a number of puzzles relating to interstate war and state formation.[37] However, unqualified reliance on the physical components of territories can also lead to overdeterministic or indeterminate analyses. For instance, the European landscape has barely changed in the last couple of centuries, but the ways in (and reasons for) which states fought over territory displayed significant variation that can hardly be explained solely by environmental change or technological innovations such as railways.[38] Physical geography matters, but it is not destiny and therefore cannot explain numerous trends and patterns in armed conflict all by itself.

The second version of the materialistic perspective portrays territory as a "resource generator": states fight over territory because controlling territory allows states to extract resources and gain strategic advantage. Stripped to its very basics, this interpretation is associated most closely with neorealists and (IR) liberals. For neorealists, state survival in an anarchical system depends on amassing sufficient material power, a function of territorial control.[39] Considering that the earth's landmass is a limited good, the quest for power (or survival) then traps states in a territorial zero-sum game. Despite all their differences from neorealists, IR liberals start from the same perspective that posits territory primarily as a resource generator.[40] Unlike neorealists, IR liberals argue that, in the post–World War II era, economic and financial interdependence has rendered wars of territorial conquest (almost) extinct, simply because the marginal (economic) returns for fighting over territory have decreased tremendously.[41]

Resource-oriented approaches to the relationship between territory and war offer essential insights. In the end, territories do host material resources

---

and racism," most notably by Nazi ideologues and strategists for planning and justifying military aggression and mass murder. See Kearns 2009, 9; Ashworth 2011, 284.

[36] Parker 1998, 49; Kaplan 2012; Grygiel 2006; Dodds and Atkinson 2000, xiv; Kearns 2009, 23; see also Flint 2006; Megoran 2010. One of the key proponents of neoclassical geopolitics, Colin Gray (1991) suggests that a country's political posture to a large extent follows from its history, and its history to a large extent follows its geographical setting.

[37] Kennedy 1987; Mearsheimer 2001. Also see Porter 2015; Herbst 2000.

[38] On the impacts of railways on warfare, see Onorato et al. 2014. Also see Cederman et al. 2011 for the greater debate. Also see Kadercan 2012.

[39] Waltz 1979; Mearsheimer 2001. On the role of "survival assumption" in neorealism, see Kadercan 2013.

[40] On IR (neo)liberalism, see Keohane 1984; Powell 1991; Snidal 1991.

[41] In the twentieth century, this idea can be traced to Norman Angell (1910). The idea, which lost its appeal especially after World War II, was revived during the course of the 1980s, most notably by Richard Rosecrance (1986). Also see Rosecrance 1999; Brooks 1999; and Brooks 2011.

30 Conceptual and Theoretical Framework

over which states compete. However, an approach that focuses exclusively on material resources alone cannot easily explain several important dynamics.[42] For example, neorealists have a hard time accounting for the transformation in European warfare during the revolutionary and Napoleonic era without invoking ideational factors such as nationalism, which are (or should be) left out of their decidedly materialistic perspective.[43] Liberals, in turn, cannot easily explain why territory remains a salient and persistent source of disputes and conflict: if the main reason for territorial disputes and conflicts is concern for resources, we should expect territory to become increasingly irrelevant in a globalized and interdependent world. This, however, is not the case.

The third branch of the materialistic perspective focuses on the demarcation-related features of territory, or the "tangible dimensions of territorial size, shape, and proximity to neighboring territories within an interstate framework."[44] Overall, as Johnson and Toft point out, these studies are not typically unified or organized around a central theoretical premise.[45] A certain common characteristic of this line of research is an overwhelming emphasis on quantitative analysis.[46] Most notably, scholars such as John Vasquez have studied in great detail the impacts of contiguity and distance between states on the likelihood of armed conflict.[47] Paul Huth, Thorin Wright, and Paul Diehl, in turn, have scrutinized the interaction between domestic and international variables in order to explain the salience of territorial issues in interstate conflicts and disputes.[48] Other IR researchers such as David Carter, Hein Goemans, Beth Simmons, and Kenneth Schulz have examined the association between (Westphalian) borders and territorial disputes.[49]

While quantitative approaches have made considerable contributions to our understanding of territory's place in world politics, they also tend to treat the "character" of territory as a constant. Similar to the other approaches highlighted above, the relevant studies rarely, if at all, define territory in specific terms. Furthermore, this version of the materialistic perspective often equates the term "territoriality" with the conventional wisdom on Westphalian territoriality. This tendency then makes it difficult to tackle or even consider

---

[42] As Le Billon (2001, 563) highlighted, "The availability *in nature* of any resource [or lack thereof] is . . . not in itself a predictive indicator of conflict."

[43] Kadercan 2012.

[44] Newman 2006a, 86. Also see Diehl and Goertz 1988; Vasquez 1993; Huth 1996; Vasquez and Henehan 2001a; Vasquez and Henehan 2001b; Huth and Allee 2003; Carter and Goemans 2011.

[45] Johnson and Toft 2014.

[46] In Monica Toft's words (2014, 192), "Most of the research on the relationship between territory and war has taken a statistical turn."

[47] Vasquez 1993. Also see Starr 2013.

[48] Huth 1996; Wright and Diehl 2016.

[49] Carter and Goemans 2011; Goemans and Schultz 2017; Schultz 2017; Simmons 2005a, 2005b; Carter 2010; Goemans 2006. Also see Walters 2006; Abramson and Carter 2016.

Territory, War, and the "Territorial Trap"   31

alternative territorial arrangements, paving the way for what George Lawson calls a "not only ahistorical, but also ahistoricist" understanding of world politics.[50] For example, it may be true that, as Starr highlights, "territory is literally of always high value";[51] however, even a cursory reading of global history and present-day world politics reveals that the "value" attributed to territory has shown great variation across time and space.

Constructivist approaches to territory and territoriality, in turn, suggest that the "value" (and meaning) attached to territory is usually in the eye of the beholder and is driven, to a large extent, by ideational and social (or intersubjective) dynamics.[52] In IR, scholars such as Friedrich Kratochwil, John Ruggie, and Richard Ashley can be seen as pioneers of this approach. For Kratochwil, territoriality is "not a simple concept, but comprises a variety of social arrangements that have to be examined in greater detail."[53] Employing the term "territorial orders," Kratochwil examines the differences and similarities between demarcation principles associated with empires and the modern state ideal. According to Ruggie, the origins of different forms of territorial models can be traced to the institutionalization of "knowledge," or ideas, about the relationship between space and politics.[54] Ruggie then draws a comparison between the modern understanding of territoriality and the medieval order.[55] Upholding a critical IR perspective,[56] Richard Ashley contests the dominant interpretations and readings of the international space, which are usually presented as static, timeless, and universal "facts" of political life. According to Ashley, critical IR scholars should explore the "historical emergence, bounding, conquest, and administration of social *spaces*" while simultaneously exposing the fact that sovereign state boundaries are "plastic divisions of political space."[57]

More recently, scholars such as Jordan Branch, Jeremy Larkins, and Kerry Goettlich have explored the socially constructed and historically contingent nature of territoriality in European and colonial history.[58] In addition, Ian Lustick, Monica Toft, Ron Hassner, and Stacie Goddard have scrutinized the notion of "indivisible territory" in great detail,[59] examining the mechanisms

[50] Lawson 2006.

[51] Starr 2005, 398.

[52] On this point, see Shelef 2016. Territories also have a strong "emotive" component. See Solomon and Steele 2017, 269.

[53] Kratochwil 1986, 27–28.

[54] Ruggie 1993, 169.

[55] Ruggie 1993, 169; see also Teschke 1998, 346; Penrose 2002, 283; Hirst 2005, 27, 28–32.

[56] On critical approaches to IR, see Barkawi and Laffey 2002.

[57] Ashley 1987, 409, 421. One illustrative example of this line of work is offered by the Identities, Borders, Orders group. See Albert et al. 2001.

[58] Branch 2014; Larkins 2010; Goettlich 2019. Also see Strandsbjerg 2010.

[59] Lustick 1993; Toft 2003; Hassner 2009; Goddard 2009. Also see Fearon 1995; Reiter 2003; Wagner 2000; Walter 2009.

32 Conceptual and Theoretical Framework

through which certain territories can be perceived as indivisible by numerous actors and lead to war and intractable conflict. Similarly, arguing that not all territories are of equal value in the eyes of different actors, Shelef explores the social construction of "homeland."[60] Scholars such as Mark Zacher, Tanisha Fazal, and Boaz Atzili emphasize the social and political construction of the global territorial arrangements at the interstate level, pointing toward the impacts of the so-called territorial integrity (or border fixity) norm on patterns of interstate and intrastate conflict.[61]

While a constructivist theory of territorial conflict holds the greatest potential to examine the relationship between territorial ideas and war in novel ways, there currently exists no comprehensive approach to the relationship between the socially constructed nature of territories and organized violence. Scholars who deal with the broader and macrohistorical topics, such as Ruggie and Kratochwil, do not directly deal with the association between territory-as-an-idea and organized violence. Researchers who directly examine the association between the socially constructed nature of territories and armed conflict, in turn, have yet to engage the aforementioned association from a macrohistorical perspective, or through a broader theoretical framework. To be precise, this is not a criticism of IR constructivism. To the contrary, these observations point toward the promise of constructivism, in the context of the relationship between territory, territoriality, and organized violence.

Note that constructivist approaches to territory go well beyond IR. In fact, the socially constructed nature of spatial arrangements has attracted considerably more attention in political geography than it has in IR.[62] According to Hakli, the "constructivist perspective was adopted so as the avoid the historical near-sightedness often implied in approaches which treat scientific abstractions in ahistorical and universalizing manner."[63] Political geographers also agree that the study of territory needs to "move beyond the traditional discourse of demarcation, proximity, size and shape of territories."[64] In this

---

[60] Shelef 2016. Also see Mylonas and Shelef 2014.

[61] Zacher 2001; Fazal 2007; Atzili 2012. As long recognized not only by political scientists but also by students of international law and sociology, the United Nations institutionalized a norm that made it rather unacceptable for states to wage wars of conquest, which is also backed by actual sanctions from the member states. As Murphy (1990, 536) highlights, article 2(4) of the UN Charter stipulates that "all members shall refrain in their international relations from the threat or use of force against the territorial integrity or political independence of any state."

[62] On the relevant literature, see Storey 2012; Delaney 2005. For a general introduction to the broader literature on territory in the context of human geography, see Yılmaz 2018. The initial impetus for this research came from the works of philosophers such as Michel Foucault and Henri Lefebvre. For Foucault (1986, 252), "Space is fundamental in any form of communal life; space is fundamental in any exercise of power." Lefebvre, in turn, focuses his attention on the ways in which territorial totalization occurs in the context of the nation-states (Lefebvre and Nicholson-Smith 1991). Also see Sack 1986.

[63] Hakli 1994, 26. Also see Le Billon 2001.

[64] Newman 2006a, 109.

reading, "Territories are not frozen frameworks where social life occurs"; instead, they are made (and remade) through social and individual action.[65] Therefore, territory and territoriality are as much about society as they are about physical space.[66]

Especially from the early 1990s onward, political geographers began to focus on the various configurations of territory in the context of world politics, paving the way for the rise of so-called critical geopolitics. Critical geopolitics refers to a broad research program that primarily addresses the ways in which different territorialization mechanisms are employed by core powers and hegemonic states.[67] The term has also served as a potent rallying point for geographers who are interested in international politics as well as numerous critical IR scholars.[68] Beyond (but not entirely independent of) critical geopolitics lies the work of scholars such as John Agnew and Stuart Elden, among many others.[69] This particular scholarship examines the multifaceted, historically contingent, and fluid nature of territorial arrangements in the context of global politics in great detail.[70]

That being said, mainstream IR and political geography have evolved almost in total isolation from one another.[71] The interaction between IR scholars and political geographers over the study of territorial conflict has been minimal so far. Scholars from one discipline, apart from notable exceptions,[72] tend to either ignore or dismiss the research carried out in the neighboring discipline. Even more likely, many IR scholars and political geographers may not even be fully aware of the research on the other side of the disciplinary fences.

---

[65] Passi 2003, 110.

[66] Murphy 1990, 532.

[67] Power and Campbell 2010, 243; Blouet 2004, 327; Dalby 2010, 281; Toal 1996; Toal and Agnew 1992, 192; Mamadouh 1999.

[68] This is hardly surprising, for "The emergence of critical geopolitics was coeval with the development of critical theories of international relations from the late 1980s onwards, especially in the work of Richard Ashley, James Der Derian, Michael Shapiro, and Rob Walker" (Power and Campbell 2010, 343).

[69] For example, Agnew 2009; Elden 2009, 2013. Also see Dalby 2010.

[70] For a detailed analysis, see Kadercan 2015. Also see Graham 2011. More recently, the debates in political geography over territory have taken a turn toward the history of ideas and political theory. The most influential work along this line thus far is Elden's *The Birth of Territory*. Elden is particularly interested in the conceptual origins of territory, which he argues are rarely examined or even questioned. In particular, Elden examines a wide variety of texts from ancient Greece to seventeenth-century Europe to show how the notion of territory developed as a political subject in Western practice and thought. Following his former work (especially Elden 2009), Elden (2013, 10) conceptualizes territory as a political technology and emphasizes the ways in which "the legal and the technical" interact with respect to the relationship between geography and politics. Also see Minca et al. 2015; Antonsich 2011.

[71] Two exceptions stand out. First, as already mentioned, critical IR and critical geopolitics robustly interact with each other to the extent that it is difficult, and perhaps meaningless, to differentiate between the two. The second area where interdisciplinary interaction already exists entails methodology. Some IR scholars increasingly use spatial analysis tools such as ArcGIS in their quantitative analysis, especially in conflict studies (or what is sometimes referred to as "peace science"). For example, see Flint et al. 2009, 827; Starr 2005, 387. On "peace research," see Dunn 2018.

[72] For a recent attempt, see Atzili and Kadercan 2018.

34 Conceptual and Theoretical Framework

An interdisciplinary approach that brings together insights from IR and political geography is not only exceptionally promising, but also more feasible than usually assumed. Such an endeavor is exceptionally rewarding because of two factors. First, paradoxically, the fact that IR scholars and political geographers have so far barely engaged with each other points toward a relatively uncharted intellectual territory, which can be explored in productive ways. The second factor follows from the logic of comparative advantage: as a discipline, IR research has long focused on the causes, conduct, and consequences of armed conflict (probably more so than any other discipline in social sciences), and political geographers have studied the conceptual, theoretical, and empirical dimensions of territory and territoriality in far greater detail than IR scholars have.[73] By forgoing interdisciplinary dialogues on the topic of conflict over territory, both IR scholars and political geographers miss out on numerous important insights that may already exist on the other side of the disciplinary fence. In other words, an interdisciplinary dialogue makes it unnecessary for both IR scholars and political geographers to reinvent the wheel, especially if the other side has already accumulated relevant research and insights.

Of course, for interdisciplinary research to take hold, "promise" is not sufficient; such an approach also needs to be feasible. The theoretical, epistemological, and methodological distance and barriers between IR and political geography are not imaginary. While an ever-increasing penchant for social scientific aspirations and an emphasis on causal inference and hypothesis-testing have long dominated mainstream IR,[74] much of the research in political geography has been fueled by postmodernist approaches and political philosophy,[75] which privilege "how" questions (as opposed to "why" questions that aim to provide causal explanations for certain phenomena).[76] These being said, constructivist approaches to territory offer a potential beachhead for interdisciplinary synergies.[77] To be precise, in political geography, there is an ongoing debate on the importance of the material aspects of territory,[78] but,

---

[73] As Colin Flint (2003, 166) maintains, "Geographers need a closer engagement with issues of war and peace, and with conflict studies in general." On the topic, also see Moore 2013; Moore 2019.

[74] Most notably, King et al. 1994.

[75] According to Peter Taylor (2002, 391), the "distance" between the social sciences and political geography follows from the particular historical evolution of the field: "Political geography lies at the periphery of human geography, which itself never established itself within the core of social science."

[76] Van Houtum 2005, 676. Also see Koopman 2016.

[77] Calls for further interdisciplinary dialogues between IR and political geography can be traced to Kahler and Walter 2006. More recently, Atzili and Kadercan (2017) initiated a dedicated effort to bring together IR scholars and political geographers. Also see Kadercan 2015.

[78] For the debate, see Usher 2020.

Territory, War, and the "Territorial Trap"   35

overall, both IR constructivists and most political geographers reject what can be referred to as materialistic determinism.

Furthermore, the very basic tenets of IR constructivism are inherently compatible with the research in political geography. An illustration can help drive home the point. IR constructivists emphasize the role of norms in world politics. These norms can be defined as a "matrix of constitutive principles that govern the behaviors of members of a given social group."[79] Political geographers would adhere to a similar, almost identical, interpretation of spatial ideas and institutions, which effectively "regulate behavior, reduce uncertainty by institutionalizing conventions, signal expectations, and reveal information."[80] Ergo, there already exist common analytical grounds between constructivist IR scholars and political geographers, which remain yet to be explored in depth.

To move forward with such an interdisciplinary approach (or simply to pursue a research agenda to formulate a constructivist theory of territorial conflict), two core issues, both of which have long been identified by political geographers, need to be addressed: conceptualizing territory and acknowledging the so-called territorial trap.[81] In the study of international politics, "territory" is a term that is commonly invoked but rarely defined.[82] In Stuart Elden's words, territory is "unhistorically accepted, conceptually assumed, and philosophically unexamined."[83] The common practice is to either leave the terms "territory" and "territoriality" undefined or take them for granted by assuming that their meanings are "self-evident."[84] Yet another misleading assumption is that territory is the product of the Westphalian ideal of clearly demarcated space over which states exercise exclusive sovereign rights. However, the Westphalian understanding of the space-politics relationship does not reflect a universal standard but constitutes only one of many possible spatial-political arrangements.[85]

---

[79] Spruyt 2000, 68.

[80] Spruyt 2000, 69.

[81] Agnew 1994.

[82] Elden 2010, 799–800; see also Ruggie 1993, 174; Vollaard 2009, 688. Marco Antonisch (2009, 795) suggests that "territory has been generally treated by different disciplines as a simple aspect of something more relevant to be studied, for example, sovereignty (in IR), culture (in anthropology)." According to Banai et al. (2014, 99), territory is "one of the most under-theorized concepts" in political theory. For a review of the existing perspectives in political geography, see Mountz 2013. For recent debates on territory and territoriality in political theory, see Stilz 2009; Miller 2012; Nine 2008; Simmons 2001. The lack of attention to territory and territoriality has also been a feature of historical sociology. For an extended argument, see Chapter 3.

[83] Elden 2005, 10.

[84] Elden 2010, 800. Also see Barkin and Cronin 1994, 107. In addition, some IR scholars may equate territory with geography, but these terms are not synonymous. See Agnew 2009, 29.

[85] Biggs 1999; Murphy 2002, 208; Penrose 2002, 283; Newman and Paasi 1998, 187. Also see Newman and Paasi 1998, 187; Branch 2014; Goettlich 2019; Ruggie 1993; Kratochwil 1986; Biggs 1999; Larkins 2010;

36 Conceptual and Theoretical Framework

The second (and related) obstacle to interdisciplinary cross-fertilization is what John Agnew dubbed as the "territorial trap." In an influential article, John Agnew (1994) argues that IR theory is built on three geographical assumptions that effectively limit its understanding of territory. The first assumption entails the reification of "state territories as set or fixed units of sovereign space," which in turn serves to "dehistoricize and decontextualize processes of state formation and disintegration."[86] Second, modern IR theory draws upon the polarity of domestic and international politics, which then obfuscates the ways in which these two dimensions interact. The third component of the territorial trap, in turn, involves viewing "the territorial state as existing prior to and as a container of society," which artificially normalizes the complicated and multifaceted nature of space-society-politics interaction simply by assuming away its complexity. Without recognizing the flawed and misleading nature of these assumptions, Agnew argues, IR cannot move beyond the territorial blindfold that not only limits but also distorts its theoretical and historical vision.[87] Overall, Agnew's territorial trap intervention points toward "the need to look at alternative and competing spaces of political practice."[88] Note that while the territorial trap remains one of the most influential interventions in political geography, it has had relatively minimal impact on the ways in which IR scholars think about their geographical assumptions.[89]

The territorial trap comes with two particular side effects. First, it makes it difficult to conceive the nature, or even existence, of alternative territorial arrangements across time and space. Geographical and spatial assumptions of IR—that is, assumptions about "the frameworks that organize the world in spatial terms and locate these actors, processes, and events, both in relation to each other and to world politics more generally"[90]—are built on our understanding, or idealization, of the nation-state. However, as Siniša

---

Mukerji 1997; Murphy 2010, 771; Agnew 1994; Strandsbjerg 2010, 29; Williams 2006, 6; Caporoso 2000; Buzan 2010, 97, 182; Kadercan 2015.

[86] Agnew 1994, 59.
[87] Murphy 2010.
[88] Murphy 2010, 771.
[89] As Solomon and Steele (2017, 277) maintain, even though more than twenty-five years have passed since the publication of Agnew's article on the territorial trap, "Much of IR theory remains wedded to the spatial assumptions that Agnew and others critiqued." Political geographer Alexander Murphy (2010, 770) argues that IR falls into the territorial trap because of "a disciplinary preoccupation with institutional, as opposed to geographical, arrangements that came out of the rise to dominance of a particular spatial scale of political organization and social life as the modern state system took root around the world." Similar critiques have also been launched by anthropologists, targeting their own discipline, if not IR. For example, see Smith 2005, 834.
[90] Barkawi and Laffey 2006, 334.

Malešević puts it, nation-states constitute a "historical anomaly."[91] As Tarak Barkawi argues, the relevant biases confine mainstream IR to the study of the nation-states, or the ideal of Westphalian state, and portray other political forms—most notably, empires—only as a minor note, even though colonial arrangements survived well into the second half of twentieth century.[92] For example, according to Andreas Wimmer, by 1900, more than 60% of the globe was governed by imperial rule or some form of colonial dependency; the same ratio was roughly 40% in 1920, and more than 20% in 1960.[93] Put bluntly, IR's geographical vision (which privileges the "modern state" at the expense of alternative political forms such as empires) hardly reflects the territorial realities of even the twentieth century, where it is supposed to apply best.

The second side effect of the territorial trap is that it renders the evolution of the present-day global territorial arrangement relatively unproblematic. Conventional accounts provide a linear and Eurocentric narrative that starts from the birth of the territorial state in Europe during the seventeenth century, only to end with the global "spread" of the Westphalian model in the twentieth. These narratives treat extra-Westphalian territorial models as aterritorial anomalies that, sooner or later, had to (or have to) converge on the Westphalian baseline. As students of global transformation who take a *longue durée* perspective have long recognized, such transformations are "multilinear"[94] and can hardly be reduced to linear and teleological narratives.[95]

In sum, if the goal is to examine the association between armed conflict and territorial ideas and associated practices across time and space, IR research can benefit greatly from the existing research in political geography and, accordingly, needs to take the task of conceptualizing territory (and territoriality) more seriously, and do so in a way that would help scholars "escape" the territorial trap.

In this setting, this study offers an analytical framework that identifies different territorial models, and then examines the two-way relationship between such models and war. Doing so, it builds on a pragmatic and interdisciplinary approach to the relationship between the socially constructed nature of territories and organized violence.

---

[91] Malasevic 2013. For a similar point, see Sassen 2008, 40. Barkawi and Laffey (2006, 334) argue that the same assumptions lead to Eurocentric historical geographies. Also see Kaplan 1999, 35. Note that the present-day global territorial arrangement itself is best conceptualized as a heterogeneous system co-constituted reflexively by different, and sometimes incompatible, territorial ideas and practices. See Agnew 2017.

[92] Barkawi 2004.

[93] Wimmer 2012, 2.

[94] Buzan and Lawson 2015, 23.

[95] Meadwell 2001, 166.

38 Conceptual and Theoretical Framework

Research Methodology

As far as the research methodology is concerned, I follow Buzan and Lawson's call to cultivate "methodological and epistemological pluralism, across disciplinary boundaries."[96] Overall, *Shifting Grounds* aims to address dynamics of "wide scope . . . in contrast to more narrowly parsed research puzzles designed to test theories" and "fill in gaps within research traditions."[97] The relatively uncharted nature of the topic, in turn, lends itself to an eclectic and pragmatic approach.[98]

Of course, eclectic research also comes with its own risks. Most notably, efforts to synthesize insights from different fields of research can lead to artificial cross-fertilization.[99] Without any analytical checks and balances, pragmatism can also prompt researchers to adopt an "anything goes" perspective. To avoid falling into this analytical trap, I follow Friedrichs and Kratochwil's advice and aim to profess "an appropriate degree of epistemological and methodological [self-]awareness."[100] Accordingly, I pursue two strategies. First, I neither intend nor claim to offer a universal and monocausal explanation for the relationship between territorial ideas and war. My intention is to offer a novel way to think about that relationship, not "the incontrovertible foundations of knowledge."[101] To quote and borrow from John Hutchinson, who has recently written a monograph on the relationship between nationalism and war, "The aim of this book is to offer general insights into the different relationships between warfare and [territorial ideas] over the *longue durée* rather than to establish 'scientific' conclusions."[102]

The second strategy I uphold involves the specific explanatory and methodological perspective I adopt in this study: abduction.[103] Friedrichs and Kratochwil classify abduction as a strategy, or a compromise, halfway between induction and deduction.[104] The intention is neither to "impose an abstract theoretical template" (deduction) nor to infer "propositions from facts" (induction).[105] The typical situation for abduction is when social scientists

[96] Buzan and Lawson 2015, 332.
[97] Sil and Katzenstein 2010, 412.
[98] As Friedrichs and Kratochwil (2009, 702) highlight, in the study of world politics, "The time has come for a pragmatic turn in research and methodology." For a similar approach to pragmatism in social sciences, see Flyvbjerg 2001.
[99] Sil and Katzenstein 2010, 414, 425.
[100] Friedrichs and Kratochwil 2009, 707.
[101] Friedrichs and Kratochwil 2009, 725.
[102] Hutchinson 2017, 11.
[103] On abduction as a logic and methodology of discovery, see Paavola 2004. According to Franke and Weber (2012, 686), abduction-based research in IR should aim for "not verification or falsification, but arguments for prospects and limitations of a theory in relation to well-defined problematic situations."
[104] Friedrichs and Kratochwil 2009.
[105] Friedrichs and Kratochwil 2009, 710.

"become aware of a certain class of phenomena that interests [them], but for which [they] lack applicable theories."[106] The main objective of abduction is detecting "patterns of similarity and difference that allow for the identification of regularities within an otherwise confusing field of research."[107]

Abduction usually entails "a comparative case study method."[108] Case sampling often follows a "'most important' or 'most typical' case design"[109] and focuses on "paradigmatic examples."[110] In this context, *Shifting Grounds* makes use of what Bent Flyvbjerg refers to as "paradigmatic cases," which are best suited to developing a metaphor or establishing a novel framework.[111] As far as case selection is concerned, this study builds on three criteria. First, the selected cases represent paradigmatic examples, which can serve as what Harry Eckstein referred to as plausibility probes.[112] Broadly speaking, plausibility probes involve an "intermediary step between hypothesis generation and hypothesis testing and . . . include 'illustrative' case studies."[113] Therefore, the intention is not to "test" the theory with the selected cases; instead, plausibility probes test—that is, if they actually "test" anything—how far the theory can go to provide plausible explanations for outcomes.[114]

The second criterion entails juxtaposing, when possible, both premodern and modern (or at least "old" and "new[er]") cases for each conceptual category.[115] The purpose is to discourage the notion that some territorial orders are a thing of the distant past. Third, the case selection method—again, when possible—involves including both Western and non-Western cases. Similar to the temporal criterion, the aim is to drive home the point that certain territorial ideas can hardly be categorized (or dismissed) as belonging exclusively with Western or non-Western geographies.

In terms of the first question of concern, I organize the case studies as follows. First, I examine the mosaic and monolithic orders through the paradigmatic cases of France and Prussia/Germany.[116] In order to highlight the differences between the two orders, I trace the relationship between territorial

---

[106] Friedrichs and Kratochwil 2009, 709.
[107] Friedrichs and Kratochwil 2009, 716.
[108] Friedrichs and Kratochwil 2009, 719, 715.
[109] Friedrichs and Kratochwil 2009, 718.
[110] Friedrichs and Kratochwil 2009, 717.
[111] Flyvbjerg 2006.
[112] Eckstein 1975. Plausibility probes can be seen as preliminary studies that are used to determine whether further research is warranted. Also see Thomas 2011.
[113] Levy 2008, 3.
[114] I'd like to thank an anonymous reviewer for this insight.
[115] On the potential benefits of invoking premodern cases in IR. also see Grygiel 2013.
[116] Since mosaic and monolithic orders are artifacts of Western ideas and practices, I limit my discussion to these two European cases, with the caveat that the same analysis can be extended to numerous other cases.

40 Conceptual and Theoretical Framework

ideas and war in these two cases across time, before and after the rise of nationalism as a vital component of state-sponsored ideologies.[117] Next, I scrutinize two paradigmatic examples of amorphous orders: the Ottoman Empire and the British colonial expansion and rule in South Asia. These two examples help drive home the point that amorphous territoriality is neither exclusively premodern nor categorically non-Western. Finally, I trace the relationship between virulent orders and war in two distinct paradigmatic cases: France during the Revolutionary and Napoleonic Wars and the group known as ISIS, which differ from each other in temporal and geographical terms.

As for the second question, that is, the impacts of wars on territorial ideas, once again I turn to paradigmatic cases. All wars may affect territorial ideas; but, if this claim has merit, the most visible (and arguably, substantial) impacts of wars on such ideas would be associated with wars of world-historical importance. More specifically, following the convention in IR theory,[118] I scrutinize four "systemic wars": the Thirty Years' War, the Revolutionary/Napoleonic Wars, World War I, and World War II. This case selection strategy also helps address the second core criterion: from a temporal point, it allows us to trace the impacts of systemic wars in both the distant past and the previous century. Furthermore, departing from the conventional practice in the relevant IR research, this study examines the impacts of these wars not only in the Western world, but also in non-Western geographies. The treatment of these wars in a sequential manner aims to provide a macrohistorical "analytic narrative,"[119] which traces the impacts of systemic wars on the evolution of the present-day global territorial arrangement.[120]

Overall, the case selection strategy aims to offer a macrohistorical and global examination of—or "a long-term and global perspective"[121] on—the interactive relationship between different forms of territoriality and war, broadly defined.[122] In fact, if one's intention is to break free from the analytical

---

[117] Following Haas (1986, 726), the term "nation" can be conceptualized as a socially mobilized body of individuals, believing (or imagining) themselves to be united by some set of characteristics that differentiate them from outsiders, striving to create or maintain their own state. Nationalism, in turn, is a "political principle which holds that the political unit and the national unit should be congruent" (Gellner 1983, 1). At the heart of nationalistic discourses lies the idea of a bounded political community, members of which relate to each other through shared cultural practices and heritage (Hutchison 2017).

[118] For example, Ikenberry 2001; Braumoeller 2019.

[119] Bates 1998.

[120] I take narrative to be "the organization of material in a chronologically sequential order, and define the focusing of the content into a single coherent story, albeit with subplots" (Stone 1981, quoted in Levy 1997, 27). On analytical narratives see Buthe 2002; Levi 1997; Bates et al. 1998; Parikh 2000; Downing 2000; Carpenter 2000; Elster 2000; Skocpol 2000; Pedriana 2005. Also see Levi 1997 for an argument on the relationship between history and political science (with a focus on IR). On macrohistorical research, see Collins 1999.

[121] Wimmer 2012, 7.

[122] Also see Tilly 1984.

blindfold that John Agnew dubbed the territorial trap, a macrohistorical and global examination of different forms of territoriality is not only desirable, but also necessary.[123] At this juncture, a disclaimer is in order. This book pursues a *longue durée* approach and covers a wide variety of empirical ground from early modern Europe to ISIS, or from the French Revolution to British colonialism in South Asia and beyond. Doing so, it draws mostly on secondary sources and existing literatures on the relevant subjects, consulting different perspectives to distill plausible interpretations of the cases under scrutiny. Of course, historians can question some of the aforementioned interpretations, as historians do. For a research project with a broad historical canvass such as this one, this dynamic is almost inescapable. Even when dealing with a single case with a temporal range of, say, a decade or two, there exist multiple interpretations. The variety of such (sometimes conflicting) interpretations exponentially proliferates when dealing with multiple, multitemporal cases. In this context, throughout the book, I have done my best to take note of the existing debates and differences of opinion in the relevant literatures.

Contributions

Conceptually, *Shifting Grounds* makes a case for taking territory and territoriality more seriously than mainstream IR does. Doing so, it introduces the territorial orders framework as a means to address the (conceptual) limitations of mainstream IR theory. Theoretically, this study offers the blueprints of a constructivist theory of territorial conflict that aims to examine the trends not only within the so-called Westphalian system but also beyond it, both temporally and geographically.

Shifting Grounds also has implications for the ways in which mainstream IR approaches the historical evolution of the so-called modern state system. For example, this study makes the case that we are living neither in the "Westphalian" territorial model that was institutionalized in 1648 nor in a version of it that became a reality later in the eighteenth or nineteenth centuries; instead, the present-day global territorial arrangements are based on ideas that rose to prominence only with the twentieth century. Similarly, *Shifting Grounds* challenges the narrative that the modern state system emerged endogenously in the West and then "spread" to the rest of the world through a linear process; from its early days, the aforementioned system evolved in the presence of imperial hierarchies and ethnocentric biases, the legacies of

---

[123] Also see Sassen 2008, 20.

which are also reflected in the present-day global territorial arrangements. In this sense, the so-called sovereign territorial order[124] is much less "innocent" and egalitarian than usually assumed.

Shifting Grounds is also the first dedicated monograph-length attempt to cross-fertilize interdisciplinary interaction in terms of the relation between territory, territoriality, and conflict. The immediate goal is to advance our understanding of the relationship between territorial ideas and armed conflict. More broadly, the aim is to establish a platform that will facilitate further interdisciplinary dialogues.

Finally, the territorial orders framework helps interpret not only the past, but also the present territorial arrangements across the globe. As the final chapter will highlight, the insights offered in this study can be applied to a wide variety of topics ranging from so-called state failure, the legacies of (geographical) racism in IR as well as international politics, the nature of territorial conflict in the twenty-first century, and the Russo-Ukrainian War.

Conclusion

Territory and territoriality play central roles in both international politics and IR. The existing research usually takes one or more of the following approaches: evolutionary, materialistic, and constructivist. Of these, the constructivist approach holds the greatest potential to explore the role of "territorial ideas" in world politics, especially in the context of armed conflict. IR constructivism, in turn, can benefit greatly from the research in political geography. For such interdisciplinary dialogues to flourish, two challenges need to be met: IR research should more explicitly define "territory" and move beyond what John Agnew dubbed the territorial trap.

This study is one such attempt, and, by building on insights from both disciplines, it pushes forward three arguments. First, territories are essentially social and political constructs. Second, territorial ideas affect wars. Third, wars themselves can also transform territorial ideas. Without further specification, these claims are bound to remain abstract. In this context, the next chapter offers a conceptual and analytical framework to develop these claims in more specific terms.

---

[124] See Simmons and Goemans 2021.

3
Territorial Orders and War

> Just as none of us is outside or beyond geography, none of us is completely free from the struggle over geography. That struggle is complex and interesting because it is not only about soldiers and cannons but also about ideas, about form, about images and imaginings.
>
> —**Edward Said**[1]

Territory is what states and societies make of it. This observation has two immediate implications about the relationship between territory and war. First, how states (or state elites) conceive territory will affect their military and political strategies.[2] Second, states use organized violence not only to capture territory, but sometimes also to transform the territorial ideas and associated practices in target areas or to "reterritorialize" them. How states fight and conclude wars, in this sense, may have significant impacts on territorial ideas. In other words, not only do territorial ideas affect how states fight, but wars themselves may also influence the same ideas. As political geographer Colin Flint put it, "War and geography are mutually constituted and socially constructed."[3]

Without further elaboration, these claims remain abstract. The task ahead, then, is to first conceptualize territory and territoriality in terms of their ideational dimensions and then analytically categorize different territorial ideas in order to examine the two-way relationship between such ideas and armed conflict. To this end, the remainder of this chapter unfolds in four steps. The first section conceptualizes territory and territoriality in a way that would make it possible to move beyond the so-called territorial trap.[4] The second section introduces the territorial orders framework. In the third section, I outline how different territorial orders affect state elites' military and political objectives and strategies. The final section elaborates on the mechanisms

---

[1] Said 1994, 7.
[2] Anderson 1996, 36.
[3] Flint 2005, 4.
[4] Discussed in Chapter 2.

Shifting Grounds. Burak Kadercan, Oxford University Press. © Oxford University Press 2023.
DOI: 10.1093/oso/9780197686690.003.0003

44 Conceptual and Theoretical Framework

and processes through which wars can influence the transformation of territorial orders.

Moving Beyond the Territorial Trap: Core Concepts

Following the work of Robert Sack, most political geographers agree that "territories are the product of human agency and this agency is usually referred to as 'territoriality.'"[5] Territoriality is "a primary geographical expression of power" as well as "a geographic strategy that connects society and space."[6] It follows that (political) territoriality is less about physical space per se than about population management in a particular area, or how political power is projected over space to organize and control social and political behavior.[7] In this sense, territory emerges when social actors take measures to demarcate physical space for political purposes and attempt to organize the sociospatial aspects within this confined space.[8]

Two key concepts lie at the heart of this perspective: territorialization and reterritorialization.[9] *Territorialization* refers to the practice of utilizing social, political, and cultural strategies in order to construct boundaries and control as well as manage the organization of social behavior within bounded space. This practice involves defining the scope, extent, and nature of political authority and influencing the cultural as well as emotive affiliations of human groups with respect to spatial arrangements.[10] An illustration may help: in its most abstract form, territorialization occurs when a human group discovers a previously uninhabited piece of land, sets up internal as well as external boundaries, and then explicates rules of social and political conduct within the demarcated space, while also attributing emotive and cultural meaning to it.

Reterritorialization is the act of transforming the preexisting demarcation principles and ideas as well as associated practices that regulate sociospatial organization in a given area.[11] In its simplest form, reterritorialization can occur in two ways: the transformation can be triggered either exogenously

---

[5] Sack 1986; Penrose 2002, 279; see also Gottmann 1973.

[6] .Sack 1986, 19; Penrose 2002, 279.

[7] Taylor 1994, 151; Paasi 2003, 111; Kadercan 2015.

[8] In this reading, territory is best seen as a "politico-institutional space" (Antonsich 2009, 795). Also see Soja 1971, 33. On the relationship between boundaries (as "social processes") and territoriality, see Paasi 1998.

[9] On reterritorialization, see Edney 2009; Adelman and Aron 1999.

[10] On the concept of "spatial socialization," see Koch 2015. On social spatialization, that is, the constant social construction of the spatial, see Shields 2013.

[11] There also exist debates about the concept of "deterritorialization." I follow Antonsich (2009, 33) and maintain that—under most circumstances—"any deterritorialization is also a form of reterritorialization."

(for instance, due to direct interference or intervention from external actors) or endogenously (that is, without overwhelming interference from external political actors). Following the abstract illustration above, externally induced reterritorialization takes place when a group arrives at an already-inhabited location—for example, colonizers arriving in the "New World," or Americas—and establishes itself in social and political terms.[12] The arrival of the new group may transform the nature as well as the extent of existing boundaries and sociospatial arrangements. An extreme example of exogenous reterritorialization is the narrative usually attributed to the fall of Carthage in the Third Punic War (143 BC). According to the conventional wisdom, Romans defeated the Carthaginians and plowed over the city of Carthage, even sowing salt into the soil; the inhabitants, in turn, were either killed or enslaved. The details of this narrative are not supported by conclusive evidence, but the narrative itself can still serve as an abstract illustration for exogenous reterritorialization in its extreme form.[13]

In turn, endogenous reterritorialization refers to the transformation of territorial ideas and practices in the absence of overwhelming interference from outside actors. In such cases, local political actors either invent novel ideas and practices or adopt (and adjust) existing ones to reshape the nature of boundaries and sociospatial arrangements. The European Union experiment constitutes one such example: the member states, without being compelled to do so by external actors, engage in activities that aim to abolish—or, at the very least, diminish—the "internal" boundaries between them, while also transforming the legal and administrative structures that directly affect (and are affected by) the relevant sociospatial ideas and practices. Among many similar cases, the modern Siamese experience constitutes another example of internally driven reterritorialization: as Winichakul masterfully showed in his *Siam Mapped*, the Kingdom of Siam appropriated the dominant territorial ideas and practices in the Western world in order to reconstruct Siam into a nation-state, which culminated in the creation of modern-day Thailand.[14]

Overall, territory as a social and political construct emerges through territorialization, and its nature (or constitutive properties) can change through reterritorialization.[15] That territory is socially and politically constructed

[12] For example, Adelman and Aron 1999.
[13] In most cases—when compared with the Carthage illustration—the nature and scope of (externally induced) reterritorialization is rarely determined by the agency of a single political actor. Instead, reterritorialization usually involves cooperative and/or competitive interaction between multiple actors.
[14] Winichakul 1994.
[15] Note that, in political geography and IR, there are two distinct views on territory and territoriality. The first distinction involves whether we are referring to *the* territory or territories. *The* territory interpretation is best reflected in Stuart Elden's *The Birth of Territory*. Elden explores the term "territory" from a "history of ideas" perspective and traces its modern-day interpretation across time and space. One implication is

46 Conceptual and Theoretical Framework

does not necessarily mean that it is conjured from thin air.[16] According to Jan Penrose, "*Space* is present whether anyone knows about it or not, but space only becomes a *place* when it acquires a 'perceptual unity,' and it only becomes a territory when it is delimited in some way." '[17] For territories to exist in any meaningful sense, the demarcation and sociospatial organization principles associated with them also need to be periodically and systematically reified through institutionalized practices.[18] This conceptualization points toward the existence of three interrelated dimensions that collectively constitute territories: the physical/geographical (or topographical) features of space (or land),[19] demarcation of space, and the sociospatial organization of this demarcated space.[20]

More specifically, demarcation involves the process of delineating and compartmentalizing space for social and political purposes.[21] Demarcation of space will determine the modes of transactions of goods and services, the mobility of people across compartmentalized spaces, and the "tangible" features of territory such as the size and location of political units and their proximity and contiguity vis-à-vis each other. Sociospatial organization involves assigning and enforcing political, social, and cultural functions, and a particular "meaning" to demarcated space. The intention is to define society's social and political identity in terms of a spatially defined entity in order to regulate and manage social as well as political behavior. The political and social organization of demarcated space can follow from the domination of one social group by another, political cooperation and competition, social engineering, or historical contingency.[22]

Defining territory and territoriality in explicit terms is a necessary first step for moving beyond the territorial trap, but if the purpose is to examine the

---

that other sociospatial arrangements that preceded the modern-day interpretation cannot easily be defined as territory in identical terms. The alternative interpretation, in turn, takes "territory" as a modular arrangement; so there is not *the* territory, but there can, and do, exist different territories. Similarly, some scholars take "territoriality" in terms of modern/Westphalian understanding of territoriality, which implies that "territorial" behavior directly speaks to our present-day understanding of (Westphalian) territoriality. In this, I follow the dominant opinion in political geography: there are different territories as well as different modes of territorial behavior, which can't be reduced to the characteristics usually (and, sometimes mistakenly) attributed to the ideal of the Westphalian state. See Agnew 2009 for an extended debate.

[16] See Kadercan 2015.
[17] Penrose 2002, 279.
[18] Fall 2010; Newman 2015.
[19] On relevant debates, which I do not engage in this study, see Elden 2010. On "land," resources, and territory, see Rosecrance 1999, 48, and Agnew 2009, 35. As Strandsbjerg (2010, 8) highlights, scholars such as Lefebvre also recognize that the physical environment itself is also an essential component of territory.
[20] See also Elden 2010.
[21] For more on the concept, see Findlay and Lundahl 2017.
[22] Furthermore, as Anderson and O'Dowd (1999, 598) highlight, "The 'container' and 'contents' are mutually formative."

two-way relationship between territory and armed conflict, further conceptual modifications are required. The two core concepts that also need to be addressed are the state and war. Put bluntly, "What it means to be a state varies from time to time and from place to place."[23] However, despite this rather all too obvious dynamic, mainstream IR scholarship tends to treat the state, or the "modern state," as the primary unit of analysis.[24] The most common definition of state is based, either implicitly or explicitly, on Max Weber's interpretation of the term: "a political organization that successfully claims the monopoly of the legitimate use of physical force within a given territory."[25] Many IR scholars may treat this conceptualization as a near-universal gold standard. However, Weber himself admitted that this particular definition applied to only a specific type of political organization, which presumably was conceived (or idealized) as the European nation-state of the late nineteenth and early twentieth centuries.[26]

Therefore, while the Weberian definition may be useful for examining the territorial nature of a particular kind of state, that is, the modern nation-state, with the same logic, the same conceptualization does not easily lend itself to appropriate analysis when the subject is a polity that is built on different territorial ideas, practices, and institutions.[27] In this sense, the particular conceptualization that lies at the heart of Weberian historical sociology—which informs many IR scholars' understanding of state—"offers no way out of the territorial trap."[28]

---

[23] Sheehan 2006, 3.

[24] Even the "systemic" neorealist theories take the "state" as the main actor in international politics; for example, Waltz 1979, Mearsheimer 2001. For a macrohistorical criticism of this position, see Maier 2016.

[25] Swedberg 1998, 56.

[26] Note that opinion on Weber's understanding of the "state" is divided. On the one hand, scholars such as Barkawi (2016, 208) argue that "Weber warned us that his definition of the state applied only to the European states of his day. State, force, society, and territory relations vary historically; they do not necessarily take trinitarian form, even in a world formally organized around the sovereign state." On the other hand, other scholars, such as Hakli (2001, 407), suggest that Weber had no conception of human society outside the system of the so-called nation states and "accepted national units as historical ultimates never to be integrated and surpassed, and thus was nationalist both methodologically and politically." Regardless, both perspectives agree on the idea that Weber's definition of the (modern) state refers to a specific form, that is, European nation-state ideal, as it was conceived during the course of late nineteenth and early twentieth centuries.

[27] Barkawi 2016, 209.

[28] Larkins 2010, 30. Larkins (2010, 29) traces the reification of territory to the nineteenth-century political thought, primarily to the ideas of Weber, whose "desire to master space" propelled the idea that "politics and history were ultimately determined by spatial factors such as states' size, location, and the distance between them," privileging, and effectively reifying, the demarcation-oriented features of territories at the expense of their constitutive properties. Strandsbjerg (2010, 11) concurs: with few exceptions, "Weberian historical sociology remains silent about the spatial transformations which accompany the development of the sovereign territorial state." On the lack of attention to territory and territoriality in historical sociology, also see Neep 2017, 467. According to Strandsbjerg (2010, 9), the leading figures of the field, such as Charles Tilly, consider territory "a generic thing containing the same meaning over time." Even scholars such as Michael Mann, whose conceptualization of society explicitly invokes sociospatial arrangements, refrain

48 Conceptual and Theoretical Framework

As far as this study is concerned, I define state as a political organization that controls, if at times in a limited fashion, space-society relations in a geographically defined domain. States also provide public services and governance to their inhabitants in return for taxation or tribute, while also acting as the dominant, if not the sole, provider of organized violence. Note that this definition may appear "fuzzy" to some IR scholars. My claim is not that IR research should redefine "state" in this way. However, if our purpose is to examine the wide variation in politics-space-society nexus from a world-historical perspective, we should also consider alternative territorial arrangements that go beyond the so-called modern state.

If the purpose is to examine the variable nature of territorial war across time and space, war is the second concept to be revisited. Just as the term "state" refers to a specific political-territorial ideal in IR, war refers to a particular way to utilize organized violence. In IR literature, especially in quantitative studies, war is defined as an armed conflict that leads to at least one thousand battle deaths per year.[29] Furthermore, "To qualify as a participant in a war, a country must either sustain a minimum of one hundred battle-related fatalities or have a minimum of a thousand armed personnel engaged in active combat."[30] The relevant data sets, usually affiliated with the Correlates of War (COW) project,[31] often take 1816 as the starting point. However, the dominant definitions of (and approaches to) war in IR inadvertently tilt our understanding of territorial conflict toward Eurocentrism, which is yet another aspect of the territorial trap.[32]

Most notably, the dominant approaches to the study of war may distort our understanding of the trends in organized violence in the past. For example, these approaches portray the nineteenth century as a "remarkably peaceful one."[33] However, this interpretation "hides the fact that European powers were

---

from exploring the spatial implications of political power (or vice versa) in great detail (Strandsbjerg 2010, 9). Anthony Giddens (especially 1985, 89), in turn, takes historicizing territoriality more seriously.

[29] This definition has been qualified in more sophisticated ways (e.g., see Braumoeller 2019), and can be traced to Singer and Small 1972.

[30] Braumoeller 2019, loc. 1556.

[31] On COW, see Frederick et al. 2017. Note that the relevant research in IR has also recognized the persistence of "extra-state wars," that is, "wars between an established country and some entity that has not been formally recognized as a country, such as a colony" (Braumoeller 2019, loc. 1553). On this point, also see Barkawi 2018, 322. However, such cases are usually treated differently from "normal" (or "conventional") wars. In Braumoeller's (2019, loc. 1797) words, "The causes of international conflict are overwhelmingly seen in the political science literature as being different than those of colonial conflict or nonstate conflict, much as homicides are seen as having different causes than death by lung cancer or death by sharkbite." One main reason is lack of equivalent statistical techniques to analyze trends in extrastate wars in tandem with state-on-state wars (Braumoeller 2019, loc. 1806).

[32] Barkawi (2016, 206–8) makes a similar argument. Also see Chapter 8.

[33] Braumoeller 2019, loc. 1761.

waging imperial wars on other continents."[34] Europe might have enjoyed a relative "territorial peace" between 1815 and 1914, but much of the rest of the world experienced considerable conflict and violence over territory during the same time. Furthermore, in Eurocentric approaches to conflict, war and peace are also easily distinguished, and wartime and peacetime refer to different temporal dimensions.[35] However, "Wars can be conducted by proxy, informally, by deniable means, defeating the armed representatives of alternate political orders and possibilities in other peoples' countries."[36] These conflicts, in turn, have been dubbed "small wars," or "wars that occurred as a result of intervention in, and conquest of, non-European countries."[37]

Overall, limiting the definition of war to the conventional usage of the term in IR categorically leaves out numerous forms of armed conflict that aimed at territorial expansion (or reterritorialization of target areas). In this context, I define territorial war as the use of organized violence by a state or state-like entity, either directly through its central armed forces or proxies, to expand (or defend) direct or indirect control of physical space and the society attached to space, as well as to reterritorialize the target areas (or preserve one's "territorial way of life").[38] Building on these definitions, the next section elaborates on "territorial orders."

The Territorial Orders Framework

I define territorial order as the collection of *aspirational ideas* and associated state-led efforts that aim to regulate the ways in which the state should demarcate space and organize space-society association within the state's domain.[39] Territorial orders are aspirational in the sense that they do not necessarily reflect reality.[40] Instead, territorial orders are ideas about how the state-society-space nexus should be ordered. Therefore, these orders are best seen as ideals that state elites strive for, as well as what Max Weber referred to as "ideal types."[41] More often than not, states may lack the capacity to fully enforce the

---

[34] Malešević 2010, 133.
[35] Malešević 2010, 200.
[36] Malešević 2010, 206.
[37] Barkawi 2004, 21.
[38] This definition of war is in alignment with the one offered by Levy and Thompson (2011, 3): "a sustained, coordinated violence between political organizations." Also see Barkawi 2016, 200.
[39] The territorial orders framework essentially involves a series of "metaphors" and, can be seen as an "attempt to impose analytical order on always messy historical reality" (Malešević 2017a, loc. 1358).
[40] On the relationship between aspirational principles (or "territorial strategies") and "actuality," see Novak 2011. Also see Agnew 2015, 44.
[41] Psathas 2005.

50 Conceptual and Theoretical Framework

territorial order they envision. However, while territorial orders may not fully reflect the facts on the ground, as aspirational ideas through which state elites also legitimize their political authority, they can exert significant influence on the "real world," affecting states' geopolitical objectives as well as methods and strategies for fighting wars over territory.[42]

For a territorial order to emerge, at least two conditions beyond physical/ geographical attributes need to hold.[43] First, the physical space needs to be demarcated. *Demarcation* of space refers to the mechanisms through which political organizations compartmentalize and scope the extent of their spatial reach. For the sake of simplicity, demarcation principles can be categorized into two types: rigid borders and fluid frontiers. Fixing borders requires specific and linear division of state territories, and efforts to enforce such division.[44] In order to exist even at the ideational level, the ideal of rigid borders requires relevant cartographic knowledge as well as a modicum of infrastructural power to enforce boundaries, so that borders can be identified on maps and then enforced, if imperfectly. In addition, for such territorial regimes to be sustainable at the regional (or global) level, states adhering to the ideal of rigid borders need to share an understanding over territorial sovereignty. Fluid frontiers,[45] in turn, involve relatively flexible and multifaceted strategies that demarcate "state spaces,"[46] either without the benefit of, or by rejecting, specific and linear division of state territories.[47] Adherence to fluid frontiers makes it unnecessary to commit to the principle of territorial sovereignty. In fact, in numerous cases, building on fluid frontiers as the fundamental demarcating principle also implies rejection of other states' claims to territorial sovereignty.

The second condition for a territorial order to emerge is organization of space-society relationship: demarcated space should also be politically and

---

[42] Note that "territories are not necessarily state spaces at all (Agnew 2015, 46). In other words, territories, broadly speaking, may emerge independent of states and state-like entities. However, in this study, in order to remain in direct conversation with IR scholarship (where the emphasis is on states, however defined), I limit my discussions to what political geographers as well as spatially oriented historians and sociologists refer to as "state space." On the concept, see Brenner et al. 2003. For a recent intervention, see Neep 2017.

[43] This two-dimensional approach follows Kahler 2006, 3.

[44] Note that "frontiers are seldom 'natural.'" Boundaries, in many cases, are "artificial" or "political" (Findlay and Lundahl 2017, 85). Also see Sahlins 1989.

[45] Frontiers can be defined as "broad bands of territory or zones where large-scale movements of populations differing in ethnic, linguistic, and religious composition have been jumbled together with no clear lines of demarcation separating them" (Rieber 2015, 952–953).

[46] Neep 2017. According to Paasi (2009, 213), the role of the state is not merely to organize space, but also to act as a "creator of meaning." The territorial orders framework suggests that "spatial meanings" are aspirational ideas that states build on in order to organize sociospatial arrangements.

[47] The geographic mobility may also be a temporary phenomenon; for example, facing the threat of Napoleon, the Portuguese court was moved to Brazil in 1807, with Rio de Janeiro serving as the capital of the Portuguese state for thirteen years.

Territorial Orders and War   **51**

socially organized in a way that regulates and coordinates individual as well as group behavior. Again, for the sake of simplicity, organization of social and political dynamics in demarcated space can be thought in terms of homogenous or heterogeneous arrangements. Homogenous governance arrangements involve state efforts to unify and standardize legal, administrative, and political practices as well as institutions in order to establish a modicum of uniformity and conformity with respect to the relationship between space and society. States that envision a modicum of sociospatial homogeneity within their domains can pick from one or more of the following paths: proselytizing, assimilation through education/re-education, population transfers, and/or ethnic cleansing. Such models are in contrast with heterogeneous territorial systems, which stand for institutions and practices that aim to organize space-society relationship in multilayered, context-dependent, and diverse forms.

This two-dimensional approach to territorial orders, as can be seen in Figure 3.1, reveals four possibilities. The first is "mosaic" territoriality, which is built on fixed borders with heterogeneous sociospatial organization. The so-called Westphalian states before the rise of nationalism, for instance France during the eighteenth century, adhered to mosaic orders: such political entities aimed to demarcate state space and carve up areas of sovereign domains through specific borders, but did not necessarily seek ethnocultural, ideological, or civic uniformity. The second category is "monolithic" territoriality,

	Demarcation of State Territories	
	Fixed Borders	Fluid Frontiers
Homogenous	*Monolithic* "Spasmodic" territorial wars Strong incentives to reterritorialize *Example: Nation-states*	*Virulent* War as a continuous process Strong incentives to re-territorialize *Examples: Revolutionary states, ISIS*
Heterogeneous	*Mosaic* "Spasmodic" territorial wars Little incentive to re-territorialize *Example: prenationalism Westphalian states*	*Amorphous* War as a continuous process Little incentive to re-territorialize *Examples: Most premodern empires, pre-Westphalian "composite states" of Europe*

Organization of Space-Society Relationship (row label, left of table)

Figure 3.1 Territorial orders and war.

52   Conceptual and Theoretical Framework

which is built on the combination of fixed (or rigid) borders and homogeneous organization of space-society relationship. The best example of monolithic territoriality is the nation-state ideal. This ideal draws on the notion of "inviolable homeland"[48] with "hard" borders, and the idea that social identities within this putative homeland should be projected onto a specific area.[49] Conversely, state space should be defined in terms of a uniform social identity, where "uniformity" is usually defined in ethnocultural, ideological, or civic terms.[50] For historical as well as geographical reasons, modern Japan comes closest to this ideal.[51]

The remaining categories—amorphous and virulent orders—distinguish themselves from the first two with respect to demarcation principles: neither territorial order is built on the notion of rigid borders. Instead, states that adhere to these orders, either by choice or out of necessity, envision the spatial extent of their political authority in terms of fluid and flexible frontiers. At least in theory, these territorial orders also reject the concept of mutual [territorial] sovereignty, which is epitomized—or idealized—with the Westphalian arrangement. "Amorphous"[52] territoriality entails the combination of fluid frontiers and heterogeneous organization of the space-society relationship. From a world-historical perspective, amorphous orders have been more the rule than the exception. Many premodern states as well as empires adhered to this order and did not recognize linear borders,[53] while also refraining from attempts to homogenize sociospatial configurations within their domain.[54]

The final category is "virulent" territoriality, where fluid frontiers are mixed with an intention (on the part of state elites) to achieve sociospatial homogeneity. Some universalizing empires—arguably, the Holy Roman Empire during parts of its reign—professed virulent territoriality in the past and aimed to unify social arrangements, most commonly, in terms of religion.[55] An extreme version of virulent territorial order, more specifically, was adopted by Nazi Germany; Nazi Germany aimed to expand indefinitely in Europe and Eurasia while also "purifying" the lands under its rule, if in racial

---

[48] Kadercan 2018.

[49] On territoriality and nationalism, see Murphy 2013.

[50] As Etherington (2010, 333) highlights, even civic nationalism is essentially territorial.

[51] On the differences between Tokugawa Japan and modern Japan vis-à-vis social and political homogeneity, see Ringmar 2012.

[52] Culcasi (2016) uses the term "amorphous territory," but not in the same fashion.

[53] For example, as Matthew Longo (2017a, 759) highlighted, Roman imperium was "not territorially circumscribed."

[54] Mann 1986.

[55] For example, Opello and Rosow (1999, 37) point toward the "Christianization of Europe" during the eighth century, which can be seen as an attempt at sociospatial homogenization; for example, "In 785, Charlemagne ordered 4,500 pagan Saxons . . . to convert . . . or die."

terms.[56] In the modern era, revolutionary states that uphold universalizing ambitions, at least in their early days, also profess virulent territorial orders.

Note that a state can also profess "dual territoriality" by adhering to multiple territorial orders at the same time, but in different locations.[57] For example, European states and colonizers in the "New World" conceived Americas—different from their vision of Europe—as "empty spaces" and experimented with territorial ideas and practices that were not (or could not be) upheld in Europe at the time.[58]

How Territorial Orders Affect War

State elites' geopolitical assumptions and vision about sociospatial arrangements—or their territorial ideas—affect, if not entirely determine, how states fight over territory. In general, the notion of fixed borders renders territorial war a "spasmodic"—or discrete—undertaking. War entails an identifiable beginning (prior to which there is an established territorial status quo), a series of battles, and a specific conclusion where a new territorial status quo yet again based on fixed borders is established.[59] For states that adhere to the principle of fluid frontiers, alternatively, territorial war is a continuous enterprise that can also be carried out through "hybrid warfare."[60]

States that aim to homogenize the space-society relationship, in turn, have strong incentives to radically reterritorialize what they perceive as target areas and transform them in their own image. Intention to radically reterritorialize target areas can trigger high levels of violence, which may also spread to the civilian populations. Adherence to heterogeneous spatial-social

[56] In the words of Malešević (2010, 139), Nazi Germany sought "an ethnically, physically and heterosexually pure society."

[57] Agnew (2009) does not utilize an identical terminology, but the core ideas, at least from an analytical perspective, are similar.

[58] Larkins 2010; Branch 2014. A caveat is in order. While the territorial orders framework involves the dichotomous categorization of the two critical dimensions of territorial orders, that is, ideas about demarcation and sociospatial organization, these two dimensions can also be conceived as graduated spectrums, not merely dichotomous categories. For example, most modern federal nation-states profess a territorial vision that is more "relaxed" than unitary ones when it comes sociospatial homogeneity: while present-day Italy and Germany both adhere to monolithic orders, for instance, the territorial order of the former, as a unitary state, presupposes a more homogeneous sociospatial association than the latter. Similarly, while the practice of "rigid" borders became dominant, at least in Europe, throughout the course of the nineteenth century, the so-called border fixity norm of the post-1945 era hardened the existing borders in more robust terms, suggesting that there are also different degrees to border rigidity. In this study, I limit my discussions to the aforementioned four territorial models for the sake of simplicity, while also recognizing that territorial orders can be analyzed through a spectrum-based framework. On the relevant topics, see Ziblatt 2006 and Atzili 2012, respectively.

[59] For a similar point, see Guilmartin 1988, 721–725.

[60] On this concept, see Murray and Mansoor 2012.

54 Conceptual and Theoretical Framework

arrangements, alternatively, creates disincentives for states to radically reterritorialize their targets. Under such circumstances, abstention from radical reterritorialization efforts can limit the intensity of armed conflict, and the likelihood of large-scale civilian victimization might be lower. Also note that adopting a heterogeneous approach to space-society association does not always guarantee that the depth and scope of reterritorialization efforts will be limited. For example, some states, usually empires, may profess a heterogeneous approach to sociospatial organization in target areas while also pursuing a divide-and-conquer (and then rule) strategy. In these settings, sociospatial arrangements can undergo considerable transformation, and do so without homogenization.

Mainstream IR research collapses the territorial ideas and practices in the modern state system under the conventional understanding of the so-called Westphalian territoriality. This tendency ossifies the idea that the territorial practices of the "modern states" have remained relatively unchanged for more than three centuries. Existing data sets and case studies then scrutinize the relevant wars that took place in the modern state system by building on the assumption that while economic factors, military technology, and demographic dynamics might have undergone major shifts since 1648, the dominant understanding of (Westphalian) "territoriality" has remained constant. A key argument of this study is that the so-called Westphalian understanding of territoriality is often misunderstood and cannot be conceived as an unchanging "constant" of the modern state system. Instead, the modern state system has been dominated by two distinct territorial models, mosaic and monolithic, each associated with different modalities of war. The fact that these two territorial models are typically collapsed under the conventional Westphalian narrative makes it necessary to offer a detailed analysis from a comparative perspective.

When mosaic orders are dominant in a regional or global state system, state elites have little incentive to homogenize the sociospatial organization not only within their domains, but also in their targets. Societies in targeted areas, in turn, will be less inclined to resist territorial conquest, and state elites will be unable (or unwilling) to mobilize masses in the entirety of their domains to put up a fierce defense. In relation, state space will be seen more in terms of a "divisible" good than it would have been if the dominant territorial ideas resembled monolithic territoriality. As a corollary, state elites will have little incentive to invest heavily in territorial defense for the preservation of the territorial integrity of the state for its own sake. Furthermore, mosaic territoriality will allow states to deal with the sunk cost dilemma fallacy more effectively. When the expected costs of fighting over territory far exceed the expected material and strategic benefits, for example, states will find it easier to terminate the conflict. Similarly, redistribution of territory that had been deemed ex ante divisible will not necessarily lead to revanchism or protracted disputes over territory in the aftermath of the wars.

When combined, these dynamics will contribute to, if not determine, three broad trends in territorial conflict. First, incentives on both sides—potential conquerors and defenders—will dampen the severity[61] of war (and the scale of civilian victimization), of course, when compared with monolithic orders. Second, "territorial deterrence" will be rather weak, because the potential defenders cannot easily and credibly signal that they would (or could) exponentially escalate the conflict to preserve the territorial integrity of the state per se. Accordingly, even a momentary weakness on the part of the potential defender can easily motivate the potential aggressors to launch wars of opportunism, as revisionist actors would have reason to hope that they can swiftly grab some land and then hold onto it. Third, by way of dampening the severity of conflicts (and the magnitude of civilian victimization) and encouraging opportunistic wars, mosaic territoriality will render interstate wars a more frequent—or at least ubiquitous—practice.

When monolithic territorial order is the dominant aspirational model in a regional or global state system, by contrast, states aim to homogenize (and often radically transform) the sociospatial organization not only within their own domains, but also in target geographies. Defending states as well as societies, in turn, will have strong incentives to put up a fierce resistance to protect their "territorial way of life." These dynamics then make it both easier and more expedient for state elites to mobilize masses in the entirety of their domains to put up a fierce resistance. In relation, state space will be seen more in terms of an "indivisible" good. Accordingly, state elites will have strong incentives to invest heavily in territorial defense for the preservation of the territorial integrity of the state for its own sake. Once war breaks out, states will have difficulty dealing with sunk costs, as they will be extremely sensitive to the prospects of losing even small chunks of territory. Even when the expected costs of fighting over territory far exceed the expected material and strategic benefits, for example, states will find it extremely difficult to terminate the conflict. As a corollary, territorial losses will likely trigger revanchism and/or protracted disputes. In such cases, the relevant states find themselves in a political-military limbo where they are reluctant to rush into an all-out war over disputed territory, but also cannot reach a long-term solution to the dispute.

---

[61] Levy (1983) defines severity in terms of battlefield deaths excluding civilians.

56 Conceptual and Theoretical Framework

Collectively, these dynamics contribute to three trends in war over territory. First, the aforementioned incentives, on average, render war over territory more severe than it would have been in the presence of mosaic territoriality. Second, in the presence of monolithic territoriality, territorial deterrence will be relatively robust (if not perfect), because the potential defenders can credibly signal that they would exponentially escalate the conflict to preserve the territorial integrity of the state per se. The prospects of a war that will most likely involve disproportionate costs—that is, disproportionate when compared with the material and strategic stakes involved—will then create ex ante incentives for parties to conform to the territorial status quo, limiting, but not eliminating, wars of opportunism. Broadly speaking, state elites will approach war initiation with caution, making war more of a rare event. Third, while the aforementioned mechanism discourages opportunistic campaigns, it also has a particular side effect: Obsessed with even marginal territorial losses, a group of states that deem their territorial possessions as indivisible goods, or inviolable homelands, may paradoxically find themselves facing an intense security dilemma, even (or especially) when the actual likelihood of suffering an attack at any given time is negligible. As a result, as far as the origins of wars are concerned, fear of losing territory will be a more common motive than territorial opportunism.

When state elites adhere to amorphous orders, they aim neither to establish rigid borders nor to homogenize society-space association. War for territory is seen as a continuous undertaking, which can be carried out through both set-piece battles and gradual incursions that may include numerous measures that go beyond conventional warfare. The aim is not merely to expand areas of sovereign (or direct) rule, but also to establish suzerainties and spheres of influence, tasks that do not always require radical reterritorialization of the target areas. States that profess amorphous territoriality can also engage in substantial reterritorialization. However, even then, the intent is not to impose sociospatial homogeneity but to restructure the human terrain to make it easier to establish control and extract resources.

Different from mosaic and monolithic orders, amorphous territoriality does not easily lend itself to quantifiable and comparative analysis. An emphasis on the "frequency" of territorial wars, for example, may fail to capture the trends in armed conflict precisely because the methods through which frequency is measured take war as a discrete event with a beginning and an end. Similarly, measuring and comparing "severity" is also problematic, since the existing data sets in IR research rarely engage conflicts that do not qualify as conventional (or "interstate") war.[62] These being said, it is still possible to

---

[62] For a recent attempt to address this issue, see Miller and Bakar 2022.

push forward the following claim: amorphous orders, when compared with virulent orders, are usually associated with less violence, broadly defined. The reason is simple: the state elites do not seek to establish sociospatial homogeneity.

In the presence of virulent orders, state elites reject the notion of rigid borders and, when possible, aim to expand indefinitely, while also going to lengths to homogenize the space-society association in their own image. Just as it is the case with amorphous territoriality, states that adhere to virulent orders envision territorial war as a continuous process, and aim to expand the spatial extent of their authority not only through conquest, but also by creating spheres of influence, satellites, and dependencies. What separates these two territorial models is the following: virulent territoriality implies an emphasis on homogenizing societies within and beyond the relevant states' domains, which is closely associated with their incentives to radically reterritorialize target areas. The Soviet experience during the early stages of the Cold War presents an important example. The early Soviets not only aimed to expand their sphere of influence indefinitely, but also to radically alter the territorial order in their target areas such as Central and Eastern Europe, most notably by establishing ideological-societal uniformity in their satellites, sometimes through violent means (e.g., Hungary in 1956 and Czechoslovakia in 1968).

Similar to amorphous orders, until or unless appropriate data sets are constructed, virulent orders do not always lend themselves to comparative [quantitative] analysis in terms of dimensions such as frequency and severity. That being said, it is possible to make two "soft" claims. First, as mentioned above, all else being equal, virulent orders tend to be associated with a higher magnitude of violence and civilian victimization than amorphous orders. Second, in cases where it is possible to assess and compare the quantifiable trends in conventional warfare (e.g., revolutionary/Napoleonic France, Nazi Germany), virulent orders are likely to lead to far more severe conflict than mosaic orders, on par with and sometimes even more so than monolithic orders.

Bellicose Origins of Territorial Orders

Just as territorial ideas affect the ways in which states fight their wars, the reverse is also true: how states fight and conclude their wars can influence territorial ideas. Wars destabilize the existing territorial arrangements, and postwar settlements usually involve efforts to construct a new equilibrium. During the relevant processes, political actors strive to generate new

58 Conceptual and Theoretical Framework

territorial ideas, or modify and appropriate existing ones, usually with un-expected consequences. How wars affect territorial ideas, in turn, plays out differently in symmetrical and asymmetrical relationships. When political actors (intersubjectively) define their relationship in relatively symmetrical terms—for example, in an arrangement where they mutually recognize each other's territorial sovereignty—the ways in which wars affect territorial ideas will be different from cases where the relationship is conceived in asymmet-rical terms, for example, in colonial (or "quasi-colonial")[63] arrangements.

From a world-historical standpoint, I make two central claims. First, the so-called systemic wars played important and nonlinear roles in shaping the evolution of the present-day global territorial arrangement. More specifi-cally, as will be discussed in detail in Chapter 7, the Thirty Years' War, the Revolutionary and Napoleonic Wars, World War I, and World War II, and how major political actors approached postwar settlement efforts, triggered categorical shifts in how state elites, and eventually societies, envisioned the "appropriate" demarcation as well as sociospatial organization principles. The second claim is that the so-called systemic wars affected the transformation of territorial ideas and practices through different mechanisms in the West and non-Western world.

Note that the claim here is not that wars constitute the only—or the single most important—drivers of change in territorial ideas and associated practices in general, or territorial orders in particular. Territorial ideas may undergo transformation due to shifts in ideas about political authority, ideas about war itself, cartographic knowledge, or state capacity.

Ideas about the nature of political authority most certainly have an impor-tant impact on how state elites and societies conceive territory and territo-riality. Most notably, ideas emanating from legal scholars either about the concept of sovereignty and interstate war can be said to have influenced the territorial practices of the so-called Westphalian states. For example, Jeremy Larkins examines the transformation of territorial imageries from a *longue durée* perspective, tracing the rise of present-day territorial ideas about the extent and scope of political authority to the Reformation, long before the Peace of Westphalia.[64] Ideas (or norms) about war itself as an "appropriate" practice can eventually affect territorial ideas, if indirectly. Most notably, John Mueller argues that how societies conceived the practice of war has been undergoing a transformation during the course of the last century, and war it-self has become an unacceptable practice.[65] Changing ideas about war, in this

---

[63] For example, Kayaoğlu 2010.
[64] Larkins 2010.
[65] For example, see Mueller 1989. Also see March and Olsen 2006.

context, can also transform territorial ideas: if war itself, regardless of its territorial underpinnings, becomes a socially unacceptable practice, this transformation can also affect how societies and state elites conceive territory and territoriality.

Territorial ideas are also largely affected by the visual representations of geography, encapsulated with maps. For example, as Jordan Branch highlighted, even as a "concept," the sovereign state owed much of its existence to the emergence of modern cartography.[66] Branch argues that how territorial systems are constituted as spaces of political practice in a particular context depends on the technologies available to the relevant actors as well as the dominant forms of "knowledge." According to Branch, technology and knowledge vary tremendously across time and space, and these variations have had remarkable subsequent impacts on how political organizations have evolved. More specifically, the rise of modern cartography from the seventeenth century onward acted as a critical factor that allowed the emergence of territorial sovereignty and the so-called modern state system. Even then, cartography did not instantly or swiftly transform the dominant territorial ideas and practices in Europe, but was part of a long-term process that reached maturity only in the early nineteenth century.

Of course, territorial ideas do not exist in an ideational vacuum, but they are also affected by state capacity, usually defined in terms of what Michael Mann dubbed infrastructural and coercive power.[67] As already mentioned, even to exist as an aspirational set of principles, territorial orders require a modicum of state capacity to monitor and enforce certain territorial practices. For example, monolithic territorial orders, which lie at the heart of the nation-state ideal, require a modicum of infrastructural and coercive power to exist even at the aspirational level, for two reasons. First, as far as demarcation is concerned, monolithic orders require state capacity to monitor and enforce the practice of rigid borders and act as the main, if not always the sole, arbiter of what and who can enter or leave the state space. Second, monolithic orders also require a certain level of state capacity to (even try to) homogenize sociospatial organization. Most notably, states that adhere to monolithic territoriality aspire to survey their population and create a shared sense of belonging and emotive attachment to the state space through education and what Michael Billig referred to as "banal nationalism."[68] As Michel Foucault, Anthony Giddens, and James Scott have long highlighted, nation-states also

---

[66] Branch 2014.
[67] Mann 1986.
[68] Billig 1995.

60 Conceptual and Theoretical Framework

try to "discipline" the social groups or individuals who are deemed "outliers" through either assimilation efforts or "othering" mechanisms that help unify a majority at the expense of minorities.[69]

These points being said, wars may act as catalysts that can trigger large-scale change, emboldening some territorial ideas at the expense of others. For example, as highlighted by numerous scholars,[70] the Thirty Years' War and the Peace of Westphalia did not "create" ideas that did not exist previously; the war and postwar settlement institutionalized some of the existing ideas and practices, if implicitly, at the expense of alternatives. Similarly, and more obviously, World War I did not "invent" the notion of homeland, which is an exemplar of the monolithic order, but war efforts (including propaganda) as well as postwar settlements emboldened and even ossified it in numerous countries in Europe (and beyond) as an aspirational model.

Overall, my argument on the impacts of wars on territorial ideas is built on three fundamental premises. First, wars and postwar settlements can trigger substantial reterritorialization. Second, the impacts of wars on territorial ideas are rarely dictated by a single political actor; the relevant processes usually play out in relational terms. The third premise involves so-called systemic wars: all wars may have impacts on territorial ideas, but given their scale and severity (as well as the magnitude of the postwar settlement efforts), systemic wars can have substantial and long-lasting impacts on territorial ideas. The extent and nature of the transformation triggered by systemic wars, in turn, will differ in symmetrical and asymmetrical (or anarchical and hierarchical) settings.

Wars as Processes of Reterritorialization

All wars can embolden some territorial ideas at the expense of others, leading to significant changes in sociospatial arrangements. In addition, wars can act as "mythmoetour," or constituting myth,[71] leading to the generation of sociospatial memories (real or imagined).[72] While wars can affect territorial ideas in various ways, I emphasize three specific mechanisms (and

---

[69] Foucault 1977; Giddens 1986; Scott 1998. Also see Marx 2003. On the relevant mechanisms, also see Neep 2017, 477; Mukerji 2011; Strandsbjerg 2008. The relevant state efforts, in turn, require administrative, bureaucratic, and coercive capabilities, not to mention financial and economic means. Michael Mann (1986, 112–114) refers to this process as "social caging." Also see Malešević 2010, 74. As Hakli (2001, 415) highlights, maps and surveys also play an important role in this process. For an example of the relevant mechanisms in practice, see Brown 2001.

[70] For example, Spruyt 1994.

[71] Hutchinson 2017, 52.

[72] These territorial myths are usually cultivated and institutionalized selectively. See Herb 2004.

associated processes). First, the transformation of territorial ideas and associated practices can be imposed by outside actors. For example, after World War II, not only were Germany's borders redrawn, but the virulent territoriality that lay at the heart of German geopolitik was also curbed and systematically eliminated by both the Allied powers and the Soviet Union. Second, wars can enable (or motivate) local actors to initiate institutional transformation of territorial ideas. The experience of modern Turkey in the aftermath of World War I and the War of Turkish Independence (1919–1923) can offer some insights into the relevant processes.[73]

Third, postwar settlements can entail collective reterritorialization efforts among major participants, usually the victors. Under such circumstances, the relevant actors aim to lock in their interests and prevent a similar conflict. Such efforts can then reshape territorial arrangements that go beyond the location of boundaries, triggering transformation in ideas about the nature of boundaries and appropriate ways to conceive sociospatial organization. Most notably, World War II and postwar settlements established the prominence of the monolithic orders across the globe, if as an aspirational model.

War for Territory in Relational Terms

Reterritorialization is rarely a unilateral process: transformation of territorial ideas and associated practices usually involves interaction between multiple actors. One key element that affects the reterritorialization process is the nature of the relationship between the actors. While this "nature" may take many shapes, for the sake of simplicity, I focus on one key element of the relationship: whether the relevant actors conceive of their intersubjective association in symmetrical or asymmetrical terms. In this context, wars' impacts on territorial ideas work differently in symmetrical and asymmetrical settings.

(A)symmetry is best defined in terms of not only relative material capabilities, but also ideational and intersubjective dimensions of the relationship. In fact, under certain circumstances, ideational and cultural factors that define the relational as well as intersubjective nature of the association can play a more important role than solely material dynamics. For example, European states colonized numerous geographies across the globe and exerted their authority over existing polities, with little concern for the right to autonomous rule. By contrast, at least until the Napoleonic Wars, the relationship among the European states were quite different: out of the three hundred or so states

---

[73] On the case of Turkey, see Özkan 2012.

62 Conceptual and Theoretical Framework

and state-like territorially defined units in Europe, none other than Poland ceased to exist as a result of war and/or conquest.[74]

Similarly, for instance, the French relationship with Monaco and Morocco displayed categorical differences in the past: France recognized the autonomy of the former despite Monaco's lack of military capabilities, while denying self-rule to the people of Morocco—whose military capabilities and material power far exceeded that of Monaco—for almost half a century between 1912 and 1956. In other words, for the French state elites (and some segments of the French society) "Monaco" and "Morocco"—as territorial units—were not equal. These dynamics cannot be explained solely by relative material power alone, and point toward the existence of an intersubjectively defined territorial (a)symmetry, which is usually left out of the leading IR theories.

Note that the aforementioned "territorial asymmetry" has direct implications for debates over the anarchy-hierarchy duality in IR theory.[75] While dominant approaches such as neorealism, liberalism, and some segments of constructivism usually start from the assumption that international politics is anarchical, scholars such as David Lake have made the case that global politics is innately hierarchical.[76] A territorial perspective, in this context, suggests that hierarchy has been more of a norm than an exception in world politics. It follows that, while present-day global territorial arrangement emerged in—and into—what IR theory dubs an "anarchical" environment in the West, the evolution in much of the rest of the world took place in the presence of territorial hierarchy.

So how do wars affect the transformation of territorial ideas in symmetrical and asymmetrical relations (or anarchical and hierarchical settings)? As mentioned, wars destabilize the territorial status quo. To be precise, wars don't merely change the location of the borders; they can also transform the meaning of boundaries and the organization of the sociospatial arrangements. When actors intersubjectively perceive and define their relationship in symmetrical terms, postwar settlements will usually lean toward problem-solving, a process that will aim to establish a new territorial equilibrium. Asymmetrical relationships usually reflect the struggle between hegemonic forces and the weaker actors. The "weaker" actors may resist the imposition of hegemonic territorial ideas and practices or may attempt to appropriate such ideas and practices in order to destroy, or at least diminish, the hierarchical relationship.

---

[74] Osiander 2001.
[75] On anarchy-hierarchy debate, see Griffiths 2018; Butt 2013.
[76] Lake 2011. Also see Zarakol 2017.

Systemic Wars and Territorial Orders

The third premise involves so-called systemic wars: all wars may have an impact on territorial ideas, but given their scale and depth (as well as efforts for war settlement), systemic wars can have substantial and long-term impacts. Emphasis on great—or systemic—wars is a common theme in both IR and historiography.[77] Systemic wars commonly result from system-wide tensions that could not be resolved through peaceful means and more limited wars. Victorious powers aim to avoid similar conflicts in the near future and establish an arrangement that will be stable while also benefiting them. The associated processes do not always work out the way that original initiators wanted, and the outcome is rarely, if ever, determined by the preferences of a single designer.[78] Transformation of territorial orders as a result of systemic wars can be seen through the prism of "punctuated equilibrium." The concept of punctuated equilibrium, as it is used by Hendrik Spruyt in his research on the rise of territorial states,[79] maintains that "the dominant forms of state frequently change in spurts, in punctuations of equilibrium, separating long eras of no more than incremental alteration."[80] The claim here is that systemic wars act as large-scale catalysts that trigger significant changes in dominant territorial ideas and practices, tilting the balance in favor of one set of ideas at the expense of others.

Following from the previous premise, I argue that systemic wars will have differential impacts on territorial ideas in anarchical and hierarchical (or symmetrical and asymmetrical) settings. In anarchical (or symmetrical) settings, the transformation efforts, if not the actual outcomes, will usually reflect the interests and priorities of great powers and will take the form of collective "problem-solving." In hierarchical (or asymmetrical) settings, the primary determinant of the transformation will be the struggle between the center and periphery, which will take place not only in the material sphere, but also at the ideational level about the nature of boundaries and sociospatial organization.

As will be discussed in more detail in Chapter 7, in the Western world, the mechanism through which systemic wars led to the transformation of territorial orders often entailed problem-solving. The participants in the postwar settlements attempted to address the perceived problems that led to war in the first place by setting a new ideational gold standard over the question of how to demarcate space and organize space-society association, usually with

---

[77] Manela 2007, 20; Gilpin 1981, 36; Barkin and Cronin 1994, 114.
[78] Gilpin 1981; Ikenberry 2001; Braumoeller 2019.
[79] Spruyt 1994.
[80] Tilly 1995, 811.

64 Conceptual and Theoretical Framework

unintended consequences. In the non-Western world, systemic wars affected the transformation of territorial orders through two mechanisms. First, these wars disrupted, if temporarily, the hierarchical relationship between the Western states and local populations, creating opportunities for the local elites to challenge the hierarchy. Second, the local elites appropriated the aspirational territorial models that were institutionalized in the West in the aftermath of systemic wars—especially the monolithic order—to both undermine the legitimacy of the territorial hierarchy and galvanize support from local populations, with different levels of success.

Conclusion

From a world-historical perspective, territorial ideas show great variation across time and space. Different territorial ideas, in turn, can have an influence on how states and societies approach armed conflict over territory. Similarly, wars themselves can transform how states and societies conceive of territory. Building on these insights, this chapter offered a theoretical framework that differentiated between four territorial models (or territorial orders), each of which is categorized with respect to two key dimensions that collectively make up territories: demarcation principles and idea(l)s about sociospatial organization. The chapter specified two key arguments. First, each territorial order will affect how states and societies fight their wars over territory in different ways. Second, wars themselves, especially systemic wars, have had a drastic influence on the transformation of territorial orders. In the next four chapters, I elaborate on these claims by building on numerous paradigmatic examples.

PART II
HOW TERRITORIAL IDEAS
AFFECT WARS

4
Rigid Borders, Spasmodic Wars
Mosaic and Monolithic Territorial Orders

> We all felt for Frederick, but what did we care for Prussia?
> —**Johann Wolfgang von Goethe**[1]

> Think of [Alsace-Lorraine] always; speak of [it] never!
> —**Leon Gambetta**[2]

Borders lie at the heart of present-day world politics. Borders—if sometimes mostly in theory—demarcate the spatial extent of political authority and exert significant influence over what, or who, can travel across them. They also have a direct influence on identity formation, by way of differentiating between "insiders" and "outsiders."[3] The notion of territorial sovereignty, a foundational principle of the modern state system, is directly defined in terms of borders. As John Agnew pointed out, "Borders matter . . . both because they have real effects and because they trap thinking about and acting in the world in territorial terms."[4]

Historically speaking, the rise of borders—as we understand them today—is usually traced to the Peace of Westphalia. Scholars such as Stephen Krasner, Andreas Osiander, Benno Teschke, and Sebastian Schmidt have debunked the myths surrounding the Westphalian arrangement,[5] but the term "Westphalian system" is still widely used, usually for heuristic purposes. However, while the notion of Westphalian sovereignty has long been debated in IR, the concept of Westphalian territoriality is rarely questioned and usually taken for granted.[6] According to the conventional wisdom, the territorial model—or ideal—on

---

[1] Quoted in Morgenthau 1949, 118.
[2] Quoted in Pratt 1914, 223.
[3] On politics of borders, see Vaughan-Williams 2009; Longo 2017b.
[4] Agnew 2008, 175. Also see Newman 2006b.
[5] Krasner 1999; Osiander 2001; Teschke 2003; Schmidt 2011.
[6] See Chapter 2.

Shifting Grounds. Burak Kadercan, Oxford University Press. © Oxford University Press 2023.
DOI: 10.1093/oso/9780197686690.003.0004

which the present-day state system is built reflects the Westphalian arrangement. This line of thinking comes with a corollary: globalization may have recently challenged the territorial practices emanating from (or attributed to) the Peace of Westphalia, but the core ideas associated with Westphalian territoriality themselves have also remained relatively unchanged in the last four centuries.

This chapter contests the conventional wisdom and pushes forward two central claims. First, the dominant territorial model in the present day is affiliated with the Westphalian ideal, but it is also categorically distinct from it.[7] While the original Westphalian territorial ideal was built on mosaic territoriality (which stipulated rigid borders and heterogeneous sociospatial organization), the dominant territorial model since 1945 is the monolithic ideal (which emphasizes the combination of rigid borders and homogeneous sociospatial organization). Historically speaking, the difference between mosaic and monolithic orders—or the transformation of mosaic orders into monolithic ideal—can be traced to the rise of nationalism, which eventually transformed how states and societies conceived the appropriate path to sociospatial organization.[8]

The conflation of the territorial underpinnings of prenationalism Westphalian states and the nation-state ideal, or mosaic and monolithic territorial orders, can be traced to two dynamics. The first is the overwhelming emphasis on the "sovereignty" side of the term "territorial sovereignty," which limits discussions of the "territorial" component. Conflating sovereignty and territoriality leads to reducing the latter to the former, which obfuscates the fact that (state) territories are constituted not only by demarcating space for political purposes but also through the organization of sociospatial arrangements within bounded space. The second dynamic is the "stickiness" of the territorial trap and the "nationalistic" (or nation-state oriented) lenses associated with it. More precisely, the territorial trap entails a nation-state-centric reading of world politics, and the past and present of international politics since the Peace of Westphalia is usually viewed through the lenses of the nation-state ideal.[9] The territorial orders framework suggests that it is not the early Westphalian understanding of territoriality that is projected onto the nation-state ideal. In fact, just the reverse is true: the territorial underpinnings associated with the nation-state ideal are projected onto the prenationalistic era, where territory and territoriality entailed different ideas and practices. It

---

[7] Kadercan 2018.

[8] Paasi 2003, 116; White 2000. Note that while nationalism may not be the sole driver of sociospatial homogenization efforts, from a world-historical perspective, it has served as the most robust and visible factor.

[9] Etherington 2010, 324; Penrose 2002, 294; Smith 2005, 834; Kadercan 2012.

follows that the so-called Westphalian territoriality is not withering away in the face of globalization; it already withered away, if gradually, with the rise of nationalism as a core component of state ideologies.

The second broader claim is that mosaic and monolithic orders are associated with different patterns in war or different kinds of territorial conflict. This broader claim can be broken down to two categories. First, the theory, as highlighted in Chapter 3, suggests that, when compared with mosaic orders, monolithic orders, on average, help render armed conflict less frequent (or ubiquitous) but more severe events. This is a rather "soft" claim, for reasons to be explained below. The second, and "harder," claim is that why states fight (over territory), how they fight, and how they conclude their wars show great divergence across mosaic and monolithic orders; states in both mosaic and monolithic orders do fight over territory, but territory means categorically different things in these orders, with significant implications for how state elites and societies think about the causes, conduct, and consequences of territorial conflict. For example, on average, mosaic orders are affiliated more with wars of territorial opportunism, while monolithic orders are more likely to lead to wars of territorial fear (or fear of losing even small pieces of territory). War termination, in addition, is a much more challenging task in monolithic orders than it is in mosaic orders.

From a macrohistorical perspective, since they are defined by an emphasis on discrete borders, both mosaic and monolithic orders are essentially European constructs. In this chapter, I examine the relationship between mosaic and monolithic orders and war in the European state system through two paradigmatic cases: France and Prussia/Germany. Two factors render these cases paradigmatic. First, both France and Prussia/Germany were great powers that fought numerous wars, making it easier to trace the impacts of territorial ideas on armed conflict. Second, nationalism became a core component of state ideology in these two cases earlier than most, if not all, alternative cases.[10]

These two cases, when compared with other cases examined in this study (with the exception of the revolutionary/Napoleonic France) stand out for two, interrelated, reasons. First, France and Prussia/Germany have long occupied a central place in the very geopolitical environment and time period, the so-called modern state system, that attracted considerable attention in IR scholarship, including quantitative approaches. Second, the trends in severity and frequency of war in the modern state system have been scrutinized by numerous IR scholars. Therefore, since the softer claims in this chapter involve

[10] For a similar approach to case selection, see Posen 1993.

70   How Territorial Ideas Affect Wars

severity and frequency of interstate war in the European state system, an engagement with the relevant data sets and (quantitative) analyses is expedient.

When it comes to the relationship between the causal mechanisms offered in this chapter and the relevant data sets, there exist three main issues. First, in the study of war (in IR), data collection efforts usually deal with the post-1815 period.[11] The extensive research on the general patterns in war, exemplified by—but not limited to—Correlates of War (COW) project, has amassed an impressive array of data sets, but rarely treats the pre-1789 (or, more precisely, pre-1815) era in a similarly robust fashion, which makes the task of intertemporal comparisons rather challenging. Second, the main data set that scrutinizes a broader temporal scope in the European state system, originally compiled by Jack Levy,[12] focuses on great powers, or wars where at least one great power was an active participant. This emphasis, when combined with the fact that Levy follows the COW project's criterion for which conflicts classify as "war" (at least one thousand battle deaths), leaves out some severe conflicts between "small powers" and smaller (less severe) armed conflicts over territory. For example, the Balkan wars of 1912 and 1913, which led to more than half a million casualties (not all of which were necessarily battle deaths) and reshaped the territorial landscape of southeastern Europe, are missing from Levy's data set. There are recent attempts to construct a more comprehensive (and less Eurocentric) data set that, in the future, may allow for a concrete assessment of the claims offered in this study.[13]

Third, the existing data sets do not include sufficient information to actually test the relevant claims, for a simple reason: not surprisingly, these data sets do not include "territorial ideas" (or, as a proxy, the salience of nationalism in state ideologies) as a dimension of concern. This limitation makes it practically impossible to assess the relative (statistical) importance of territorial ideas vis-à-vis other potential explanatory variables such as (dyadic) balances of power, military technology, or demographic factors through multivariate analysis.

These being said, some of the existing data sets can still be consulted, if merely in terms of descriptive statistics. For example, in terms of frequency of war (where at least one participant was a great power), Levy's data set lists thirty-two armed conflicts that took place in Europe and Eurasia between 1648 and 1789. For the period between mid-nineteenth century (from 1848 onward) and 1945, the same data set lists thirteen wars. This comparison does

---

[11] For example, see Gleditsch 2004; Min 2021; Clauset 2018.
[12] Levy 1983.
[13] Miller and Bakar 2022.

not offer direct evidence for this chapter's claims, but it suggests that, at the very least, these outcomes are compatible with these claims. Even with Levy's emphasis on great powers, his findings for the period between 1648 and 1789 suggest that war was rather ubiquitous in Europe: in this period, the number of "peaceful" years in Europe (excluding the wars Europeans fought beyond Europe and Eurasia) was 27, as opposed to 114 years of war.[14] For the period between 1848 and 1945, according to the same criteria invoked above, there were 27 years of war and 70 years of peace. Again, these comparisons can hardly provide any direct support for the claims; they just show that the claim that war was more frequent (or at least ubiquitous) in the first period than in the second is compatible with Levy's data set.

Severity, in turn, is a trickier concept to assess. Following the convention in IR, most studies measure severity in terms of battle deaths. This chapter makes the additional claim that monolithic territoriality increases not only the severity of conflict (as the term is traditionally used in the literature) but also the risk of civilian victimization when wars over territory break out. To my knowledge, the existing data sets do not include this dimension, especially in terms of the period before 1789. Still, we can use severity as a partial proxy for the broader claims. Levy's original assessment about the overall trends in severity are rather inconclusive. The fact that Levy's original analysis compares these trends in terms of centuries, as opposed to certain historical benchmarks, also makes it difficult to draw hard conclusions. For example, in terms of the severity of war during the seventeenth century, Levy lists twenty-six wars, four of which are parts of the broader Thirty Years' War.[15] This puts average battle deaths (per war) at 154,500 with a median of 24,000. If we exclude the Thirty Years' War, which was an anomaly in terms of duration and severity, the average becomes 88,544, with a median of 15,000. These findings are still valuable for a number of tasks, but without historical context, it is difficult to pinpoint specific trends that could contradict or conform the claims offered here.

Lars-Erik Cederman, Camber Warren, and Didier Sornette offer a more nuanced analysis of the changing patterns in severity from a macrohistorical perspective.[16] These scholars build on Levy's data set and expand it by making use of the COW data sets, reaching a conclusion that conforms to the arguments offered here: the severity of interstate war displayed a systematic increase from the late eighteenth and early nineteenth centuries onward.

---

[14] Arguably, the most prolonged period of Europe-wide peace was seven years. See Kadercan 2011.
[15] Levy 1983, 88–91.
[16] Cederman et al. 2011.

72 How Territorial Ideas Affect Wars

Cederman, Warren, and Sornette also offer a nationalism-oriented explanation, making the case that mass mobilization that came with nationalism led to a fundamental shift in the very state system and the nature of interstate war, amplifying the severity of armed conflict. In a recent study, Charles Miller and Shuvo Bakar pursue an ambitious project to create an extensive data set that includes cases that go back in history as far as 1483 BC.[17] These authors also compare and contrast two data sets, one compiled by Peter Brecke,[18] the other compiled by the authors themselves by drawing on Tony Jacques's extensive dictionary of more than eight thousand battles.[19] In terms of battle deaths over time, the comparison suggests a certain trend that is similar, if not identical, to the one highlighted by Cederman, Warren, and Sornette: when compared with the previous periods, the severity of wars displays a remarkable increase from the nineteenth century onward, especially in the data set the authors built by drawing upon Jacques.[20]

Note that my claim here is not that the arguments offered in this study explain the changing patterns in the overall frequency and severity of armed conflict in the state system, however that system is defined. In fact, as highlighted above, without appropriate operationalization of the variable of concern, territorial ideas (which, in turn, would need to be coded on a case-by-case basis), such an analysis would not be feasible. My claim is more modest: the existing data sets and quantitative analyses, at least to an extent, are compatible with my arguments.

In terms of France and Prussia/Germany, it is safe to make the case that, following the general trends in European warfare, interstate armed conflict was, on average, a more severe enterprise from the second half of the nineteenth century onward, when compared with the period between 1648 and 1789. At the same time, such wars became far less frequent and ubiquitous, of course, when compared with the prerevolutionary era. Especially in terms of frequency and/or ubiquity of war, Brecke's data set can offer some insights.[21] Brecke's data set, when compared with the COW project or Levy's data set, is far less systemized, and mostly incomplete. However, at the same time, the list of armed conflicts that Brecke includes goes far beyond these more systematic attempts. Brecke's data set is difficult to sift through, but a brief overview points toward a far more nuanced picture, especially in the period before the French Revolution. Admittedly, Brecke's data set provides more support for

---

[17] Miller and Bakar 2022.
[18] Brecke 1999.
[19] Jaques 2007.
[20] Miller and Bakar 2022, 8.
[21] Brecke 1999.

the French case than it does for Prussia. This may be partially explained by the fact that France was already a great power by 1648, while Prussia established itself as a middle power only by the mid-eighteenth century. Simply put, France had far more opportunity (and capability) to wage wars than Prussia did, at least until the mid-eighteenth century. Still, a brief overview of the descriptive statistics can be helpful.

Even when we exclude France's colonial wars in Americas and Asia, its military engagements in North Africa, and the French (military) interventions vis-à-vis revolts and rebellions in Europe, Brecke's data set strongly confirms that for France between 1648 and 1789, armed conflict was ubiquitous. During this time, France participated in seventeen armed conflicts, big and small.[22] Of course, France was not always at war during all these wars, but these armed conflicts, overall, point toward sixty-five years of peace, as opposed to seventy-six years of war between 1648 and 1789.[23] If we assume that the House of Hohenzollern stands for both Brandenburg and Prussia in Brecke's data set, the Hohenzollerns participated in twelve armed conflicts during the same period, big and small.[24] Again, Prussia (or the Hohenzollerns) was not always at war during all these wars, but these wars, collectively, point toward a period of fifty-seven years of conflict and eighty-four years of peace in the immediate geopolitical vicinity of Prussia.[25]

In sum, the relevant data sets do not make it possible to directly test the implications of the theory, as it applies to the European state system before and after the rise of nationalism as a core component of state ideologies. That being said, the existing data sets and quantitative analyses, on average, are compatible with the predictions of the theory.

The remainder of this chapter unfolds in three steps. The first section offers an analysis of the relationship between mosaic territoriality and war in France and Prussia before the French Revolution. The second step elaborates on the

---

[22] These wars, as listed in Brecke's data set, are the following: Franco-Spanish War (1650–56), Anglo-Spanish War (European leg, 1656–59), Habsburg-Ottoman War (1663–64), Second Anglo-Dutch War (1665–67), Candian War (1667–69), War of the Devolution (1667–68), the French Conquest of Lorraine (1670), Dutch War (1672–78), Reunion War (1683–84), France-Genoa conflict (1684–85), the French Conquest of Luxembourg (1684), War of the Grand Alliance (1688–97), War of Spanish Succession (1701–14), War of Quadruple Alliance (1717–1720), War of the Polish Throne (1733–35), War of Austrian Succession (1740–48), Seven Years' War (1756–63).

[23] The author's calculation, based on Brecke's data set.

[24] These wars are listed in Brecke's data set as follows: Brandenburg-Poland (1655–56), Brandenburg-Sweden (1657–60), Dutch War (1672–78), Danish-Swedish War (1675–79), War of the Grand Alliance (1688–97), Second Northern War (1700–21), Prussia-Sweden (1715–20), War of the Polish Throne (1733–35), First Silesian War (1740–42), Second Silesian War (1744–45), Seven Years' War (1756–63), War of Bavarian Succession (1778–79). Note that I have excluded three cases: War of Austrian Succession (not to double-count Silesian wars), Prussia-Neuburg War (1651, since little information exists on the topic), and Scheldt War (or Kettle War of 1785, due to lack of casualties).

[25] The author's calculation, based on Brecke's data set.

74 How Territorial Ideas Affect Wars

ways in which nationalism affected the dominant territorial ideas in the so-called European state system. In the third section, I offer a brief overview of the association between monolithic territoriality and war in France and Germany between the late nineteenth century and 1945.

Mosaic Territoriality and War in France and Prussia, 1648–1789

The European state system before the French Revolution could be defined in terms of mosaic territoriality.[26] Broadly speaking, the theory and practice of the original Westphalian interpretation of sovereignty involved three key dimensions: (1) the domain of authority;[27] (2) mutual recognition of the spatial extent of "in-group" states; (3) identity of the sovereign.[28] The first pillar stipulated that all issue domains in a clearly demarcated sphere should be under the sovereign's jurisdiction. Accordingly, the relevant spatial and geographical imageries highlight the notion of sovereignty, defined in terms of absolute authority over clearly defined and compartmentalized spaces.[29] Besides, to function, the Westphalian arrangement also required an external, or relational, arrangement: a system of mutual recognition, where each "member" state operating within the state system acknowledged, if not always respected, the sovereignty of other members.[30] These two dynamics may not all by themselves have "fixed" the existing borders indefinitely, but, together, they allowed for relative territorial stability between states that adhered to mosaic (or monolithic) orders.[31]

The third pillar of the Westphalian territorial model followed from the dynastical legacy of the early modern Europe: it was the monarchs who were

---

[26] As will be discussed in more detail in Chapters 6 and 7, prerevolutionary Europe also harbored numerous "territorial abnormalities," such as the empire and city-states, which can hardly be conceived in terms of mosaic territoriality. In this chapter, the focus is on the so-called modern states, the epicenter of most IR research.

[27] Spruyt 1994; Sassen 28, 32–33; Anderson 1996, 17.

[28] Hall 1999.

[29] Larkins 2010; Mylonas 2012.

[30] Sassen 2008, 81. On the concept of territorial sovereignty see Agnew 1994; Kratochwil 1986; Krasner 1999; Osiander 2001; Ruggie 1983, 1993; Spruyt 1994; Teschke 2003; and Tilly 1990. While John Herz (1957) suggested that the Westphalian states, in principle, were construed as impregnable "territorial shells," as Stephen Krasner pointed out, the impregnability of state territory was a theory that was hardly grounded in reality. States occasionally violated and disregarded the territorial sovereignty of others, and collectively turned a blind eye to such incursions. This dynamic, however, does not suggest that aspirational ideas in general, or territorial models in particular, have exerted little influence on world politics. The relevant ideas define the spectrum of acceptable behavior and incentives of political actors, enabling some actions while also constraining others.

[31] Parvin and Sommer 1980, 2.

sovereigns. As Benno Teschke pointed out, the treaties of the seventeenth and eighteenth centuries entailed the rulers, not states per se, as corporate entities:[32] "Before the emergence of nation-states . . . [the] relationship between rulers and their subjects was primarily marked by the idea of 'verticality' and heterogeneity."[33] In such a setting, individuals were not concerned all that much with the ethnic background of their rulers or their own ethnic kin.[34] The absence of popular sovereignty had important implications for ideas about sociospatial organization: the society did not have an attachment to the entirety of the state space (which was usually, if not always, conceived in terms of monarchy), and monolithic ideal did not take root. As sociologist Anthony Smith pointed out, "Pre-nationalist outlooks tend[ed] to treat territory simply as 'land' to be worked and settled."[35]

Put differently, before nationalism's rise to prominence, the dominant territorial ideas in the modern state system did not demand sociospatial homogeneity and were in fact built on heterogeneity.[36] In the words of Charles Tilly, the early Westphalian states "either [did] not penetrate very deeply or left that penetration to largely autonomous intermediaries" and "have [not] homogenized their populations."[37] Accordingly, masses living inside the borders of a given polity were culturally and politically fragmented.[38] This fragmentation deprived the inhabitants of the state of an all-encompassing and inclusive imagination to visualize the territorial belongings of the state as their homeland.[39] As Jeremy Black put it, "In much of Europe monarchs ruled what were often legally distinct territories and their possessions lacked either a shared sense of the past or often one of present interests."[40] Not surprisingly, the masses had little attachment to the entirety of the territory controlled by the state that ruled over them.

The lack of association between the society and state space came with both advantages and disadvantages for state elites. Before the age of nationalism, losing territory meant losing access to resources, which was by no means a favorable outcome, but the loss of territory per se did not necessarily increase the likelihood of losing office (or, more specifically, the throne). A direct

[32] Teschke 2003. 238. Also see Osiander 2001, 145.

[33] Hakli 1994, 40. As Peter Wilson (1999, 86) highlights, "Even in the republican regimes of Venice, Genoa, and the Dutch, political power was displayed through a court and hereditary nobility, alongside narrow representative assemblies."

[34] Wimmer 2012, 1.

[35] Smith 1981, 191.

[36] Teschke 2003, 203, 232, 233, 239.

[37] Tilly 1994, 140. Also see Mann 1995; Tilly and Ardant 1975; Hutchinson 1987.

[38] Sahlins 1990, 1427–1428.

[39] Schelling 1966, 27–28.

[40] Black 1990, 179.

76 How Territorial Ideas Affect Wars

implication of such an environment for the territorial politics of the age was the fickleness of the borders. Despite the fact that the modern states were construed as "territorial shells"[41] (in theory, if not in practice), borders were not set in stone; in fact, they were in constant flux as a result of not only wars but also royal marriages and purchases.

The ease of territorial "trades" was striking. Before the rise of nationalism, European states—or more precisely, monarchs—were able to treat the territories they controlled like commodities that could be swapped, bought, or sold.[42] As Clausewitz wrote, the typical state of the time "behaved as though it owned and managed a great estate that it constantly sought to enlarge—an effort in which the inhabitants were not expected to show any particular interest."[43] Accordingly, the sovereign states of the seventeenth and eighteenth centuries could treat the lands they controlled primarily as commodities that could be "cut and pared like Dutch cheeses."[44] Evan Luard refers to the ease of such exchanges as follows:

> To suit the convenience of states, territories were swapped around in unscrupulous dealing. Sicily was handed over from Spain to Savoy in 1740, exchanged in 1720 for Sardinia, and 20 years later joined with Naples and awarded to a foreign prince. Parma and Piacenza were awarded to the same prince in 1732, transferred to Austria in 1739, and transferred yet again to his brother in 1748. Tuscany was handed to the duke of Lorraine in 1739, while the unsuccessful contender for the Polish throne was compensated with Lorraine, and Poland handed to the elector of Saxony.[45]

In such an environment, while states frequently fought for territorial aggrandizement, they had relatively little tolerance for the military costs—both blood and treasure—that were associated with territorial defense and expansion. Big, decisive battles were avoided, and military commanders of the period such as Marshall de Saxe and Marlborough were applauded as much for their skills in avoiding decisive—and potentially costly—battles as for their

---

[41] Herz 1957.

[42] Hutchinson (2017, 33) argues that "sacralization of the land" in Europe preceded the eighteenth century.

[43] Clausewitz [1832] 1976, 589. Also see Howard (1976, 75). Land could also be exchanged as dowry, as can be seen in the case of Anne of Denmark in the late sixteenth century, whose marriage to James VI brought Orkney and Shetland Islands to Scotland. Furthermore, in many cases, considerable chunks of state territory also literally belonged to the monarchs. "Around 1740," for example, "almost a quarter of [Prussia's] surface area was directly owned by the Crown" (Schieder et al. [2000] 2016, 53).

[44] May 1933, 20.

[45] Luard 1987, 156–157.

performance in actual conquests.[46] Strategic thinking about territorial defense, in this reading, was much more practical and cost-sensitive when compared with the age of nationalism. The famous fortification-oriented defense system that Marquis de Vauban initiated in the second half of the seventeenth century, for example, was an unprecedented effort on the part of France to defend its borders.[47] The logic of fortification depended on a rather "thin" and multilayered defense strategy that would, if need arose, allow aggressors to march into French territory and hold substantial chunks of land for extended periods of time, so that the French forces could interfere with adversaries' command and communications. By contrast, the Maginot Line that the French built right after World War I did not endeavor to cut the costs of defense. It was not only an extremely costly undertaking, but also designed to prevent even temporary breaches of the territorial integrity of the French state. The Maginot Line was built, in historian Judith Hughes's words, "to assure the inviolability of the nation's territory."[48]

The prominence of mosaic territoriality in the prenationalistic era, in turn, also made decision to go to war comparatively easy. It was no coincidence, from such a vantage point, that the health of the monarchs was a good predictor of wars. The prospect of leadership change implied a momentary weakness. Such perceived weakness provided other states with a window of opportunity for conquest, with dynastic claims serving as no more than "an opportune sham."[49]

Overall, the case of France between the Peace of Westphalia and the French Revolution offers a set of illustrative examples. Along with Spain and England, France is usually accepted as one of the "prototypes" in the context of the age of the modern states.[50] By the sixteenth century, France, with its inclination to form a centralized state, might have appeared somewhat of an anomaly to many contemporaries, but, from the second half of the seventeenth century onward, it also began to emerge as a territorially defined modern state which inspired other polities across Europe. Broadly speaking, France was one of the "winners" of the Peace of Westphalia. The French "triumph at Westphalia," to be precise, "lay less in the extent of her immediate annexations than in destroying Habsburg predominance and laying the foundations for her own

---

[46] Clausewitz [1832] 1976, 590. As John Wolf (1951, 68) highlights, Marlborough was hailed as the "winner of 'bloodless victories.'" Of course, such an approach, shared by most of Marlborough's contemporaries, prolonged the duration of most conflict.

[47] Duffy 1985b, 1–20, 71–97; Black 1994, 97–99.

[48] Hughes 1971, 199.

[49] Black 1987, 8. Especially after 1648, the main underlying motivation behind claims to succession was "demand for more territory" (Luard 1987, 101). Also see Holsti 1991.

[50] On the origins of the French state, see Collins 1997.

78　How Territorial Ideas Affect Wars

future expansion."[51] In fact, the Peace did not mean the end of the "state of war" for France. For France, the state of war ended only in 1659, when France and Spain signed the Treaty of Pyrenees, setting the grounds for one of the most durable delineated borders in modern European history.

In the era following the Peace of Westphalia, probably the most relevant figure in France is Louis XIV. Being crowned at the age of four in 1643, Louis played only a minor role in France's domestic and foreign politics until 1661. Having inherited a rather strong state from his former mentor and chief minister, Cardinal Jules Mazarin, Louis spent his first half a decade in power consolidating his domestic authority, in the face of confessional tensions and antitaxation revolts. Overall, the remainder of Louis's reign was marked by almost incessant fighting.[52] Louis was involved in five wars: the War of Devolution (1667–68), the Dutch War (1672–78), the War of the Reunions (1683–84), the Nine Years War (1688–97), the War of Spanish Succession (1701–14).

The bellicose nature of Louis's reign has prompted some spectators to consider the French king as a proto-Napoleon with similar ambitions to conquer and remake the entire European continent. Arguably, this interpretation has been partially fueled by the anti-France discourses of the time (which, given the threat that Louis's France posed to numerous geographies for more than half a century, is not surprising) and partially by an anachronistic reading of the past. Many historians now agree that Louis and Napoleon were two different political animals operating in categorically different political and social environments, who professed categorically different policy objectives.[53]

It is true that Louis aimed for a "bigger" France and had a keen interest in expanding his state's territorial base, either through war or through dynastic claims and purchases. In that, however, Louis was not all that different from most of his contemporaries. Louis was operating in a geopolitical landscape where "rulers looked on their states as their personal property."[54] As John Lynn argued, for the rulers of the time (including Louis), "The proper prize of war was territory."[55] According to Frank Tallett, territory was "a dominant concern" for the rulers of the time.[56] Therefore, rulers who sought to increase their standing in European politics had few options other than expanding their territorial base. Also note that this "system" was viable and feasible at the

---

[51] McKay and Scott 1983, 4.

[52] Lynn 1999, 364.

[53] Chapter 7, in turn, will make the case that the prerevolutionary and revolutionary territorial ideas among the French leadership were at great variance.

[54] McKay and Scott 1983, 16. Also see Giesey 1983, 207.

[55] Lynn 1999, 29. Also see Black 1990, 2.

[56] Tallett 1992, 19.

Rigid Borders, Spasmodic Wars **79**

time in Europe, partially because the mosaic territoriality made it possible to carve up territories without much of a backlash from the relevant societies.[57]

Beyond his exceptionally long tenure, what separated Louis from his contemporaries was not his objectives per se, but the fact that he ruled over the strongest state in Europe at the time, which afforded him the luxury of territorial ambition. That being said, Louis still behaved in line with the existing norms of his time, which prioritized wars of limited territorial objectives. Put differently, while Napoleon aimed to remake the European landscape, Louis just wanted a bigger share within the existing arrangements. As Lynn put it, while "Napoleon dictated" (or aimed to do so), "Louis negotiated," and did so within the bounds of the existing norms and arrangements of his time.[58] In relation, the conduct of war during the age of Louis XIV simply followed the existing practices embedded within the ancient regime.[59] Battles and sieges were inherently indecisive, rulers and military commanders tended to prioritize attrition over decisive engagements, and diplomatic negotiations and actual fighting were inherently interlinked, arguably considerably more so than it would be possible in the age of nationalism.[60] Once again, the "fusion" between actual fighting and negotiations over territory followed from mosaic territoriality; territories, the ultimate prize over which states fought, were deemed divisible goods, which made it much easier to negotiate over them. The fact that rulers pursued limited territorial objectives, in turn, also made it possible for rulers to simultaneously wage wars "without becoming merged in a generalized struggle."[61]

The War of Devolution (1667–68) was Louis's first war for territory.[62] In 1660, Louis XIV had married Maria Theresa, the Spanish ruler Philip IV's daughter, following a bilateral compromise—neither Maria Theresa nor her children from Louis XIV would ever lay claim to the Spanish throne and, in return, Louis would be paid five hundred thousand gold *ecus*. Philip IV died in 1665, leaving Carlos II as his sole heir. Taking advantage of the political uncertainty in Spain that accompanied the ascension of a sickly four-year old to the throne, Louis pressed a claim: because the promised sum had never been paid, it was Maria Theresa who should be accepted as the rightful ruler of Spain. Eventually, Louis led his seventy-two-thousand-strong army into the Spanish Netherlands in 1667.

---

[57] Tallett 1992, 244.
[58] Lynn 1999, 375.
[59] Lynn 1999, 367.
[60] Lynn 1999, 3.
[61] Wolf 1951, 54.
[62] On this conflict, see Lynn 1999, 105–158.

80 How Territorial Ideas Affect Wars

Louis XIV might have favored an outcome where his wife would assume the Spanish throne. However, the main reason he took his wife's claim to the throne "very seriously" was that it offered the pretext to "annex strategically important areas" in Flanders through an opportunistic campaign.[63] In a matter of weeks, France found itself facing a coalition of England, Sweden, the Dutch Republic, and Spain. Despite the magnitude of the territorial stakes involved and the size of the forces fielded, the participants were able to settle on an outcome after suffering a total of only four thousand casualties. This relatively brief engagement, however, led to "very impressive" border changes.[64] French forces withdrew from the Spanish Netherlands, but Louis XIV was allowed to keep twelve newly conquered cities through the Treaty of Aix-la-Chapelle (1668). In line with the theory's predictions, while peace was achieved without steep costs, it was not sustainable in the long term. For Louis XIV, the settlement was just a "breathing spell" before launching yet another opportunistic campaign in 1672 in the Netherlands.[65]

In fact, Louis "deliberately" began to plan an attack on the Dutch "as soon as" the War of Devolution was formally over.[66] This is hardly surprising. Even back in 1667, Louis was primarily interested in the Spanish Netherlands.[67] From such a vantage point, while Louis's territorial gains during the War of Devolution were limited, the war still provided him what he sought: "an enclave in the Spanish Netherlands."[68] Building on this enclave, Louis merely bided his time, and went to lengths to break up the Triple Alliance between Sweden, the Dutch Republic, and England (which was formed as a response to Louis's incursions into the Spanish Habsburg territories) before launching into yet another war of territorial conquest.[69]

In 1672, having been convinced that a window of opportunity finally revealed itself, Louis launched an offensive on the Dutch, which led to the outbreak of the Dutch War. In this sense, the War of Devolution and the Dutch War "are best seen as one, broken by a four years' truce."[70] Louis hoped to make considerable territorial gains through a quick and limited war, and the initial French attacks on the Dutch proved to be a success for Louis. However, the fact that Louis wanted to retain his early conquests while also making a move for Franche-Comte—especially considering the contra-France alliance

---

[63] McKay and Scott 1983, 20.
[64] Roosen 1976, 19.
[65] Wolf 1968, 211.
[66] McKay and Scott 1983, 25.
[67] Holborn 1964, 69.
[68] McKay and Scott 1983, 21.
[69] Lynn 1999, 109.
[70] Lynn 1999, 105.

Rigid Borders, Spasmodic Wars **81**

that formed between the Dutch, the Holy Roman Empire, and Spain (among others)—"backfired," and Louis was eventually forced to withdraw from much of the Dutch territory by 1674.[71] The conduct of war, to a large extent, once again followed the existing patterns; much of the struggle between France and its rivals was dominated by lengthy sieges and blockades, with only three major battles (in Seneffe, Cassel, and St Dennis), none of which yielded decisive outcomes for any of the participants.[72]

The Dutch War was finally settled in 1678, with the Peace of Nygemen (or Nijmegen). For Louis, the war yielded a "net gain," at least in territorial terms. France agreed to return the Dutch territories it occupied in the initial stages of the war but, in return, acquired Franche-Comte as well as numerous provinces such as Ypres and Cassel from Spain. Overall, France might have failed to preserve its earlier conquests, but the French leadership considered it a success, for two reasons. First, as mentioned above, France ended up taking over a number of coveted provinces; according to Peter Wilson, the War of the Devolution and the Dutch War allowed Louis to make the "largest territorial gains of the last 250 years of the French monarchy."[73] Second, Louis proved to his rivals that he could actually fight a long war against multiple foes and still impose a peace that would be favorable to France.[74]

Beyond these relatively well-known wars, we can also talk about what came to be referred to as the "Reunions," which paved the way for the War of the Reunions in 1683. This episode rarely, if at all, attracts the attention of IR scholars, presumably because it hardly qualifies as a "great power war," as the term is traditionally employed. However, the Reunions episode provides important insights into the ways in which organized violence and territorial aggrandizement related to each other in the prenationalistic era in Europe. Emboldened by the Peace of Nymegen, Louis spent the next five years following the Dutch War in order to acquire pieces of territory alongside its borders, and did so through "a strange mix of legality and force."[75] Louis drew upon obscure legal claims to legitimize his small-scale conquests, and when such claims failed to provide any sort of legal alibi, Louis still went ahead and took over target areas. The violent seizure of Strasbourg in 1681 is a case in point; France had no real legal basis to claim the city, but still took over it in the context of the Reunions.[76]

---

[71] Ekberg 1974.
[72] Lynn 1999, 158.
[73] Wilson 1999, 79.
[74] McKay and Scott 1983, 35.
[75] Lynn 1999, 37.
[76] Lynn 1999, 37.

82 How Territorial Ideas Affect Wars

Broadly speaking, "If [the Reunions] was not war in name, it was war in fact."[77]

The Reunions episode is directly related to mosaic territoriality, in two ways. First, France could actually target the relevant territories rather easily, in full knowledge that none of the great (or smaller) powers of the time deemed such territories to be indivisible parts of their national homelands. Second, the Reunions episode was closely associated with the "evolution" of mosaic territoriality, as it reflected the ambiguities embedded with this aspirational model. More specifically, "During the second half of the seventeenth century, the concept of state borders was in the process of evolution."[78] Still, the Peace of Westphalia and the Peace of Nymegen pointed toward more specific delineation of state spaces across Europe, a tendency that put the remaining feudal or quasi-feudal entities at a significant disadvantage. Treating Westphalia and Nymegen as legitimizing tools, Louis took advantage of the "confused realities of frontiers at the time" and went to lengths to absorb such entities with "radical determination."[79] Louis's piecemeal conquests eventually prompted Carlos II to formally declare war on France in 1683, sparking the War of the Reunions. Spain and France ended the war with the Truce of Ratisbon in 1684. France kept almost all of its territorial gains, other than Courtrai and Dixmude, which were returned to Spain.[80] While IR scholarship has barely taken any interest in it, historians such as John Lynn refer to the War of Reunions as Louis's "briefest and most successful war."[81]

The French successes during the Reunions prompted further territorial opportunism on the part of France. The result was the Nine Years War.[82] More precisely, Louis aimed to expand France's territorial base, and expected another short conflict along the lines of the War of the Reunions.[83] In fact, the War of the Reunions and the Nine Years War were inextricably linked. The initial French attack in 1688 targeted France's German neighbors, and aimed to compel them to ratify the French gains in the Truce of Ratisbon.[84] As the very name of the war suggests, Louis's hopes for the repeat of the War of the Reunions proved to be overly optimistic. Louis's continuous attempts to expand triggered a Europe-wide balancing coalition comprising almost all key actors in the European state system, from the Dutch Republic to England,

---

[77] Lynn 1999, 160.
[78] Holborn 1964, 161.
[79] Holborn 1964, 161, 82.
[80] Holborn 1964, 169.
[81] Lynn 1999, 169.
[82] On the conflict, especially the religious aspects associated with it, see Onnekink 2009.
[83] Lynn 1999, 191.
[84] Lynn 1999, 264.

Rigid Borders, Spasmodic Wars **83**

from Austria to Portugal, not to mention Spain and Sweden. The conduct of war, once again, followed the existing patterns. In fact, the most significant fighting in the war took place around the French borders and could be defined as collection of "largely indecisive" sieges and maneuvers.[85]

How the war was finally concluded in 1697 with the Peace of Ryswick, in this context, provides insights about mosaic territoriality. Most notably, France agreed to a certain peace that could hardly be justified in terms of either the costs of the war (which negatively impacted France) or the French military performance (France had not suffered a substantial military defeat in the battlefields). Most notably, Louis surrendered Casale and Pinerolo to Spain, which was a widely unpopular decision in France at the time. The main reason for Louis to agree to such generous terms, in turn, had to do with questions over Spanish succession; Carlos's health was rapidly declining, and the Spanish king had no direct heir. In such a landscape, Louis aimed to "curry favor in Madrid," planning ahead for the crisis over the Spanish throne and, by implication, Spain-ruled territories.[86] Note that such pragmatic decisions over territory are not easily made in the presence of monolithic territoriality, epitomized in the nation-state ideal. For example, given the prominence of monolithic territoriality, it would not be comparably easy for Germany to return Alsace-Lorraine to France in order to curry favor in Paris during the decade leading up to World War I. That this very counterfactual may sound rather bombastic only helps drive the point home: what could be seen as "normal" in the age of mosaic territoriality would appear almost unimaginable in the age of monolithic territoriality, and vice versa.[87]

Louis's next and final war, the War of Spanish Succession, attracts more attention in IR scholarship. The conduct of the war followed patterns already highlighted above. Causes of the war largely followed from the half-century-long saga that fused dynastic claims with territorial ones in the context of the Spanish throne.[88] In fact, the crisis over Spanish succession was a direct reflection of mosaic territoriality: given that sociospatial homogeneity was a main concern for neither the rulers of Europe nor the "ruled," the rulers could easily took it upon themselves to slice and dice through various territories as if they were divisible and substitutable goods.

---

[85] McKay and Scott 1983, 49.

[86] McKay and Scott 1983, 49. Also see Gagliardo 1991, 259.

[87] Louis's deal with Savoy, epitomized in the Treaty of Turin of 1696, is yet another example. In order to free up around thirty thousand troops who were needed elsewhere, Louis made a secret deal with Savoy, allowing Savoy to "capture" a number of strategic outposts and provinces in Italy. See Wolf 1951, 49.

[88] On the legal complexities of the day, in the context of the Spanish succession, see Dhondt 2011.

84 How Territorial Ideas Affect Wars

Note that the French involvement in the war is sometimes traced to Louis's alleged ambitions to rule both France and Spain, as part of his desire to impose French hegemony all across the Continent. This interpretation, however, is usually contested on two grounds. First, Louis did not necessarily intend to wage a decade-long conflict over the Spanish throne in the first place. Instead, the complexity of the competing dynastic claims over the Spanish throne prompted Louis to consider numerous "partition" deals, most notably with William of Orange, in order to prevent a full-blown conflict. Carlos II's final will pointed toward Louis's own grandson, Philip (Duke of Anjou), placing Louis between a rock and a hard place, or between honoring Carlos's will on behalf of his grandson and the partition deal France struck with William of Orange, the king of England, Ireland, and Scotland. Facing two inherently imperfect choices, Louis opted for his grandson's claims in 1700, which eventually pitted France against the Dutch and the British, who declared war in 1702. Second, after four decades in power and numerous wars under his belt, Louis understood that the idea that a single ruler could rule both France and Spain was not a viable one, especially in the ancient regime.[89] Therefore, Louis's policy objectives were rather limited: prevent encirclement by the Habsburgs and, if possible, expand French territory into the Spanish domains.[90]

The decade-long conflict involved more than a dozen states and entities in Europe, and came to an end with the Peace of Utrecht (1713–15). Louis's grandson Philip became the king of Spain, with the condition that no single ruler would ever lay claim to both French and Spanish thrones. For Louis, it was a costly war that ate up considerable resources, but, in the end, the aging French king prevented the risk of yet another encirclement attempt by the Habsburgs. France was also able to hold on to its earlier conquests and even added "some minor pieces of territory."[91]

In fact, the Peace of Utrecht itself speaks volumes about the implications of mosaic territoriality for interstate politics. Note that, especially in IR, the Peace of Utrecht is sometimes interpreted as a turning point with respect to balance-of-power politics. The conventional wisdom suggests that, through Utrecht, European great powers committed to a system where the "balance" in European politics were to be preserved intentionally through balancing coalitions and compensations, so that none of the great powers could emerge as a continent-wide hegemon. What's missing from most relevant debates in IR is the fact that the relevant arguments are usually defined in terms of

[89] Thomson 1954, 113–114.
[90] McKay and Scott 1983, 58.
[91] Lynn 1999, 359.

"balances of relative power," without necessarily defining what "power" entailed in the context of the day. Upon close inspection, said "balance" reveals itself to have been based on territory. In principle, if not always in practice, a great power's territorial losses in a certain geography were to be compensated by gains elsewhere, and vice versa. Frederik Dhondt refers to this arrangement as "territorial balance"; for Dhondt, the Peace of Utrecht institutionalized this existing practice and extended it to the entirety of Europe.[92] Note that such an arrangement would not necessarily (or perhaps could not) function when monolithic territoriality is dominant. Most notably, nation-states cannot easily trade their provinces as if they are divisible and substitutable goods, at least as easily as European states could trade during the course of the eighteenth century. This observation has a direct implication for IR research on the concept of balance of power: the kind of specific practice that was institutionalized at Utrecht was necessarily built on mosaic territoriality, which implies that at least some of the insights to be gained from the study of balance of power during the eighteenth century are not easily applicable in the age of the nation-states.

Between Louis XIV's reign and the French Revolution, France continued to engage in numerous conflicts in Europe, ranging from the War of the Quadruple Alliance (1718–20) to the War of the Polish Succession (1733–35). Of all the relevant conflicts, the Seven Years' War (1756–63) is the one that attracted the most attention, for understandable reasons. In the words of economic historian Larry Neal, "The Seven Years War is an anomaly from whatever angle of approach one chooses to study it."[93] The severity of the war, which Levy lists at 992,000 battle deaths,[94] far exceeded most of the conflicts since the time of the Peace of Westphalia, and the war was truly "global" in geographical terms. These being said, as far as France was concerned, the origins of the Seven Years' War had less to do with Europe per se than with the "colonial question" between England and France.[95] Still, the dynastic nature of the territorial politics of the day almost guaranteed that a colonial conflict between England and France would also have significant repercussions in the Continent: George II was not only the king of England, but also the Elector of Hanover, a dynamic, when combined with the intricate alliance configurations of the time, that turned the colonial question into a European one. Overall, the Seven Years' War proved to be a disaster for France beyond

---

[92] Dhondt 2011, 371.
[93] Neal 1977, 20.
[94] Levy 1983.
[95] Ropes 1889, 147.

86 How Territorial Ideas Affect Wars

Europe; France lost considerable colonial possessions.[96] However, within Europe, "France ceded no territory."[97] Broadly speaking, in Europe, the Seven Years' War involved much higher stakes for yet another great power, Prussia.

Prussia is the second case of concern with respect to the relationship between mosaic territoriality and war in prenationalistic Europe. Of course, just as it is the case with Germany,[98] "When is Prussia?" and "Where is Prussia" are two questions with no self-evident answers. The origins of the Prussian state goes back at least to the rise of the House of Hohenzollern in the sixteenth century. In 1525, Albert von Hohenzollern, the last grand master of the Teutonic Knights, converted to Lutheranism and eventually established himself as the Duke of Prussia (or Brandenburg-Prussia, to be precise).[99] Operating within the fluid and complicated networks of the geography it inhabited, the House of Hohenzollern eventually emerged as a secondary (perhaps even tertiary) player within the empire by the seventeenth century. In 1701, the Hohenzollern Duke of Brandenburg-Prussia was crowned king, not as "king of Prussia," but as "king in Prussia."[100]

"Where was Prussia?" is an even more difficult question to answer. The reason has to do with the fact that while Prussia eventually emerged as a modern state by the nineteenth century, its origins had a lot to do with the complicated territorial arrangements associated with the Holy Roman Empire and remnants of feudalism. Put simply, where Prussia was and where the Hohenzollerns reigned defied any simplistic categorizations. Philip G. Dwyer sums up the level of complexity as follows:

> The heterogeneous character of the state was reflected in the titles that preceded the Prussian king's name. He was Margrave of Brandenburg, Duke of Pommern, Magdeburg and Cleves, Prince of Minden and Halberstadt, Count of Mark and Ravensburg and Prince of Neuchatel, to name but the most important. Not only were these territories spread over a large area of northern Europe, but Prussia enjoyed no natural boundaries that helped protect it from outside aggression. Furthermore, Prussia was not a uniquely German state, but rather a religious and political hybrid, a non-national state—although not to the extent that Austria was.[101]

---

[96] Note that the argument here is that European states' approach to the relationship between war and territory took different paths in Europe and in non-European geographies. On this point, see Chapter 5.
[97] Scott 2011, 447.
[98] Gagliardo 1991, 1.
[99] See Dwyer 2014, locs. 1113–1129.
[100] On this episode, see Gagliardo 1991, 293–311.
[101] Dwyer 2014, loc. 580.

As far as wars were concerned, Prussia was a "late bloomer"; from 1740 onward, however, it was engaged in almost every major European conflict in the eighteenth and nineteenth centuries.[102] This trend sometimes paves the way for a certain interpretation: perhaps, Prussia was exceptionally bellicose, even by the standards of its time. However, as Philip Dwyer emphasizes, there was "nothing out of the ordinary" about Prussia's behavior, and states like Britain, Austria, and Russia were "engaged in even more conflicts over the same period of time."[103] Still, a few factors rendered Prussia an outlier. First, Prussia was victorious, or at least was not the defeated party (in terms of territorial losses), in almost all of the conflicts it participated until the Revolutionary Wars.[104] Second, Prussia can easily be construed as an aggressor in almost all of these wars. The third factor that renders Prussia an outlier, and can also explain the second one, has already been mentioned: simply put, Prussia aimed to become a great power, or at least a "state" in the traditional sense, but it did not possess a compact and contiguous territorial base to do so. Prussia's original (dispersed) territorial possessions provided strong incentives to launch wars of aggrandizement. In other words, expansion and conquest were not practices peculiar to the Prussian state; what made Prussia an outlier was that it was "hungrier" than most other comparable states and eventually developed the military capabilities to address the aforementioned hunger.

Also note that while Frederick II has sometimes been lionized in German nationalistic discourses and imageries, neither a sense of "German nationalism" nor a desire to "unify Germany" drove the Prussian rulers' foreign policy postures during the seventeenth and eighteenth centuries. Both the constitutional and cultural makeup of the empire, and the mindset of the Prussian leaders, precluded such tendencies.[105] In other words, while Frederick's wars are sometimes associated with (German) nationalistic discourses, the wars that Prussia fought during the course of the seventeenth and eighteenth centuries had little to do with (German) nationalism, as we understand the term today.

In fact, as far as the seventeenth century was concerned, Prussia pursued a rather "pacific" foreign policy.[106] Prussia's first ever large-scale military engagement was in the Second Northern War (1655–60) between Sweden and Poland, during the time of Frederick William, also known as the Great Elector. Prussian troops saw some action during the Battle of Warsaw

---

[102] Dwyer 2014, loc. 882.
[103] Dwyer 2014, loc. 884.
[104] Dwyer 2014, loc. 885.
[105] Black 1990, 180.
[106] Gagliardo 1991.

88 How Territorial Ideas Affect Wars

(1656),[107] but for Prussia the war was already "very safe" when it entered it.[108] The Great Elector's successors, especially Frederick I (reigned 1701–13) and Frederick William I (1713–40) went to great lengths to establish a competent, well-organized, and disciplined army. By the time Frederick William died in 1740, he had already more than doubled the size of the army (compared with 1713),[109] and while Prussia was still a minor player in European politics, its military establishment attracted the attention and admiration of many in Europe.

When Frederick II, also known as Frederick the Great, took over power in 1740, he faced a paradox: his state possessed one of the most (qualitatively) strong armies in Europe, but Prussia's territorial possessions were exceptionally dispersed and vulnerable. Furthermore, Prussia was "a third—or, at best, second—rank power,"[110] which played an important role only within the empire and northern Europe, on par with entities such as Saxony and Hanover.[111] Frederick was fully aware of Prussia's status, referring to his state as "a kingdom in name, but an electorate in fact."[112] The fact that the Hohenzollern's territories were "widely scattered" particularly worried Frederick; Prussia's territories were "exposed and scattered across half the continent . . . from enclaves in Westphalia through the heartlands of Brandenburg, Pomerania and Magdeburg in central Germany, astride the rivers Elbe and Oder, to distant East Prussia."[113] From such a vantage point, it was not surprising for Voltaire to refer to Frederick as the "king of the border strips."[114]

Similar to Louis XIV, Frederick operated in an environment where wealth and prestige followed from controlling territory, which was deemed infinitely more "divisible" when compared with the age of nationalism. To make Prussia and himself "great," Frederick desperately needed to expand and further secure his territorial base, and wars of conquest appeared to be one viable way to accomplish the aforementioned goals. Frederick already had a list of "potential territorial gains" as early as 1740, which included Polish Prussia, Swedish Pomerania, and the Duchy of Mecklenburg and Jülich-Berg.[115] Similar to most European rulers of the time, Frederick was inclined to "wage short wars for limited territorial ends."[116]

---

[107] Holborn 1964, 57.
[108] Gagliardo 1991, 310.
[109] Dwyer 2014, loc. 799.
[110] Dwyer 2014, loc. 3992. Also see Ropes 1889, 155.
[111] Dwyer 2014, loc. 525.
[112] Dwyer 2014, loc. 3979.
[113] Dwyer 2014, loc. 4029.
[114] Dwyer 2014, loc. 4035.
[115] Dwyer 2014, loc. 4122.
[116] McKay and Scott 1983, 164. On Frederick the Great's wars, see Showalter 1996.

The War of the Austrian Succession (1740–48) was triggered by Frederick's first daring attempt to expand Prussia's territorial base, into Silesia.[117] At the time, Silesia was a coveted region, for it hosted a large and industrious population as well as considerable resources.[118] For Dwyer, Frederick's reasons for targeting Silesia can be summarized "with two words": "sheer opportunism." In 1740, just as Frederick the Great came to power in Prussia, Charles VI of the House of Habsburgs died, leaving his hereditary domains to his daughter, Maria Theresa. Charles VI had already convinced the German states that a female heir could inherit the Habsburg domains through the Pragmatic Sanction of 1713. However, Frederick decided to exploit the momentary weakness in the Austrian state,[119] presumably encouraged by three factors. First, while Maria Theresa would eventually prove herself a competent leader in the coming decades, in 1740, she was a young and untested, not to mention controversial, leader.[120] Second, Austria had long been dealing with the Ottoman threat from the east, and most of its army was still stationed in Hungary or Transylvania.[121] Last, Tsarina Anna had died only a few days before Charles VI, prompting Frederick to believe that Russia would not be in the best position to assist Maria Theresa, if it came to that.[122] Note that Frederick decided to invade Silesia eight days after Charles VI died;[123] considering the time it would take for the news to reach Berlin, it is safe to conclude that Frederick had already set his eyes on Silesia and was simply waiting for the right time.

Drawing upon an obscure treaty from the mid-sixteenth century, the Prussian ruler asked for Silesia in return for Prussia's recognition of Maria Theresa's authority.[124] When Maria Theresa turned down what she saw as a "proposal of robbery, punctuated by blackmail," Frederick swiftly occupied Silesia.[125] Frederick intended to fight a war with "limited territorial ends" and "had no intention of provoking a partition of Austria or a general war."[126] With

[117] The War of the Austrian Succession led to a total of 356,000 casualties in eight years (Clodfelter 2002, 82). The casualty rate, however, was partially a function of the global scale and the duration of the conflict, as well as the number of great powers involved. On this war, see Hochedlinger 2003, 246–264.

[118] According to McKay and Scott (1983, 175), "By his conquest of Silesia, Frederick the Great increased the resources and population of Prussia by almost a half."

[119] Frederick, in his alleged "confessions," clearly highlights his motives and admits his opportunism (Treitschke 1915, 67).

[120] Ingrao 1994, 150.

[121] Dwyer 2014, locs. 4174–4175.

[122] Tuttle 1883, 49; Black 1999, 102.

[123] Dwyer 2014, loc. 4160.

[124] Note that it was not only Frederick who intended to take advantage of the opportunity; "the Saxons, Spanish, and Piedmontese all entered claims at the expense of the Austrian body politic" (Duffy 1985a, 23). Also see Gagliardo 1991, 314.

[125] Marriott and Robertson 1915, 121.

[126] McKay and Scott 1983, 164.

hindsight, we now know that Prussia rose to prominence and Frederick became "Great" over the course of his reign. However, Prussia's military and political might in 1740 "was far from obvious to contemporaries."[127] Frederick's plan to capture Austrian territory was in fact a highly risky, opportunistic gamble that could have led to adverse territorial consequences for the fledgling Prussian state. Arguably, considering that Frederick's political survival was not directly influenced by his ability to preserve the territorial integrity of the Prussian state per se, this was a gamble that Frederick was willing to take. In fact, the expansion of the conflict into a multifaceted war with numerous participants caused the conflict to last much longer than Frederick had envisioned.[128]

The conflict between Prussia and Austria was formally concluded in 1748. However, Prussia fought for less than half of the time between 1740 and 1748. In fact, for Prussia, there were two wars, the First Silesian War of 1740–42 and the Second Silesian War of 1744–45, both fought over the coveted province.[129] Broadly speaking, the series of clashes between Austria and Prussia, as well as France, lasted until 1745 and was formally concluded with the Treaty of Aix-la-Chapelle (1748), through which Prussia recognized Francis Stephen, Maria Theresa's husband, as the Holy Roman emperor and, by implication, Maria Theresa as the rightful ruler of Austria.[130] The price for recognition turned out to be Silesia, which Maria Theresa—albeit reluctantly—agreed to pay.

Frederick's second "big" war was the Seven Years' War. Most notably, Frederick triggered the European leg of the conflict by invading Saxony in 1756. This has led some scholars to consider Frederick's decision a "blatant act of aggression."[131] It is true that Frederick was the aggressor, but, arguably, his main motivation was not territorial aggrandizement per se, but breaking up an anti-Prussian coalition preventively before the aforementioned coalition had a chance to strike Prussia.[132] More specifically, by invading Saxony, Frederick aimed to "scare Russia into neutrality," while also sending a clear message to other German states and state-like entities about Prussia's inclination to hold onto its previous conquests.[133] According to Gagliardo, "Whatever long-range dreams Frederick may have entertained about further territorial conquests, it seems clear that his attack on Saxony was prompted

---

[127] Wilson 1998, 243.

[128] The expansion of the war was fueled by incentives for other states, ranging from France to Saxony, for territorial "booty" that can be captured from belligerents (Fischer-Fabian 1981, 199).

[129] Dwyer 2014, loc. 4195.

[130] For the intricate territorial redistribution that followed the treaty, see Ingrao 1994, 157–158.

[131] Dwyer 2014, loc. 855.

[132] Dwyer 2014, loc. 4340.

[133] Ingrao 1994, 174.

by defensive considerations."[134] Frederick's preventive war, as is well-known, backfired, and Prussia found itself fighting three great powers (France, Austria, and Russia), among others such as Sweden, at the same time.

As already highlighted above, the Seven Years' War can be seen as an "anomaly" in the context of the ancient regime. The territorial orders framework's predictions about the typical motivation for launching wars in systems dominated by mosaic territoriality, that is, opportunism (as opposed to fear), also does not fully apply to Frederick's decision to invade Saxony. Regardless, Frederick's specific conduct during the war can still provide insights about the association between mosaic territoriality and war. One of the striking facts about the Seven Years' War is that Frederick fought against overwhelming odds for almost a decade but was still able to avoid defeat and significant territorial losses. One common explanation for Frederick's impressive success involves the death of Tsarina Elizabeth in 1762, which paved the way for the ascension of Peter III to the Russian throne. Peter III, who harbored much less animosity toward Frederick than Elizabeth did, instantly ceased all military campaigns against Frederick, "saving" the Prussian ruler, if indirectly. Russia's decision to withdraw from open hostilities most certainly contributed to the outcome, but cannot all by itself account for how Frederick was able to make it all the way up to 1762 without suffering a crushing defeat.

Another explanation involves Frederick's acumen as a military commander and a strategist. Frederick's accomplishments and perseverance as a military commander, especially in this war, deserves some credit. Most notably, Frederick chose to "lead from the front"; for seven years, the Prussian king visited Berlin only once, spending almost all of his time managing (and sometimes micromanaging) the war effort. His main strategy, that is, fighting one adversary at a time (when possible), while also avoiding battles against coalition partners all at once, probably was the key element behind Frederick's success. However, the territorial orders framework suggests that Frederick's aforementioned strategy was a possibility in the first place thanks to the prominence of mosaic territoriality. Recall that the Hohenzollerns' possessions were widely scattered across central and northern Europe, exposing Prussia to invasion through multiple fronts. During the Seven Years' War, however, Frederick was able to transform this vulnerability into strength, and could do so mainly because the notion of "inviolable homeland" was a key motive for neither the Prussian king nor the inhabitants of the Prussian territories.

More specifically, Frederick made the strategic decision to abandon the Westphalian territories and East Prussia and focused his attention on the

---

[134] Gagliardo 1991, 325. Also see Dwyer 2014, loc. 4352.

central (territorial) core of his kingdom. In other words, while his opponents might be hoping for Frederick to fight and defend all of his territories, which would have considerably weakened him in the face of a wide variety of adversaries, the Prussian king easily identified his territorial priorities and acted accordingly.[135] Consequently, for Prussia, the Seven Years' War was fought mostly in Pomerania, Brandenburg, Silesia, Saxony, and Bohemia. This allowed Frederick to reduce the "disadvantages of encirclement and the lack of defensible frontiers" and maximize "the benefits of a compact position for most of the struggle."[136] Note that such decisions are not equally feasible and even actionable in the presence of monolithic territoriality, which ossifies the notion of indivisible homeland. This does not mean that such decisions cannot be made, say, in nation-states. They obviously can be made in nation-states, but leaders would be much more reluctant to make them, if for nothing else, due to the risk of adverse reactions from their respective societies. For example, it would have been difficult for the leadership in Wilhelmine Germany to willingly "give up" some parts of the German homeland during the initial stages of World War I, even when such a decision might have made perfect sense from a military-strategic perspective. Put simply, what was "doable" in the presence of mosaic territoriality eventually became almost "unthinkable" when monolithic territoriality became the key aspirational model (and vice versa).

In the end, Frederick survived the war, and fully established Prussia's status as a great power. When the war was over, Frederick chose to pursue a much more restrained foreign policy posture. Seven years of incessant fighting, when combined with the fact that, despite all his ingenuity, Frederick barely survived the conflict, eventually convinced the Prussian ruler to keep a lower profile in matters of war and peace during the remainder of his tenure.[137] Beyond the Seven Years' War, Frederick's military engagements remained remarkably limited and were confined to smaller-scale conflicts such as the War of the Bavarian Succession (1778–79).[138] Broadly speaking, Frederick left an important legacy: having inherited a secondary or even tertiary state, he made Prussia a great power through use of arms and skillful diplomacy. Of course, this legacy would be soon tested by the immediate impacts of the French Revolution.

Overall, the cases of France and Prussia provide insights into the relationship between mosaic territoriality and war. Before the advent of nationalism

---

[135] Dwyer 2014, loc. 4450.
[136] Dwyer 2014, loc. 4450.
[137] Dwyer 2014, loc. 4764.
[138] Holborn 1964, 258.

as a core component of state ideologies, European rulers considered territory the ultimate prize, but, paradoxically, territories were also deemed relatively divisible, and sometimes even substitutable goods. Redistribution of territory through wars and even marriages was a recurring theme of interstate politics. Even the much-debated "balance-of-power politics," as the term applied to the eighteenth-century Europe, was built on the fact that territories could be sliced and diced in order to establish a sense of "territorial balance" among the great powers. The relevant dynamic rendered the decision to go to war relatively easy and kept the severity of conflict over territory, on average, limited. Wars of opportunism were also more common than wars of fear (or wars triggered by fear of territorial loss). The most important structural transformation in Europe, in this context, followed from the rise of nationalism as a core component of state ideologies.

Nationalism, Territoriality, and the European State System

The rise of nationalism is a much-contested topic. Two specific questions lie at the heart of the debate: Where and when did nationalism "rise"? According to most scholars, the rise and diffusion of nationalism first took place in Europe.[139] However, focusing on "Europe" as a sociogeographic collective does not reveal all that much, for a simple reason: even in Europe, the rise of nationalism as a core component of state ideologies was not an evenly distributed phenomenon. Well into the twentieth century, nationalism and the notion of popular sovereignty existed side by side with alternative doctrines such as the imperial patriarchy of the Habsburgs[140] or the multicultural sultanate of the Ottomans, not to mention nationalism's cosmopolitan archrival, socialism. In fact, in contrast with the conventional wisdom, nationalism remained weak in many polities until the early twentieth century, even in geographies such as the Balkans.[141] Furthermore, the states' "nationalizing" policies have not always met with unqualified success, perpetuating what Bjork refers to as "national indifference."[142] Put simply, it was clear that

---

[139] For example, Hobsbawm 1991. For an exception, see Anderson 1983.

[140] On the notion of imperial patriarchy, see Healy 2004.

[141] Malešević (2012), for example, highlights that nationalism has been a less significant driver of politics in the Balkans than conventional wisdom on the region's rampant nationalism may predict. Also see Tilly 1994, 137.

[142] Bjork 2008, 6, 34. For example, Bjork (2008, 196) maintains that in Upper Silesia, regional elites were "unenthused about union with either Berlin or Warsaw" in the aftermath of World War I. Upper Silesia is an example where nationalism does not exert its influence in the geographical periphery of a state (or multiple

94 How Territorial Ideas Affect Wars

nationalism was emerging as a constitutive property of the state system by the turn of the twentieth century.[143] However, state-sponsored territorial nationalism took hold in some states earlier than others, prompting a situation of uneven development.[144]

"When did nationalism rise?" is an even more intricate question. Nationalism, to be sure, might have existed as an idea before the late eighteenth century; Liah Greenfeld has masterfully traced the origins of the idea of nation to the English literary texts of the sixteenth century,[145] and the writings of the early eighteenth century romantics such as Herder reveal unmistakably nationalistic characteristics sometimes with distinctly geographical underpinnings.[146] Anthony Marx examined nationalism's religious origins in cases such as fifteenth-century France, Spain, and England.[147] John Hutchinson, in turn, claims that "nationalism and national communities formed much earlier during the early Middle Ages."[148] The primordialist students of nationalism, most of whom take issue with the claim that nations are merely social constructs, similarly argue that nationalism as an idea and practice has its roots in eras far earlier than the French Revolution.[149]

However, nationalism (as an ideology) did not exert a significant impact on interstate politics and territorial conflict until the late eighteenth century.[150] While the historical origins of the idea of nationalism are open to debate, most scholars agree that "nationalism as an 'ism' hardly existed prior to the French Revolution."[151] Accordingly, it is difficult to claim that nationalism played an important role in how state elites and societies conceived territory before 1789.[152] However, portraying nationalism as a virus that broke out in 1789 and then spread across the globe through a linear process with lightning speed would be historically inaccurate and misleading. While the French Revolution can be taken as a robust reference point—which can also be associated with the idea of nation *une et indivisible*[153]—nationalism did not take over France (or Europe) immediately after the Revolution.

---

states). In contrast with these studies, Sahlins (1989) argues that national consciousness may emerge at the edges of state territories, sometimes earlier than it does in the center.

[143] Hall 1999.
[144] Gellner 1983. Also see Wimmer 2012, 4; Hutchinson 2017, 94.
[145] Greenfeld 1992.
[146] On the ideational currents of the eighteenth century, see Outram 1995.
[147] Marx 2003. Overall, Marx's focus is on the early modern period.
[148] Hutchinson 2017, 3.
[149] For a survey, see Coakley 2018.
[150] Hobsbawm 1991.
[151] Herz 1950, 161.
[152] Tilly 1994, 138.
[153] Schulze 1991, 48.

These being said, the Revolution still played an important role in setting the grounds for the rise of nationalism (and monolithic territoriality), if through a nonlinear mechanism. The French Revolution is best conceptualized as an exogenous shock that destabilized the equilibrium that had sustained and perpetuated mosaic territoriality.[154] As mentioned above, before the rise of nationalism and its adoption by states led to a change in the constitutive properties of territory, state elites showed little interest in pressuring the societies over which they ruled to homogenize sociospatial organization within the state space. Accordingly, state elites also had little incentive to penetrate deeper into society in order to mobilize significant resources and defend territory for its own sake. Such measures would entail either offsetting the traditional social structures on which their authority was based, or granting masses further rights and privileges.[155] That no single monarch was willing to deviate from the norm unilaterally (which would put their domestic political prospects at risk) ensured that wars over territory would not necessitate excessive resource mobilization efforts, helping rulers keep the costs of war relatively limited.[156] In such an environment, rulers had little incentive to escalate their war efforts to defend their territory and, paradoxically, found starting wars to capture territory from other states a relatively easy decision to make. In this context, the French Revolution disrupted the equilibrium that shielded the rulers from the masses vis-à-vis their foreign policy choices over territory by making the masses, at least in France and Prussia, "stakeholders" when it came to the defense of states' territories. The Revolution also allowed the elites who successfully embraced and utilized this relationship to mobilize unprecedented resources for their war efforts.

Following Napoleon's defeat in 1815, however, monarchs in Europe did their best not to encourage and exploit, but to contain and defuse nationalism because of the challenges it posed to their sovereignty and political privileges.[157] Doing so, they attempted to move back to the equilibrium that the French Revolution and subsequent war efforts had crushed. However, nationalism (as a political ideology) proved too potent and overwhelming for ruling elites to contain,[158] and too tempting to pass up as an outlet that could be utilized for resource mobilization. Increasingly, leading European states embraced the relevant ideas and political principles associated with nationalism by the second half of the nineteenth century.[159] In the words of

---

[154] See Chapter 7.
[155] Levi 1997; Palmer 1986, 92.
[156] Kadercan 2012.
[157] Howard 1976, 94–95; 1983, 161–162.
[158] According to Hew Strachan (2001, 4), "Nationalism [could be] moderated but not deflected."
[159] Weber 1976; Breuilly 1994.

96 How Territorial Ideas Affect Wars

political geographer Peter Taylor, by the second half of the nineteenth century, a number of European states "discovered the efficacy of [nationalism] and nurtured it" and eventually "[hitched] their destinies to nationalism."[160]

More specifically, the rise of nationalism is closely associated with the concept of popular sovereignty, which eventually transferred the identity of the "sovereign" from the person of the monarch to the putative "people." As James Mayall recognized, the idea of popular sovereignty "could have been advanced without tying it to nation";[161] however, over the course of the nineteenth and twentieth centuries, these two concepts became interchangeable.[162] In this sense, the rise of nationalism simultaneously "[vested] sovereignty in the people and [linked] territory to the [putative] nation."[163]

Furthermore, nationalism also involves "transference of loyalty from kinship groups or local and regional levels to the larger national group."[164] In nationalistic discourses, the putative nation simultaneously refers to a phenomenon that is both plural and singular. The nation is plural in the sense that it refers to a collective of individuals who share certain characteristics that separate them from "other" social, cultural, or political groups. The term also invokes "singularity," reducing the collective to a homogeneous and unitary actor with its own "national will" and "national interest."[165] These dynamics have a direct implication for the aspirational sociospatial organization principles within the state's borders. Just as the state space "belongs" to the nation, the nation itself also belongs to the state space. In this reading, nationalistic discourses anthropomorphize both the collective of individuals who make up the putative nation and the (national) state space: to the collective are attributed the characteristics of a single, unique, and faceless individual with its own will and interest, and the state space is often portrayed as the physical (or spatial) reflection of the same individual.

In nation-states that adhere to monolithic orders, just as in mosaic orders, demarcation of the state space—which is, or should be, congruent with the "national space"—is defined in rigid and explicitly bounded terms. The immediate territorial implication of this line of thinking is that such communities should also be bounded in geographical terms (and, consequently,

---

[160] Taylor 1994, 156.

[161] Mayall 1990, 149–150. According to Alexander Murphy (2013, 1218), "Enlightenment political theorists [Locke, Rousseau, and Mill] argued that sovereignty should be vested in the people, which they understood to be relatively homogeneous, cohesive social collectivities sharing common cultural characteristics."

[162] Wawro 2003.

[163] Buzan and Lawson 2015, 4.

[164] Knight 1982, 521.

[165] Paasi (1996, 55) calls this process "national territorial socialization." Also see Hooson 1993; Paasi 1999; Williams and Smith 1983; Yiftachel 2002.

separated from other social groups). In political geographer Alexander Murphy's words, "The modern concept of nationalism is inextricably tied to territory in that nationalism is rooted in the relationship between a group with a self-conscious cultural-political identity and a discrete territory."[166] The main distinctive characteristic of the nationalistic understanding of borders is what exactly borders (should) delineate: while borders in prenationalistic Westphalian states focused on compartmentalizing the extent of sovereign jurisdiction, for a nation-state, borders also act as "cultural containers."[167] Put differently, national borders, in theory, are supposed to distinguish and isolate one cultural group (or even the culture itself) from other cultural groups. In order to accomplish this goal, nation-states tend to sacralize the state space,[168] and borders are "associated with powerful images, symbols, and (sometimes invented) traditions."[169]

Accordingly, unlike prenationalism Westphalian states, which were to a large extent "composite states" that ruled multiethnic, multilingual societies through heterogeneous administrative and political arrangements, nation-states strive to organize space-society relationships in homogeneous terms.[170] Political geographers have long identified the spatial aspects of this dynamic.[171] For example, according to Alexander Murphy, nationalism is essentially about "the bond between a people and its territory."[172] Jouni Hakli argues that nationalistic discourses and practices aim to homogenize "space through standardization of the day-to-day life in spheres of language, thought, and routine" through the enforcement of a uniform language and education system and the "creation of an iconography to erase existing local differences."[173] In this sense, in a nation-state, the dominant territorial imagination is "particularistic," as Liam O'Dowd has highlighted, and aims to establish "homogenization of administrative forms, culture, and citizenship within fixed territorial borders."[174] For Guntram, nationalism entails reterritorializing the state space, which, "taken to its extreme," may pave the way for a "nationalist cleansing of the landscape," with the intention of reconfiguring territory in uniform terms.[175]

---

[166] Murphy 2013, 1215. Also see Lefebvre and Nicholson-Smith 1991, 280–281.
[167] Taylor 1994, 155. Also see Colas 2007, 62.
[168] Taylor 1994, 155–156.
[169] Anderson 1996, 3.
[170] On the role of legitimacy in nationalistic discourses, see Wimmer 2012.
[171] Sociologists have also long examined the social homogenization efforts involved with nationalism, with less attention to the spatial dimension. For example, see Malešević 2010, 141; Tilly 1994, 133.
[172] Murphy 1990, 536.
[173] Hakli 1994, 41, 48–54.
[174] O'Dowd 2010, 1042.
[175] Herb 1999, 23. It is true that, as Peter Taylor highlighted, the idea(l) of the nation-state has been more myth than reality, since all states have their share of "cultural mixes" that include minorities. Consequently,

98 How Territorial Ideas Affect Wars

Overall, sociospatial homogenization remains a core component of state-led nationalization efforts, and state institutions aim to "systematically homogenize their subjects in cultural [and/or] ethnic terms."[176] Accordingly, governance mechanisms strive to impose a modicum of standardization—which can be defined in terms of linguistic, ethnic, racial, cultural, civic, or religious unity and conformity—in legal, administrative, political, and cultural dimensions within state territories.[177] Even in multiethnic countries like the United States, the "American people" are defined as a homogeneous entity, at least to the extent that they share some basic characteristics that categorically separate them from non-Americans, with strong ties to a specific area, the American homeland.

In sum, societies in nation-states—in principle if not always in practice—are engaged (or are expected to engage) in a direct and organic relationship with the state's territorial belongings. To the state space, in turn, is attributed more of an "identity" in the form of the homeland.[178] States promote the notion of an inviolable homeland, striving to create a close association between society and territory. To accomplish these tasks, nation-states channel and shape the extent and foci of the spatial attachments of the inhabitants of a state. Thanks to states' "monopoly of legitimate education"[179] as well as the salience of "banal nationalism"[180] in dominant nationalistic discourses, maps are anachronistically projected into an invented past of commonness in order to construct spatially defined imagined communities.[181] As highlighted in Chapter 2, territoriality that comes with nationalism is essentially different from elemental inclinations sometimes attributed to evolutionary territoriality. What is peculiar about nationalism is individuals' willingness to care not only for their immediate surroundings but also for the entirety of the imagined and inviolable homeland, most parts of which they will never visit.[182]

---

in practice, nationalistic discourses involve what sociologist Andreas Wimmer (2008, 1000) refers to as "asymmetrical consensus": in numerous cases, not every citizen of the putative nation-state agrees on who qualifies as conational (or who would also be an equal stakeholder in the "homeland"), but there is usually a majority who believe themselves to be in the same cultural category defined as the dominant national group. For a similar argument, see Wimmer 2012, 117.

[176] Wimmer 2008, 991.
[177] Tilly 1994.
[178] Barkin and Cronin 1994.
[179] Gellner 1983, 34.
[180] Billig 1995.
[181] Darden 2014.
[182] Anderson 1983; Billig 1995; Jones 2008. Of course, as Hutchinson (2017, 41) warned us, "A statist account [of nationalism] fails to explain why populations should love their cage." As Malešević (2010, 11) highlighted, nationalism can seen as a "centrifugal" ideology backed by strong organizational capacity, and the strength of this ideology can be explained by "mutual reinforcement" between the "top-down" nationalizing efforts emanating from the states and "bottom-up" demands from within the society.

Most notably, state-led nationalism in France followed a more linear path than it did in Prussia/Germany. The French Revolution sowed the seeds of (state-led) French nationalism, and the French state eventually took measures to cultivate a sense of territorially defined national belongingness. Of course, the process was linear only when compared to Germany; as Eugene Weber has masterfully shown, nationalization of the inhabitants of France took almost a century after the Revolution, culminating only during World War I.[183]

For Prussia, and later Germany, nationalism constituted a highly contested domain. In France, the French state could and did play an important role in defining the French nation and its spatial extension. Before 1870, there was no comparable entity to serve a similar function for the German-speaking populations, broadly defined. Consequently, there existed no single interpretation of "German nationalism"; instead, as Geoff Eley identified, there was a competition between different understandings of nationalism,[184] most notably between liberal/republican and monarchical interpretations, the latter of which paradoxically "fused" the notion of "'unlimited' monarchical sovereignty with popular representation."[185] The failed revolutions of 1848, and the refusal of the Prussian king to subject his will to the liberal and republican (yet still nationalist) movements, eventually paved the way for the rise of a state-led (German) nationalism emanating from Prussia.

The fact that German unification took place only by 1870–71, and only under the heavy hand of Prussia, complicates a direct comparison with France.[186] However, it is also possible to claim that by 1870, even though German states had concerns about their coethnic Prussians, they were willing to side with Prussia to stave off France, which posed more of a threat to what they increasingly began to see as German lands. The case of Württemberg is illustrative. One of the smaller German states, Württemberg initially opposed Prussian ambitions for unification and even fought against Prussia in 1866 in the Austrian-Prussian war. However, Württemberg joined Prussia against the perceived French threat in 1870 and voted for unification. In doing so, in the words of Alon Confino, Württemberg was expressing "a German national feeling that was impossible to negate in 1870–71."[187]

---

[183] Weber 1976.

[184] Eley 1991, 161.

[185] Dwyer 2014, loc. 6684.

[186] On this point, see Lepsius and Campbell 1985.

[187] Confino 1997, 21. According to Confino (1997, 13), "Germany's modern national memory began in 1871." In this context, "Before 1871 there was a history of the Germans and German history, but no history of Germany; only thereafter did Germany history proceeded as a single development."

100 How Territorial Ideas Affect Wars

In the decades after the German unification in 1871, territorial nationalism in Germany became increasingly robust. The German state was an active agent of the (re)territorialization efforts in the new state space, and also benefited from (and, appropriated) the *Heimat* tradition in German-speaking geographies, if selectively. According to Guntram Herb, *Heimat* sought to "create a feeling of belonging among the members of the nation by attaching the collective group to the national territory" and served to "foster national similarity."[188] *Heimaten* could be both local and national, but, at the end of the day, they "informed the ideal of one, unique nationality."[189] The German state's efforts to embolden monolithic territoriality were selective, and some geographical memories needed to be forgotten, and some new ones needed to be invented. As Alon Confino pointed out, "To share a common past, Germany needed to modify, perhaps even obliterate" the memory of distinct ideas about Germany.[190] In such a setting, "Prussians needed to forget the victory, citizens of the small German states to forget the defeat, and all to forget Austria."[191] In fact, this selective approach to geographical memories was hardly surprising. Article 1 of the German constitution of 1871, for example, clearly delineated the territorial scope of the "German" nation, which virtually left out substantial swaths of territory where German-speaking populations lived (e.g., in Austria), and instead emphasized the indivisibility of the homeland, as specified in the document.

In sum, while the German path to monolithic territoriality differed from France, where state-led nationalism had earlier roots and evolved through different processes, the result was similar. By the late nineteenth century, emphasis on the ideal of a clearly demarcated and unique state space, which would be inhabited by a homogeneous population (however defined), played an essential role in how state elites and a considerable segment of the society perceived their relationship to geography.[192]

The next section briefly examines the association between monolithic territoriality and war through the cases of France and Germany.

---

[188] Confino 1997, 158.
[189] Confino 1997, 158.
[190] Confino 1997, 15.
[191] Confino 1997, 15.
[192] As Eugene Weber (1976) documented, the process of nationalization even in France was not complete until World War I.

Monolithic Territoriality and War in France and Germany, 1870–1945

The Franco-Prussian War of 1870–71 is an exemplary case where we can observe the early impacts of monolithic territoriality on war, for four reasons.[193] First, the steps leading up to the war were at odds with the typical wars of the seventeenth and eighteenth centuries.[194] While Prussian chancellor Bismarck most surely welcomed the acquisition of Alsace-Lorraine, his primary goal before the outbreak of the war was not to capture land from France but to crush Bohemian and Saxon resistance to the idea of a unified Germany under Prussian leadership.[195] Broadly speaking, Bismarck needed an "external threat to weld Germany together,"[196] and there was no better threat than the French one. In other words, for Bismarck, the war aims were essentially territorial (fostering the idea of a greater Germany under Prussian leadership), but the nature of these aims was categorically different from, say, those professed by Frederick the Great (capturing territory through an opportunistic campaign). Reportedly, Bismarck eventually came to recognize the decision to take over Alsace-Lorraine was "mistaken,"[197] presumably because he came to appreciate the sense of territorial revanchism it triggered and perpetuated in France. French willingness to fight Prussia, in turn, derived not from a penchant for territorial acquisition, but from the rise of Prussia and the territorial fear it provoked.[198]

Second, the Franco-Prussian War was brief but remarkably costly by seventeenth- and eighteenth-century standards. France suffered about 240,000 casualties, while the number for Germany neared 135,000.[199] Third, the war also signaled that territory had acquired a new meaning for the society and consequently for the ruling elites. Charles XII of Sweden and Louis XIV in 1713, Francis II of Austria in 1805, and Frederick William III of Prussia in 1806 had lost substantial chunks of territory after wars, but these losses did not propel a domestic challenge to their political survival. In contrast, Napoleon III was immediately deposed after the Battle of Sedan in 1870 (never to return

---

[193] On the Franco-Prussian War, see Wawro 2005. For A. J. P. Taylor (1957, 264), the Austria-Prussian War of 1866 was the last cabinet war, and the Franco-Prussian War of 1870–71 was necessarily an affair of the people. Also see Luard 1987, 162.

[194] Koch 1978, 265–267.

[195] Marriott and Robertson 1915, 370. Michael Howard (1983, 43) also suggests that the priority in von Moltke's war plans was "almost entirely . . . the defence of German territory." According to historian Otto Pflanze (1990, 490), "Bismarck's major war aim was not the conquest of French soil, but the voluntary acceptance by the south of the north German constitution without essential change."

[196] Crankshaw 1981, 253.

[197] Hillgruber 1981, 4.

[198] Marriott and Robertson 1915, 121, 361–362; Black 2001, 138; Taylor 1957, 204.

[199] Addington 1984, 101.

to power, or even France), an outcome pointing to the robustness of the relationship between loss of territory and ruler prospects. Napoleon III might not have been aware of the nature of the relationship, but it is safe to assume that his downfall sent a clear message to other European leaders who established their political authority on the basis of their role as the agent of the "principal," or the people: try not to lose pieces of the homeland.[200]

A fourth dynamic was reflected in the nationalist reaction to the German occupation of the French homeland. In the aftermath of Sedan, the "Government of National Defense" sustained the war efforts for months, which, according to Michael Howard, was a departure from the "normal customs of warfare observed by the regular armies and the traditional statesmen of Europe" in the previous centuries.[201] The main force behind this attitude, which prompted a "savage war of peoples,"[202] was the territorial nationalism propelled by the idea that France should not yield "an inch of [French] territory."[203] The war eventually ended with France ceding Alsace-Lorraine to Germany. According to John Keiger, while France also had to pay a considerable indemnity, loss of Alsace-Lorraine was the "most serious blow to France."[204] Loss of homeland territory triggered a sense of revanchism in France that was best captured in Leon Gambetta's famous words, "Think of [Alsace-Lorraine] always; speak of [it] never!"[205]

The question of Alsace-Lorraine eventually "formed the foundation of Franco-German mythologies of national enmity for the next half-century and beyond."[206] To be precise, the so-called Alsace-Lorraine question was a "predominantly" French concern; in France, literature, commentaries, works of popular art, and even the education system continuously presented Alsace-Lorraine as a region that was "toiling under Teutonic yoke and pining endlessly for the return of the French rule." In such depictions, these provinces were also commonly anthropomorphized, usually as (French) women or children "held hostage by barbaric Germans."[207] Of course, the aforementioned "question" eventually lost some of its salience by the early twentieth century. Still, the French refusal to publicly renounce these provinces proved to be "an obstacle to any form of agreement between Paris and Berlin because it was

---

[200] Kadercan 2012.
[201] Howard 1981, 571.
[202] Howard 1981, 232.
[203] Voiced by French statesman Jean Favre, quoted in Taylor 1957, 212. General Trochu echoed the sentiment, suggesting that this was a "war to the bitter end" and "not a mile of territory, not a stone of the fortresses was to be ceded to the enemy" (Pratt 1914, 189).
[204] Keiger 1983, 5.
[205] Quoted in Pratt 1914, 223.
[206] Nolan 2005, 27.
[207] Nolan 2005, 70–71.

interpreted as a sign that the neighboring state's revanchist intentions had been concealed, but not revised."[208] The drive for recovering these provinces after they had been separated from the French homeland by force of arms did not immediately trigger a new Franco-German war. Such a drive, however, played an important role in strengthening France's acceptance of the idea of another war with Germany and shaped French war aims in World War I.[209]

There are a multitude of explanations of the origins of World War I. In the words of historian Donald Kagan, "No war has produced so long and heated a debate about its causes as the First World War."[210] A dominant, if not universal, element in most of the relevant accounts is the notion that the war can be construed as an accident, blunder, or a tragedy fueled by insecurity, fear, and "a vein of fatalism,"[211] not as a byproduct of territorial greed.[212] According to historian Hew Strachan, for example, the drive for "territorial expansion . . . was not a cause of the First World War."[213] Of course, this does not mean that territory played no role in the outbreak of World War I; while warring parties, once the conflict deepened, began to define their aims in terms of territorial acquisition,[214] leading up to the war, it was "territorial fear" (fear of losing parts or all of what was considered inviolable homeland), rather than territorial opportunism, that drove the incentives of the rulers. In his influential book *Cataclysm*, David Stevenson also argues that the combatants fought not for gain, but "to avoid a negative," suggesting that "they fought from fear."[215] For Donald Kagan, in the spring of 1914, "None of the major powers wanted war."[216]

Of course, the debates over the origins of World War I cannot be settled here. However, a counterfactual could be utilized to push the argument that Wilhelmine Germany was not inherently driven by a sense of territorial opportunism, at least in Europe. Arguably, if territorial opportunism had been a key driver of Wilhelmine Germany's decisions over war and peace (as had been the case for, say, Louis XIV or Frederick II), one would expect Germany to go to war in 1905, when numerous factors put it at an advantageous position, as opposed to 1914, when Germany enjoyed none of the advantages it did in 1905.[217] More specifically, in 1905, Russia suffered a crippling defeat

---

[208] Hewitson 2000, 583.

[209] Tuchman 1962, 28–43.

[210] Kagan 1996, 205.

[211] Clark 2012, 333.

[212] Howard 1976, 10; Bridge and Bullen 1980, 177–178; Taylor 1957, 514–515, 517; Turner 1970; Copeland 2000.

[213] Strachan 2001, 37.

[214] On the dynamic nature of "war aims" during World War I, see Goemans 2000.

[215] Stevenson 2004, 35.

[216] Kagan 1996, 187.

[217] Hillgruber 1981, 17; Rosenberg 1970, 66–67.

104 How Territorial Ideas Affect Wars

at the hands of the Japanese. The defeat also triggered uprisings from within Russia, making it extremely difficult for the tsar to join a combined military effort against Germany in any meaningful way. As of 1905, French support for Russia, especially in terms of industrialization efforts and the construction of extensive railways, had yet to mature. France was still reeling from the aftershocks of the Dreyfus affair, and its alliance with Britain had yet to lead to any tangible commitments from London. Of course, counterfactuals cannot prove a point all by themselves. Still, they can help make a point: certain conditions that could have made a war of territorial opportunism almost a certainty in the age of dynastic monarchies, given the categorically different meaning territory acquired due to the rise of nationalism, did not result in war in 1905. When war finally broke out in 1914, how it was fought was also categorically different from the wars of the (dynastic) past.

The interaction between France and Germany also lends itself to interpretation from the perspective of the theory. Given that German forces immediately occupied French territory in the opening stages of the war, France found itself in the difficult position of having to recover the occupied provinces regardless of the cost.[218] The series of offensives on the German defenses culminated in a cycle of ever-increasing casualties for both parties. Similarly, the German strategy also involved taking advantage of French willingness to hold and recapture homeland territory even when the strategic rationale dictated otherwise. The Battle of Verdun (1916) constitutes an exemplar. In Verdun, according to one common interpretation, the German aim was not to capture territory, but to set up a "death trap" and "bleed [the French] white."[219] Note that we can compare the territorial attitudes of France and Germany not only with their own past behavior, but also with contemporaries that did not profess similar nationalistic ideologies. Russia and Austria-Hungary, for example, differed greatly from Germany and France in terms of war aims and attitudes to war termination. According to Michael Howard, "left to themselves," Russia and Austria-Hungary "almost certainly" would have "declared a truce and patched up a compromise peace," even if that meant parting ways with some of their territories.[220] This was hardly a viable option for France and Germany.

The impacts of monolithic territoriality on the causes and conduct of World War II, in turn, are more nuanced, partially due to the territorial consequences of World War I. While border changes after great power wars had been typical

---

[218] Ross 1983, 19; Strachan 2001, 59.

[219] Keegan 1998, 303, 308; Black 2002a, 50; Howard 2002, 76; Chickering 1998, 67.

[220] Howard 2002, 45. To be precise, Howard refers not to the outbreak of the war, but to what could have happened after the war proved very costly.

in past centuries, post–World War I redistribution led to the rise of two specific problems for the international order. First, in cases where the salience of nationalism had already established the inviolability of some state territories in the pre-1918 era, most notably in Germany, division of perceived homelands triggered and sustained a strong sense of territorial revanchism.[221] This territorial revanchism, which was built on the understanding that the inviolable German homeland was unjustly violated and therefore it should be made whole again, was also ingrained in the society's collective geographical memories. For example, maps that showed the German state space before and after Versailles in tandem (so that spectators could easily identify which parts of the homeland were lost) were widely circulated, even in schools.[222]

While territorial revanchism cannot account for the causes of World War II or the German strategy during the war all by itself, it can partially explain Hitler's meteoric rise to power as well as the support he was able to secure from the German society in the initial stages of the war.[223] Arguably, Hitler exploited the sentiments in Germany that followed from attachment to monolithic territoriality and was able to push forward a radical interpretation of virulent territoriality, which not only legitimized but also encouraged indefinite territorial expansion.[224]

Another unintended consequence of the post–World War I settlements derived from the mismatch between the demarcation and sociospatial organization of the new territorial units. Many new states such as Yugoslavia and Czechoslovakia were founded not on the principle of "self-determination," but as a result of geopolitical considerations of great powers, which hardly made for coherent or strong territorial arrangements. This dynamic effectively hindered the social and political construction of inviolable homelands in these states. That these new states did not have sufficient time and strong institutions to construct a salient sense of monolithic territoriality encouraged revisionist states to seek expansion at their expense, as exemplified by the German approach toward Czechoslovakia and Austria during the late 1930s.[225]

---

[221] Mearsheimer 2001, 189; Eyck 1970, 12–13. Also see Miller 2007; Van Evera 1994.

[222] Dijkink 2005, 121.

[223] Geyer 1985, 102.

[224] Note that while the conventional wisdom tends to portray Nazi Germany as a state with "too much" nationalism, the argument here is that Nazi Germany's territorial vision was categorically different from that of the typical nation-state, and therefore better defined in terms of virulent territoriality.

[225] The case of the Soviet-Finnish war (1939–49) provides a contrast. Considering that the notion of "homeland" was more robust in Finland, it is not surprising that the Finnish resistance was much fiercer than the cases mentioned above. The Finnish borders eventually proved "breakable," though the cost of such acquisition for the Soviets was more than three hundred thousand casualties.

106   How Territorial Ideas Affect Wars

Monolithic territoriality also played a role in the conduct of World War II, albeit to a lesser extent than World War I. Two relevant dynamics may be highlighted. First, recognizing the importance of territorial integrity for French society (and in order to prevent large-scale resistance), Germany did not formally annex French territory, even the much-disputed Alsace-Lorraine, during its wartime occupation. Second, despite the supranationalist ideological underpinnings of their regime, when pressed by Nazi Germany, the Soviets found it both expedient and necessary to retreat to the discourse of an inviolable homeland—built on the (territorial) narrative of the so-called Mother Russia—in order to garner support for their war efforts.[226] This development highlights the salience of the discourse of inviolable homeland (or mosaic territoriality in general) vis-à-vis interstate wars of the twentieth century.

A final question to address, at this juncture, is the following: Why pick the end of World War II as an endpoint for the cases of France and Germany? The answer has to do with the impacts of World War II and postwar settlements that aimed to redesign the global territorial order on France and Germany. As will be discussed in more detail in Chapter 7, postwar settlements entailed what is sometimes referred to as a "border fixity norm," or the idea that no state should unilaterally capture territory from another through the use of force.[227] From the perspective of the territorial orders framework, the relevant arrangements aimed to "freeze" existing monolithic orders in many parts of the world, including Europe.[228] Furthermore, postwar arrangements led to the creation of an interstate community, which eventually took the form of the European Union, and made it nearly unthinkable for France and (West) Germany to consider war over territory. Therefore, given the robustness of the border fixity norm, and the ideational as well as institutional impacts of postwar settlements on France and Germany, there is little reason to trace the relationship between monolithic orders and war in these two cases beyond 1945.

Conclusion

This chapter made the case that mosaic and monolithic territorial orders are distinct and are best associated, respectively, with the early Westphalian state

---

[226] Overy 1998, 156.

[227] Atzili 2012.

[228] Of course, German experience should refer to not one, but two Germanies. On the different paths to reterritorialization in East and West Germany after World War II, see Herb 2002.

system and the nation-state ideal. Mosaic orders promote the idea of clearly demarcated borders and a heterogeneous approach to sociospatial organization. Monolithic orders, while they share the demarcation principles of mosaic territoriality, come with an intent to homogenize the organization. In a regional or global system where mosaic territoriality is dominant, wars tend to be frequent but less severe, and war for territory is driven more by opportunism than fear. In the dominance of monolithic orders, wars are relatively less frequent, but they can be more severe, especially when territorial stakes are involved. Fear of losing territory, in turn, may play a more critical role than opportunism (to gain more territory). Historically speaking, the transition from mosaic to monolithic territoriality can be traced to the rise of nationalism as a core component of state ideologies. This chapter first highlighted the similarities and differences between mosaic and monolithic territoriality, and then traced the relationship between the relevant territorial ideas and interstate wars by focusing on Europe in general, the cases of France and Prussia/Germany in particular.

Note that the French and Prussian/German cases are paradigmatic, in the sense that these two cases, when compared with numerous experiences across the globe, come closer to the "ideal type(s)." Accordingly, as far as mosaic and monolithic orders are concerned, different experiences are likely to follow different tempos and trajectories. However, monolithic territoriality dominates present-day world politics, if mostly as an aspirational ideal. In many cases, as will be discussed in more detail in Chapter 7, the facts on the ground and the monolithic ideal have contradicted each other, leading to numerous conflicts as well as chronic instability, especially during the twentieth century. Some of these contradictions still exist in present-day politics. In this sense, exploring the differences between mosaic and monolithic territoriality, while also highlighting the association between monolithic territorial ideas and interstate war, can shed further light on not only the past but also the current state of affairs in world politics.

This chapter dealt with the so-called modern state system, which lies at the heart of most IR research. In the next two chapters, I depart from the "norm" in IR theory, that is, thinking of territoriality and war almost exclusively in terms of the modern state system, and examine two territorial orders, amorphous and virulent, that cannot be easily examined through the dominant geographical assumptions of IR research.

5

Fluid Frontiers and Forever War I

Amorphous Territorial Orders

The map is not the territory.

—Alfred Korzybski[1]

Rigid and clearly demarcated borders lie at the heart of the dominant perception of the relationship between international politics and geography. We tend to interpret world politics through the lenses of modern-day maps, which differentiate between different political units by way of well-defined, linear, and clearly demarcated borders. As John Agnew highlighted, this geopolitical imagery lies at the heart of the so-called territorial trap.[2]

The so-called territorial trap is so robust that it prevents an overwhelming majority of the public, as well as IR scholars, from directly engaging the historically contingent nature of borders, as we understand them today. The impacts of the territorial trap on present-day geopolitical imageries reveal themselves most visibly through the ways in which historical states are projected onto political maps in modern-day scholarship (or the broader public imagination): more often than not, scholars illustrate the spatial extent of historical states via linear and clearly demarcated Westphalian borders. This practice precludes recognizing the fact that, across time and space, leaders and inhabitants of many states and state-like entities envisioned boundaries in different terms. Paradoxically, dismissing or ignoring the alternative territorial arrangements across time and space also makes it difficult to fully understand the nature of so-called Westphalian territoriality. To paraphrase Erik Ringmar's comments on the study of the so-called international system in IR (and replacing "system" with "territoriality"), "Although there have been many [territorial models] throughout history, it is the contemporary Westphalian

---

[1] Korzybski 1933, 750.
[2] Agnew 1994. For a detailed discussion, see Chapters 2 and 3.

Shifting Grounds. Burak Kadercan, Oxford University Press. © Oxford University Press 2023.
DOI: 10.1093/oso/9780197686690.003.0005

[territoriality] that repeatedly is investigated—as though it were possible to understand it purely on its own terms."[3]

This chapter and the next examine two territorial orders—amorphous and virulent—that are built on the rejection (or dismissal) of the so-called Westphalian borders. When these territorial orders guide state elites' (and, society's) conception of the space-society-politics nexus, states' approach to war differs from mosaic and monolithic orders: territorial war is seen not as a discrete event with a clear beginning and an end, but as a continuous undertaking, which itself can also be carried out through hybrid warfare and gradual encroachments. In this sense, the "frequency" of wars becomes less relevant for understanding the patterns in territorial conflict. Amorphous and virulent orders differ from each other in terms of sociospatial organization, and these differences lead to diverging approaches to the ways in which organized violence is utilized for territorial expansion (or defense): while amorphous orders are usually associated with mild(er) forms of reterritorialization (which may limit the extent and scope of violence), adherence to virulent orders usually lead to radical reterritorialization (which may trigger severe conflict). Accordingly, in comparison with amorphous orders, virulent territoriality may lead to more severe conflict and may be associated with a higher risk of civilian victimization.[4]

This chapter scrutinizes the relationship between amorphous orders and territorial conflict through two paradigmatic cases: the early period Ottoman Empire (between the fourteenth and seventeenth centuries) and British colonial expansion and rule in South Asia, primarily—if not exclusively—during the course of the nineteenth century. As already discussed in Chapter 3, I employ three criteria for case selection, for both amorphous and virulent territorial orders. Following the abduction-oriented case study research, the first criterion entails "paradigmatic cases," or cases where the relationship between territorial ideas and territorial conflict is salient and therefore easily visible. Second, the cases differ from each other in terms of their origin: the British case is decidedly "Western," and the Ottomans stand for a wide variety of non-Western cases.[5] Such an approach intends to avoid both ethnocentric and

---

[3] Ringmar 2012, 1.

[4] Note that my approach differs from scholars such as Andreas Wimmer (2012, 27), who do not differentiate "universalizing empires" from revolutionary states. My categorization starts not from "state forms," but from different territorial models. In that sense, some universalizing empires (e.g., Nazi Germany) adhered to territorial principles that are closer to most revolutionary states, of course, when compared with empires such as the British Empire.

[5] The claim here is not that the Ottoman case is a "special" one that deserves attention. Just the reverse: it is emblematic one for premodern cases, similar to countless others. At the same time, I am not claiming that all similar entities professed *identical* territorial ideas and associated practices; the actual contents of such territorial ideologies are bound to differ from each other in numerous dimensions, though they may converge on principles over demarcation and sociospatial organization.

110 How Territorial Ideas Affect Wars

essentialist interpretations, which could potentially associate amorphous territorial order exclusively with Western or non-Western experiences.

Third, the cases assigned to each territorial order differ from each other in temporal terms, and an "older" case is juxtaposed to a "newer" one. The rationale behind the temporal variation is straightforward: these two territorial orders are not dominant in present-day world politics, but this does not mean that they are necessarily "old" (or premodern) or "new" ideational models. Also, for both amorphous and virulent territorial orders, case selection entails picking an "extreme" example side by side with a relatively more moderate representative. More specifically, the analysis offered here suggests that the Ottomans adhered to a more robust version of amorphous territoriality than the British Empire did, with differential impacts on patterns of armed conflict and reterritorialization efforts. This method allows for observing the variation from within each territorial order.

The remainder of this chapter is organized into three main sections. First, I provide a general discussion on amorphous territorial orders. In the second section, I examine the case of the early Ottoman Empire. The third section offers an analysis of the British colonial expansion and governance in South Asia, especially during the course of the nineteenth century.

Amorphous Territorial Orders

The combination of fluid frontiers and heterogeneous organization of the space-society nexus that lies at the heart of amorphous orders is an attribute of numerous political organizations ranging from premodern empires (or colonizing states) to pre-Westphalian European states. From a world-historical perspective, it is safe to argue that amorphous territoriality has been the norm, not the exception. As Charles Tilly highlighted, for most of world history, states built on societal heterogeneity and "some form of indirect rule" to govern their territories.[6] Such political entities also demarcated their territories through "fuzzy frontiers," the limits of which were never truly identified. Premodern empires, which can be defined as "composite, multiethnic, and multi-religious political [formations] in which relations between center and periphery are regulated through flexible and negotiated arrangements,"[7] constitute a paradigmatic category.[8] In empires, "[Middlemen] with a territorial

---

[6] Tilly 1994, 133. Also see Kaplan 1999, 39; Anderson 1996, 17.

[7] Barkey and Godart 2013, 85.

[8] Such empires also have not incorporated the "Westphalian model of multilateral recognition" (Dijkink 2005, 125).

base play a central role in key practices, and . . . [the] power bargains between the center and the middlemen are not uniform, neither ideally nor in practice."[9] Operating through what Nexon and Wright refer to as "heterogeneous contracts,"[10] "imperial systems" can be conceived as composite, instead of consolidated, polities. Such empires were not "territorially consolidated because they were never territorially demarcated"[11] and comprised "numerous boundaries" and "patchy arrangements of power units," which were intrinsically flexible.[12] Many empires tended to prefer (or at least were comfortable with) a heterogeneous approach to how they organized social identities.

Of course, empires come in different forms and shapes, and some empires may profess territorial ideas and practices that cannot be examined exclusively in terms of amorphous orders.[13] However, most empires in history adhered to two principles that lay at the heart of amorphous territoriality: demarcating territory in fluid and flexible terms, and refraining from homogenizing the sociospatial organization within and beyond their domains. As Matthew Longo has highlighted, "Empires have frontiers, frequently taken to be zonal in nature."[14] These frontiers are usually fluid and permeable.[15] In this sense, frontiers did not serve the purpose of a "container" that geographically "enclosed the polity within its perimeters."[16] Most empires considered frontiers to be "lines of communication" that helped them penetrate areas beyond their spatial reach.[17] Not only premodern empires, but European empires of the nineteenth and twentieth centuries also adhered to similar demarcation principles. As Buzan and Lawson comment, "The image of a late nineteenth-century map of the world in which imperial territories are represented by a single color is . . . highly misleading," mainly because empires were built on fragmented territories and porous borders.[18] The colonial state space, under such circumstances, was hardly defined in ethnic or nationalist terms and, consequently, was not bound by ethnicity, nationality, or even culture.[19] It is true that some empires, most notably the Roman and

[9] Jordheim and Neumann 2011, 155.

[10] Nexon and Wright 2007, 254.

[11] Yurdusev 2004, 18.

[12] Winchakul 1994, 79.

[13] Note that I do not engage the "varieties of empires" debate, which is beyond the scope of this study. For example, Luttwak (1976, 22–23) differentiates between "territorial empire" (direct control) and hegemonic empire (indirect rule). Michael Mann (1986) makes a similar distinction between empires of domination and territorial empires. John Darwin (1997), in turn, distinguishes between formal and informal imperialism. On the conceptual roots of empires and imperialism, see Jordheim and Neumann 2011.

[14] Longo 2017a, 763.

[15] Munkler 2007, 5–6. Also see Paasi 2003 and Isaac 1990.

[16] Longo 2017a, 765.

[17] Longo 2017a, 765. For similar interpretations, see Zhang 2001, 47; Emiralioğlu 2012, Brauer, 1–3, 5, 67.

[18] Buzan and Lawson 2015, 132.

[19] Wimmer 2008, 991.

112 How Territorial Ideas Affect Wars

Chinese, built geographical markers such as walls, which may lead modern-day observers to think that "hard borders," as we understand them today, were adopted as the ultimate principle of demarcation much earlier than the so-called Westphalian system. However, these walls and other geographical markers did not set the limits of the imperial state space. For example, setting up a fixed border was not the principle that defined the Great Wall of China; instead, the Great Wall served as a defensive barrier through which the Chinese dynasties could employ a strategy of "build and move" in order to expand their spatial reach.[20]

For many imperial rulers, not committing to set boundaries made it possible to lose territory without facing domestic backlash. At the same time, this flexible geopolitical vision reflected, and also perpetuated, an unbounded penchant for territorial expansionism. In the words of Opello and Rosow:

> A traditional empire was, theoretically, expandable to encompass the entire globe because such empires did not have fixed borders. Imperial borders were merely frontiers that marked the empire's temporary outer limits where its army happens to have stopped and could be moved outward at will. In other words, the boundaries of a traditional empire did not demarcate an area of exclusive territorial jurisdiction based on a shared national identity, but defined a flexible zone of military and economic contact between the empire and the peoples outside of it.[21]

Unlike the ideal-type Westphalian state (or the nation-state), for most empires, territorial expansion did not necessarily imply the extension of sovereign authority to newly conquered lands. In addition to exerting direct territorial control (usually in their core domains), many empires also sought to project "informal and indirect power" in target areas.[22] Put differently, while ambition for continuous expansion might be a shared aspect of imperial geopolitics, the expansion itself did not need to take place in the form of direct territorial rule. Empires, at least most of them, also aimed to expand their spheres of influence.[23]

---

[20] Longo 2017a, 766.

[21] Opello and Rosow 1999, 9.

[22] O'Dowd 2010, 1040.

[23] On this point, I differ from scholars such as Steinmetz (2005, 342), who suggests that there exists a category of "nonterritorial empire," which involves "control of space rather than the annexation of territory and sovereignty." The main reason for disagreement follows from my definition of territory and territoriality, which builds on political geography, and the absence of a similar, or even an alternative, definition in most scholarly research on the subject.

As far as ideas and associated practices concerning sociospatial organization are concerned, most empires, in contrast with nation-states, did not seek cultural homogeneity.[24] In most empires, rules and norms that govern the society showed considerable variation.[25] Put differently, imperial governance relied on institutional heterodoxy and decentralization; therefore, empires cannot be easily conceptualized as "monolithic spaces."[26] As Charles Tilly highlighted, most empires in history "have usually favored some identities over others, but have neither homogenized their populations nor faced serious threats that subject peoples would rebel in the name of their distinctness."[27] In fact, these empires actively encouraged and cultivated cultural heterogeneity,[28] fostering what can be called "chaotic pluralism."[29] The relevant governance and administration practices emphasized parceling out the empires' hegemony, or at least tolerating "subhegemonies."[30] Such systems typically entailed indirect governance through local subsidiaries, or clients, through cooperation and co-optation.[31]

Put simply, most empires refrained from sociospatial homogenization. However, this dynamic does not necessarily imply that empires were "benign spaces of heterodox cooperation."[32] In order to expand their spatial reach, in addition to more direct forms of organized violence, most empires co-opted and empowered some local groups at the expense of others while also practicing outright repression. Ergo, the claim here is not that empires (or other state forms) that professed amorphous territoriality were necessarily more "peaceful" and "tolerant" than states that adhered to other territorial orders. The claim is that while amorphous territoriality led to reterritorialization efforts in target areas, it did not entail an intent to homogenize sociospatial arrangements.

In the next two sections, I examine the Ottoman Empire and the British colonial rule in South Asia through the lens of the territorial orders framework.

---

[24] Malešević 2017a, 4–5; Kumar 2010, 121. Hall and Malešević (2013, 16) argue that the relationship between empires and nation-states is more organic and transient, since "Many European nation-states had been empires, in the sense that they had expanded from a core to incorporate diverse territories, and then they sought to establish overseas empires of their own."

[25] O'Dowd 2010, 1042. Also see Munkler 2007.

[26] Buzan and Lawson 2015, 129, 131.

[27] Tilly 1994, 133.

[28] Kumar 2010, 121.

[29] Buzan and Lawson 2015, 131.

[30] Steinmetz 2005, 356.

[31] Opello and Rostow 1999, 9. For a discussion of the Roman Empire, Opello and Rostow 1999, 25.

[32] Buzan and Lawson 2015, 133.

The Ottoman Empire

When European states came of age around 1500, statesmen and scholars viewed the Ottoman Empire as a geopolitical giant. Although a transcontinental empire by 1500, the Ottoman state had humble beginnings. When the House of Osman was established in 1299 on the northwestern edge of Asia Minor by a "minor march lord,"[33] it was one of the smaller Turkic *beyliks* (emirates) in an expansive archipelago of post-Seljuk principalities and not the most likely candidate for a future regional hegemon. By the end of the fourteenth century, however, this "insignificant frontier state" had subdued most of the emirates in the region and extended its power into Europe,[34] epitomized with the conquest of Constantinople in 1453. By 1453, Black writes, "No Christian state matched Mehmed [the Conquerer's] power, and the Ottoman Empire became the most important state in Europe,"[35] posing a military threat to Europe "that could be given a parallel and historical validation by comparison with the Persians of Antiquity."[36] The Ottomans' political and military might continued to expand. Not only did the Ottomans subdue the Mamluks of Egypt in 1517 and establish the Ottoman sultans as caliphs, but they also made extensive gains in Europe, most notably laying siege to Vienna in 1529.[37]

Until the nineteenth century, the Ottoman Empire professed amorphous territoriality. More specifically, especially in their first three centuries of existence after 1299, the Ottomans adhered to fluid frontiers instead of strict borders and preferred a heterogeneous approach to sociospatial organization over a homogeneous (or, more accurately, homogenizing) one. Professing amorphous territoriality, in turn, affected the ways in which the Ottomans drew upon organized violence to expand (or defend) its territorial reach. The Ottomans conceived war for territory as a continuous enterprise, while also taking advantage of an innate ability to contract when necessary, and do so without necessarily contradicting their geopolitical vision. The Ottomans refrained from radical reterritorialization efforts and did not aim to homogenize sociospatial arrangements. This did not mean that the Ottomans left the areas they conquered "as was"; the empire engaged in substantial reterritorialization efforts especially in some regions, most notably through

---

[33] Kunt 1995, 4.

[34] İnalcık 1973, 3.

[35] Black 2002b, 56.

[36] Black 2010, 18.

[37] For a comparative perspective over Ottoman Empire in the context of other great powers in history, see Mikhail and Philliou 2012.

population transfers and provision of selective incentives to local populations in order to encourage conversion to Islam, but even then the aim was not to impose sociospatial homogeneity. The Ottomans' amorphous order eventually imploded when they attempted to implement a modicum of sociospatial homogeneity throughout the course of the nineteenth and twentieth centuries.

In the next two subsections, I first elaborate on the demarcation and sociospatial organization principles in the early Ottoman Empire and then examine the relationship between territorial ideas and armed conflict.

Demarcation and Sociospatial Organization

The Ottomans built their method of territorial demarcation on the basis of fluid frontiers, which were never set and could expand or contract whenever opportunities or challenges presented themselves.[38] Put differently, the Ottomans did not consider land in terms of discrete pieces of real estate. Territory was seen more in terms of a "fuzzy" continuum, with no real endpoints or beginnings. Similar to numerous nomadic Turkic tribes who left Central Asia centuries ago and made it to Asia Minor only by the late eleventh century, the Ottoman founding fathers professed a modicum of "spatial portability." In other words, until the early fourteenth century, the Ottoman founding fathers did not define state space in terms of a specific region. By the turn of the fourteenth century, the Ottomans established the core of their state space in northwest Asia Minor, but did not set any specific boundaries, presenting themselves as a frontier state facing Christian lands.

The Ottomans' frontier-oriented geographical imagery did not solely follow from their intrinsic desire to project their own territorial vision to their environment. Instead, the Ottomans also pragmatically adopted territorial practices that would best fit their strategic environment. In Cemal Kafadar's words, "If anything characterized [the area where the Ottomans operated], it was mobility and fluidity."[39] Operating in a fluid geopolitical environment, the Ottomans rose to prominence partially because they were able to master the art of territorial flexibility. More specifically, the Ottomans mixed geopolitical pragmatism and religious references, and the latter were selectively invoked to serve the former.[40]

---

[38] For a similar interpretation of Muslim territoriality, see Parvin and Sommer 1980, 5, 14.

[39] Kafadar 1995, 140.

[40] The Ottomans were not unique: "Muslim principles of territorial expansion and unfixed boundaries could . . . arguably be cited as a case of opportunism" (Parvin and Sommer 1980, 8).

116   How Territorial Ideas Affect Wars

As far as the organization of the space-society relationship is concerned, the Ottomans, similar to many other premodern empires in history, strictly adhered to heterogeneous governance arrangements.[41] Their flexibility and heterogeneity, in so many ways, were a function of the origins of the Ottoman institutions and the makeup of the populations they ruled. While the Ottomans are usually depicted as primarily an Islamic empire, the Ottoman imperial system evolved or "was derived" from numerous sources including the Byzantine Empire as well as Turkic and nomadic traditions, not to mention previous Near Eastern models of administration.[42] Such diversity in design is not surprising given the temporal and spatial extent of the empire. In the words of Göçek, "[The Ottoman Empire's] temporal reign traversed the modern and premodern eras, and its geographical land mass covered parts of Eastern Europe, the Balkans, Asia Minor, the Arabian Peninsula, and North Africa."[43] The complexity of the Ottoman institutions only increased with further expansion, as the empire "became increasingly heterogeneous as it spread over three continents."[44]

Note that while the Ottoman state was imperial in design and purpose, it also cannot easily be defined as colonial in the sense that the term is used in the context of European colonialism.[45] There are at least two key differences. First, the Ottoman territorial possessions were largely contiguous. Second, in relation, while the Ottoman court was dominated by Sunni Muslims, the Ottomans were not necessarily "alien" to the societies they ruled over. Additionally, they recognized as well as acknowledged the diversity of the populations within their domain. From a historical point of view, this is hardly surprising. The Ottomans "started as the rulers of a predominantly Christian population"[46] and "owed great deal of their success to the cooperation of local Christian elements."[47]

The early Ottoman state-builders, accordingly, did not aim to transform the society-politics-space association by imposing a master "one size fits all" model of governance. The ideological and institutional structure employed by the Ottomans "appealed as much to the Muslim as the non-Muslim peoples of the empire, refraining from the imposition of an absolute creed or understanding of one religion, one completely unified and cohesive system."[48] In a

---

[41] Especially, Barkey 2008.
[42] Yurdusev 2004, 17; Angelov et al. 2013.
[43] Göçek 2013, 74.
[44] Karpat 1977a, 2.
[45] Göçek 2013, 79.
[46] Barkey 2014, 471.
[47] Veinstein 2013, 121.
[48] Barkey 2014, 472.

landscape where "the frontiers of faith were wide, moveable, and difficult to control,"[49] the Ottomans opted for institutional flexibility and pragmatism. This also meant that they shied away from imposing sociospatial homogeneity on the "porous borderlands between Christianity and Islam."[50]

As Karen Barkey recognized, as the Ottomans struggled to control this diverse terrain, they "made decisions based on immediate concerns."[51] In such a system, "The state [created] conflict [of interest] within the provincial command structure, projecting a shifting rationale for provincial groups to remain loyal to the state."[52] This political system made it both expedient and necessary for the Ottomans to work through local networks of social and political authority. The local notables, in turn, "found the imperial framework acceptable as long as its demands remained limited to the exercise of limited sovereignty," which was the case at least until the nineteenth century.[53]

Put differently, compared with most of its counterparts in the West, "The Ottoman Empire was observably more pluralistic in its sociopolitical and imperial policies, at least judged by the norms of its era."[54] The pluralistic and [seemingly] tolerant nature of the imperial policies followed from the Ottomans' intentions to expand their spheres of influence while also ensuring the continuing obedience of both Muslims and non-Muslims. The result was a relatively "diverse and tolerant society based on the simultaneous division and integration of communities into the state, while providing them with internal autonomy to organize and lead their peoples in their own traditional ways."[55] The reflection of such diversity was also present in what Al-Qattan refers to as "territorialization of law" in the Ottoman Empire, which established a flexible and fluid system that mediated between Sharia, *kanun* (traditional law), and local/religious practices.[56]

Most notably, the Ottomans' population management practices were built on the so-called millet system, which granted different religious groups considerable autonomy.[57] The millet system allowed Ottoman rulers "to efficiently organize the empire's population into communities and to devolve power to trusted intermediaries and community leaders."[58] This did not imply a democratic system that reflected unadulterated tolerance. Non-Muslims

---

[49] Brummett 2015, 75.
[50] Barkey 2014, 472.
[51] Barkey 1991, 710.
[52] Barkey 1991, 700.
[53] Keyder 1997, 32.
[54] Iyigun 2015, 30.
[55] Barkey 2014.
[56] Al-Qattan 2007, 201–212.
[57] On millet system, see Barkey 2005.
[58] Barkey and Gavrilis 2016, 24.

118 How Territorial Ideas Affect Wars

were excluded from public offices and subjected to special taxes called *jizyah*. The early Ottomans also occasionally targeted religious minorities. For example, in 1512, Sultan Selim I sanctioned the massacre of thousands of Alawites who allegedly allied with the Ottomans' arch-nemesis to the east, the Safavid Empire. Regardless, like previous Islamic states,[59] the Ottomans created strong incentives for non-Muslims to convert, but did not pursue a top-down homogenizing strategy.

Territorial Ideas and War

The Ottomans envisioned territorial expansion as a continuous enterprise, but they had little incentive to radically reterritorialize target areas.[60] The notion of fluid frontiers, in relation, privileged "gradual encroachments" over "rapid conquests."[61] The Ottomans' notion of territorial expansion differed from modern European states with respect to the relationship between power-projection and acquiring and holding territory. While the early modern European experience was usually associated with territorial change via grand battles in war, the early Ottomans, who also fought their share of conventional, set-piece battles for territorial expansion, conceived conquest as an ongoing enterprise that could also be carried out through continuous small-scale raids.

Adherence to fluid frontiers also came with an open-ended penchant for territorial aggrandizement. Note that the Ottomans professed a version of what can be called the "geopolitics of jihad," which shaped how they envisioned the political-spatial nature of the globe. Stripped to its basics, geopolitics of jihad portrays the world in binary terms, separated between *dar al-Islam* (land of Islam, or "the whole territory in which the law of Islam prevails") and *dar al-harb* (land of war, or "any contested or contestable territory which [is] not under Islamic rule").[62] The lines separating these two geographical imageries are neither sharp nor concrete; instead they are "vague and blurred."[63] Waging war on the *dar al-harb* for territorial conquest is deemed not only legitimate, but also a religious duty to be fulfilled. Consequently, boundaries

---

[59] In Hugh Kennedy's (2007, 374) words, "The [earlier] Muslim conquerors put little or no pressure on the recently subjected populations to convert to Islam."

[60] Guilmartin (1988, 726) refers to this process as "the perpetual war of raid and counter-raid." Note that modern-day Salafi jihadism adheres to a similar understanding with respect to perpetual conflict (Celso 2016).

[61] Milner 1876, 12.

[62] Parvin and Sommer 1980, 3.

[63] Brauer 1995, 44.

that separate *dar al-Islam* and *dar al-harb* can only be temporary. Not surprisingly, this geopolitical vision is built on the rejection of other political entities' claims to sovereignty. Note that this vision does not suggest that there would be open conflict at all times; there can be episodes of relative peace, but these are merely seen as temporary truces in a continuous war of conquest (or, conversely, a continuous war for the defense of *dar al-Islam*). In this sense, the geopolitics of jihad draws upon the notion of fluid frontiers, the extent of which is "determined by the fortunes of war."[64]

A closer look at the Ottoman thinking reveals that the empire's geographical philosophy entailed a more sophisticated and flexible version of geopolitics of jihad. Simply put, the Ottomans consciously conceived a "third" category, in addition to *dar al-harb* and *dar al-Islam*: *dar al-sulh*, or the lands of peace (or reconciliation), which can be defined as "an area in which the practice of Islam is permitted but not under the protection of a Muslim ruler."[65] In the Ottoman context, the term stood for the "Ottoman vassal principalities and other tribute-paying administrations."[66] In this sense, the Ottomans considered their boundaries in terms of potential for continuous expansion, even if this expansion entailed a flexible and multilayered form that included *dar al-sulh*. The Ottomans' version of geopolitics of jihad, which also included *dar al-sulh*, suggests that the Ottomans did not think of the global-territorial arrangement in binary terms defined as spaces of war versus spaces of Islam, but were cognizant—and tolerant—of the societal gray zones (with many shades of gray, that is) that were not amenable to religion-defined homogeneity, a factor that played an essential role in the Ottoman way of war and territorial expansion.

The notion of fluid frontiers entailed not only a drive for expansion but also an ability to contract with relative ease. Of course, such territorial flexibility was not peculiar to the Ottomans; many non-Westphalian entities including those existed in medieval and early modern Europe operated on similar terms.[67] However, a crucial element that followed from the Ottomans' adherence to "Muslim territoriality" made it relatively easy for the empire to legitimize territorial contraction: the concept of hegira.[68] Terrorism experts are familiar with the term, which stands for emigration.[69] Numerous jihadi

---

[64] Brauer 1995, 28.

[65] Parvin and Sommer 1980, 5. The early Islamic empires had pragmatically invented this category (among others) as a means to legitimize reconciliation with rival non-Muslim political entities, especially after their initial expansion came to a halt.

[66] Arı 2004, 41.

[67] However, there are also differences of "degrees of flexibility" among extra-Westphalian empires. For example, Hugh Kennedy (2007, 363) notes that the confines of the Roman Empire were defined with firmer frontiers than early Islamic empires, which defined their frontiers rather "hazily."

[68] This term is also known as *hijrah* or *hijra*.

[69] For example, see Uberman and Shay 2016, 16–19.

120   How Territorial Ideas Affect Wars

leaders and groups, ranging from American-born propagandist Anwar al-Awlaki to ISIS,[70] have invoked the concept, calling Muslims living in Western countries to emigrate to "lands of Islam" and join Salafi jihadi groups. However, research on "Muslim territoriality" suggests that the concept's origins also have a distinctly spatial component,[71] one that has usually been ignored in terrorism research.

"Hegira" refers to a specific incident in 622.[72] That year, facing overwhelming pressure and threats from their enemies, Prophet Mohammed and his followers left Mecca for Medina in a move that modern spectators would call strategic withdrawal. The relocation of the infant "Islamic state" was fraught with numerous hardships, and the Prophet could return to Mecca in 629, and only after numerous trials and tribulations. The psychic and physical suffering during hegira was immediately interpreted in terms of a test from God, as well as the price for ultimate victory. Hegira left a legacy for Muslim territoriality, rendering it not only acceptable but also advisable for Muslims to relocate, *when faced with overwhelming odds and threats*. In principle, hegira is not "a setback but a necessary precondition for the eventual return to the homeland."[73] Those who undertake hegira, in turn, "are viewed with compassion."[74] The concept of hegira, in this context, made it easier for the subsequent Islamic states, including the Ottomans, to pragmatically withdraw from areas where they faced overwhelming military challenges[75] and do so without contradicting their claims to Islamic statehood.[76]

Overall, the Ottoman grand strategy involved a "great deal of pragmatism and flexibility."[77] The Ottomans frequently invoked references to religious duty for continuous expansion (in the name of Islam) to galvanize support from Muslim populations. However, the empire also sought opportunities anywhere it could: "in pursuit of territory, booty, and power" the Ottomans did not hesitate to "attack co-religionists, ally with former enemies, or hire warriors from any background."[78] More specifically, the Ottoman vision for

---

[70] For example, *Dabiq* 3. *Dabiq* is ISIS's English-language online journal.

[71] Parvin and Sommer 1980, 3; Ahmad 1976.

[72] As Hugh Kennedy (2007, 48) highlights, hegira "marks the beginning of the Islamic era."

[73] Hobbs 2005, 310.

[74] Parvin and Sommer 1980, 4, citing Quranic verses 16:11–111.

[75] Ahmad 1976.

[76] Note that the argument here is less about the reputational costs, defined in terms of interstate politics than about the logic of survival: the loss of territory per se did not put the Ottoman rulers at considerable risk of losing power and facing post-tenure punishment. In that, the Ottoman rulers were not all that much different from their counterparts in prerevolutionary Europe. The relationship between territorial losses (or gains) and the reputational aspects between multiple states (broadly defined) constitutes an interesting and promising research agenda, but a complete analysis of this relationship also goes beyond the scope of this study. I would like to thank an anonymous reviewer for bringing up this point. On the logic of political survival, see Bueno de Mesquita et al. 2005. On reputational costs, see Tingley and Walter 2011.

[77] Agoston 2007, 77.

[78] Darling 2000, 138.

territorial expansion was built on three components: (1) a "moving" frontier that would help the Ottomans to attract and motivate fighters while also placing continuous, if gradual, pressure on their neighbors, (2) "co-opting" the social groups that were living on the edges of the empire by providing them with selective incentives, and (3) minimizing resistance and maximizing cooperation from the local populations in the newly acquired lands (which served as stepping stones for further expansion).

As highlighted above, the Ottomans adhered to a moderate version of the geopolitics of jihad that allowed for a third category: *dar al-sulh*. Doing so, the Ottomans acknowledged and tolerated (societal) "gray zones" in their domains and spheres of influence. Put differently, the early Ottomans aimed to expand, but they were willing to do so even if that meant merely extending their *sphere of influence*, without imposing social uniformity and conformity or direct rule in target areas. In this context, the Ottomans refrained from extreme forms of reterritorialization efforts and exercised relatively mild interference with the local arrangements in the newly conquered areas, at least in the short term. According to Halil İnalcık, the Ottoman conquests involved two stages.[79] The first was a period of suzerainty, which would be replaced by a more direct form of control following the elimination of native dynasties. This process took a long time and did not aim at transforming the social and political structure in the conquered lands, which were usually preserved in their pre-Ottoman administrative boundaries:[80] "The Ottomans often conquered territories without fundamentally transforming their own peculiar rules of reproduction be it legal, ideological, and even material."[81] For example, the conquests in the Balkans did not lead to major disruptions in economic and social life, and the Ottoman rule "provided room for the continuity of local traditions and life patterns."[82]

Even when the Ottomans transitioned into İnalcık's "second stage" of eventually liquidating the local nobility, such acts were not always "resented by the masses who had little in common with the [nobility] and had often suffered grievously from arbitrary rule."[83] As a result, Ottoman rulers often succeeded in co-opting the masses in newly conquered areas. Overall, the spatial extent of the Ottomans expanded considerably between the fourteenth and seventeenth centuries. However, the Ottoman rulers refrained from radically transforming the sociospatial organization within the spatial-political

---

[79] İnalcık 1954, 103.
[80] İnalcık 1954, 108.
[81] Nişancıoğlu 2014, 336.
[82] Minkov 2004, 34.
[83] Sugar 1977, 274–75.

122 How Territorial Ideas Affect Wars

order in the lands they conquered. Such a "hands-off" approach to governing people and space helped the Ottomans expand their territorial reach.

The Ottomans' vision of continuous and gradual expansion reveals itself best in the so-called *ghaza* (ghazi warfare), a "well-established tradition of frontier warfare."[84] "Ghazi," in its traditional interpretation, stood for the Islamic knight, the protector of the Islamic realm and a heroic conqueror. Ghazi bands constituted only one component of the Ottoman grand strategy for territorial expansion. The Ottomans also had significant conventional capabilities—most notably, a central standing army—to match their objectives,[85] but ghazi warfare can illustrate how amorphous territoriality can resonate in territorial war and expansion.

Most notably, the Ottomans used the ghazi bands for continuous harassment and softening of the frontier populations.[86] In the Ottoman state, warfare was usually depicted in terms of desultory frontier raiding, not grand battles, which was a significant attribute of the ghazi order.[87] The term "ghazi" was at the center of decades-long debate in Ottoman historiography, which makes it necessary to elaborate further on the subject. While the early interpretations of the ghazi tradition represented the institution as a religion-fueled and exclusively bellicose enterprise, more recent literature established the tradition's pragmatic and sophisticated nature. To begin with, the ghazi order was not strictly or exclusively bellicose. The frontier society that hosted and produced the majority of the ghazi fighters was both tolerant and diverse. In fact, the ghazi order acted as "the most powerful and inclusive unifying device available to conquerors on the frontier, more so than tribalism, origin, religion, language, or culture."[88] Furthermore, while the ghazi practice had its roots in Islamic thought, it was not driven solely by religious concerns.[89] The Ottoman sultans often invoked the ghazi ideal, but "the ideal served more as a legitimizing ideology than as an organizing principle of the state."[90]

Put differently, the ghazi tradition, at least in the way that the Ottomans employed it, was built on pragmatism and aimed at integrating new territories to the imperial system in a cost-effective fashion. In Darling's words, the ghazi order was "inclusive rather than exclusive, aiming at the attachment

---

[84] Emiralioğlu 2014, 15. The term *ghaza*, which preceded the Ottomans, is closely associated with jihad. On similarities and differences between the two, see Kafadar 1995, 79–80. Also see Veinstein 2013, 173. Ottomans were not the only polity using the ghazi ideology in Asia Minor (Çolak 2015, 18). On *Ghaza* (or *ghazawat*) tradition before the Ottomans, see Haug 2011.

[85] See Kadercan 2014.

[86] Panaite (2000, 78) calls the ghazi tradition a "political instrument."

[87] Kafadar 1995.

[88] Darling 2000, 157.

[89] Gürkan 2013.

[90] Dale 2010, 55.

Fluid Frontiers and Forever War | **123**

of new territories and new adherents by whatever means proved successful, whether violent or pacific."[91] As Halil İnalcık emphasized, the ghazi tradition had a distinct emphasis on keeping the empire's subjects content with their everyday lives.[92] For example, between 1299 and 1402, when the ghazi order exerted its influence in the newly conquered Christian-majority areas, especially in the Balkans (but also Asia Minor), it extracted only limited taxes and relieved the locals of personal tasks they had been held responsible for by their (former) Byzantine and Latin rulers.[93]

The ghazi method of territorial expansion was a form of hybrid warfare. The relevant tactics included continuous and systematic harassment, infiltration, co-optation, and intimidation. The intention was to "soften" the target areas for full-scale invasion or gradual incorporation into the Ottoman domain. Ghazi bands used both positive and negative incentives. Ghazi conquests were carried out in stages: an initial infiltration and intimidation campaign was usually followed by co-optation of the locals, which itself was accompanied by a gradual exertion of political and social influence.[94] Once the Ottomans completed the "infiltration" stage in a target area, the next step was to expand their authority by co-opting the locals, which required flexibility and pragmatism in managing the society-space-politics relationship.

The above discussion does not imply that the Ottoman rule emphasized respect for the local arrangements for their own sake, or always kept the intensity of reterritorialization efforts at a bare minimum: pragmatism drove the tolerance (and not the other way around), and the Ottomans did not leave the conquered areas as they were. Therefore, it would not be appropriate to paint a rosy (or anachronistic) picture of the Ottoman Empire. For example, when faced with opposition from the local lords, "In order to make their new conquests secure, the Ottomans used an elaborate system of colonization and mass deportation."[95] The associated reterritorialization efforts, at times, entailed forced migration of rival Turcoman tribes from Asia Minor to the Balkans, a territorial strategy that restructured the sociospatial organization in both regions.

Note that the narrative above applies best from 1299 until the seventeenth century. From the early seventeenth century onward, the Ottoman expansion in Europe stagnated. As the European states began to define and defend their boundaries in more concrete terms, the Ottomans were compelled to

---

[91] Darling 2000, 137.
[92] İnalcık 1973, 66.
[93] Karpat 1977b, 86.
[94] Kadercan 2017.
[95] İnalcık 1954, 122. Also see Doumanis 2013, 23.

accept, or at least live with, a more bounded frontier in Europe, even though they might have desired differently. The collapse (or implosion) of the traditional Ottoman territorial order followed the Westernization efforts initiated rapidly in the second half of the nineteenth century. These efforts involved efforts to remake the state institutions on the basis of the Western nation-state model. There were two interrelated motives behind such efforts. The first was the extent and scope of the military defeats suffered at the hands of European powers as well as Russia.

Until the nineteenth century, Ottoman rulers considered military defeats primarily as a military problem and refrained from large-scale political and administrative reforms, focusing primarily on military reformation. By the early nineteenth century, however, the Ottomans' increasing inferiority on the battlefield eventually convinced their leadership to emulate the Western institutions not only in the military but also in administrative and political dimensions. Second, by the nineteenth century, European states were able to interfere with the ways in which the Ottomans ran their institutions. In general, the Ottomans were pressurized into undertaking two contradictory transformations in their domestic order. On the one hand, the outside powers wanted the Ottomans to become more like a European nation-state with respect to managing their territories. On the other hand, the Ottomans had to allow the external powers to project legal and political authority within the same domain.

These pressures culminated in the so-called Tanzimat Fermanı of 1839 (also known as the Imperial Edict of Gulhane). The so-called Tanzimat reforms constituted the first major attempt at transforming the very fabric of the Ottoman state. The reforms aimed to impose uniformity in taxation, military service, property rights, and law.[96] Attempts to homogenize the space-society-politics nexus and impose "harder" borders eventually led to numerous internal conflicts and rebellions within the empire.[97] A major driving factor was the clash between the traditional flexibility of the Ottomans' amorphous territorial order and the rigidity of the order that the Ottoman elites were trying to impose in a rather top-down and "rushed" fashion. According to Göçek, "Western European practices and institutions adversely impacted the fluidity of Ottoman identity," and eventually "Identities became more solid and stratified, introducing publicly visible inequality and enmity among social groups."[98] In such a landscape, the Westernization effort, which involved

---

[96] On Tanzimat Fermanı, see Shaw and Shaw 1976, 55–272.
[97] Zubaida 2002, 205; Makdisi 2002.
[98] Göçek 2013, 88.

uniformity and centralization in the space-society-politics nexus, "was not congenial to autonomous provinces"[99] that lay at the heart of the traditional Ottoman territorial order. At the very extreme, the "geographical claim" of such undertaking "implied massive ethnic cleaning,"[100] which also meant that the Westernization efforts turned the Ottomans' previously amorphous territoriality on its head. Centralization and homogenization efforts then clashed with the territorialization of nationalistic and ethnic claims, facilitating the implosion of the entire system.

In sum, the Ottomans' territorial ideas and practices, especially in the first three centuries of their reign, can be seen as a paradigmatic representation of amorphous territoriality. Adherence to amorphous territoriality, in turn, affected the Ottomans' geopolitical vision as well as the ways in which the Empire approached territorial conflict and expansion. The Ottomans' territorial vision and associated practices eventually imploded in the face of monolithic territoriality's increasing salience within and beyond their domains.

The British Empire in South Asia

Amorphous territoriality is not exclusively a characteristic of premodern states or non-Western empires. The so-called modern states have also professed amorphous territorial orders, if beyond their core territories. More specifically, numerous European states adopted geopolitical visions that can be referred to as dual territoriality; that is, they adhered to monolithic (or mosaic) orders in their core territories (or Europe) while also professing amorphous territoriality in their colonial possessions.

While mainstream IR does not always directly engage the imperial (or colonial) roots of the so-called modern state system,[101] even a crude reading of world history reminds us that "there is no sharp break between the age of empires and the era of nation-states."[102] In fact, the rise of the modern nation-state in Europe and the European expansion to the rest of the world (in the form of colonialism) "occurred simultaneously,"[103] and, nation-building and imperialism went "hand-in-hand."[104] Under these circumstances, especially from the nineteenth century onward, there existed a "contradiction" (or

---

[99] Göçek 2013, 533.
[100] Keyder 1997, 41.
[101] Barkawi and Laffey 2006.
[102] O'Dowd 2010, 1043.
[103] Barkawi and Laffey 2002, 113. In Barkawi's (2016, 209) words, "Western polities have complicated histories, mongrel histories of nation and empire."
[104] Buzan and Lawson 2015, 3, 35.

126 How Territorial Ideas Affect Wars

"territorial hypocrisy") in the territorial ideas and practices of many European countries.[105]

The territorial orders framework suggests that many European states conceived of their actual or potential colonial possessions in terms of amorphous territoriality: the demarcation principles of the "colonial [state] space" were based on fluid and flexible frontiers, and there was no impetus to homogenize sociospatial organization in target areas. In fact, many colonial powers consciously preferred heterogeneous organization of sociospatial arrangements, as this approach allowed them to govern on the cheap, at times through the principle of divide and conquer (and rule). This geopolitical vision affected how European colonizers utilized organized violence to fight their wars of territorial conquest, as well as how they drew upon military and paramilitary force to sustain as well as deepen their authority. Unlike the "conventional" wars that were fought in Europe, the colonial wars over territory were usually based on what Tarak Barkawi referred to as small wars.[106]

Of the European colonizing states, Britain during the nineteenth century stands out as a paradigmatic case. As John Darwin put it, "No other power developed more varied and far-reaching imperial relationships than Victorian Britain."[107] Of course, a brief examination of the British case does not—in fact, cannot—capture all the subtleties and the variety of ideas and practices involving imperial territoriality in modern history all by itself. However, it can still serve a heuristic purpose at the conceptual and analytical level, while also driving attention to some of the broader commonalities. In this study, I focus on the relationship between territorial ideas and conflict in South Asia, for two reasons. First, a more comprehensive survey is beyond the scope of this study. Second, of all the areas that the British Empire colonized, South Asia can be seen as the central pillar of the imperial arrangement.[108]

The British presence in South Asia in general, India in particular, can be traced to 1612.[109] The British initially engaged in numerous conflicts with both European powers such as the Dutch, the French, and the Portuguese, and local powers like the Marathas. Britain's incursion into South Asia focused on colonial India and was initially carried out through the East India Company, whose effective rule in India began as of 1757, following the conquest of Bengal. In 1761, the British finally overwhelmed its sole remaining competitor, France, and emerged as the dominant European power in

---

[105] O'Dowd 2010, 1043.
[106] Barkawi 2004.
[107] Darwin 1997, 630.
[108] Doyle 1986, 236; Kiernan 1969, 32.
[109] On the gradual conquest of India by the British, see Lawrence 1997.

the subcontinent. The East India Company was a chartered entity, but the British Empire still exerted significant, sometimes decisive, influence on the company's operations. For example, the company's economic and political authority was "severely circumscribed" by Pitt's India Act of 1784.[110] Furthermore, from 1779 onward, there were always some royal regiments in India.[111] Following the Mutiny of 1857, the British Empire exerted direct rule in India in 1858 and governed the subcontinent until 1947. In the next two subsections, I examine the territorial ideas that empowered and shaped the British colonial expansion, and the relationship between such ideas and organized violence.

Demarcation and Sociospatial Organization

As far as demarcation principles are concerned, the British Empire in South Asia, just like many of its contemporaries hailing from Europe, did not conceive its spatial reach in terms of "sovereign territorial lines," but instead emphasized "spheres of influence, hegemonies, and other kinds of juridically informal arrangements" that included different forms of indirect rule.[112] As highlighted above, the British geopolitical vision entailed dual territoriality (or territorial hypocrisy). Buzan and Lawson capture the essence of this duality, especially with respect to the rise of nationalism: the notions of nationalism and popular sovereignty legitimized state borders in the so-called modern state system (thereby ossifying what I refer to as monolithic orders) in Europe, but at the same time emboldened a geopolitical vision that portrayed non-Western geographies as "alien" (or empty) spaces into which expansion was both acceptable and desirable.[113]

Put differently, at the ideational level, the global-territorial vision associated with European powers during the age of colonization, epitomized with the British Empire, implied that while the boundaries within the so-called (European) state system was identifiable and collectively recognized, the spaces beyond this enclosed system comprised open-ended and fluid frontiers, waiting to be "explored" and controlled by the Europeans.[114] For example, during the "scramble for Africa," the notions of "fixed boundaries,

---

[110] Betts 1975, 57.

[111] Kiernan 1998, 23.

[112] Barkawi 2018, 320.

[113] Buzan and Lawson 2015, 35. Also see Betts 1975, 19.

[114] Note that I do not differentiate between the British geopolitical visions dominant in the metropole and in the colonies, as my argument is that elites in both geographies shared similar territorial ideas. On this point, see Roy 2015, 69–70.

sovereign independence and non-intrusion into territory not one's own," which are usually used to define the "international system," were easily discarded when European states including Britain were considering the sociospatial future of the African continent.[115] It is true that, in Africa, European powers eventually demarcated, or carved out, territories among each other; but that is the point: the European powers considered the geographies they carved as "empty." In such a setting, it was only the European states who could decide how colonial spaces were to be demarcated.[116] A similar practice was also upheld in North America: with the Rush-Bagot convention of 1817, the sovereign states with presence in the region "fixed the lines separating political communities in North America," but "no one consulted the [Native Americans]."[117]

European ideas about non-Western geographies were in alignment with, as well as fueled by, numerous ideational trends that were dominant in Britain (and, Europe) such as racism, ethnocentrism, capitalism, and social Darwinism. According to Buzan and Lawson, "Nationalism sacralized borders and represented those outside these borders as alien, while liberalism, racism, and, on occasion, socialism legitimized expansion into these alien spaces," leading to "the re-articulation of imperialism as a progressive practice."[118]

One crucial component of this geopolitical vision was ethnocentrism, which was also propelled by the self-adopted British (and European) mission to "civilize" uncivilized populations and geographies. As Malešević put it, "The ever-increasing popularity of Darwinist interpretations of social life combined with the imperial doctrine of *mission civilisatrice* provided the key ideological glue for imperial expansion."[119] Even prominent liberal thinkers of the time favored this expansionary vision, under the pretext of universalizing principles.[120] For example, thinkers such as John Stuart Mill, Thomas Macaulay, and Jeremy Bentham supported British imperialism.[121] In this sense, "Western—or perhaps even more specifically, British—exceptionalism became abstract universalism through the institutional vehicle of empire."[122]

---

[115] Parker 2010, 116.

[116] On the partition of Africa, see Foeken 1995.

[117] Adelman and Aron 1999, 823. On this point, I differ from Hendrik Spruyt (2000, 74), who argues that "modern colonial empires recognized fixed territorial limits to their claims to jurisdiction." Western empires did recognize fixed territorial limits in their overseas (or colonial) domains, but only vis-à-vis each other. As will be highlighted in detail, Western powers considered most non-Western geographies to be open and empty frontiers, especially during the course of the nineteenth century.

[118] Buzan and Lawson 2015, 127.

[119] Malešević 2010, 133.

[120] Sartori 2006.

[121] Sartori 2006, 624; Kolsky 2015, 1223.

[122] Sartori 2006, 626.

Fluid Frontiers and Forever War | **129**

Furthermore, the rise of capitalism, especially in the British context, fueled a penchant for acquiring new markets and resources. As Rosa Luxemburg highlighted, by its very nature, the capitalist system needed to expand and do so almost indefinitely.[123]

Overall, the combination of social Darwinism, the sense of a "civilizing mission," and drive for securing and exploiting new markets ossified a geopolitical vision not all that different from the Manichaean version of the geopolitics of jihad: instead of differentiating between "land of war" and "land of Islam" (*dar al-harb* and *dar al-Islam*), the dominant British thinking differentiated between "land of the civilized" and "land of the uncivilized." This geographical dichotomy made it not only feasible but also desirable to expand, almost indefinitely, into the "other side" through military force, coercion, or co-optation. As far as the land of the "uncivilized" was concerned, at least in principle, the scope of the nineteenth-century British imperialism was "limitless."[124] In such a setting, "overseas expansion was a constant, not an intermittent" dynamic.[125]

The aforementioned "civilizational spatial divide" was also codified into international law. As Anthony Anghie argued, the territorial hierarchy, and all the injustices and inequalities associated with it, was embedded within the [presumably] universalizing, and universal, principles of modern international law.[126] By unilaterally setting up a "universal" and unquestioned (or unquestionable) set of principles that constituted "international" law throughout the nineteenth century, European powers including Britain institutionalized what can be called "differential sovereignty,"[127] a dynamic that has also been identified by IR scholars such as Edward Keene.[128] The European (or Western) states, in this reading, enjoyed a sort of territorial equality among each other, which they denied to countless non-Western societies and the so-called backward territories[129] they inhabited.

Put simply, international law was instrumentally deployed to "reorder colonized spaces and bodies."[130] One notable example is the concept of terra nullius, or "territory belonging to no one."[131] The concept had been in use during the course of the seventeenth and eighteenth centuries, and portrayed

---

[123] Etherington 1982, 9.
[124] Darwin 1997, 628.
[125] Betts 1975, 4.
[126] Anghie 2007; Kennedy 1997.
[127] Mahmud 2010, 11.
[128] Keene 2002.
[129] Lindley 1926.
[130] Mahmud 2010, 15.
[131] Castellino 1999, 547.

the non-Christian geographies simply as "ownerless" spaces.[132] During the course of the nineteenth century, the content of the relevant discourses changed, but the substance remained practically the same: terra nullius began to refer to spaces that did not belong to a "civilized state."[133] Under such circumstances, colonial geopolitical thinking recognized no boundaries beyond its European/Western core, and conceptualized non-Western spaces as either "plentiful worlds" or "empty worlds,"[134] bolstering the "mythologization of the colonial landscape as an empty space."[135]

In sum, driven by a mix of social Darwinism, racial biases, and a civilizing mission, while also armed with the support of modern international law (the establishment of which was not independent of British efforts), the British colonial elites conceived the extra-Western spaces in terms of fluid frontiers, which could be explored and controlled if and when feasible.[136] In regions such as colonial India and Afghanistan, "The frontier of the British Empire did not end with a line of the map, but rather faded out as influence became more tenuous, and knowledge more sparse."[137] Discourses of the imperial frontier, in turn, not only allowed but also motivated the British Empire, among other European empires, to "furnish license to occupy and subjugate coveted spaces that were represented as being empty,"[138] and do so through organized violence when necessary.

Note that the British did not "destroy" existing strict and clearly delineated boundaries in South Asia; even before the arrival of the British and their ascendancy in the region from the mid-eighteenth century onward (if, indirectly through the East India Company), the "demarcation of political units [was] essentially loose and porous."[139] Put differently, the British empire did not "break the borders" in South Asia, since there existed barely any borders, as we understand them today. Instead, the British manipulated the existing territorial fluidity[140]—most notably, in terms of three frontier categories, that is, protectorates, neutral zones, and buffers in-between—to exert influence its influence, if sometimes in an indirect and informal fashion.[141] The British

---

[132] It is possible to trace the origins of this line of thinking to the Treaty of Tordesillas, which aimed to divide the so-called New World, signed between Spain and Portugal in June 1494, and which was supported by Pope Alexander VI's edict *Inter caetera divinae* a month earlier. On this point, see Mahmud 2010, 9–10.

[133] Mahmud 2010, 9–10.

[134] Clement 2019.

[135] Noyes 1992, 7. On colonialism and the emergence of a distinct colonial spatiality, see Carter 1988.

[136] Note that some historians such as Galbraith (1960) argue that the British expansion was not driven by a penchant for expansionism per se, but that the British continued to expand due to a sense of geopolitical vulnerability. On this "expansion for security" perspective, see Mearsheimer 2001 and Chapter 2.

[137] Bayly 2014, 455.

[138] Mahmud 2010, 24.

[139] Mishra 2016, 9.

[140] Mishra 2016, 13.

[141] Darwin 1997, 617.

eventually leaned toward attempts to fix its frontiers, but almost invariably when faced with a challenge from another great power. For example, the so-called Great Game between Britain and the Russian Empire eventually led to the creation of Durand Line in 1893, which aimed to establish Afghanistan as a buffer zone between the two empires.[142]

As far as sociospatial organization is concerned, the British Empire adopted a heterogeneous approach. Of course, sociospatial heterogeneity was neither imposed upon nor introduced to South Asia by the British. Not surprisingly, the territorial ideas and practices in the region did not align with the monolithic ideal rising to prominence in Europe. The administrative, cultural, and political landscape in South Asia has long been defined in terms of multilayered and fluid arrangements.[143] In such a setting, the British territorial expansion followed a gradual process. Similar to the Ottomans, the British Empire's initial encroachments in the region entailed "working with" the existing sociospatial arrangements. For example, in southern Goalpara, "The advent of British rule . . . merely conformed much to previous practice."[144] Overall, two factors can explain the initial British preference for a relatively light footprint in South Asia. First, the East India Company and later the empire itself, as many empires have done, preferred to rule on the cheap, and radical and swift attempts at reterritorialization might have triggered a societal backlash, which would only exponentially amplify the cost of expansion and governance. Second, the British were not under any illusions about the social, political, and cultural complexity and fluidity in South Asia; instead, the colonial agents were well aware that most parts of the region could be best conceived as "conceptually heterogeneous" entities.[145]

Regardless, the British in South Asia, especially colonial India, eventually attempted to impose a modicum of geographical "rationality" to what otherwise resembled an unmanageable conundrum through the use of surveys, mapping, and new administrative and economic zones.[146] In the words of Bernardo Michael, "When confronted by the continued persistence of fuzzy boundaries and patchy territorial mosaics, arising out of a complex and shifting structure of agrarian entitlements, colonial officials took recourse to modern surveys and mapmaking as a scientific solution to the problem of space in South Asia."[147] Not surprisingly, the relevant efforts, on numerous

---

[142] On this dynamic in the so-called age of empires, see Mbembé and Rendall 2000.
[143] Mishra 2016, 7.
[144] Misra 2005, 215.
[145] Bayly 2014, 448; Betts 1975, 12.
[146] Edney 2009.
[147] Michael 2017, 38.

132 How Territorial Ideas Affect Wars

occasions, led to confrontations between "indigenous and colonial notions of political space."[148] Most notably, the British "reconfigured" space-society association in colonial India by placing pressure on nomadic groups, manipulating (sometimes inadvertently) patterns of urbanization, and building railways. All these efforts effectively reterritorialized the entire subcontinent, if in uneven ways.[149]

The British attempted to impose a "scientific" geographical order onto South Asia primarily in order to maximize its extractive capabilities and minimize the costs of governance. However, as mentioned above, the intention was not to help establish sociospatial homogeneity in the subcontinent. Furthermore, the British efforts to create a spatial order through which they could effectively identify, cultivate, and exploit the economic sources and human capital in South Asia amounted to little more than a "largely incomplete project."[150] The patchy local arrangements, dispersed territories, and ever-shifting as well as contingent nature of the indigenous political systems could not be easily reconciled with the rational and scientific understanding of the state space that dominated British geographical thinking. During the process, the British also had to recognize and appropriate indigenous territorial ideas and practices. In this sense, the colonial reterritorialization of South Asia did not entail a "one-way" (or top-down) process where European territorial ideas and practices were unilaterally imposed onto indigenous spaces.[151] Instead, the reterritorialization of the subcontinent followed an interactive dynamic, where the British and numerous indigenous social and political groups affected each other's spatial ideas, norms, and institutions, almost on a continuous basis. Christopher Bayly draws an interesting parallel between the British and the Ottoman Empires; according to Bayly, while colonial India was becoming "more British," British India was also becoming more like the Ottomans in particular, or non-Western empires in general.[152]

As highlighted above, the British did not seek to promote sociospatial homogeneity across colonial South Asia.[153] On the contrary, the British encouraged sociospatial heterogeneity in order to expand into, pacify, and govern the subcontinent through "divide and rule" mechanisms.[154] The British intent to preserve (and, eventually, manipulate) heterogeneous arrangements

---

[148] Misra 2005, 220.
[149] Novak 2011, 752. On the impacts of railways on identity politics in India, see Chatterjee 1993.
[150] Michael 2017, 53.
[151] Bayly 2014, 450.
[152] Bayly 2007, 334.
[153] Evangelical missionaries initially attempted to "Christianize" the indigenous populations, but these attempts were relatively ineffective, and they were downplayed in the aftermath of the Mutiny of 1857–58. On this point, see Hutchins 2015, 3–19.
[154] Barkawi 2017, loc. 628.

in South Asia was most visible in the colonial legal arrangements. Not all that different from the Ottoman Empire's millet system, the British in South Asia also encouraged and eventually institutionalized a legal structure that differentiated between social groups in religious and ethnic terms. For example, the "Plan for the Administration of Justice" of 1772, overseen by the East India Company, institutionalized separate laws for Muslims, Hindus, Christians, and white colonizers or settlers.[155]

Arguably, promoting sociospatial heterogeneity had a strategic logic behind it: minimizing both the cost of colonial governance and risk of anti-colonial uprisings or resistance. Put simply, the alternative to encouraging heterogeneity—that is, a direct imposition of sociospatial homogeneity—was a double-edged sword. On the one hand, the attempts to superimpose sociospatial homogeneity would likely instigate reactions from different segments of the society. Such reaction, in turn, could weaken Britain's grip on South Asia[156] or trigger a substantial increase in the resources that the British needed to commit to the administration (and, pacification) of the subcontinent. The Mutiny of 1857–58, in this context, was a reminder that the British hold over South Asia was in fact more fragile than initially thought, and European encroachments were not always well received.[157] Therefore, even though the British Empire imposed direct governance in colonial India after the mutiny, it did not necessarily accelerate colonial efforts to impose sociospatial homogeneity.[158] On the other hand, even if the British could successfully establish a modicum of sociospatial homogeneity in geographies such as colonial India, the long-term consequences of the relevant efforts might have brought more harm than good for the empire: a socially and politically unified India, for example, could more easily resist and challenge the metropole. From the perspective of the territorial orders framework, the British Empire ruled through amorphous territoriality and had little incentive to establish monolithic territoriality in South Asia.

Under such circumstances, the British had all the incentive to manipulate the heterogeneous terrain to their advantage and do so by playing one ethnic or communal group against the others (and vice versa) through sophisticated patron-client networks.[159] In fact, the colonial agents did not always merely take the existing cultural, religious, and ethnic differences at their face value;

---

[155] Kolsky 2015, 1230.
[156] On this dynamic, see Hechter 2000.
[157] Barkawi 2017, loc. 668.
[158] For example, despite the empire's engagement in a number of centralization efforts, it also allowed more than five hundred princely states to exist. On this point, see Mishra 2016, 8.
[159] Cooper 2004, 260: Kiernan 1969, 52.

the British also manipulated or reinterpreted existing societal categories,[160] sometimes inventing and imposing new ones. Mishra summarizes this "mix and match" approach adopted by the British as follows: "Sometimes people from the same socio-cultural and identity adherence were divided into two or more political units and in some other cases, less related socio-cultural groups were put into one political unit."[161]

Territorial Ideas and War

As highlighted in the previous subsection, Britain, like many European contemporaries, conceived of the non-Western geographies as open spaces, which were waiting to be "discovered," cultivated, and "civilized." This geographical understanding was built on the notion that there could be only temporary frontiers between the British and the polities and societies in South Asia. In this sense, the notion of fluid frontiers propelled a penchant for continuous expansion and violent conflict. Numerous scholars share the idea that European empires of the modern age perceived territorial expansion through continuous use or threat of organized violence. As Isabel Hull put it, "The colonial situation itself was identical to war."[162] Tarak Barkawi identifies the main distinction between intra-European wars and colonial war: while the Western states conceived of the relationship among them in binary terms, that is, war and peace, their approach to actual and potential colonies entailed the notion of "permanent war."[163]

The British expansion and rule in South Asia involved near-permanent use of violent means and tactics. Broadly speaking, this expansion entailed remarkable flexibility. The colonial agents employed a multitude of methods and various forms of violence and repression. Accordingly, the British territorial expansion was carried out through different paths and sequences in different parts of the subcontinent. In the words of John Darwin, "Frequent oscillation between different forms of expansion was the hallmark of flexible imperial thinking."[164] At the cost of oversimplification, it can be argued that the British territorial expansion and governance built on four different, if related, paths: conventional wars against major local competitors in the region,

[160] Barkawi 2018, 320.
[161] Mishra 2016, 8.
[162] Hull 2005, 332.
[163] Barkawi 2016, 205.
[164] Darwin 1997, 621.

gradual raids and other punitive measures, selective co-optation, and what is usually referred to as "lawfare."

The initial British incursions into colonial India involved numerous military campaigns against local power-holders. Most notably, between 1760 and 1820, the East India Company fought four wars with Mysore and three with the Marathas.[165] Open conflicts with local powers were in fact a crucial part of initial British incursions in India. For example, between 1767 and 1799, the British and Mysore were at peace for only ten years out of twenty-three.[166] To be precise, conventional military campaigns helped the British subdue indigenous military powers, but were a far cry from being the only, or main, mechanism of territorial expansion and control.[167]

More specifically, these relatively conventional military operations did not play a "decisive" role in the colonization of India, as some scholars have argued.[168] Instead, the British expansion is best conceived as a gradual and continuous enterprise. At the conventional war level, the myth of British technological and organizational superiorities as key to ultimate subjugation of the subcontinent has long been debunked.[169] When the British first encountered the local Indian powerbrokers such as Mysore, the Siths, and the Marathas, there existed no real asymmetry in military and organizational domains.[170] As far as military hardware was concerned, mainly thanks to trade with, and support from, Britain's European rivals such as France, the indigenous powerbrokers enjoyed parity with British colonial forces in India. Mysore, Marathas, and Sikhs also benefited from European mercenaries and officers for organizing and training their forces. In fact, the British ended up appropriating the unconventional forms of organized violence that were already dominant in South Asia. For example, Randolf Cooper argues that, as early as the late eighteenth century, "the East India Company's armies began to look and function more like other Indian armies."[171]

In addition to conventional military campaigns, which were being fought using more and more non-Western tactics and through heavy reliance on local troops serving for the East India Company (later, directly for the British Empire), the British also continuously launched raids to punish, coerce, and deter local groups. This is hardly surprising. During the course of the nineteenth century, low-intensity conflict and resistance to colonial rule was

---

[165] Cooper 2005, 540.
[166] Barua 2005, 76–88.
[167] On these wars, see Barua 2005.
[168] Cooper 2005, 543. Also see Lynn 2003.
[169] Cooper 2005.
[170] Cooper 2005.
[171] Cooper 2005, 541.

"virtually constant," a dynamic that compelled the British to exert constant pressure on the discontented indigenous groups.[172] The notion of "turbulent frontiers," which needed to be "pacified" and eventually controlled, played an essential role in shaping the British attitude toward the use of organized violence. For instance, the British waged "constant war" on India's northwestern frontier for almost a century, from formal annexation in 1858 until independence in 1947.[173] Between 1849 and 1879 only, the colonial agents launched at least thirty-seven expeditions on the frontier.[174] It is difficult to assess how "severe" the relevant military and paramilitary engagements actually were, for two reasons. First, the existing data do not allow for such evaluation. Second, the British records tended to focus more on the casualties suffered by the British and their local proxies, and did not pay much attention to the casualties suffered on the other side. Still, such operations were a typical component of the British colonial-territorial expansion and rule in South Asia. Most notably, Kiernan argues that the British owed their "paramountcy" in India to these "small operations"; collectively, the military effort that went into these "small" operations rivaled European battlefields before 1789.[175] The emphasis on "frontier fighting" eventually led Lord Kitchener, who assumed the post of commander in chief of India in 1903, to establish a "small, highly trained frontier army" to deter and punish discord among the local populations.[176]

In the first thirty years of British direct rule, the northwestern frontier witnessed "more than forty punitive expeditions in which crops were destroyed, livestock were slaughtered, and entire villages were burned to the ground by colonial troops."[177] Elizabeth Kolsky succinctly summarizes the nature of colonial warfare on the frontier, as both a tactic and language: "As a tactic, it paved the way for colonial pacification and control. As a language, British administration argued that violence was the only sign system the 'rude and savage' people on the frontier understood."[178]

In such a setting, the colonial agents of the British Empire adopted not only the military tactics of the indigenous forces but also the dominant tactics of violence and coercion in the region. For example, the British and their local auxiliaries systematically engaged in punitive blockades and retaliatorily seizures.[179] The colonial violence also entailed symbolic acts that aimed to

---

[172] Buzan and Lawson 2015, 183.
[173] Kolsky 2015, 1224.
[174] Kiernan 1998, 69.
[175] Cooper 2005, 37.
[176] Barua 2005, 128–129.
[177] Kolsky 2015, 1224.
[178] Kolsky 2015, 1223.
[179] Kolsky 2015, 1225.

"discipline" the local populations: for instance, the British forces and their local auxiliaries occasionally burned the corpses of their deceased opponents for public display, a practice intended to terrorize religious groups that conceived such measures as anathema into submission.[180]

In addition to outright violence, the British in South Asia also drew upon selective co-optation of the locals in order to facilitate territorial expansion and control. Not all that different from the Ottomans, the British aimed to win the "hearts and minds" of the conquered soldiers and peasants by "combining traditional Indian with British administrative systems."[181] The colonial agents supplemented "sticks"—that is, targeted blockades and punitive expeditions—with "carrots" such as construction of roads and opening of army ranks.[182] In relation, the British rule in South Asia established client networks, empowering certain indigenous groups at the expense of others, thereby making effective use of local auxiliaries to pacify the subcontinent.[183] Similar to the Ottomans, the relevant mechanisms also involved what can be referred to as "discriminate tolerance." In such a setting, the colonial agents aimed to exercise organized brutality in a selective fashion, which rewarded the obedient and punished the dissident.[184] Giorgio Agamben's interpretation of the concept of "zones of exception"[185] can also help explain the dichotomy between legal tolerance and organized brutality. In geographies where the indigenous populations acted in line with British interests, colonial agents provided a sense of "order." Geographies where the British faced resistance, in turn, were rendered "exceptional spaces." In these zones of exceptions, the colonial agents and their proxies could engage in numerous aspects of organized brutality and intimidation to pacify "lawless and turbulent" people.[186]

Colonial co-optation was most evident in the armed forces. The British efforts toward territorial expansion and control drew heavily upon indigenous soldiers, who were categorized and selected according to their perceived (martial) "race." In this sense, "Indian regiments were doing most of the work of conquering India" for the British.[187] A relevant form of co-optation involved "political intrigue and bribery."[188] More specifically, when dealing with their opponents, the British (and the East India Company before the imposition of direct rule) not only drew upon its military capabilities but also

---

[180] Kolsky 2015, 1237.
[181] Cooper 2005, 542.
[182] Novak 2011, 749.
[183] Barkawi 2016, 210; Newbury 2000.
[184] Cooper 2004, 268.
[185] Agamben 1998, 2005. Also see Vaughan-Williams 2009.
[186] Kolsky 2015, 1244.
[187] Kiernan 1969, 42; Krieg and Rickli 2019, 20; Kiernan 1998, 51.
[188] Barua 2005, 112.

co-opted the officers and troops of its adversaries (such as the Marathas or the Sikhs) with bribes, or by integrating them to the British ranks.[189]

Indirect means of suppression were also backed by what is often called "lawfare," or "the effort to conquer and control indigenous peoples by coercive use of legal means."[190] More specifically, colonial violence was supplemented with a discriminate legal system that allowed the British to "conquer and control indigenous peoples by the coercive use of legal means."[191] In this context, in "the geo-legal space of colonialism,"[192] violence spoke "through"[193] the colonial laws.

In sum, the British incursions into South Asia were closely associated with colonial and territorial ideas and practices, which are best encapsulated with amorphous territoriality. As will be discussed in more detail in Chapter 7, the rise of nationalism, when combined with the effects of both World War I and World War II, eventually led to the collapse of the British colonial rule, also reshaping the dominant territorial ideas in the subcontinent. In the post–World War II era, monolithic territoriality emerged as the dominant aspirational model in South Asia, just as in many other parts of the world. Again, as will be discussed in Chapter 7, swift and accelerated transitions from amorphous territorial orders (in practice) to monolithic territoriality (as an aspirational model) may potentially lead not only to interstate and intrastate conflict, but also to intracommunal tensions, for two reasons. First, attempts to impose monolithic territoriality in geographies that have long been governed through fluid and flexible demarcation principles and sociospatial heterogeneity can lead to numerous crises, as it was the case for the Ottoman Empire during the late nineteenth and early twentieth centuries. Second, competing factions may all adhere to the primacy of monolithic territoriality as an aspirational model (which is embedded in the ideal of the nation-state), but can also disagree over both the location of the borders and the criteria around which the space-society association should be homogenized. Both conditions existed in most parts of South Asia. Most notably, postcolonial territorial arrangements triggered a series of conventional wars between the newly established Pakistan and India, not to mention intracommunal violence. In this sense, how the British expanded into and ruled in South Asia, that is, by manipulating the existing amorphous territorial orders to its advantage, has had long-term and substantial impacts on the trajectory of territorial disputes and conflicts in the subcontinent.

[189] Barua 2005, 113, 119.
[190] Comaroff 2001, 306.
[191] Mahmud 2010, 16.
[192] Mahmud 2010.
[193] Newman 2004, 577.

Conclusion

From a world-historical perspective, amorphous territorial orders have been more of the norm than the exception. Countless polities adhered to flexible, fluid, and porous demarcation principles while also conceiving the space-society nexus in heterogeneous terms. How the relevant states and societies defined their relationship to territory and territoriality, in turn, has had an impact on how said states and societies approached the relationship between organized violence and territorial expansion and control. More specifically, amorphous territoriality is usually associated with an understanding of continuous war and reluctance to homogenize the space-society association in target areas. This chapter aimed to trace the relationship between amorphous territoriality and organized violence in two distinct cases: the early Ottoman Empire and the British experience in South Asia during the nineteenth century.

The analysis suggests that (amorphous) territorial ideas affect, if not determine, the patterns and processes of organized violence in these cases. Not only similarities but also differences between these two cases point to the subtle relationship between territorial ideas and organized violence. Most notably, the Ottomans professed a more robust version of amorphous territoriality than the British did in South Asia. Consequently, reterritorialization efforts in target areas were relatively modest, again, when compared with the British experience. Regardless, as will be explored in more detail in Chapter 7, the ways in which both empires drew upon amorphous territoriality for territorial expansion and governance have had long-term consequences for present-day global-territorial arrangements.

6

Fluid Frontiers and Forever War II

Virulent Territorial Orders

> State boundaries are the product of a deficient human mind. . . . The revolution does not recognize borders and frontiers, it will go through them.
>
> **—Ayatollah Khomeini[1]**

Monolithic territorial order, which is reflected in the nation-state ideal, has been the "ideational hegemon" since the end of World War II.[2] Mosaic territoriality, while it is usually conflated with the monolithic territorial order, is also no stranger to the students of international politics: the so-called Westphalian state before the rise of nationalism was essentially based on this aspirational model. Put differently, existing scholarship does not necessarily differentiate between mosaic and monolithic orders, but, if intuitively, it is familiar with both models. Chapter 5 also established that amorphous territoriality, from a world-historical perspective, has been the norm, not the exception. While mainstream IR does not always deal with the territorial underpinnings of extra-Westphalian polities and systems, certain aspects of amorphous territoriality, especially as it was upheld by historical empires, were recognized by scholars such as John Ruggie, Hendrik Spruyt, Andreas Osiander, and Friedrich Kratochwil.[3]

Virulent territorial orders, by comparison, not only are relatively rare, but also rarely register as a distinct category in IR research and beyond. A common practice is to "normalize" states and state-like entities that adhere to virulent territoriality as overambitious nation-states or empires. For example, sociologist Andreas Wimmer considers Nazi Germany to be an empire with overarching goals.[4] I do not contest similar categorizations. Ergo,

---

[1] Quoted in Buzan and Lawson 2015, 141.
[2] Chapters 2 and 4.
[3] Ruggie 1993; Kratochwil 1986; Spruyt 1994; Osiander 2001.
[4] Wimmer 2012, 27.

Shifting Grounds. Burak Kadercan, Oxford University Press. © Oxford University Press 2023.
DOI: 10.1093/oso/9780197686690.003.0006

the territorial orders framework does not start from "types" of political organizations (nation-states, empires, and the like) and then ascribe different territorial ideas and practices to them. Instead, the intention is to start from a broad analytical framework that establishes different territorial models and then try to "situate" past and present examples with respect to the same framework on a case-by-case basis. Once we move beyond the territorial trap and consider different territorial ideas from a (decidedly simple) two-dimensional framework that scrutinizes demarcation and sociospatial organization principles, virulent orders reveal themselves as a distinct category, with numerous examples in history from Nazi Germany to numerous revolutionary states and state-like entities.

As highlighted in Chapter 3, "virulent" territoriality entails the combination of fluid frontiers with an intention (on the part of state elites) to achieve sociospatial homogeneity. Just as it is the case with amorphous territoriality, states that adhere to virulent orders envision territorial war as a continuous process and aim to expand the spatial extent of their authority not only through conquest and extension of direct sovereignty, but also by creating spheres of influence, satellites, and dependencies. What separates virulent territoriality from amorphous territoriality is the emphasis the former model places on homogenizing societies within and beyond the relevant states' domains, which is closely associated with their incentives to reterritorialize target areas in radical. Accordingly, virulent orders are usually associated with severe and continuous conflict.

The burden of this chapter is to examine the relationship between virulent orders and territorial conflict by building on two paradigmatic cases: revolutionary and Napoleonic France and the group known as the Islamic State, or ISIS. Following the case selection mechanism in the previous chapter, I employ three criteria. The first criterion, again, follows from abduction-oriented case study research: both cases are paradigmatic in their own sense. France can be taken as paradigmatic,[5] since it is the first potent example in modern history where a state decided to remake the entire European (or world) politics in its own image by way of territorial expansion and, arguably, possessed the potential military prowess to do so. Of course, there are other revolutionary states in history, such as Soviet Union, Maoist China, and revolutionary Iran; but, as historian William Sewell highlighted, the French case has been the original template in modern history that inspired the subsequent attempts to remake global (or regional) territorial arrangements.[6] Since my

[5] Hobsbawm 1962, 54.
[6] Sewell 1996. Also see Keitner 2000.

argument is that virulent territoriality is a common, if not universal, feature of universalizing revolutionary states, France offers a unique opportunity to assess this claim's validity.

ISIS, in turn, is a counterintuitive but important case that can help flesh out the relationship between virulent territoriality and armed conflict. It is counterintuitive in the sense that it is usually not accepted as a "real" state, and perhaps there is a risk in attributing "statehood" to an organization that thrived on terrorism and genocide. Note that my intention here is not to attribute statehood to a terrorist organization. Instead, the aim is to widen the scope of our understanding of territory and territoriality by scrutinizing an organization that controlled and governed large swaths of land for years, while also adhering to spatial ideas that are utterly antithetical to the dominant territorial inclinations in present-day world politics. In this sense, ISIS's territorial experiment can potentially reveal insights about the extent to which territorial ideas can vary, even in the present day, and how such ideas may affect organized violence.

The second criterion for case selection involves the origin of the cases: the French case is obviously Western, just as ISIS is a non-Western example. As argued in the previous chapter, juxtaposing Western and non-Western experiences could prevent our succumbing to ethnocentric and essentialist interpretations (such as claiming that virulent territoriality is an exclusively Western or non-Western phenomenon). Third, the cases differ in terms of temporality; an older case is juxtaposed to a newer one. This approach aims to highlight that virulent territoriality is neither an archaic remnant of the past nor a recent invention. Finally, the cases are different from each other vis-à-vis the "robustness" of virulent territoriality. More specifically, ISIS professed a much more extreme version of virulent territoriality than revolutionary and Napoleonic France did. This difference makes it possible to observe the variation in the impacts of virulent territorial ideas on organized violence.

The remainder of this chapter is organized into three main sections. The first section entails a general discussion on virulent territorial orders. Second, I offer an examination of revolutionary and Napoleonic France. The third section, in turn, examines the relationship between ISIS's territorial vision and its efforts for territorial aggrandizement as well as governance.

Virulent Orders

As mentioned above, virulent territorial orders, which are built on an understanding of fluid frontiers and sociospatial homogeneity, have constituted an exception. Overall, when virulent territoriality is dominant in a polity, (state) elites perceive war as a continuous enterprise, and they have incentives to completely reconfigure the existing sociospatial arrangements in target areas in their own image. Territorial expansion, in this context, can be carried out through conventional battles, but, at the same time, it can take the form of gradual incursions. Different from monolithic orders (reflected in the nation-state ideal), and similar to amorphous orders (a hallmark of numerous historical empires), virulent territoriality also makes it easier for state elites to withdraw from occupied areas when faced with formidable military challenges, for a simple reason: state elites' political prospects are not necessarily tied to the preservation of the integrity of the state space for its own sake. Compared with amorphous orders, state elites may find it easier to motivate the masses for war efforts, as they are guided and fueled by an overarching and universalizing (or totalizing) ideology.

Some universalizing empires—an example, arguably, is the Holy Roman Empire during parts of its reign—professed virulent territoriality in the past and aimed to unify sociospatial arrangements, most commonly, in terms of religion. An extreme version of virulent territorial order, more specifically, was adopted by Nazi Germany, which aimed to expand indefinitely in Europe and Eurasia while also "purifying" the lands under its rule in racial terms. As Michael Geyer put it, "Hitler's power depended on the terrorist cleansing of the body politic at home, annihilation, and on the production of space abroad, war of conquest."[7] According to political geographer Guntram Herb, the concept of Lebensraum, which lay at the heart of German geopolitik, was in fact an argument for limitless, or unbounded, expansion.[8] Hitler, in particular, denounced numerous Westphalian principles, including sovereignty and nonintervention,[9] suggesting that he intended not merely to create a large Germany that would exist in a regional system of Westphalian states (or nation-states), but to break the entire system and its territorial underpinnings, at least in Europe and Eurasia.

The territorial orders framework suggests that, in the modern era, universalizing revolutionary states—at least in their early days—also profess virulent territorial orders.[10] To students of revolutions, this should hardly come as a surprise. A revolution can be defined as a "collective mobilization that attempts to quickly and forcibly overthrow an existing regime in order

---

[7] Geyer 1992, 101.

[8] Herb 2002.

[9] Holsti 2016, 47.

[10] On different interpretations of revolutionary movements and states, see Malešević 2017a, chap. 6; Lawson 2019.

to transform political, economic, and symbolic relations."[11] As Buzan and Lawson highlight, "Revolutions [symbolize] the march of progress, standing for irresistible and irreversible change."[12] In addition, many revolutions are universalistic (and universalizing) in their aims. That is, unlike cases such as the American Revolution (which, in fact, did not entail total destruction and reconstruction of the existing social, political, and economic institutions), universalizing revolutions are built on claims to "ultimate" truths, which need to be spread throughout the globe (or a wider region).[13] Such universalizing revolutionary movements are associated with "ideals of universal society and global insurrection."[14] Consequently, revolutionary movements pose a challenge to the existing "ground-rules of international society,"[15] including existing ideas and practices that involve sovereignty, diplomacy, international law, and territorial arrangements. Accordingly, territorial ideas associated with revolutionary movements and states tend to differ from nation-states, prenationalism Westphalian states, or most (if not all) historical empires.

IR scholars, along with historians and sociologists, have long studied the causes and consequences of revolutions.[16] However, the same scholars rarely scrutinize the territorial visions of revolutionary states. Arguably, this trend has an easily understandable explanation: historically speaking, revolutionary states have not remained truly revolutionary for a long time. Put differently, the revolutionary states or state-like entities in modern history have either been stripped of their revolutionary zeal by their adversaries through use of force, or compelled by international pressures to adapt to the Westphalian territorial arrangement of fixed borders.[17] Even without external intervention or pressures, revolutionary leaders who eventually assume power may realize the gap between their utopian ideals and the difficulties of actually running a state and may be forced to give up their initial revolutionary and universalizing aims.[18] Regardless, universalizing revolutionary states or regimes in the modern era have intended to either eradicate the Westphalian order or establish a sphere of influence where the Westphalian understanding of sovereignty no longer applies.[19] As IR scholar Kalevi Holsti put it, Napoleon assaulted the very fabric of the Westphalian system, and the "Bolshevik leaders were

---

[11] Lawson 2019, loc. 244.
[12] Buzan and Lawson 2015, 141.
[13] Lawson 2019, loc. 964.
[14] Lawson 2019, loc. 980.
[15] Lawson 2019, loc. 980.
[16] For an overview, see Lawson 2019.
[17] Calvert 1984.
[18] Buzan and Lawson 2015, 146.
[19] Arguably, the Soviet Union's approach to East Europe during the Cold War can be taken as an example of the latter.

dreaming of world revolution and the total destruction of the Westphalian system."[20]

Put differently, revolutionary states such as revolutionary France, the early Soviet Union, or Maoist China might eventually end up working with the existing Westphalian borders for pragmatic reasons, but their early geopolitical visions considered them to be temporary obstacles that needed to be demolished, suggesting that their ideal demarcation principle was built on fluidity, not rigidity. In sum, most revolutionary states initially aim to expand indefinitely and intend to homogenize the societies not only within but also beyond their domains, usually in ideological terms. Accordingly, (Westphalian) borders are seen as a temporary nuisance to be eventually destroyed, and the state elites' aim is to transform the sociospatial arrangements within and beyond their domains to impose territorial uniformity. In the next two sections, I examine the relationship between virulent orders and armed conflict in two cases: revolutionary/Napoleonic France and ISIS.

Revolutionary and Napoleonic France

Revolutionary and Napoleonic France is no stranger to the students of social sciences. In particular, sociologists, IR scholars, and diplomatic as well as military historians have long examined the causes, conduct, and consequences of the Revolutionary and Napoleonic Wars extensively.[21] While "benchmarks in IR" has recently become a contested issue in the literature,[22] the French Revolution remains one of the two foundational reference points in IR, second only to the Peace of Westphalia. The impacts of the French Revolution on international politics are usually examined in terms of the ideological transformation it triggered, or the notion of nationalism with which it is usually associated.[23]

Despite their interest in this episode, IR scholars have rarely fully engaged the territorial transformation triggered by the Revolution in ways that go beyond the location of the borders, and the elimination of numerous states and state-like entities. Until the French Revolution, the dominant territorial conceptions and practices in France were built on the conventional

---

[20] Holsti 2016, 46.

[21] Some prominent examples are Walt 1996; Halliday 1999; Schroeder 1994; Blanning 1986; Schulze 1991; Feher 1990; Best 1982; Blanning 1996; Hunt 1984; Doyle 1988; and Stone 2002. Also see Skocpol 1979, especially 51–67. On Skocpol's treatment of the Revolution, see Sewell 1985 and Skocpol 1985.

[22] Buzan and Lawson 2015.

[23] Herz 1957; Huntington 1993; Fukuyama 1992.

prenationalism Westphalian state: fixed borders and a heterogeneous approach to space-society relationship. The space-society association in France was representative of the monarchies of the day:[24] monarchs were considered to be the principle sovereigns over state territories, and societies over which they ruled did not (or were not necessarily expected to) have a close association with the entirety of the territorial belongings of the state.[25] The organization of the space-society relationship, in this context, entailed multilayered and nonuniform legal, political, and administrative arrangements.[26] In the words of Malcolm Anderson, the events of August 1789 triggered a process that eventually "swept away [spatial] abnormalities" and led to "a radical reorganization of the internal borders."[27] Put differently, the Revolution led to an about-face in the French territorial order, transforming the state's approach to both demarcation and organization of space, with direct implications for French geopolitical objectives and war efforts.

Demarcation and Sociospatial Organization

The rise of the bourgeoisie and the Enlightenment during the course of the eighteenth century, when combined with the popular unrest and financial troubles fueled by wars, set the stage for the French Revolution.[28] The catalyst of the political avalanche that evolved into the French Revolution came with the Bastille incident of July 12. Despite all the mythmaking that followed the incident, the outbreak of the Revolution simply entailed an antimonarchical small-scale uprising where a mob of one thousand or so Parisians took over the Bastille prison that held "four forgers and three madmen" and "no political prisoner."[29] From a tactical point of view, the sole benefit of capturing Bastille for the protestors came from the ammunition that was stored in the bastion. Symbolically, however, the fall of Bastille highlighted the vulnerability of the regime.

The Bastille episode, in this reading, constituted what William Sewell calls a "historical event."[30] According to Sewell, historical events "tend to transform social relations in ways that could not be fully predicted from the gradual changes that may have made them possible" and "reshape historiography,

---

[24] Bukovansky 2009, 68.
[25] Kadercan 2018. Also see Chapter 4.
[26] Especially Sewell 1985. Also see Anderson 1996, 19.
[27] Anderson 1996, 23.
[28] Skocpol 1979, 51–66. Also see Tilly 1993, 163.
[29] Sewell 1996, 849. Also see Kadercan 2012.
[30] Sewell 1996, 843.

imparting an unforeseen direction to social development and altering the nature of the causal nexus in which social interactions take place."[31] From an ideological standpoint, "Republicanism was the original model of popular sovereignty" that followed from the French Revolution.[32] Inspired by ideas about the universalistic equality of men,[33] the thrust of the Revolution entailed a struggle in the name of the people of Europe, for the rights of men, against the kings and other oppressors.[34] The new ideological direction of the French state reflected these cosmopolitan and republican ideals.[35]

Domestically, the revolutionary elites tried to solidify their rule by rewiring the state institutions in the image of the new state ideology.[36] The attempts to establish a new calendar and eradicate the role of religion from political life had a strategic logic behind them: the revolutionaries aimed to uproot the very ideological foundations of the old regime. However, while they were united against the monarchy, the revolutionaries hardly constituted a monolithic group; different factions had different aspirations over the trajectory of the Revolution. In the face of fierce competition against each other, the contending factions ended up reproducing the more radical aspects of the revolutionary philosophy through what Jack Snyder has dubbed (ideological) "outbidding."[37] More specifically, competing political factions tried to improve their credentials in the eyes of the relevant domestic audiences by supporting policies that resemble "truer," or more radical, interpretations of the Revolution.[38] The consequent radicalism, which eventually peaked during the Reign of Terror between June 1793 and July 1794, exerted a significant impact on the conduct of domestic politics of the French state.[39]

The radicalization of the revolutionaries' thinking also affected—in fact, was coconstituted by—the changing ideas about territory and territoriality in general, aspirational principles about demarcation of the state space and sociospatial organization in particular. As highlighted above, the

---

[31] Sewell 1996, 843.

[32] Meadwell 1999, 40. Also see Greenfeld 1992, 10.

[33] One can plausibly argue that the "universality" of the aforementioned ideas was largely limited to the European world, including the settler colonies (North America, Oceania) but probably excluding the rest of the world, colonized or otherwise. In other words, "international society," as the term was construed during the eighteenth and nineteenth centuries, entailed significant Eurocentrism. On this point, see Keene 2002, 60–96.

[34] Hendrik Spruyt (2002, 133), even though he recognizes the power of the democratic principles ignited by the French Revolution, argues that these ideas led to increasing levels of integration and identification of subjects and rulers.

[35] For the republican aspects of the Revolution see Meadwell 1999.

[36] Sewell 1996.

[37] Snyder 1991. For an application of this logic to religion, see Toft 2007.

[38] On this argument, see Kadercan 2012.

[39] On "Terror," see Mayer 2000, 171–225.

Revolution might not have been born radical, but it became quickly radicalized.[40] Rejection of the Westphalian arrangement was an immediate consequence of such radicalization. As historian Janet Polasky highlights, "The revolutionaries and their ideas ignored national borders that figure so prominently on maps and in history books."[41] Such a cosmopolitan and expansionist approach was in fact ingrained in the Declaration of Rights of Man and Citizen on August 26, 1789: the revolutionaries made claims over not only the French but all humanity.[42] In Arno Mayer's words, "From its creation, the French Revolution was at minimum a trans-European event."[43] To summarize, revolutionary France "worked with" the Westphalian borders when necessary, but the geographical conceptions of the state elites pointed toward a much more "fluid" understanding of boundaries, of course, when compared with other European powers.

The transformation that the Revolution triggered regarding the organization of space-society relationship was even more radical. In William Sewell's words, the Revolution "totally redefined the nature of the French state and society."[44] In particular, "The revolutionaries annihilated all legally established corporations and set out to build a new state."[45] The revolutionaries, for example, abolished the multilayered institutional arrangements that regulated domestic territorial control almost overnight, on August 4, 1789,[46] and initiated a process of "radical re-organization of the internal boundaries of the country."[47]

Through extensive "reform of the territorial administration," revolutionary France replaced traditional provinces, which displayed significant divergence from each other, with territorial units called "departments," with the explicit intention of establishing "geographic uniformity" across the country.[48] Such uniformity, in turn, allowed revolutionary France to eliminate the "profound differences of language, law, custom, and belief" within the society, to create "a more homogeneous and unified nation."[49] Put differently, revolutionaries intended to "proselytize and mobilize the masses"[50] and establish a "single

---

[40] For example, Sewell 1985, 71.
[41] Polasky 2015, 8.
[42] Blanning 1986, 77–78; Desan 2013, 86.
[43] Mayer 2000, 544.
[44] Sewell 1990, 538.
[45] Sewell 1990, 538.
[46] Sewell 1985, 62–63, 69, 77.
[47] Anderson 1996, 23.
[48] Sewell 1985.
[49] Nelson 2013, 74. As recognized by scholars such as Barry Posen (1993), the rise of mass armies also contributed to the process. Of course, as Eugene Weber (1976) highlighted, such homogenization efforts took almost a century to reach their ultimate objective.
[50] Skocpol 1979, 170.

homogeneous [territory]."[51] Note that Napoleon also accelerated the relevant processes, most notably with the introduction of "Code Napoleon," a unified legal system to be exercised throughout the entire French territory, and later across Europe.[52]

Overall, the revolutionary territorial ideas conceived demarcation of the state space in terms of fluid frontiers. Also, the revolutionaries considered a modicum of sociospatial homogenization to be the ultimate goal, both within and beyond the existing borders. A disclaimer is in order. My claim is not that revolutionary and Napoleonic France adhered to an extreme version of virulent territoriality, as, for example, Nazi Germany or ISIS did. Instead, the claim is that, *when compared with prerevolutionary France as well as France's European contemporaries*, revolutionary and Napoleonic France's territorial vision is better defined in terms of virulent orders than mosaic (or monolithic) territoriality. In the next subsection, I briefly examine the relationship between territorial ideas and war.

Territorial Ideas and War

The virulent territorial ideas associated with the Revolution eventually paved the way for all-out warfare in Europe. The severity and ubiquity of interstate war during the Revolutionary and Napoleonic Wars have long been established by contemporaries like Clausewitz, military historians, and IR scholars.[53] For instance, according to Jack Levy's study on great power wars, the Revolutionary and Napoleonic Wars stand out in terms of severity; with 2.5 million battle deaths, these wars are even more severe than the Thirty Years' War, for which Levy lists around 2 million.[54] In terms of ubiquity or frequency of interstate war, the Revolutionary and Napoleonic Wars, even if we exclude the smaller conflicts, witnessed nine wars, that is, seven coalitional wars, the Peninsular War (1807–14), and the French invasion of Russia in 1812; between 1792 and 1815, there was not a single year of peace in Europe.

As IR scholar Stephen Walt has noted, the revolutions create an extremely volatile threat environment among competing factions by leading to a mutually shared sense of uncertainty about each other's intentions, which may spiral into crises and even war.[55] One relevant concept from IR theory is

[51] Hobsbawm 1962, 55.
[52] Mayer 2000, 540–541. However, the Declaration of the Rights of Man and of the Citizen was "incomplete," as it did not apply to natives and slaves living in French colonies (Malešević 2017a, loc. 5129).
[53] For example, Cederman et al. 2011.
[54] Levy 1983, 88–91.
[55] Walt 1996.

150   How Territorial Ideas Affect Wars

"security dilemma."[56] Security dilemmas emerge when competing states find it difficult to both assure others of their (benign) intentions and alleviate their own concerns about their competitors' intentions. Under such circumstances, even if all relevant states may initially be concerned primarily with their own security, defensive or precautionary measures taken by one actor can be perceived as preparations for aggression by another (and, vice versa), fueling a spiral of mutual mistrust and enmity. Since revolutionary states usually indulge themselves in inflammatory rhetoric, it becomes more difficult for the relevant states to prevent the spiral from leading to open conflict. Furthermore, counterrevolutionary states may perceive a structural weakness in their revolutionary opponents (since revolutions usually come with domestic turmoil and ambiguity), creating incentives for launching preventive wars.[57] Arguably, both of these conditions—security dilemma fueled by aggressive rhetoric and incentives for preventive war on behalf of the counterrevolutionary states—apply to the case of the Revolutionary Wars.

In this context, the geopolitical vision of the revolutionaries, which—if mostly at the discursive level—aimed to destroy the existing borders and remake all of Europe in their own image led to "a Manichean ideological environment where war had to be won regardless of the number of dead."[58] Revolutionary thinking drew upon the belief the revolutionaries had access to a "universal and singular truth," which should serve as a "blueprint of an ideal social order."[59] The (aspirational) spatial reach of this ideal social order, in turn, was not limited to the borders of France and, if necessary, could be expanded through the use of force. This line of thinking was best reflected in a speech delivered by Jacques Pierre Brissot, a parliamentary deputy of the French Republic, in the Convention in November 1792: "[We] cannot be calm until Europe, all Europe, is in flames."[60] As Hobsbawm identified, revolutionary France waged a war of unlimited aims, and for revolutionaries, war "oscillated between the maximum victory of world revolution" and the "maximum defeat," which meant military catastrophe and regime change in France.[61]

Therefore, even before Napoleon rose to power, the revolutionaries professed "unabated" expansionism.[62] A question that needs to be addressed at this juncture is the following: Did the French rulers profess a modicum of

---

[56] On security dilemma, see Jervis 1978.
[57] Walt 1996.
[58] Malešević 2010, 132. Also see Howard 1976, 81.
[59] Malešević 2010, 132.
[60] Quoted in Sheridan 1994, 465.
[61] Hobsbawm 1962, 66.
[62] Blanning 1986, 176; Bukovansky 2009, 194; Stirk 2016: 51; Mayer 2000, 557.

instrumental rationality in combining their actual and potential military capabilities with their revolutionary territorial conceptions? While scholars such as Paul Schroeder claim that France never stood a chance of dominating Europe,[63] there is also reason to think that French leaders were not being entirely irrational when defining the geographical scope and nature of their territorial objectives. France was the most powerful land power of its time and the cultural epicenter of Europe. Besides, its leaders could draw on particular ideologies such as antimonarchical republicanism and/or nationalism to mobilize the masses for their war efforts and co-opt societies in their target areas. That Napoleon came close to categorically transforming the Westphalian system is a testimony of such potential military and political might.

In addition, revolutionaries, acting on "Revolutionary Messianism," also sought to export revolutionary ideas to other countries through unconventional means such as interfering with the domestic politics of their rivals, not only across the continent, but even in the British Isles.[64] The revolutionaries, especially in the first couple of years following 1789, had good reason to believe that their ideology's appeal might be far-reaching. Especially in the Low Countries, the Rhineland, Switzerland, Savoy, Italy, Ireland, and Poland, there existed numerous social groups who displayed initial sympathy for the developments in France.[65] One example of the Revolution's initial popularity among European intelligentsia can be found in the reaction of Johann Gottlieb Fichte to the developments in France. Most notably, Fichte is known as the orator of the German call to arms of 1807, usually credited with being one of the intellectual founding fathers of modern German nationalism. In his address to the German nation in 1807, which followed the Prussian defeat at the hands of Napoleon in Jena the previous year, Fichte likened the revolutionary French to the Romans of the first millennium and asked Germans to stand up against the values and ideas that contradicted their nationhood just as their ancestors had done more than a millennium ago vis-à-vis the Roman culture.[66] When the Revolution came in 1789, however, Fichte, just like many European intellectuals of his time, had openly welcomed and championed the cosmopolitan and universalistic underpinnings of the transformation in French political life, and even promoted the spread of the ideals that emanated from the Revolution. The Revolution's appeal across Europe was not limited to intellectuals or economic elites. Revolutionary ideas and practices also promised hope to the discontented masses in Europe, who might have

---

[63] Schroeder 1994.
[64] On this point, see Blanning 1986, 159; Polasky 2015, 249–259; Desan 2013, 88.
[65] Hobsbawm 1962, 79.
[66] Moore 2009.

152 How Territorial Ideas Affect Wars

found the new French regime's antiaristocratic policies—especially those that involved land reforms—rather attractive.[67]

Revolutionary France's approach to demarcation and organization of space influenced its military and political strategies in two ways: it helped frame (revolutionary) war as a continuous process and created incentives for the French to homogenize space-society relationship in target areas. That (elites in) revolutionary/Napoleonic France saw war as a continuous undertaking requires little elaboration. Driven by both fear of forceful regime change and an ever-expansionist ambition, France fought numerous conventional wars with its enemies between 1792 and 1815. According to Arno Mayer, "The consolidation of the Revolution at home and its export by means of endless foreign war were closely connected."[68]

Note that while virulent territoriality prompted a geopolitical vision that aimed to expand continuously and remake the sociospatial arrangements elsewhere in Europe, it also had implications for conflict from within France.[69] Most notably, encouraged and supported by clerical and promonarchical elements within and beyond France, the peasantry in Vendee and Brittany resisted the central government's reterritorialization efforts. The revolutionaries responded harshly, eventually leading to the deaths of around 160,000 out of 800,000 inhabitants of these two regions.[70] This response, justified in "strictly universalist terms," could be seen as an act to cleanse (or homogenize) the revolutionary state space.[71]

The dominant discourses concerning the foreign affairs of the new French regime, in turn, dictated that the Revolution was not a local but a universal one. Therefore, for the Revolution to succeed, it should be spread across Europe.[72] In Onuf's words, "The revolutionaries' universalistic pretensions were manifest in their determination to liberate the benighted peoples of Europe and to wage total war against a reactionary 'Conspiracy of Kings.' "[73] In the face of revolutionary outbidding, even pragmatists who might have preferred to keep the Revolution "local," that is, within the borders of the French state, were compelled to commit to the idea that the French state should be the vessel of a universal revolution. The radicalization of domestic and foreign politics by 1792 rendered the French state the epicenter of antimonarchical political sentiments in Europe.

---

[67] For example, see Keegan 1994, 352.
[68] Mayer 2000, 541.
[69] Hibbert 1980, 107–162; Schama 1990, 616–638; Doyle 1988, 174–196.
[70] Malešević 2010, 132.
[71] Malešević 2010.
[72] Schama 1990, 616–638.
[73] Onuf 2004, 174.

The revolutionary rhetoric eventually evolved into unabated expansionism, leading many to frame the Revolution as "a crusade for universal liberty."[74] The Edict of Fraternity, issued in November 1792, made it clear that the French state aimed to "export the French Revolution" with the promise of fraternity and help to all peoples who wish to recover their liberty.[75] The mix of cosmopolitanism, antimonarchical sentiments, and revolutionary zeal eventually primed revolutionary France to reject the existing territorial arrangements in Europe, including the "fixity" of the existing borders.[76] The revolutionary doctrine "denied the legitimacy of all states not founded upon the compact the revolutionaries believed had constituted their own nation"[77] and defied "the whole system of [monarchical] geopolitics."[78] In particular, revolutionary France denounced the very treaties—or "the entire system of international law as understood by the governments of the day"[79]—that established the Westphalian borders. Put simply, the foreign policy of revolutionary France, especially from 1793 onward, "pushed far beyond the prudent limits of the *Ancien Regime*."[80]

Revolutionary France also aimed to reterritorialize its targets in radical terms through an extensive sociospatial homogenization campaign. The geographies that fell under direct or indirect French rule went through significant social, political, and economic transformation.[81] Through their conquests, the French armies "not only brought bayonets, but also law codes" that regulated property ownership, monarchical rights to territorial control and governance, and administrative reforms.[82] Such efforts aimed to transform the European territories in the image of the Revolution: "The revolutionary idea of self-determination for other nations," for example, "demanded political organization in accordance with a French administrative model."[83] Overall, "The set of reforms the French imposed in the territories that they conquered were extensive and radical."[84]

As highlighted above, the French elites aimed to export the revolution through the use of arms. In the last decade of the eighteenth century alone,

---

[74] Daly 2016, 18.

[75] Malešević 2017a, loc. 3110.

[76] The notion of "natural frontiers" had a place in the French courts, but its usage was fluid and depended largely on the context, achieving its present-day meaning only by the mid-nineteenth century. On this point, see Sahlins 1990.

[77] Stirk 2016, 54. Also see Walt 1996, 56.

[78] Desan 2013, 88.

[79] Stirk 2016, 40; also Blanning 1986, 75; Mayer 2000, 571.

[80] Mowat 1924, 105.

[81] Broers 2014, 60.

[82] Daly 2016, 20.

[83] Keitner 2000, 20.

[84] Acemoglu et al. 2011, 3286.

the Republic was able to mobilize at least 2,080,000 men.[85] The War of the First Coalition lasted until 1797. That Britain had joined the fight after the execution of Louis XVI in early 1793 also turned the confrontation into a global one. When the war was finally over between France and Austria, the French armies now controlled Belgium, a substantial chunk of Italy, and the Rhineland. Despite the costs incurred by all parties during the War of the First Coalition, the peace between France and the old regime was short-lived. The incessant sense of insecurity and distrust between the revolutionary elites (who were convinced that the Habsburgs would lead the way in another attempt at rolling back the revolution) and the monarchs of the old regime (who were particularly concerned with the French attempts at creating satellite republics all around Europe, such as the Parthenopean Republic in Naples and the Helvetic Republic in Switzerland) led to the War of the Second Coalition in 1798.

The War of the Second Coalition eventually established a strategic stalemate in Europe. Both the monarchies of Europe and the revolutionary regime were unable to subdue or overthrow the other side. While the new regime established following the Revolution survived the reactionary onslaught launched by the monarchies of Europe, it failed to convert the rest of Europe into a collection of pro-France republics. Furthermore, the French regime's revolutionary zeal paradoxically fueled anti-French sentiments in most parts of Europe, especially in the vicinity of France, where most of the fighting took place. Reluctant to impose additional taxes on the already aggravated French populace, the revolutionary elites chose to pay for the Revolutionary Wars by the age-old method of "living off the land," a method employed cunningly by many European princes from Gustavus Adolphus to Frederick the Great. Adopting this method, the French army extracted the resources necessary for the campaigns from the territories that lay outside the (traditional) borders of France and, occasionally, the French army embarked on campaigns simply to pay for the expenses of the army.[86] The self-entitled "liberators" started to be perceived not as liberators but as malign conquerors doing the bidding of the expansionist French revolutionary elites, if not that of an expansionist king.[87] Therein lay the radical shift: the expansionist kings of the past refrained from radical reterritorialization efforts; the revolutionaries aimed to reterritorialize the target areas, which created a societal backlash and enmity.

[85] Clodfelter 2002, 119.
[86] Mearsheimer 2001, 281.
[87] Luard 1987, 57.

The trajectory of the competition between France and its rivals entered a new phase with Napoleon Bonaparte's ascension to power in 1799. Whether Napoleon should be considered as a revolutionary or an imperialist is open to discussion. On the one hand, scholars such as Martyn Lyons argue that Napoleon was "the heir and executor of the French Revolution, not its gravedigger or liquidator."[88] On the other hand, it can easily be argued that Napoleon was not a revolutionary, and that he merely appropriated the early revolutionaries' achievements and momentum in order to create a personalistic empire. From the lenses of the territorial orders framework, whether Napoleon is labeled as a revolutionary or aspiring emperor (in the traditional sense) matters little; Napoleon built on virulent territoriality professed by the revolutionaries, and his reign entailed a penchant for continuous expansion and sociospatial homogenization efforts within and beyond France.

However, it would be misleading to argue that Napoleon aimed to establish a "greater France," for instance, as Louis XIV aspired to do. Arguably, Napoleon's geopolitical vision was more cosmopolitan than nationalistic.[89] According to Connelly, Napoleon's long-term plans involved creating a multinational and multilingual European (as opposed to "French") state; in this reading, for Napoleon, the French Empire was only the first step toward a unified Europe.[90] Examining Napoleon's rule of the satellite kingdoms in great detail, Connelly reaches the following conclusion: "The history of the satellite kingdom confirms that Napoleon progressively centralized control of his empire until he seemed bent on founding a European government in which national states had no part."[91] In this sense, just as Napoleon strove to impose uniformity within the European landscape, the struggle against him was one of "diversity against standardization, of tradition against innovation."[92] Put differently, it is merely semantics whether Napoleon was the heir of the Revolution, or merely an opportunist who drew upon the societal and political energies released by it in order to create his personalistic empire. From a territorial point of view, his geopolitical vision is best encapsulated with virulent territoriality.

That Napoleon was also the harbinger of near-continuous (conventional) war in Europe requires little elaboration: during his reign, he was "at war with at least one power for all but fourteen months."[93] In addition to territorial

---

[88] Lyons 1994, 2. Broers (2014, 125) also refers to Napoleon as the "direct heir" of the Revolution.
[89] Broers 2014, 269.
[90] Connelly 1965, 339.
[91] Connelly 1965, 333.
[92] Broers 2014, 270.
[93] Holtman 1950, xii.

156 How Territorial Ideas Affect Wars

expansion, Napoleon not only adhered to but also accelerated the homogenizing principles associated with the territorial conceptions of the Revolution, which, again, aimed at destroying the traditional Westphalian order. Not only did Napoleon create numerous "sister republics" across Europe that defied both demarcation and organization principles of the "old" Westphalian territorial order, he also eliminated "territorial abnormalities" that survived the original Westphalian arrangement. For example, the Holy Roman Empire was abolished in 1806, along with ecclesiastical territories, free imperial cities, and about 112 small German states, reducing the number of territorial entities in Europe from roughly 300 to fewer than 40.[94] Feudalism was also virtually eradicated in the lands that Napoleon ruled over or subjugated.[95]

Remarkably few European geographies were spared from Napoleon's reterritorialization efforts. Napoleon took over, directly or indirectly, Bavaria in 1800, Tuscany in 1801, the Cisalpine Republic (later, the Kingdom of Italy) and Helvetic Republic in 1803, northwest Germany (restructured as the Duchy of Berg) in 1804, Naples, Lucca, and the Batavian Republic (renamed Kingdom of Holland) in 1805, Neuchatel, Baden, Württemberg, and Nassau in 1806.[96] Napoleon's reterritorialization efforts escalated following the twin treaties of Tilsit, signed between France and Russia in 1807. Having pacified its final continental rival, Napoleon strove for "the ruthless reordering of the European mainland."[97] In 1807, Napoleon established parts of Germany as the Kingdom of Westphalia, and substantial chunks of Poland as the Grand Duchy of Warsaw. Some of these satellite entities were then directly subsumed into direct French rule; most notably, in 1810, Napoleon annexed the Kingdom of Holland, which was reorganized into nine French departments.[98]

With the exception of the Grand Duchy of Warsaw, "Napoleon imposed various of his institutions"[99] in all the provinces that fell under France's direct or indirect rule.[100] In fact, Napoleon did not hesitate to initiate reforms in newly conquered or subjugated territories, even before the actual fighting had ended.[101] As Hobsbawm highlighted, in geographies annexed or subjugated, "The institutions of the French Revolution and the Napoleonic Empire were automatically applied, or were the obvious models for local administration."[102] When they attempted to reterritorialize the rest of Europe, neither

[94] Acemoglu et al. 2011, 3289; Daly 2016, 20; Mowat 1924, 111.
[95] Hobsbawm 1962, 90.
[96] Owen 2010, 142.
[97] Broers 2014, 46.
[98] Broers 2014, 202.
[99] Owen 2010, 143.
[100] Broers 2014, 93.
[101] Broers 2014, 35.
[102] Hobsbawm 1962, 90.

Napoleon nor his predecessors questioned whether the ideas and practices they were trying to inject in the newly conquered or subjugated geographies were "desired" by the local populations.[103] Instead, Napoleon, following his predecessors, aimed to establish "uniformity" in law, bureaucracy, and even education, without the consent of local populations.

That Napoleon tried to create a "uniform body of law"[104] across Europe with the establishment of the Napoleonic Code requires little elaboration. In addition to attempts to impose legal homogeneity, Napoleon also rationalized tax systems and seized lands that belonged to the church. In the areas that fell under French rule or influence, Napoleon made sure to appoint French officials to key judicial and administrative posts to oversee the establishment of territorial uniformity.[105] As highlighted above, Napoleon's long-term plans for Europe entailed a pan-European vision. Accordingly, Napoleonic France attempted to co-opt or enlist members of the European intelligentsia and bureaucracy as well as politics.[106] Note that the Napoleonic vision of a unified Europe had supporters in satellite kingdoms and beyond. According to Connelly, there were many non-French bureaucrats and politicians in the newly subjugated geographies who "suppressed their sense of nationality to labor for . . . [the] Europe" that Napoleon envisaged and "saw themselves as functionaries of a European government, at home anywhere in Europe."[107] In this sense, Napoleon's efforts at reterritorialization also relied heavily on selective co-optation of the local power brokers, or bureaucrats, whom Hobsbawm defines as "[auxiliaries] to French conquest."[108]

Napoleon's sociospatial homogenization efforts did not remain limited to substantial reforms in legal, bureaucratic, administrative, and financial domains, but also extended to education. For example, in the newly created Grand Duchy of Warsaw, the French "extended and completely revised the system of government control of education."[109] Similarly, Murat, acting as Napoleon's chief agent in Naples, decreed a system of education that was almost entirely built on the French model. In the Italian Republic (later the Kingdom of Italy), Napoleon also took measures to impose a French-style public education system, which eventually contributed to the "moral unification of the country."[110]

---

[103] Broers 2014, 263.
[104] Broers 2014, 53.
[105] Broers 2014, 78.
[106] Broers 2014, 264.
[107] Connelly 1965, 338.
[108] Hobsbawm 1962, 81.
[109] Holtman 1950, 133.
[110] Holtman 1950, 133.

158 How Territorial Ideas Affect Wars

In sum, the revolutionary territorial conceptions played a significant role in driving French ambitions to expand indefinitely while also reorganizing the space-society relationship in target areas in radical terms. Napoleon was eventually defeated, first in 1814 and finally in 1815. Napoleon's defeat, in turn, marked the end of virulent territoriality in France and beyond. The victorious great powers restored the French monarchy and the prerevolutionary French borders, with only minor changes. The so-called Vienna system aimed to prevent the resurgence of virulent territoriality and revolutionary movements in Europe, and the great powers of the time were, at least initially, not sympathetic to nationalism and its territorial extension, monolithic territoriality.[111] In so many ways, the victorious great powers wanted to reestablish mosaic territoriality as the aspirational gold standard in Europe.

Ironically, as will be discussed in Chapter 7, the Revolutionary and Napoleonic Wars rendered mosaic territoriality more of a reality, rather than merely an aspirational ideal that did not apply to many geographies in Europe. These wars eradicated the territorial abnormalities embedded within the early (pre-Revolution) Westphalian system, paving the way for "a general rationalization of the European political map," which "in terms of political geography," also meant the end of the "European middle ages."[112] However, again, as will be discussed in Chapter 7, while the Revolutionary and Napoleonic Wars made mosaic territoriality more of an achievable goal in Europe, they also paradoxically triggered a process where nationalism, and monolithic territoriality, would emerge as the ideational hegemon in the coming centuries.

Islamic State

The group known as the Islamic State (ISIS) is usually seen as an anomaly in the modern state system.[113] While essentially (or originally) a terrorist organization with a radical and ultraviolent ideology, ISIS also controlled and governed large swaths of territory in Iraq and Syria, and made claims to statehood.[114] That being said, the claim that the broader ISIS conflict was in fact exceptionally severe and violent requires some elaboration, for a simple reason: while the group wreaked political and social havoc in Iraq and Syria,

---

[111] See Chapters 4 and 7.

[112] Hobsbawm 1962, 88.

[113] On ISIS, see Cockburn 2015; Warrick 2015; Stern and Berger 2015; McCants 2015; Byman 2015; Weiss and Hassan 2015; Fishman 2016; Wood 2016; Fawaz 2016; Al-Tamimi 2014; Fromson and Simon 2015.

[114] ISIS never made claims about Westphalian-style statehood; in fact, ISIS branded itself as a state that directly challenged the so-called modern state system and its underpinnings.

the magnitude of the violence ISIS caused still pales in comparison with some of the interstate wars in the region such as the Iran-Iraq War (1980–88), which resulted in around half a million battlefield deaths and one hundred thousand civilian losses.[115]

The key factor that renders ISIS an exceptionally violent (territorial) actor is "scale," which reveals itself best through a comparison. For instance, the Iran-Iraq War entailed two sizable nation-states (with a combined population of or more than fifty million) that fully mobilized their resources for war efforts. During this almost decade-long conventional war, Iran and Iraq consistently fielded military forces that at times exceeded half a million soldiers in total. Of course, modern warfare is about more than just the size of the armies, it is also about the quality and quantity of the relevant military hardware. Even at the outset of the conflict in 1980, that is, before the war itself escalated the arms race between Iran and Iraq, the two countries collectively possessed more than four thousand tanks, almost two thousand artillery pieces, and around four hundred combat aircraft.[116] As energy-abundant powers, both Iran and Iraq could spend a substantial amount of money to sustain their war efforts; in 1984 alone, for example, the total defense spending of the two countries exceeded $27 billion.[117]

By contrast, the overall scale of the ISIS conflict, defined in terms of the size of the military/paramilitary forces in the theater, the associated military hardware, not to mention the financial resources involved, was much smaller. However, given this relatively minuscule "scale," ISIS still caused considerable destruction and violence in Iraq and Syria. Most notably, even at its peak, ISIS is believed to have fielded a maximum of thirty thousand fighters at any given time, though the actual number fluctuated greatly.[118] It is true that ISIS captured some tanks from the Iraqi army, but it did not have the means and capability to operate them for long; the group never had an air force of its own. As far as finances were concerned, again, even at its very peak, ISIS could raise a maximum of $2 billion in annual revenues, only a portion of which was spent on war efforts.[119] Still, ISIS was able to do a lot of damage

---

[115] I would like to thank an anonymous reviewer for highlighting this comparison, which allowed me to clarify my position. Note that the actual numbers, in terms of battlefield and civilian deaths, are open to debate. For example, the Correlates of War (COW) project points toward a total of 1,250,000 dead. The Battle Deaths Dataset, compiled by Bethany Lacina and Nils Petter Gleditsch (2005), puts the number at around 600,000. If Iranian and Iraqi officials' statistics are to be believed, the sum is slightly more than 400,000. According to sociologist Charles Kurzman (2013), who traced the relevant censuses in both countries as well as demographic trends across time, the actual number might be even lower.

[116] Talmadge 2013, 193, 217.

[117] Talmadge 2013, 217.

[118] Beccaro 2018, 210.

[119] Cengiz et al. 2022, 27. In order to sustain its claims to statehood, ISIS had to provide a wide variety of public goods and services in the territories it governed.

with so little. In a matter of less than five years, ISIS directly killed at least thirty thousand civilians, although some estimates are considerably higher (and include deaths indirectly caused by ISIS). The group also launched genocidal campaigns against minorities such as Yazidis, while also triggering forced population transfers on a massive scale, affecting the lives of hundreds of thousands in drastic ways. ISIS's methods were also exceptionally brutal; in addition to institutionalizing practices such as slavery, the group also carried out more than seven hundred recorded beheadings between 2014 and 2020.[120]

Furthermore, of the estimated 75,000 fighters that ISIS was able to assemble between 2014 and 2019, the majority were killed in action, roughly around forty to forty-five thousand, though some estimates put the number as high as seventy thousand.[121] Few if any polities in modern history witnessed such an overwhelming KIA (Killed in Action) ratio. In addition, the local forces in Syria and Iraq who fought ISIS also suffered considerable losses. For example, the Kurdish militia in Syria, known as the YPG (People's Protection Units), suffered at least eleven thousand battlefield deaths,[122] not to mention more than twenty thousand wounded. At its face value, this number may look rather low when compared to the Iraqi and Iranian battlefield deaths. However, given that there are about two million Kurds in Syria, eleven thousand deaths amount to more than 0.5% of the total Kurdish population in the country. Adjusted for population size, a similar ratio for the United States would imply 1.8 million lives lost. In sum, if we only look at the numbers, the havoc ISIS unleashed in Iraq and Syria pales in comparison to the Iran-Iraq War. Once the "scale" is taken into consideration, ISIS reveals itself to be an exceptionally violent territorial entity.

Broadly speaking, ISIS emerged as the global public enemy number one after it took over Iraq's second biggest city, Mosul, in the summer of 2014. The origins of the group can be traced to Jama'at at-Tawhid wa Jihad (the Monotheism and Jihad Group), led by Abu Musab al-Zarqawi. Most notably, Zarqawi and his group, originally established in Afghanistan, relocated to Iraq after the US military response to the September 11 attacks. Jama'at at-Tawhid wa Jihad carried out numerous terrorist attacks in Iraq after the US invasion in 2003, and eventually pledged allegiance to Osama bin Ladin and al-Qaeda in late 2004, adopting the name Al Qaeda in Iraq (AQI).[123] However, the

---

[120] Cengiz et al. 2022, 26.
[121] Woody 2017.
[122] Cockburn 2020, 280.
[123] Note that while the group is usually defined terms of "nation-states" such as Iraq or Iraq and Syria in the West, this does not represent how similar groups define themselves in geographical terms. For example, AQI did not use "Iraq" in its title, but instead referred to the broader geographical category of "Mesopotamia."

relationship between al-Qaeda's leadership and AQI was troubled from the beginning. While al-Qaeda refrained from excessive victimization of fellow Muslims and premature attempts at establishing a state (caliphate), AQI disagreed on both accounts and "sought to subsume Iraq into a global and cosmic battle."[124]

Until he was killed in a US airstrike in 2006, Zarqawi carried out numerous attacks to fuel the sectarian divide in Iraq and experimented with territorial control in locations such as Fallujah, aiming to impose Sharia law in areas held by AQI, if briefly. After Zarqawi's death, AQI (which adopted the name Islamic State in Iraq, ISI) suffered a major setback due to two emerging dynamics. First, the United States launched what is usually referred to as the "Surge," increasing the number of troops on the ground as well as the "tempo" of anti-AQI operations.[125] Second, in coordination with the United States, the Iraqi government was able to co-opt numerous Sunni tribes who were growing disgruntled with the radical ways of AQI. Sometimes referred to as the "Sons of Iraq," these tribes turned against AQI/ISI, a development that was branded as "The Awakening" (*Sahwa*). By 2010, AQI/ISI was assumed to have been effectively marginalized in Iraq, if not ultimately defeated.

ISI was able to regroup and reorganize under the leadership of Abu Bakr al-Baghdadi, thanks to three factors. First, the Iraqi government, dominated mostly by Shia, did not fulfill the promises it made to the Sunni tribes that had fought against AQI/ISI in the first place, setting the stage for the resurgence of sectarian tensions. Second, the United States began its withdrawal in 2009, and moved its military personnel from Iraq (other than advisers) as of 2011. Third, the outbreak of civil war in Syria around 2011 allowed ISI to branch out there and exploit the sectarian tensions in not one but two countries. The gradual rise of AQI/ISI in Iraq and Syria culminated in the conquest of Mosul in 2014. Immediately afterward, Baghdadi declared himself caliph, and his organization a caliphate. The group wreaked havoc in Iraq and Syria for years, and also accepted allegiance from jihadi groups in countries such as Egypt, Libya, Afghanistan, and Nigeria (which made them part of the Islamic State, if mostly in theory). ISIS was eventually defeated in Iraq and Syria by a coalition of dozens of countries in 2019.

Scholars and analysts hardly agreed on the group's true nature, intentions, and trajectory, but they unanimously identified ISIS as a "territorial" organization. There are good reasons to consider ISIS a territorial, state-like entity.

---

[124] Ahram 2019, loc. 4524. On the rift between al-Qaeda and AQI, see especially Fishman 2016; Can 2017; and Bunzel 2016.

[125] On this episode, see Robinson 2008.

162 How Territorial Ideas Affect Wars

In 2014, ISIS not only declared itself a caliphate but, at its zenith, also ruled over a large amount of terrain in Iraq and Syria, the size of which exceeded the United Kingdom.[126] In addition, the group framed its ambitions in geographical terms, announcing that it aimed to "remain and expand."[127] In a theatrical act that involved ISIS-operated bulldozers in the Iraqi-Syrian border, ISIS also claimed to have "broken" the so-called Sykes-Picot borders, referring to the secret agreement between Britain and France (1916) that sought to carve up the Middle Eastern territories of the Ottoman Empire.[128] Furthermore, what helped ISIS emerge as a magnet for Salafi jihadists worldwide was its interest in controlling territory, not to mention its ability to do so.[129] Arguably, the group's territorial focus also rendered ISIS "a new step, a new wave, in jihadism."[130]

ISIS's approach to territory and territoriality attracted little attention from IR scholars. Political geographers, in turn, showed greater interest in the territorial underpinnings of the group. Most notably, political geographer Yosef Jabareen maintains that what makes ISIS unique is that ISIS's "conceptions of territoriality" (ideas) resemble Islamic states of the past, but its "tactics of territoriality" (practice), especially when its brutal methods are taken into consideration, distinguish it from both the Westphalian norm and past or (most) contemporary Islamic organizations.[131] However, once examined through the lenses of the territorial orders framework, the group's territorial ideas (and associated practices) resemble a radical version of virulent orders, not all that different from a revolutionary state.[132]

As far as demarcation principles are concerned, ISIS professed an approach that highlighted "fluid frontiers," which paved the way for not only gradual encroachments, but also a sense of "territorial flexibility" that rendered strategic retreats, or even relocation, feasible.[133] ISIS's approach to sociospatial

---

[126] Dobbins and Jones 2017, 52.

[127] *Dabiq* 5.

[128] Note that the so-called Sykes-Picot borders (or zones of direct and indirect control) did not match the borders that eventually emerged after World War I.

[129] McCants 2015.

[130] Fawaz 2016, 4.

[131] Jabareen 2015. Hamdan's (2016) research suggests that ISIS pursues a "pragmatic" approach in its territorial practices. More specifically, as opposed to following an inflexible strategy that can be traced to the group's religious doctrine, ISIS adapts to each area's specific social and political dynamics and behaves accordingly, only to frame its actions—in an ad hoc manner—in religious terms by *selectively* invoking Islamic texts or past practices.

[132] For example, Daniel Byman (2016) drew attention to the fact that Maoist/revolutionary insurgencies have shown an interest in holding and governing territory, for such territorial control may allow them to create "base areas" that can be used to attain the ultimate objective, regime change. Similarly, Stephen Walt (2015) suggested that ISIS is best seen as a revolutionary state that is not very different from revolutionary France and the early Soviet Union. Stathis Kalyvas (2015) suggested that ISIS resembles a revolutionary "group," not a state.

[133] Kadercan 2017.

organization, in turn, focused on homogenization, best represented by what the group defines as the principle of "extinguishing gray zones." Put differently, while ISIS claims to model its state on historical caliphates, its territorial vision was much closer to a revolutionary state (or, more precisely, Nazi Germany's geopolitical vision). ISIS's territorial practices partially resemble the Islamic empires of the past (e.g., the Ottomans), especially with respect to its methods of spatial demarcation and conquest. Simultaneously, refusing classical Islamic empires' adherence to the preservation of cultural and social heterogeneity within their domains, ISIS aimed to "homogenize" the population it rules over just like a revolutionary state, if in sectarian terms.

The next two sections examine the dominant territorial ideas in ISIS and their relationship with the ways in which the group drew on organized violence to expand and govern its domain.

Demarcation and Sociospatial Organization

ISIS categorically refuses the modern state system and its territorial trappings for their artificiality. Note that pan-Arab movements of the twentieth century also subscribed to the idea that Sykes-Picot borders were artificial.[134] However, while such movements in the region are concerned with where borders should be drawn, ISIS rejects not only the location of the borders, but also the very concept of (Westphalian) border itself.[135] ISIS's approach to demarcation can be thought of in terms of fluid frontiers.[136] ISIS positioned itself as a frontier state fighting a never-ending war in defense, and for the glory, of the Islamic lands.[137] "Sacralizing" the areas it controlled, ISIS presented the defense of what it refers to as *dar al-Islam* as well as expansion into *dar al-harb* (land of Islam and land of war, respectively)[138] as religious duty. ISIS's spatial expression is also "portable."[139] More specifically, ISIS rejects "spatial specificity," that is, defining the spatial reflection of a "body politic" in terms of a specific geographical area. The meaning ISIS attributes to its infamous black flags is illustrative. While a nation-state's flag typically represents sovereignty over a specific piece of demarcated space, ISIS's spatial extent follows the

---

[134] Ahram 2019.

[135] Hamdan 2016; Larsson 2017, 106; Jabareen 2015; Stern 2016; *Dabiq* 4, p. 18.

[136] Jabareen 2015; Gates and Podder 2015. This understanding is also associated with Islamic philosophy, which "recognized no boundaries for [Islamic] kingdom" (Parvin and Sommer 1980, 3). Also see Khadduri 1955, 46.

[137] ISIS specifically invokes the term *ribat*, which can be interpreted as frontier outpost. For example, *Dabiq* 5, p. 11; 9, pp. 8–13. On AQI's use of the concept, see Long 2009.

[138] See Chapter 5.

[139] On "portability" of state territory in so-called Muslim territoriality, see Parvin and Sommer 1980, 2.

164 How Territorial Ideas Affect Wars

flag: ISIS is where the black flags fly, whether it is Afghanistan, Egypt, Libya, Nigeria, Iraq, Syria, or beyond. It follows that ISIS does not necessarily require the lands it ruled over to sustain its claims to statehood; it merely needs some territory, somewhere.[140]

This dynamic separates ISIS from similar Salafi jihadist groups.[141] A comparison with al-Qaeda and the Taliban may help drive the point home. Similar to ISIS, al-Qaeda does not adhere to spatial specificity, but it also has remained a transterritorial network that—so far—has refrained from making the kind of territorial commitment that ISIS made between 2014 and 2019 in Iraq and Syria.[142] As far as similar radical Islamic insurgencies that have aimed to control and govern territory go,[143] the Taliban arguably comes closest to ISIS. Just like ISIS, the Taliban imposed a harsh religious order on the sociospatial aspects of life, acting as both insurgency and proto-state. However, comparing ISIS with the Taliban only highlights the distinction between the two. The Taliban commits to a "country [Afghanistan] first" understanding,[144] which suggests the group adheres to a form of spatial specificity. ISIS has long criticized the Afghanistan-based group for its provinciality[145] as well as "nationalistic tendencies,"[146] and built its own insurgency and state-building efforts on an infinitely more transnational and borderless (unbounded) principle than that which is exercised by the Taliban.[147]

Note that ISIS's geopolitical vision differs from numerous historical Islamic states such as the Ottoman Empire. As highlighted in Chapter 5, while the Ottomans adhered to geopolitics of jihad, they also incorporated a third and more reconciliatory category in their geopolitical vision (that is, *dar al-sulh*). By contrast, ISIS adhered to a radical and dichotomous vision of geopolitics of jihad. This Manichaean geopolitical vision stipulates that there can never be boundaries until a Sharia-based perpetual peace is established all over the world, and that there is no room (or space) for reconciliation. The geopolitics of jihad is also compatible with how some scholars and analysts see ISIS's intentions: "At its ideological heart, ISIS seeks to overthrow the existing world order . . . to convert all people to Islam; and to rule all Islamic

---

[140] For example, *Dabiq* 13, pp. 49–54.

[141] In fact, political geographers have shown greater interest in jihadi groups' territoriality (e.g., Flint and Radil 2009; Elden 2009; Bahgat and Medina 2013).

[142] As mentioned above, disagreements over "when" or "whether" to establish an Islamic state played a crucial role in the tensions between al-Qaeda and AQI/ISI/ISIS.

[143] Lia (2015) counts about twenty jihadi proto-states, but also recognizes that very few survived more than a year and controlled territory in any meaningful sense.

[144] Gates and Podder 2015.

[145] For example, *Dabiq* 1, p. 35; 5, p. 47.

[146] *Dabiq* 13, pp. 40, 49.

[147] Pérouse de Montclos (2016) makes a similar case for Boko Haram's provinciality.

lands and eventually the world according to its fundamentalist interpretation of Islam."[148] The group itself has also been very vocal about its intentions. For example, in July 2014, right after the declaration of the self-proclaimed caliphate, the group's spokesman announced that the "Islamic State has no borders, and its conquest will continue with God's permission."[149]

As far as sociospatial organization is concerned, the group has aimed to transform the territorial arrangements in Iraq and Syria in radical terms. Just like a revolutionary state, in fact, even more radically so, ISIS aimed to homogenize populations within its domain (and target areas), homogeneity defined in terms of neither civic nor ethnic uniformity and conformity, but extreme (Sunni) sectarianism.[150] Note that ISIS's understanding of community rejected racial, ethnic, and national identities and aimed to create "a new form of citizenship."[151] In 2014, Abu Bakir al-Baghdadi, ISIS's leader and self-proclaimed caliph, defined the self-proclaimed caliphate as a "a state where the Arab and non-Arab, the white man and black man, the easterner and westerner are all brothers."[152]

While many historical Islamic states refrained from top-down societal homogenization efforts (e.g., the Ottomans' multireligious millet system), ISIS built its ideology on an exclusive interpretation of the concept of *asabiyyah*, which stands for "kinship within the context of political organization" in Islamic thought.[153] ISIS's interpretation of *asabiyyah* considers only Sunnis *who explicitly adhere to the group's particular interpretation of Islam* as full members.[154] Not only the Shia, but also Sunnis who refuse to do so, an overwhelming majority of the greater Sunni population worldwide, are categorized as heretics. Non-Muslims, even those accepted as "people of the book," are left out of ISIS's vision of *asabiyyah*. Most notably, while ISIS imposed *jizyah* tax on Christians and Jews just like the historical Islamic states, it continued to violently target them even when these religious minorities paid their taxes.[155] The relevant practices are perfectly aligned with ISIS's geopolitical vision, which rejects *dar al-sulh*, land of reconciliation: there can be only land of Islam (as ISIS interprets it) and land of war, with no place for "gray zones."[156]

---

[148] Lister 2015, 7. Also see *Dabiq* 5, p. 3.

[149] Ahram 2019, loc. 4863.

[150] Lister 2015.

[151] Kfir 2015.

[152] Larsson 2017, 43. ISIS also saw its war-making efforts as an opportunity to forge the transnational community it seeks to create. In 2014, for example, al-Baghdadi stated that during the group's struggle, ISIS fighters' "blood mixed and became one, under a single flag and goal" (Larson 2017, 43).

[153] Mabon 2017; Ahmed 2002.

[154] Fishman 2016.

[155] Fawaz 2016.

[156] For example, *Dabiq* 1, p. 10.

Territorial Ideas and Armed Conflict

ISIS's understanding of fluid frontiers (as opposed to fixed and rigid borders) led to gradual encroachments and an ability to contract easily. The group's dedication to homogenize the space-society relationship in target areas, in turn, fueled extreme reterritorialization efforts, that is, attempts to transform the demarcation as well as organization principles vis-à-vis space-society association. Overall, ISIS's territorial vision was based on a simple geopolitical principle: degrade and destroy what the group refers to as "gray zones," or the "sociocultural [environments] where Muslim [or, more specifically, Sunni] and non-Muslim [or non-Sunni] shared the same physical environment and political institutions in a common social context."[157]

In this context, ISIS's territorial objectives are best conceived in two interrelated levels: global and regional. The driving force behind objectives at both levels follows a simple logic: degrade and destroy the gray zones. At the global level, ISIS aims to project its version of the clash of civilizations (between what the group portrays as "real" Muslims and the Crusaders) onto space.[158] The intention is to amplify the "us versus them" narrative by fueling a discourse of "our land versus their land." In order to accomplish this goal, ISIS carries out or inspires terrorist attacks on Western targets, with the intention of provoking the Western states to help destroy existing gray zones within and beyond their borders.

ISIS has been vocal about its global goals and affiliated strategy. For example, in an issue dedicated to "extinguishing the grayzone," the group's English-language journal *Dabiq* states that "the presence of the [caliphate] . . . magnifies the political, social, economic, and emotional impact of any operation by the mujahideen against the enraged crusaders. This magnified impact compels the crusaders to actively destroy the grayzone themselves."[159] Abu Bakir al-Baghdadi also made a similar point: "[If] the Crusaders today have begun to trouble the Muslims who [live] in the lands of the cross by monitoring them, arresting them, and questioning them, then soon they will begin to displace them and take them away either dead, imprisoned, or homeless."[160]

The group's regional objectives are also associated with the logic of degrading and destroying the gray zones, with a sectarian twist. ISIS leadership intended to establish a revolutionary proto-state in Iraq and Syria exclusively for Sunnis, while also drawing upon control of territory to amplify ISIS's

---

[157] Joffé 2016, 808.

[158] Huntington 1993.

[159] *Dabiq* 7, p. 62.

[160] *Dabiq* 9, p. 54.

appeal in the eyes of Salafi jihadis worldwide. Regionally, ISIS aimed to radically reterritorialize its domain in Iraq and Syria. In 2015, Bruce Hoffman wrote, "ISIS has forcibly re-drawn the map of the modern Middle East."[161] An analysis of the group's territoriality suggests that ISIS aimed not only to redraw said map, but also to "repaint" it in sectarian terms.

At the regional level, the group applied the logic of "extinguishing the grayzone"[162] in sectarian (in addition to civilizational) terms. In particular, the group sought to transform the diverse and "mixed" settlement patterns—which it perceives as gray zones—into "zones of insecurity" marked by population homogeneity, defined in terms of sectarian affiliations. With this, ISIS likely intended to keep alive the Sunni victimization narrative on which it feeds, even after the group lost its possessions in Iraq and Syria. Put differently, ISIS's strategy was based on efforts to create socially homogeneous enclaves, each defined in terms of sectarian or ethnic identities.

In line with the notion of fluid frontiers, ISIS's method of territorial conquest was built on gradual encroachments. The case of Mosul is illustrative. The group's conquest of Mosul in 2014 was initially interpreted as a "jihadist Blitzkrieg," defined in terms of a quick decisive victory achieved through extensive use of mobile shock troops in "rapid fashion."[163] A closer examination of ISIS's territorial expansion suggests that the group has "consistently followed a strategy of infiltration, assassination, and intimidation before fully controlling an area."[164] In Whiteside's words, ISIS's "seizure of broad swaths of territory was . . . preceded by years of preparation by unconventional warfare."[165] In particular, ISIS pursued a "carrot-and-sticks approach" for expansion.[166] The group aimed to gradually co-opt some segments of the Sunni population.[167] As far as "sticks" were concerned, ISIS exploited and fueled the sectarian tensions and pacified its potential Sunni opponents—especially those who joined the US and Iraqi governments during the so-called Awakening (or *Sahwa*) campaign between 2006 and 2009—through under-the-radar tactics (such as discriminate assassination campaigns) that were not immediately visible to the Iraqi and US governments. Put differently, while the battle for Mosul (2014) might have appeared "rapid" when it finally culminated, ISIS's gradual conquest of the city likely started in 2013, if not earlier.

---

[161] Hoffman 2015, 81.
[162] *Dabiq* 7.
[163] Naumkin 2014.
[164] Shatz and Johnson 2015, 4. Also see Whiteside 2016, 17.
[165] Whiteside 2014b.
[166] Whiteside 2014a.
[167] Fawaz 2016.

Examining the group's media products and behavior in Iraq, Aaron Zelin comes to a similar conclusion about ISIS's method of gradual conquest.[168] Zelin points toward five phases. The first is intelligence gathering. During this phase, ISIS infiltrates the target area to gain local knowledge through sleeper agents. In the second military phase, the group utilizes low-intensity violence to soften the population through acts that include hit-and-run murders, sniper assassinations, improvised explosive devices (IEDs), car bombs, and suicide attacks. The third phase entails attempts to co-opt the locals through dawah (public outreach) campaigns. In the fourth stage, *hisba*, the group gradually imposes Sharia rule, "reterritorializing" the target area through destruction of Sufi, Shia, and pagan shrines, tombs, and historical artifacts, or any other geographical symbol that contradicts their ideology.[169] The final phase involves the establishment of basic governance and imposition of the group's black flags.

Not committing to particular borders also had a particular benefit for the group: paradoxically, it fueled expansionist propaganda while also allowing for strategic territorial contraction in the face of severe adversity and difficulty. Doing so, ISIS pragmatically and selectively interpreted religious references in a way to serve the group's strategic and tactical needs. On the one hand, in order to signal its intention to "expand," ISIS's propaganda identified utopian targets, such as Rome[170] and Istanbul,[171] which resonate with its references to historical caliphates and prophecies. On the other hand, ISIS could also draw upon elements of what Parvin and Sommer dubbed "Muslim territoriality,"[172] which had made it relatively easy for the historical Islamic states to legitimize territorial contraction in the past.

One crucial example of ISIS's territorial flexibility involves the Syrian town of Dabiq, which was the geographical epicenter of ISIS's propaganda as well as the namesake of the group's English-language online journal. ISIS long emphasized that it had been preparing for an apocalyptic battle in Dabiq with what the group identifies as the "infidel" armies, presumably Western powers and their local allies. The battle in Dabiq, ISIS propaganda emphasized, was expected to facilitate the apocalypse. If ISIS's discourse about the geographical centrality of Dabiq is to be taken seriously, one should expect the group to place great emphasis on defending the town.[173] Instead, in October 2016, ISIS

---

[168] Zelin 2016.

[169] On how Salafi jihadist groups "reterritorialize" areas they control, see Campion 2017 and Dobos 2016. Also see *Dabiq* 2, p. 15; 11, pp. 32–33.

[170] *Dabiq*, 5, p. 3.

[171] *Dabiq*, 6, p. 83.

[172] Parvin and Sommer 1980.

[173] In fact, numerous ISIS experts expected group to make a grand stand for Dabiq, for example, Wood 2016 and McCants 2015.

hastily withdrew from Dabiq when pressed by a modest force comprised of Turkish special operations forces and the Free Syrian Army, and then changed the name of its English-language journal to *Rumiyah*. More recently, facing ultimate defeat in Iraq and Syria, ISIS declared hegira to other locations, calling its supporters and sympathizers to move to Yemen, Egypt, and Afghanistan.

In its efforts to crystallize and (re)territorialize existing sectarian/ethnic differences by creating zones of insecurity, ISIS pursued three strategies. The first was the proselytizing of those whom the group deems heretics. ISIS's interpretation of *asabiyyah* is exclusive in terms of membership, but also offers room for "redemption," of course, if the new member fully adopts the group's belief system and offers *bayah* (pledge of allegiance) to ISIS. Even Shia can be accepted as full members: the group's first spokesman, Abu Maysara al-Iraqi, and its one-time suicide campaign director in Baghdad province, were Shia who converted to ISIS's brand of Salafism.[174] The group's proselytizing efforts also entailed more subtle measures, best revealed in terms of legal arrangements, bureaucracy, and education. ISIS infamously imposed a radical version of Sharia in the domains it controlled, and severely punished those who violated the law. The group also attempted to establish a unified administrative system in Iraq and Syria, introducing its own currency in order to dominate the economic life. In addition, ISIS paid considerable attention to the education system and strove to create a generation of acolytes through extensive and enforced indoctrination of youth.[175]

Beyond proselytizing, the group also directly engaged in what Jessica Stern refers to as "geographical cleansing," a process where "minorities and enemies of the militant group either emigrate or are killed, leaving behind only Sunni Arabs."[176] Again, the case of Mosul is illustrative. Historically, Mosul hosted a mixed and diverse population in terms of sectarian, religious, and ethnic identities for centuries. ISIS's homogenizing efforts have driven away many non-Sunni groups, for example, at least one hundred thousand Christians, rendering Mosul a "Sunni-land," if temporarily. Most notably, in 2014 ISIS launched a campaign of ethnic cleansing against the Yazidis, an ethnoreligious group it considered heretics. ISIS killed and enslaved thousands of Yazidis and drove those who survived the onslaught away from the lands controlled by the self-proclaimed caliphate.

Third, similar to the group's acts of terrorism at the global level, ISIS pursued a strategy of provocation. Paradoxically, while ISIS's efforts to provoke

---

[174] Whiteside 2017.
[175] Almohammad 2018.
[176] Stern 2016.

numerous regional and global actors contributed to its military defeat, its strategy of provocation also helped the group fuel the so-called Sunni victimization narrative. The Western intervention in Iraq and Syria allowed the group to frame the struggle against ISIS as a Crusader attack on Sunnis. The atrocities of the Assad regime, involvement of Iran and its regional affiliate Hezbollah in the civil war, and the rising prominence of Shia-dominated Iraqi militia also contributed to ISIS's Sunni victimization narrative. ISIS also identified its fiercest local opponent in Syria, the Kurdish militia also known as the YPG, as a band of Marxists with an openly anti-Islamist agenda.[177]

In the end, facing a powerful multinational coalition, ISIS could not "remain" as its propaganda promised. From such a perspective, ISIS's experiment in Iraq and Syria has failed in the short term. However, the group most certainly succeeded in disturbing the sociospatial makeup of the region, perhaps in irreversible ways. Whether ISIS's short-lived efforts will yield the group benefits in the long term, either in Iraq/Syria or beyond, remains to be seen. Regardless, given the detrimental effects as well as the "flexible" nature of ISIS's virulent territoriality, the territorial orders framework suggests that the international community should remain vigilant about the group's geopolitical vision and strategy.

Conclusion

Virulent territoriality has constituted more of an exception than the rule in world politics. In addition, this distinct form of territoriality has received little scholarly attention from either IR scholars or political geographers. While they are rare from a world-historical perspective, virulent territorial orders, when they are dominant in a polity, can have far-reaching consequences for global and regional politics, for a simple reason: polities that adhere to virulent territoriality tend to strive for continuous expansion, and they aim to homogenize sociospatial arrangements within and beyond their core domains. Such polities usually profess a universalizing and totalizing ideology through which they can mobilize masses (or supporters) for their war efforts. Furthermore, states that adhere to virulent territoriality in the modern era usually pose a direct challenge to the foundations of the so-called international system and can prompt considerable instability and conflict. In the modern era, most universalizing revolutionary states and movements have professed virulent territoriality.

---

[177] For example, *Dabiq* 2, pp. 12–13; 4, p. 9; 10, pp. 30–34.

This chapter aimed to assess the plausibility, if not to test the validity, of these claims through two distinct cases: revolutionary and Napoleonic France and the group known as ISIS. While there are considerable parallels within these two cases vis-à-vis the relationship between territorial ideas and armed conflict, there is also a crucial difference: while ISIS adopted an extreme version of virulent territoriality, France adhered to a milder version, which can help explain why the former was far more brutal and violent than the latter (when we control for the relative size and capabilities of France and ISIS). Further examination of the territorial underpinnings of virulent territoriality, in turn, can help students of world politics to better make sense of not only the past but also the present and future challenges emanating from revolutionary movements and states, as well as radical transnational groups such as ISIS.

PART III
HOW WARS AFFECT TERRITORIAL IDEAS

The relationship between territorial ideas and armed conflict is not one-sided: just as territorial ideas can shape how states and societies approach war over territory, wars themselves can also influence and even transform territorial ideas. This section, comprised of a single but lengthy chapter, develops these claims by building on the territorial orders framework. In particular, Chapter 7 scrutinizes the ways in which four systemic wars —the Thirty Years' War, the Revolutionary and Napoleonic Wars, World War I, and World War II— have shaped the transformation of territorial orders across time and space. The chapter is based on a simple observation: Monolithic territorial order is the aspirational and ideational hegemon in the present day. The question then becomes: How did systemic wars contributed to the emergence of mono-lithic territoriality as the aspirational hegemon? Systemic wars and postwar settlements usually privilege one territorial order at the expense of others. The impacts of these wars, however, differ in anarchical (or symmetrical) and hi-erarchical (or asymmetrical) settings. As far as global history is concerned, this perspective suggests that systemic wars have had differential impacts on territorial orders in the Western world and the Global South. In anarchical settings, the transformation works through collective "problem-solving," and will usually be shaped by the interests and priorities of great powers. In hier-archical settings, it is the struggle between the center and periphery, in both the material and the ideational dimensions, that shapes the transformation that systemic wars trigger in terms of territorial ideas. The analysis offered in this chapter also points toward a certain insight: the legacies of Western imperialism and geographical racism lie at the heart of present-day territo-rial arrangements and imageries. In other words, the present-day territorial arrangements are more a product of Western imperialism and geographical racism than they are an "expanded" version of the territorial model typically attributed to the Peace of Westphalia.

7

Systemic Wars and the Evolution of Territorial Orders

> War creates geographies of borders, states, empires, and so on, and in turn, these geographies are the terrain over which peace is maintained or new wars are justified. Rather than being as permanent and sedate as a mountain range, the geography of war is as fluid and volatile as a lava flow.
>
> —Colin Flint[1]

Charles Tilly famously argued that the war made the state, and the state made war.[2] In particular, Tilly argued that the relationship between state-building and war-making was circular: just like states engaged in numerous wars, wars themselves as well as preparation for wars also shaped state-formation processes, and, consequently, the evolution of the modern state system. Considering that "state-building and a sense of territory have often gone hand in hand,"[3] a similar argument can be made about the relationship between territorial ideas and war: just as territorial ideas can affect how states and societies approach war, wars themselves have played an essential role in the transformation of ideas about state space. The question then becomes: how have wars affected the evolution of territorial ideas and associated practices?

Of course, the notion of territorial ideas, without elaboration, remains rather abstract. In fact, this is where the territorial orders framework can help us identify the impacts of wars on the transformation of territorial orders. As established in previous chapters, monolithic territoriality, exemplified by the nation-state ideal, has been an ideational and aspirational hegemon since the end of World War II. Then the question becomes: How did monolithic territoriality end up as the ideational and aspirational hegemon, eliminating the

---

[1] Flint 2005, 4–5.
[2] Tilly 1975.
[3] Anderson 1996, 5.

Shifting Grounds. Burak Kadercan, Oxford University Press. © Oxford University Press 2023.
DOI: 10.1093/oso/9780197686690.003.0007

appeal and legitimacy, if not always actual practice, of amorphous, virulent, and mosaic orders? More specifically, for the purposes of this chapter, how have wars affected the rise of monolithic order as the hegemonic aspirational territorial model?

As highlighted in Chapter 3, the argument here is that systemic wars act as large-scale catalysts that can lead to significant changes in dominant territorial ideas and practices. They do so by tilting the balance in favor of one set of ideas at the expense of others. More specifically, systemic wars will have differential impacts on territorial ideas in anarchical and hierarchical settings. In anarchical (or symmetrical) settings, the transformation will be driven by the interests and priorities of great powers and will usually take the form of collective "problem-solving." In hierarchical (or asymmetrical) settings, the struggle between the center and periphery, in both the material and ideational dimensions, plays a crucial role in shaping the impacts of systemic wars on territorial ideas in two ways. First, systemic wars disrupt, if temporarily, the hegemony of the metropole over subjugated geographies. Second, systemic wars and the postwar settlements create opportunities for indigenous actors in the periphery to appropriate and exploit the ideational transformation taking place in the core.

This chapter examines the impacts of four systemic wars—the Thirty Years' War, the Revolutionary and Napoleonic Wars, World War I, and World War II—on the transformation of territorial ideas and associated practices. At this juncture, three points need further elaboration. The first involves the selection of these four wars (and postwar settlements) and not others. For example, some IR scholars may argue that the Peace of Utrecht of 1713 marked a monumental shift in the diplomatic and political balance of power in Europe;[4] others point out that conflicts such as the Seven Years' War (1756–63) were fought on a global scale, with significant implications that went well beyond the European landscape.

There are two main reasons for focusing on these four wars. First, these wars are typically accepted as the key turning points in the so-called international system, and their impacts on the so-called modern state system are examined in detail by numerous IR scholars.[5] For example, according to Ikenberry, "The great postwar junctures share a set of characteristics that make them unusually important in providing opportunities for leading states to shape international order," and the new distribution of power reflects "coping with the

---

[4] For example, Osiander 1994.
[5] For example, Gilpin 1981; Hutchinson 2017; Braumoeller 2019; Ikenberry 2001; Osiander 1994; Reus-Smit 2013."

newly emerged asymmetries of power."[6] However, these studies rarely emphasize the territorial aspects of systemic wars. Revisiting these particular conflicts from the perspective of the territorial orders framework, in this context, allows me to highlight how my approach differs from or is in alignment with existing research on the impacts of these wars on the international system. More importantly, this case selection strategy reflects the "pragmatic" approach already highlighted in Chapter 2: my intention is neither to "test" the theory with these cases, nor push forward the claim that these particular wars should enjoy a superior epistemological status over others. Instead, just as in other empirical chapters, I am testing how far my theory can go to provide plausible explanation for outcomes.[7] In relation, this chapter also pursues an abduction-oriented perspective, where the theory and the selected cases are in continuous dialogue.

The second issue that requires attention involves the impacts of these systemic wars on non-Western geographies, or the Global South. Mainstream IR scholarship usually portrays these wars as "internal" feuds fought within Europe, or the Global North, and either leaves out the impacts of these conflicts on the Global South or treats them as footnotes.[8] In other words, while mainstream IR tends to refer to these conflicts as "systemic" or "global" wars, it also excludes much of the "international system" as we understand the term today as well as the globe itself. As will be discussed in detail in Chapter 8, this tendency is a reflection of what can be referred to as geographical ethnocentrism (or geographical racism) dominant in mainstream IR approaches.

This study departs from the aforementioned tendency in two ways. First, following the critical and postcolonial studies in IR and beyond, it explicitly recognizes that while these four systemic wars did break out in Europe, their impacts were not limited to the Western world: World War I and World War II in particular were fought well beyond the Global North, and they affected geographies and societies that did not even directly participate in these conflicts. Second, this chapter explicitly recognizes the West-dominated hierarchical nature of global politics, especially from the nineteenth century onward.

It follows that systemic wars not only played an important role in the emergence of the present-day territorial arrangement, but did so in the presence of "territorial hierarchy" between the Western world and much of the rest of

---

[6] Ikenberry 2001, 3, 17.
[7] I'd like to thank an anonymous reviewer for helping me clarify my position.
[8] Barkawi 2018.

the globe, especially during the nineteenth and twentieth centuries.[9] In such a setting, the evolution of territorial orders and the eventual triumph of monolithic territoriality as an aspirational hegemon cannot be portrayed as a story that begins in the Western world, which then effortlessly "spreads" to the rest of the globe. In this sense, this study recognizes the "mutual constitution of Europe and non-European world and their joint role in making history."[10] The spread of the nation-state ideal (and therefore monolithic territoriality) across the globe—especially during the course of the twentieth century—was neither generously "granted" to colonies by their colonial overlords, nor "often surprisingly consensual," as some scholars argue.[11] Instead, the relevant processes played out in the presence of colonial hegemony and institutionalized racism, which had lasting consequences.

The third dynamic that needs to be addressed is the analytic narrative offered in this chapter. Similar to scholars such as Alfred Rieber,[12] I adopt a *longue durée* account of the transformation of territorial ideas and practices. That being said, the narrative offered in this study is "multilinear rather than linear."[13] In relation, the narrative differs from alternative accounts that portray the Peace of Westphalia as a "Big Bang" that erupted in Europe, the territorial underpinnings of which then expanded to the rest of the world like a virus. For example, as will be highlighted below, mosaic territoriality emerged as a prominent aspirational model in the aftermath of the Thirty Years' War, but it became more attainable only in the aftermath of the Napoleonic Wars. Paradoxically, the Revolutionary and Napoleonic Wars also rendered mosaic order unsustainable as an aspirational model in the long run. Similarly, post–World War I arrangements emphasized the importance of self-determination (and its territorial reflection, monolithic orders), but the "right" of self-determination was categorically denied to non-European societies. Post–World War II arrangements, in turn, were more inclusive when it came to self-determination in the Global South. However, "recognition"—especially in the colonized geographies—was granted not necessarily to the "people," but often to the preexisting (colonial) territorial-administrative units.

In the next four sections, I examine the impacts of the aforementioned systemic wars (as well as postwar settlement efforts) on the transformation of territorial ideas in general, and territorial orders in particular.

---

[9] As Buzan and Lawson (2015, 25) highlight, the nineteenth century witnessed a global transformation, as "The West broke open and overwhelmed remaining bastions of the classical world (the Ottoman Empire, China and Japan), and overcame the environmental barriers."

[10] Barkawi and Laffey 2006, 330.

[11] Meyer et al. 1997, 144.

[12] Rieber 2014.

[13] Buzan and Lawson 2015, 23.

The Thirty Years' War

In Europe, the mosaic order as an aspirational territorial model rose to prominence, but not dominance, following the Thirty Years' War and the Peace of Westphalia.[14] As highlighted in Chapter 4, in IR scholarship the Peace of Westphalia has become a somewhat contested topic. In such a setting, an analysis of the relationship between the Thirty Years' War and the transformation of territorial ideas needs to acknowledge three dynamics. First, the Peace of Westphalia did not serve as "the majestic portal which leads from the old world into the new world," as Leo Gross famously argued.[15] The territorial underpinnings of the so-called Westphalian state had already began to take hold in parts of Europe, well before the Peace. Especially from the thirteenth century onward, "Rival semiautonomous units of politico-military rule began to consolidate around the idea of bounded, mutually exclusive territory and politico-military power began to centralize."[16] As political geographer Jean Gottman highlighted, the "doctrine of space portioning" matured in Europe between the fifteenth and seventeenth centuries.[17] Put simply, the Peace of Westphalia neither invented nor created the territorial ideas that are commonly attributed to it; instead, the Thirty Years' War and the Peace tilted the balance in favor of one set of existing ideas that emphasized the notion of spatially defined sovereignty,[18] at the expense of others.

Second, the Peace also fell short of establishing territorial uniformity across Europe, even at the aspirational level. As Hendrik Spruyt put it, in contrast with the popular imagination, sovereign territoriality "only entrenched well after 1648."[19] In other words, the Peace did not render mosaic territoriality the sole territorial model in Europe. From a territorial standpoint, complexities, contradictions, and "anomalies" (that is, if one is to accept the early Westphalian state as the "norm") survived well into the nineteenth century. More specifically, "in much of Europe, autonomous enclaves—cities, the estates of imperial nobles, ecclesiastical domains—remained within territorial units until the nineteenth century."[20] Under these circumstances, "Small types of political organizations not only persisted but flourished right up until the French Revolution."[21] Furthermore, the Holy Roman Empire—while its

[14] For an overview of the war, see Wilson 2011.
[15] Gross 1948, 28.
[16] Opello and Rosow 1999, 38.
[17] Gottman 1975, 33.
[18] Larkins 2010.
[19] Spruyt 2000, 69.
[20] Sheehan 2006, 6.
[21] Abramson 2017, 125.

power was diminished—survived until 1806. Put differently, "Westphalia was less a 'watershed' than an affirmation of existing practices, including the centrality of imperial confederation, dynastic order and patrimonial rule."[22]

That the Peace neither invented a new mode of territoriality nor established territorial uniformity in Europe in its immediate aftermath does not necessarily imply that Westphalia had no discernible impact on the evolution of territorial ideas. To understand that impact, a third dynamic needs to be accounted for: the impacts of the Reformation on territorial ideas and practices across Europe. Most notably, IR scholar Daniel Philpott traced the origins of the modern state system to the Reformation.[23] In particular, Philpott argues that the Reformation triggered a process that undercut the authority of the Holy Roman Empire and the Catholic Church, which then paved the way for a "revolution in sovereignty," epitomized by the Peace of Westphalia.

Like most IR scholars, Philpott is interested in the "sovereignty" component of the notion of territorial sovereignty.[24] Accordingly, he does not deal with the territorial implications of the Reformation, the Thirty Years' War, and the Peace of Westphalia in great detail. Philpott's emphasis on the Reformation, however, is worth pursuing from a territorial perspective. More specifically, the Thirty Years' War broke out and was fought in the presence of a territorial crisis, or a crisis about the appropriate territorial ideas, that can be traced to the rise of Protestantism from 1517 onward and, more specifically, the Peace of Augsburg of 1555.[25] Prior to 1517, the European landscape could be defined in terms of administrative and political heteronomy,[26] with numerous political actors ranging from early modern states like France to city-states, city-leagues, and the Holy Roman Empire, all of which were vying for competition and cooperation in a land of overlapping and fluid jurisdictions.[27]

Admittedly, the territorial orders framework can hardly provide a comprehensive picture of the territorial underpinnings of pre-Reformation Europe. Put simply, sixteenth-century Europe resembled a "heterogeneous geopolitical system."[28] In such a setting, the territorial ideas were too complicated and multifaceted to be contextualized in terms of a simple framework.[29] Still, the territorial orders framework can provide some insights that can help put the

---

[22] Buzan and Lawson 2015, 49; also Nexon 2009, 278–280.
[23] Philpott 2001.
[24] See Chapter 4.
[25] Philpott 2001.
[26] Ruggie 1993.
[27] Spruyt 1994.
[28] Teschke 2003, 218.
[29] Teschke 2003, 66.

Wars and Evolution of Territorial Orders 181

Thirty Years' War and the Peace of Westphalia into (territorial) context. As highlighted above, as far as demarcation principles were concerned, mosaic territoriality was emerging in some polities by the sixteenth century, but it was far from the norm. Before the Peace of Westphalia, there existed no supreme authority within a given territory, and "both the pope and the emperor intervened regularly in the territorial affairs" of kings and nobles.[30]

As far as sociospatial organization is concerned, while European society differed significantly in terms of culture, language, ethnicity, these differences mattered relatively less when compared with another marker of identity: religion. In so many ways, Europe was seen, both by rulers and societies, as a Christian land. Before the Reformation, the Christian community was conceived through the lenses of "the Pauline metaphor of the body of Christ," where the "members of a single organism in which all [believers in the true faith] found their identity and purposes."[31] In this context, European society was "united,"[32] at least at some level, and this uniformity was associated with the concept of *Respublica Christiana*, or Christian Commonwealth.

In the words of Opello and Rosow, "Though people were personally loyal to counts and kings, their identity as human beings was not bound up with a secular political order to which all belonged. To the extent people recognized an intersubjective social unity that linked them to people outside their immediate local surroundings, it was Christendom, that vast community of believers under the authority of the Catholic Church."[33] This principle was also enshrined in the concept of *religio vincula societatis*, which suggested that religion is the "bond that holds society together" and "religious uniformity [provides] the best foundation for stability."[34] These principles were not merely about the societies per se; they were also about territory. Put differently, the European landscape before the Reformation entailed a modicum of sociospatial homogeneity, which was defined in terms of religious uniformity. Also note that the "Christian space" was not limited to Europe, but extended to anywhere inhabited by Christians. In this sense, the community of believers "recognized no geographic limits."[35] This geographical vision implied that the "Christian space" also extended to geographies such as the Holy Land, where Christians lived in substantial numbers.[36]

---

[30] Philpott 2001, 77.
[31] Philpott 2001, 77.
[32] Philpott 2001, 77.
[33] Opello and Rosow 1999, 42.
[34] Owen 2010, 85.
[35] Sassen 2008, 38.
[36] Philpott 2001, 78.

182 How Wars Affect Territorial Ideas

The rise of Protestantism from 1517 onward challenged the perceived sociospatial homogeneity: rulers and societies were now divided across confessional lines, especially in Central and Western Europe.[37] The combination of geopolitical competition and religious tensions then triggered Europe-wide instability. Initially, the Catholic Church attempted to suppress Protestantism through military force by "encouraging monarchs who remained loyal to the Church to attack those who had converted to one of the new Protestant religion."[38] Attempts at "military erasure of Protestantism" eventually became a century-long trend: especially between 1525 and 1648, the emperor and "some combination of Catholic princes" sought to suppress and liquidate Protestantism across Europe.[39] For example, in 1525, the Swabian League of princes, backed by the Habsburgs, initiated a campaign to suppress the Protestants, which eventually led to the deaths of some one hundred thousand peasants.[40] Similarly, again in 1525, the Catholic princes of northern Germany assembled at Dessau to pledge to "exterminate" the Protestants.[41] Not surprisingly, the relevant attempts triggered a response from the Protestant princes, who sought to oust the Catholic clergy and seize church property from within their realms.[42] Again, all these attempts were essentially about territory. To be precise, these attempts were not merely about territorial conquest, they were also about the meaning of territory, and boiled down to the following question: Would the relevant territories be defined as Catholic or Protestant lands?

In such a setting, Central Europe witnessed the rise of "two mutually plans for ordering public life," which "held in common the medieval insistence that societal cohesion required religious homogeneity."[43] These contradicting views about how the space-society-religion nexus should be organized eventually led to a territorial zero-sum game between competing factions. Most notably, the emergence of the Catholic League of Dessau in 1525 triggered the rise of the Lutheran League of Torgau in 1526.[44] The tensions escalated in 1529 with the Diet of Spreyer, as the Catholic princes bonded more closely, effectively rendering Lutheranism officially illegal within the imperial domain.[45] The subsequent tensions and instability eventually paved the way for the Peace of Augsburg in 1555.

---

[37] On Luther and Calvin, see Bonney 1991, 1–76.
[38] Opello and Rosow 1999, 79.
[39] Philpott 2001, 108.
[40] Owen 2010, 91.
[41] Owen 2010, 91.
[42] Owen 2010, 92.
[43] Owen 2010, 92.
[44] Owen 2010, 94.
[45] Owen 2010, 95.

The Peace of Augsburg came with a specific stipulation: *cuius regio, euis religio* (whose the region, his the religion).[46] In the words of historian Geoffrey Parker, the Peace of Augsburg "created a layered structure of legal securities for the people of the Empire. At the top was the right of each secular territorial ruler, from the Electors down to the Imperial Knights, to dictate whether their subjects' religion was to be Catholic or Lutheran."[47] The only exceptions to this arrangement were Imperial Free Cities and the Catholic ecclesiastical states. In this sense, Augsburg "granted German princes authority over religion in their land and allowed them to establish uniformity."[48] Those who refused to convert to the religion of the ruler had two options: worship in secret (and risk persecution) or emigrate.[49] From a territorial perspective, this collective agreement can be seen as a move toward homogenization of the space-society relationship.

The Peace of Augsburg, however, failed to address, and even exacerbated, three problems. First, the Peace of Augsburg recognized only the Lutherans and did not cover Calvinism.[50] This omission not only ignored the increasing influence of Calvin and his teachings but also deepened the wedge between the Calvinists and Lutherans. Second, the Peace of Augsburg remained ambiguous about the princes who converted from one confession to another; the Peace did not establish specific guidelines regarding the people who lived in the realm.[51] Just as territory is not only about physical space but also about the relationship between space and the society, the Peace was about territorial identities; in that, it offered some radical solutions (sociospatial homogeneity defined in terms of religion) but did not, or could not, stipulate clear and viable paths that would render the associated reterritorialization efforts practical. Third, the Peace of Augsburg fueled a territorial paradox: the princes could choose to homogenize sociospatial arrangements in religious terms within their realms, but the demarcation principles that defined the spatial extent and scope of political authority still remained unclear, or at least complex and contingent.

When combined with the fluidity of boundaries and contested as well as overlapping jurisdictions, princes' efforts, or rights, to establish sociospatial homogenization within their domains set the stage for long-term instability. This is hardly surprising. By the turn of the seventeenth century, the Holy

[46] Philpott 2001, 81.
[47] Parker [1984] 2006, 18.
[48] Philpott 2001, 88.
[49] Opello and Rosow 1999, 79.
[50] Owen 2010, 155.
[51] Owen 2010, 110.

184 How Wars Affect Territorial Ideas

Roman Empire included around "1,000 separate, semi-autonomous political units, many of them very small."[52] Under such circumstances, the Peace of Augsburg instigated incentives for rulers within the empire to determine the religion of their domains, which then paved the way for oppression, rebellion, and civil wars.[53] Civil wars, in turn, carried the risk of encouraging intervention from other princes, kings, or the empire.

In sum, the Peace of Augsburg failed to solve, and even exacerbated, the existing territorial crisis that erupted in the aftermath of the Reformation. For example, in 1578, Rudolf II—who simultaneously held the titles of Holy Roman Emperor, King of Hungary and Croatia, King of Bohemia, and Archduke of Austria—ordered the closure of all Protestant institutions in Vienna, and eventually triggered a process where "scions of the major families of all Habsburg territories began to abandon the Reformation churches in favor of Catholicism" from the 1590s onward.[54] Obviously, these measures aimed to radically reterritorialize the relevant geographies. Similarly, in 1599, the Styria archduke asked Lutherans to leave his realm and burned religious books that contradicted Catholicism.[55] From 1602 onward, numerous "special courts" across the empire confiscated lands that belonged to Protestant nobles, expelled Protestant vassals, and converted Protestant churches for Catholic use.[56] The associated attempts at what can be called "sociospatial editing" not only attracted backlash from Protestant princes but also proved much less practical and viable than initially assumed. For example, in geographies such as Hungary and Transylvania, where the rulers aimed to reestablish Catholicism, "There were scarcely any Catholics left."[57]

Overall, the rulers' attempts to impose their own religion within their domains fueled chronic, territorial instability in the empire. For instance, between 1595 and 1618, there were riots or outright rebellion in almost twenty cities of the empire.[58] At the turn of the seventeenth century, the "Christian solidarity" that marked the pre-Reformation era had "expired,"[59] and, by 1617, "War certainly seemed to be in the air."[60] Again, thinking about these dynamics solely in terms of the rulers and the society would lead to an incomplete analysis, for a simple reason: these tensions were closely associated with

---

[52] Parker [1984] 2006, 15.
[53] The relevant measures also encouraged confessional oppression in geographies like France, where the Edict of Ecouen of 1559 outlawed Protestantism. See Owen 2010, 102.
[54] Parker [1984] 2006, 7.
[55] Parker [1984] 2006, 6.
[56] Parker [1984] 2006, 8.
[57] Parker [1984] 2006, 9.
[58] Parker [1984] 2006, 22.
[59] Polisensky and Snider 1978, 54.
[60] Parker [1984] 2006, 13.

the meaning attributed to territory. The relatively homogeneous Christian lands of the past century was now being fragmented into multiple territorial shards, where rulers strove to create their own sociospatially homogeneity within their own domains. The main problem was that the overlapping jurisdictions, not to mention contingent and fluid boundaries, of the time made the task virtually impossible.

The Thirty Years' War broke out amid the aforementioned territorial crisis. As is well known, the war broke out following the Bohemian Revolt in 1618, which was triggered by Protestants' concerns about the future emperor (and devout Catholic) Ferdinand II's intentions over Bohemia. The conflict escalated to a stage where competing factions attempted to establish sociospatial homogeneity through violent means. The case of Donauworth is telling. Donauworth's Protestant ruler had long denied religious freedom to Catholics, which provoked Maximilian, the Duke and later Elector of Bavaria, to enter the city and restore Catholic worship. Maximilian did not merely restore the religious rights of the Catholics; he eventually forbade Protestant worship in the city in 1620. The same year also marked the defeat of the Bohemians at the hands of their Catholic adversaries at White Mountain, which only encouraged Catholic princes to accelerate their attempts at sociospatial homogenization. In Bohemia, for example, Ferdinand II imposed a program that "blended persecution and reorganization," which left the nobility with two choices: conversion or exile.[61]

This tendency eventually led to what can be referred to as "confessional absolutism."[62] Confessional absolutism involved neither an emphasis on theology nor attempts at centralization of political authority.[63] Instead, the emphasis was on radical conservatism, which relied on the assumption that Protestant estates in Central Europe never owned (or deserved) any constitutional rights. Consequently, this understanding fueled the notion that Protestantism could (or should) be eradicated at the will of the emperor or the princes. "Recatholicization" efforts spread to many areas, including geographies such as Upper Palatine, where Catholicism had not been practiced since the 1540s.[64] In this context, the Edict of Restitution of 1629 banned Calvinism and stipulated that all Protestant gains since 1552 were to be reversed.[65] Once again, these were all attempts at radical reterritorialization.

[61] Parker [1984] 2006, 83.
[62] Parker [1984] 2006, 85.
[63] Parker [1984] 2006, 85.
[64] Parker [1984] 2006, 90.
[65] Owen 2010, 113.

The Edict of Restitution and the subsequent efforts to transform the sociospatial configurations in Protestant-majority areas such as Magdeburg eventually met with a backlash from Protestant rulers, especially the Swedish king, Gustavus Adolphus, who entered the war in 1630. The war took a different turn in 1635, in two ways. First, the warring parties signed the Peace of Prague, beginning to play down the religious aspects of the conflict.[66] Second, France entered the war on behalf of the Protestants, amplifying the geopolitical scale of the struggle. The result was a stalemate, which eventually paved the way for the Peace of Westphalia.

In the wake of the Thirty Years' War, the rulers of Europe faced significant challenges. A concern shared by almost all rulers of Europe was the extent, duration, and severity of the conflict. The war brought pillage, destruction, disease, and famine, triggering population decline in geographies affected by the struggle. For example, the Holy Roman Empire's population went from about twenty-one million in 1618 to less than fourteen million in 1648.[67] The war also affected some areas in more radical terms than others; for instance, Bohemia's population declined from three million to less than a million.[68] Under these circumstances, the rulers of Europe aimed to avoid a similar conflict and used the Peace as a platform to address the underlying causes of the war. One, if not the sole, cause of the conflict was the rulers' intentions to impose sociospatial homogeneity within and beyond their domains. Considering that these domains were usually built on multiple and overlapping authorities and claims, the relevant (radical) reterritorialization efforts paved the way for unparalleled levels of death and destruction.

Note that "problem-solving" did not reflect the preferences and design of a unitary actor, but played out in the presence of competing and sometimes contradictory priorities of different factions, each of which sought to advance its own interests. Most notably, Sweden and France sought to empower the German states at the expense of the Holy Roman Empire. France was interested in limiting the power of the empire and keeping Germany divided; Sweden, in turn, aimed to promote Protestantism "for religious as well as political reasons."[69] The German and Dutch states desired "freedom from imperial rule in their territorial affairs"[70] and aimed to emerge as territorial states "free from the temporal power of the pope, the emperor, and the entire Catholic Church."[71] Not surprisingly, the participants in the negotiations

[66] Owen 2010, 143.
[67] Malešević 2010, 114.
[68] Lockyer 1974, 368; Malešević 2010, 114.
[69] Croxton and Parker 2009, 86.
[70] Philpott 2001, 87.
[71] Philpott 2001, 107.

identified the religious divide as a problem that needed to be addressed collectively. This divide "led to civil wars as people fought over the dominant religion in their state . . . when there was a civil war, there was an opportunity for foreign states to intervene, so civil wars often sowed the seeds of foreign wars."[72] Overall, "The Peace of Westphalia recognized the role of religion in causing the war and took steps to prevent a recurrence."[73] In this sense, religion was no longer seen as casus belli.[74]

From a territorial perspective, it was not merely religion per se that triggered decades of fighting and more than a century of instability and crisis. The Reformation and the subsequent Peace of Augsburg, as mentioned above, led to a territorial paradox: numerous rulers aimed at religion-based sociospatial homogenization in the absence of (more) explicit demarcation principles, in a political landscape that allowed for overlapping and complex jurisdictions. The Peace of Westphalia addressed this territorial paradox in two ways. First, the princes could no longer dictate the religion of their realm and turned toward a modicum of "religious toleration" within their borders.[75] Second, the spatial reach of the rulers' autonomy would be defined in clearer and "harder" terms, of course, when compared with previous episodes. Put differently, the Peace negated the rulers' right to impose religion-driven sociospatial homogenization within their domains, and aimed to define the spatial reach of the rulers' political authority in more specific terms.

Note that the Peace did not establish, or even mention, the concept of absolute territorial sovereignty, as we understand the term today. In fact, neither the treaties that collectively constituted the Peace nor the negotiations that eventually led to these treaties dealt with sovereignty as a legal concept.[76] Furthermore, the principle of nonintervention, which lies at the heart of our present-day understanding of sovereignty, was not explicitly highlighted in the settlement.[77] The treaties also did not define or even mention the "general constitutional authority of states," which became a concern for lawyers and philosophers only by the eighteenth and nineteenth centuries.[78] Last but not least, the Holy Roman Empire did not cease to exist and survived well into the early nineteenth century.[79]

---

[72] Croxton and Parker 2009, 98.
[73] Owen 2010, 113.
[74] Philpott 2001, 89.
[75] Philpott 2001, 147.
[76] Osiander 1994, 78.
[77] Philpott 2001, 32.
[78] Philpott 2001, 84.
[79] Osiander (1994, 39) implies that Holy Roman Empire played a role in the preservation of even the tiniest German princedom or free city.

188 How Wars Affect Territorial Ideas

That being said, the Peace also came with certain novelties. First, its "designers meant for it to be comprehensive, governing all of Europe," and "Every power involved was accorded legal equality."[80] Overall, the treaties had 145 signatories, representing 194 European rulers, around 150 of which were German.[81] Furthermore, while they did not invoke the legal concept of sovereignty, the treaties emphasized what can be referred as "autonomy principle," which was a crucial component of the negotiations:[82] "Whatever the historical particularities of their situation, any and all actors in the system were entitled to an autonomous existence, and . . . they alone were competent to define the extent of their autonomy."[83]

Most notably, the Peace curbed the authority and political influence of the Holy Roman Empire and the Catholic Church. The fact that the negotiations were based on the principle of equality among the parties implied that the imperial authority was effectively truncated.[84] In this context, the Peace of Westphalia "neutralized the powers of the empire to interfere in the affairs of governments," and the empire lost its privilege to effectively act as a "supraterritorial entity."[85] The Peace also diminished the influence of the pope over the princes. Pope Innocent X's declaration that portrayed the Westphalia settlements "null and void" also ruled out the possibility that the church could act as a critical mediator among the rulers, a role that it had enjoyed in the past.[86]

In sum, the Peace of Westphalia overturned the sociospatial homogenization ideal introduced by the Peace of Augsburg, allowing for heterogeneous organization of space-society association within the jurisdictions of different princes. In addition, as political geographer Anssi Paasi highlighted, the Peace of Westphalia "helped to establish the dominance of a horizontal, geostrategic view of the space of states" and aligned territory with the concept of political autonomy.[87] As mentioned above, while mosaic orders were increasingly upheld by what IR scholarship tends to refer to as Westphalian states, as far as territorial arrangements were concerned, the European landscape was still "mixed." As will be discussed below, in Europe, mosaic territoriality would become more of a standard only by the nineteenth century, following the Revolutionary and Napoleonic Wars.

---

[80] Philpott 2001, 82, 83.
[81] Philpott 2001, 32; Croxton and Parker 2009, 72.
[82] Philpott 2001.
[83] Osiander 1994, 77.
[84] Philpott 2001, 85.
[85] Philpott 2001, 30, 87.
[86] Croxton and Parker 2009, 73.
[87] Paasi 2005, 19–20.

Beyond Europe, the Thirty Years' War and the Peace of Westphalia had limited direct impacts in the short run. This is hardly surprising. At the time, European states had yet to exert their hegemony in most parts of the globe. While the colonization of the Americas was in full swing, the Middle East, Asia, and Africa were not subjugated yet. The European landscape also had yet to secure itself from threats emanating from the "Rest"; for example, the Ottomans still presented a threat to the rulers of Europe, especially the Habsburgs, throughout the seventeenth century.

While a more comprehensive examination of the long-term impacts of the Thirty Years' War and the Peace in the non-Western world is beyond the scope of this study, the territorial orders framework can still provide a few insights. Arguably, the Peace reignited and ossified a Manichaean geopolitical vision that sharply differentiated between Christian lands and non-Christian geographies. The Peace might have secularized diplomatic interactions between the European rulers, but Westphalia also implied "a Christian peace for a disunited Christendom."[88] In this sense, the Peace can be seen as the reaffirmation of a Christian unity, if a qualified one, against non-Christian "others." This observation is not hyperbole. As Daniel Philpott highlights, the architects of the Peace intended to create a constitution for Christian Europe,[89] which did not include, and in fact defined itself vis-à-vis, non-Christian "others."[90] In this reading, while the Peace is usually portrayed as a move toward what Hedley Bull referred to as "international society,"[91] this "society" was in fact being defined in terms of a putative Christian (again, if qualified) unity, which was conceived as an exclusive club. IR scholar Edward Keene points toward this "duality" that lies at the heart of the so-called Westphalian system;[92] the European states' understanding of respect for sovereignty applied only to geographies ruled by Christian polities and did not include non-Christian "outsiders" and geographies. If this is the case, perhaps, what the Peace of Westphalia originally established was not the idea of an "international society" as some scholars claim; it was the idea of a (reunified) Christian society.

A similar perspective can be applied to the interaction between the (Christian) West and the "Rest" from a territorial perspective. Note that the Peace secularized diplomacy among the European rulers, not the European landscape as a whole. Most notably, the associated documents included numerous references to religion.[93] Considering that religion still played an

---

[88] Philpott 2001, 89.
[89] Philpott 2001, 20.
[90] Neumann and Welsh 1991.
[91] Bull 1977.
[92] Keene 2002.
[93] Philpott 2001, 89.

important role in social life in Europe at least until the late eighteenth century, this is hardly surprising. Put differently, the Peace was an attempt to secularize the relations between the rulers (or states), not eradicate the role of religion in social life. From a territorial perspective, for most Europeans, Europe remained essentially a Christian land.

Arguably, the Peace (re)established a common platform among Christian rulers, regardless of confessional differences. Consequently, non-Christian lands could be portrayed as empty, inferior, or savage spaces, inhabited by " 'savages,' 'barbarians,' and 'pagans.' "[94] In such a setting, the Peace of Westphalia's "secular" nature requires further investigation. If the preliminary arguments highlighted above have merit, the "secularism" attributed to the Westphalian arrangement reveals itself to be an ethnocentric "organized hypocrisy" among European rulers. European rulers jettisoned religious differences from interstate relations in Europe but reaffirmed their qualified unity vis-à-vis non-Christian societies and geographies.

The Revolutionary and Napoleonic Wars

As highlighted in Chapter 6, the French Revolution instigated virulent territoriality in France. Napoleon, in turn, also aimed to expand the French presence and influence well beyond the French borders and intended to homogenize the sociospatial organization within and beyond France. Overall, the Revolutionary and Napoleonic Wars had a paradoxical impact on the European landscape: they made it possible for mosaic orders to rise to primacy in the short run, but they also set the stage for the ascendancy of monolithic orders in the long run. These wars rendered the mosaic orders dominant in two ways. First, the number of states or state-like entities was reduced from over three hundred to around thirty, and the Holy Roman Empire ceased to exist. The remaining states, more or less, adhered to the mosaic model.[95] Second, the spread of the Napoleonic Code further established a modicum of uniformity in the space-society-politics nexus. In the words of Jordan Branch, "The states that emerged in the post-Napoleonic period were transformed from their composite and weakly centralized precursors: rulers now wiped clean the remaining medieval complexities and overlapping claims in favor of exclusive territorial rule over clearly delineated states."[96]

---

[94] Holsti 2016, 69.
[95] Arguably, the reduction in the number of territorial units also made mosaic territoriality more practical and manageable.
[96] Branch 2014, 33.

Chapter 6 already dealt with the causes and conduct of the Revolutionary and Napoleonic Wars. Put simply, the wars between 1792 and 1815 were associated with the contradiction between territorial ideas upheld by the monarchs of Europe and the revolutionaries (later, Napoleon). The victorious great powers and the newly reinstituted French monarchy were willing to accommodate the two core transformations mentioned above. Most notably, the great powers of Europe chose not to revive the hundreds of states and state-like territorial units that perished during the wars. Besides, the rationalization of the administration and legal system was left relatively intact. Overall, the transformation of the European landscape, in some areas, was "either unalterable or actually even acceptable"[97] for the great powers.

The victorious great powers still faced two core challenges. First, as Carl von Clausewitz recognized, the Revolutionary and Napoleonic Wars transformed European conflicts from "kings' wars" into "people's wars."[98] Consequently, wars of limited (territorial) aims, to an extent, were replaced by wars of unlimited objectives, where outcomes such as regime change and/ or radical reterritorialization of target areas were on the table. Under these circumstances, the great powers of Europe "feared that a renewal of revolutionary fervor would again rouse the fury of a nation in arms."[99] Second, the Revolutionary and Napoleonic Wars left a challenging legacy for the (domestic) political authority of European monarchs: the popular energies released by the war efforts—which revealed themselves in terms of populist, nationalist, liberal, and radical movements—posed direct and indirect threats to the monarchies. The Congress of Vienna of 1814–15 aimed to address these dual challenges.[100] Different from Westphalia (which was more egalitarian and inclusive), it was the great powers of Europe who were the principal architects of the so-called Vienna system. Having defeated a common and persistent enemy that threatened the old regime to its core, the great powers' interests were relatively aligned, of course to varying degrees.

In order to address the first problem, that is, the risk of another Europe-wide "people's war," the great powers attempted to establish a system the main purpose of which was to prevent the recurrence of similar threats. The system itself was built on a theory of "territorial balance or equilibrium of power."[101] The treatment of France is telling. As is well established in IR, unlike Germany after World War I, France was not severely punished in the wake

[97] Best 1982, 204.
[98] Clausewitz [1832] 1976.
[99] Woodward 1963, 8.
[100] On the Congress, see Schroeder 1994, 517–582.
[101] Holsti 2016, 157.

of Napoleon's final defeat, and both the French territory and the monarchy were restored. More specifically, France ended up losing some peripheral territories, but it "still made a gain, compared to what it possessed before the French Revolution."[102] The intention was to prevent French revanchism in particular, and instability or "power vacuum"[103] across Europe in general.

The application of the balance-of-power principle did not remain limited to France. Ideally, the principle was expected to serve as the "main criterion for the redistribution of territories."[104] Conversely, redistribution of territories was supposed to act as the mechanism through which the balance of power, however defined, would be preserved in Europe. This principle was still viable, partially because the dominant territorial model of the day was mosaic territoriality, which, as argued in Chapter 4, made it easier for rulers to exchange territory without being held responsible by the people over which they ruled. As Osiander highlights, at the time, the idea(l) of national self-determination was present, but it barely constituted a "consensus principle" among the great powers of Europe.[105] In addition, the victorious great powers (and, later, [monarchical] France) had little incentive to embrace the notion of sociospatial homogenization. As discussed in Chapter 4, monolithic territoriality would contradict the multiethnic or multilingual composition of the societies that inhabited the great powers' territories, and might also disrupt the hierarchical nature of the monarchical system. Furthermore, nationalism as an "ism" was now becoming more popular across Europe, but it was not dominant yet, as "the full implications of [this] nationalist emotion were not to be apparent until the 1840s."[106]

The second problem entailed the rise of populist or radical sentiments, which threatened monarchical rule across Europe. The popular energies unleashed and nourished by the Revolution and the subsequent wars in France and elsewhere "had already shown their proclivity to react and combine with . . . nationalism."[107] The "flirtation" between radical movements and nationalism across Europe posed a "mortal threat" to the monarchical order in Europe.[108] In this sense, Napoleon was defeated, but "the revolution had only gone underground."[109]

---

[102] Osiander 1994, 203.
[103] Gulick 1955.
[104] Osiander 1994, 226.
[105] Osiander 1994, 198. Also see Holsti 2016, 158.
[106] Wood [1964] 1984, 47.
[107] Osiander 1994, 184.
[108] Osiander 1994, 184.
[109] Osiander 1994, 190.

The populist energies posed a most formidable threat to the monarchical rulers of Europe. To be precise, the republican ideals that engulfed revolutionary France, or the concept of republic itself, did not constitute novelties all by themselves; there already existed a number of republics in Europe well before the Revolution. The French experience posed a unique challenge to European monarchies in two dimensions. First, the previous republican experiences in Europe were limited to (geographically) small political entities, but "The French Revolution had begun to experiment with the concept of representative democracy, of mandated assemblies of the people as a whole. For the first time in Europe, this made republicanism a serious possibility not confined to small communities."[110] The second factor that separated revolutionary France from previous examples of republican rule was the cosmopolitan and expansionist nature of the revolutionary ideas: the revolutionaries, and later Napoleon, did not conceive of the revolution as a "local" and geographically contained phenomenon, and attempted to infect the rest of Europe with their virulent ideology. Doing so, the revolutionaries and Napoleon could draw upon the military, economic, and political prowess of a great power in order to achieve their objectives. In this sense, the revolutionary/Napoleonic experience propelled "the conception of democratic sovereignty in a landscape where 'sovereignty from below' was out of harmony with accepted definition of rule and authority."[111] Put differently, the Revolution and the subsequent wars instigated ideas and political movements that could undermine the hierarchical social order that lay at the heart of the monarchical system.[112] This very social order, in turn, was built on, and became a possibility in the first place thanks to, mosaic territoriality.

Facing this challenge to their political authority, the rulers of the great powers had three options: "imitation kingship to disguise what was really a populist dictatorship; a kingship that was increasingly ornamental; absolutist reaction."[113] In Vienna, the great powers of (continental) Europe settled for the third option and did not tolerate "anything approaching a democracy or even a tolerably liberal oligarchy."[114] In so many ways, for the statesmen and rulers, the postwar arrangements were "all about their 'restoration.'"[115] From a territorial perspective, the great powers wanted to have their cake and eat it too: they were willing to acknowledge the transformation that more than two

---

[110] Osiander 1994, 210.
[111] Woodward 1963, 50.
[112] Osiander 194, 207.
[113] Osiander 1994, 219–220.
[114] Sinnreich 2009, 150.
[115] Best [1908] 1982, 191.

194 How Wars Affect Territorial Ideas

decades of continuous war instigated to the extent that they made mosaic territoriality more viable, but they also wanted to do away with aspirations for popular representation.

Of all the figures involved, Austrian diplomat Klemens von Metternich stands out as a key architect of the Congress of Vienna, and perhaps the most outspoken representative of the reactionary and conservative tendencies. Metternich "identified stability with stasis"[116] and was deeply concerned about the "mere introduction of democratic or nationalist [principles] anywhere in Europe."[117] The Austrian statesman "hated discontented nationalist[s]" since they posed a formidable threat to the traditional (monarchical) order.[118] In order to address this challenge, Metternich sought a "union between monarchs" as "the basis of policy which must be followed to save society from total ruin."[119] In so many ways, the "post-1815 system came perilously close to a conspiracy of princes."[120] Metternich was committed to the idea of fighting the revolution "to [his] last breath,"[121] even if the relevant attempts were doomed to fail in the long run. In the words of Andreas Osiander, "The new political ideas might be a timebomb, but at least [Metternich] would ensure that it was ticking away as slowly as possible."[122] The Revolutionary and Napoleonic Wars, however, had already established that mosaic territoriality could not remain the dominant aspirational principle in Europe in the long run.

Regardless of European monarchies' efforts, the French Revolution and the subsequent wars had initiated a process that was "impossible to reverse."[123] The great powers of Europe still tried to reverse the process, even if it meant limiting their own military capabilities. Most notably, as highlighted in Chapter 4, in the wake of the Napoleonic Wars, the leading monarchies of Europe refrained from capitalizing on mass mobilization and mass armies in order to amplify their war-fighting capabilities. Instead, European monarchs took measures to play down such (Revolution-inspired) novelties. The logic was straightforward: mass mobilization and mass armies encouraged demands for popular sovereignty (or nationalism), which threatened the traditional pillars of monarchical rule.[124] For example, Prussian rulers perceived the *Landwehr*, the militia system that helped Prussia in its war efforts against

---

[116] Sinnreich 2009, 150.
[117] Owen 2010, 146.
[118] Wood [1964] 1984, 50.
[119] Wood [1964] 1984, 51.
[120] Osiander 1994, 221.
[121] Osiander 1994, 185.
[122] Osiander 1994, 185.
[123] Osiander 1994, 232.
[124] Kadercan 2012.

Napoleon, as a challenge to the old regime, as well as a potential platform for revolutionary (or liberal) movements.[125] Accordingly, the Prussian leadership decided to defang, not strengthen, the *Landwehr* institution in the immediate aftermath of Napoleon's defeat.

In IR, the Congress System is usually portrayed as a success story that prevented a European-wide great power war for a century, until World War I. The Congress, in fact, formally met for only a handful of times, in Aix-la-Chapelle (1818), Troppau (1820), Laibach (1821), and Verona (1822), leading some scholars to conclude that the Congress System broke down within seven years and that its actual impacts are rather exaggerated.[126] Regardless, Europe did not experience a great power war until the Crimean War of 1854–56 and the wars of German unification during the 1860s.

As highlighted in Chapter 4, the French Revolution did not immediately lead to the rise of nationalism (as a core component of state ideology) and monolithic orders among the great powers of Europe, but affected numerous geographies in Europe, especially the Balkans. The new political and territorial ideas that followed from the Revolution inspired numerous political entrepreneurs and ruling elites to achieve independence for their own putative homelands. With hindsight, it can be argued that how European great powers approached the rise of state-seeking nationalism resembled how they approached (or were to approach) the principle of self-determination after World War I: the great powers supported independence movements only if such movements did not contradict their own geopolitical interests, and when the territorial consequences would come at the expense of "others." For example, while the great powers were concerned with nationalist movements within their domains, they were willing to support Greek nationalists seeking independence from the Ottoman Empire.[127]

Beyond Europe, the Revolutionary and Napoleonic Wars had the most significant and immediate impacts on Latin America. Latin America would hardly count as a non-Western geography, but there are two reasons to consider the region. First, the Revolutionary and Napoleonic Wars had lasting impacts on the territorial arrangements in Latin America, and these impacts were filtrated through the prism of colonial hierarchy between the metropoles and the periphery. Second, the two mechanisms highlighted in Chapter 3— the disruption of the metropoles' authority in the colonial geographies (due to war efforts), and the appropriation of territorial ideas in the core by indigenous

---

[125] Best 1982, 207.
[126] Woodward 1963, 56.
[127] On Greek War of Independence, see Dakin 1973.

elites and political entrepreneurs in the periphery—can be observed in Latin America.

Most notably, the Revolutionary and Napoleonic Wars disrupted and weakened the influence of the metropole in the colonies. Such disruption allowed local elites to galvanize and organize local support to break free from their colonial overlords. Napoleon, along with Spanish forces, invaded and occupied Portugal from 1807 onward, eventually forcing the Portuguese royal family to move to Brazil temporarily. In 1808, Napoleon took over Spain and installed his brother Joseph as the new king of Spain. Note that the imperial rule of Spain and Portugal in Latin America differed from, for example, that of the British in South Asia. While the British granted a modicum of autonomy to the colonial agents, Spanish and Portuguese imperial rule was "organized centrally in the bureaucracies of Madrid and Lisbon."[128] In such a setting, instability in the metropoles, a direct result of the Napoleonic Wars, disrupted the imperial grip in Latin America.

The Revolutionary and Napoleonic Wars also affected territorial ideas in Latin America. On the one hand, the revolutionary ideas rejected the traditional forms of authority and governance. In this sense, the local elites could draw upon the same ideas about self-governance and rejection of the colonial/ monarchical authority of the metropoles. From a territorial perspective, state-seeking movements in Latin America increasingly conceived the "state space" not merely as an extension of the Spanish/Portuguese empires and the "old" order, but as an independent geography that should be more representative of the local sociospatial dynamics.

Overall, the Revolutionary and Napoleonic Wars contributed to the quest for independence in Latin America, but this independence, especially when it came to territorial ideas and practices, was still heavily affected, if not entirely determined, by imperial legacies: almost without exception, the newly independent states were built on preexisting (imperial) administrative boundaries. A crucial principle that paved the way for this outcome was *uti possidetis.*[129] The principle was inspired by a maxim of Roman law, *uti possidetis ita possidetis* (as you possess, so you possess). The doctrine of *uti possidetis* was (re)formulated in the context of independence movements in Latin America, and was seen as a means to prevent or alleviate frontier disputes among Spanish colonies as well as the relations between (former) Spanish colonies and Brazil. Applied to interstate borders, the principle "treats the acquisition and possession of a state's territory as given, with no

---

[128] Philpott 2001, 154.
[129] On the concept, see Shaw 1996.

territorial adjustments allowable without the consent of the currently occupying parties."[130] The doctrine of *uti possidetis*, more specifically, does not differentiate between de facto and de jure possession and favors "actual possession irrespective of how it was achieved."[131] In so many ways, the principle can be seen as an instrument to preserve the (territorial) status quo as much as possible.

The application of *uti possidetis* to Latin America led to several challenges. First, as mentioned above, the Spanish and Portuguese Empires in Latin America differed from the British Empire in South Asia in one key dimension: while the British in South Asia (and elsewhere) tended to sharply distinguish between the home islands and the colonial possessions, the Spanish and Portuguese aimed to "export" their own administrative systems to Latin America. The independence movements that followed the Napoleonic Wars, in this context, produced "fragments of empire, but not new states."[132] Second, there existed little if any "economic or political logic" to the borders established in the 1820s.[133]

Third, while the independence movements in Latin America were fueled by a sense of nationalism, establishing a modicum of sociospatial homogeneity was a difficult task for the rulers of the newly independent states, in three ways. First, most obviously, the existing boundaries were not drawn to achieve a "match" between borders and sociospatially homogeneous groups. Second, Latin America had both creoles with European heritage and the indigenous populations. Simón Bolívar, whose anticolonialist views influenced the entire continent, summarized the challenges that the independent movements faced in the Congress of Angostura in 1819 as follows:

> [We] do not even retain the vestiges of our original being. We are but a mixed species of aborigines and Spaniards, Americans by birth and European by law, we find ourselves engaged in a dual conflict: we are disputing with the natives for titles of ownership, and at the same time we are struggling to maintain ourselves in the country that gave us birth against the opposition of the invaders.[134]

In this context, Bolívar made a case for racial mixing as the "only equalizing solution to social division."[135] However, the rift between creoles and

---

[130] Mahmud 2010, 59.
[131] Mahmud 2010, 60.
[132] Malešević 2010, 168.
[133] Malešević 2010, 168.
[134] Skurski 1996, 371.
[135] Skurski 1996, 378.

indigenous populations proved to be a critical factor that negatively impacted state-building efforts. At the heart of the problems that nation-builders in Latin America faced lay the mismatch between the amorphous or mosaic realities on the ground and monolithic ideals.

Another challenge associated with establishing a modicum of sociospatial homogeneity within the newly independent states involved "uniqueness." As highlighted in Chapter 4, nationalistic discourses uphold a worldview that portrays the world as a collection of distinguishable and unique "nations," each of which should ideally inhabit and rule its own (national) state space. In most parts of Latin America, "Anti-colonialist nationalist discourse was based on an ambiguous relationship to the past and thus to the notion of authenticity as regards origins and purity."[136] Under these circumstances, the individual newly independent states had relatively little to distinguish themselves from other Latin American states. In fact, the former colonies, with the exception of Brazil, shared numerous characteristics such as language, religion, and a (Spanish) colonial administrative legacy that could have rendered a pan-Latin American movement a possibility.[137] Arguably, Bolívar recognized this dynamic and consequently envisioned not merely "Venezuelan" nationalism and independence, but a continent-wide social movement.[138] In this sense, Bolívar "imagined the nascent nation as part of a united continent, a paragon of civilized life" and promoted "a conception of Americas as a cultural whole," with the intention of "[inverting] the existing hierarchy of world civilization."[139] From a territorial perspective, if successful, this movement would have aimed to establish a monolithic territorial order within the entirety of the Spanish-speaking parts of the continent.

Overall, the pan-Latin American movement failed, just as would be the case in pan-Arab movements in the second half of the twentieth century,[140] and the individual states adhered to their own territorial independence. In this sense, the peoples of Latin America gained their independence from the European metropoles by the early nineteenth century, but they were "stuck" with borders that were not necessarily compatible with the sociospatial dynamics on the ground.

---

[136] Skurski 1996, 375.
[137] Malešević 2010, 168.
[138] Malešević 2010. Also note that it is not a coincidence that eleven distinct nation-states in Latin America share the same national hero, Bolívar. Also see Centeno 2002, 213.
[139] Skurski 1996, 379.
[140] Katz 1993, 370.

World War I

World War I has attracted considerable attention from IR scholars as well as military and diplomatic historians. There is little consensus on the causes of the war, but almost all scholars agree that nationalist discourses and propaganda played an important role in setting the stage for the outbreak of the war, as well as its conduct and consequences. As discussed in detail in Chapter 4, nationalism is inherently a territorial ideology, best associated with monolithic territoriality. In this reading, the Revolutionary and Napoleonic Wars propelled the idea(l) that space-society association should in fact be homogeneous, an idea that was first fueled by the revolutionaries' virulent territoriality but later appropriated by nationalist ideologues. The monarchs of Europe played down, and even suppressed, the idea of sociospatial homogenization that went hand in hand with the rise of nationalism in France and beyond. However, the monolithic order—and nationalism—eventually proved to be the leading territorial principle in several countries like France and Prussia/Germany. In this reading, by the second half of the nineteenth century, some great powers turned toward nationalism to bolster their position in world politics and arrest the development of radical (or liberal) movements in domestic politics.

Bismarck's Prussia and later Germany constitute paradigmatic examples, where the state elites attempted to "tame" populist sentiments and revolutionary currents through the prism of populist nationalism. Bismarck aimed to marry "the Vienna system on the one hand with populism in the disguise of nationalism on the other."[141] The Prussian statesman had no illusions about the extent to which states could fully control the rising nationalistic energies: "One can ride a wave, but one cannot steer it."[142] Bismarck was to be proven right; by the second half of the nineteenth century, nationalism—in either its state-led or state-seeking forms—eventually turned the Vienna system into a "minefield."[143] Some states, especially those that could potentially capitalize on nationalism as a core component of state ideology, adhered to monolithic territoriality as an aspirational model. Those that remained wedded to mosaic territoriality, out of either choice or necessity, faced a challenge: the rising salience of nationalism encouraged demands for national homelands from ethnic and linguistic minorities living within mosaic arrangements. Overall, both state-led and state-seeking nationalist movements amplified the

---

[141] Osiander 1994, 251.
[142] Quoted in Osiander 1994, 250.
[143] Osiander 1994, 251.

importance of where borders were drawn. As highlighted in earlier chapters, territory is never about physical space alone, but is also about the "people." In this context, the association between space and society was increasingly filtered through nationalism.

The increasing prominence of monolithic order as an aspirational model (due to the rise of nationalism) created numerous tensions within the empires, and the tensions in the Balkans eventually paved the way for World War I. In this sense, World War I turned out to be the cataclysm that the architects of the Congress had feared: another "people's war" that brought unprecedented destruction and threatened the very fabric of traditional political, social, and economic life. At the heart of the destruction lay the very populist currents that the architects of the Vienna arrangement had tried to combat.[144]

It is almost universally accepted that the rise of nationalism (as a political ideology) heavily influenced the conduct of war. To be precise, in the decades leading up to World War I, nationalism was already becoming a powerful ideology, but its appeal was not uniformly dominant across Europe.[145] War efforts entailed "an intensive organization of social and economic life,"[146] and intensified as well as accelerated the processes through which nationalism was becoming "a dominant discursive framework for the majority of the population."[147] States that explicitly drew upon the notion of nationalism in order to legitimize and fuel their war efforts, in turn, "projected an ideological image of a unified, trans-class, trans-gender, trans-age, solidary nation confronting a ferocious adversary."[148] Obviously, this image also had a territorial reflection; nationalism also implied a singular territorial identity built on the idea of an inviolable, sacred homeland, for which all members of the nation should make sacrifices.

Note that World War I did not have a uniform impact on the societies of all warring states. As Malešević noted, wars do not automatically enhance cultural homogenization and solidarity, but can also destroy internal cohesion in some cases, an outcome that can be seen in Russia, Austria-Hungary, and the Ottoman Empire.[149] Regardless, at the ideational level, war efforts and associated propaganda emboldened and crystalized nationalism as an aspirational model, which emphasized the importance and inviolability of putative homelands.

---

[144] Osiander 1994, 250.
[145] Malešević 2010, 135.
[146] Wood [1964] 1984, 321.
[147] Malešević 2010, 137. Also see Weber 1976.
[148] Malešević 2010, 137.
[149] Osiander 1994, 188.

In the immediate aftermath of the war, the victorious great powers faced a gargantuan challenge: World War I "appeared to render the prewar international system illegitimate,"[150] a dynamic that prompted the great powers to design a new global political order. Nationalist sentiments, especially in geographies that used to be governed by empires, had emerged as a "genie" that was now impossible to force "back the bottle."[151] From the perspective of the territorial orders framework, the tensions between the monolithic ideals and mosaic realities created crucial problems that needed to be addressed. The victorious great powers aimed to address the relevant challenges they faced through two interrelated mechanisms: the self-determination principle and the League of Nations.

The principle of self-determination, originally voiced by Lenin,[152] is usually associated with US president Woodrow Wilson, who popularized the term across the globe. Wilson's vision, publicized as early as 1916, was built on two core ideas about the future of world politics: (1) political arrangements should be based on "the consent of the governed"; (2) "All political units constituted through such arrangements of consent should relate to each other as equals."[153] At face value, the principle is straightforward: all "peoples" should be able to form their own state and rule their own (clearly demarcated) territory, without interference from other states. The concept of "peoples," in this reading, reflects an implicit affirmation of nationalistic discourses. Such discourses portray a geopolitical imagery where the world's landmass is inhabited by unique and distinct nations (or peoples), each deserving its own sovereign territory. From a territorial perspective, the principle of self-determination implies the primacy of a clearly demarcated state space, which would be inhabited and ruled by a putative nation, that is, a sociospatially homogeneous group. The task for the architects of the postwar global (or European) order, then, was to redraw the borders in order to assure a modicum of sociospatial homogeneity in the newly created (or newly readjusted) state spaces. Put differently, the architects of the peace negotiations aimed to reterritorialize the European landscape in terms of monolithic state spaces.

Note that monolithic territoriality was neither invented nor created during the postwar negotiations. Instead, at the ideational (or aspirational) level, World War I and postwar settlements tilted the balance in favor of monolithic orders, at the expense of alternative territorial models. For example, Wilson did not portray the self-determination principle as an abstract construct that

---

[150] Manela 2006, 1350.
[151] Murray 2009, 238–239. Also see Wood [1964] 1984, 343.
[152] Manela 2007, 37.
[153] Manela 2007, 22.

he intended to impose on Europe (or the world), but as an "independent force already at work in world politics, one that must be recognized and implemented."[154] In this sense, Woodrow's emphasis on self-determination marked the coronation of the nation-state ideal and the monolithic territoriality that comes with it as the dominant aspirational model on a global scale, but only in theory.

The Paris Peace Conference was the epicenter of the efforts that aimed to reshape the global politico-territorial order. Some scholars—rightly so—argue that peace treaties at the end of systemic wars such as World War I and World War II resulted in the "transformation of world territorial space with the creation of over a hundred nation-states."[155] However, these peace treaties did not have uniform or linear impacts on the transformation of territorial ideas and associated practices across the globe; the story behind said transformation was rather nuanced.

In Paris, convinced that another conflict such as World War I would lead to a global cataclysm,[156] Wilson aimed no less than "the peace of the world."[157] For Wilson, the post–World War I peace should be "based upon justice and upon the aspirations of all the common people of the world."[158] However, the Paris Peace Conference was by no means an egalitarian enterprise; similar to the Congress of Vienna, it was the (victorious) great powers who decided not only what was just or unjust and for whom, but also where all the new borders would be drawn.[159] For example, thirty-two distinct countries and more than a thousand delegates were present during the negotiations that led to the Treaty of Versailles. However, the decisions were made by building on a system of "weighted voting," where the great powers of the time—Britain, France, Italy, United States, and Japan—each had five votes; Belgium, Brazil, and Serbia were allocated three votes; twelve countries had two votes; twelve participants had only one vote.[160]

The victorious great powers were the key architects of post–World War I (territorial) arrangements, but, even more so than was the case in Vienna, each power had competing interests and contradicting motives. For example, the French leadership was primarily concerned with the risk of yet another military challenge from Germany and aimed to defang Germany through

---

[154] Manela 2006, 1332.
[155] Hutchinson 2017, 177.
[156] Mee 1980, 16.
[157] Tooze 2015, 255.
[158] Mee 1980, 16.
[159] Osiander 1994, 246.
[160] Osiander 1994, 280. Note that Siam and Liberia were present in Versailles but had no way to meaningfully participate in the negotiations.

punitive measures. Britain, in turn, strove to capitalize on the collapse of the "old" empires such as the Ottomans and expand its colonial reach.[161] While the United States, under Wilson's leadership, was in favor of neither excessive punishment of Germany nor further expansion of the (Western) colonial system, Wilson was willing to accommodate his key partners. For instance, the British and the Americans agreed to dispose of the German and Ottoman empires through the so-called mandate system, well before the formal negotiations began in Paris.[162]

The Paris Peace Conference and the subsequent postwar arrangements were troubled by three challenges or problems. First, the principle of (national) self-determination implied that monolithic territoriality was the new dominant aspirational model, but most parts of Europe where territorial "reorganization" were to take place had been ruled by heterogeneous ideas and arrangements for centuries. Second, in relation, the peacemakers committed numerous blunders that contradicted not only the territorial facts on the ground (vis-à-vis sociospatial arrangements and existing demarcation principles), but also the "idealistic" prose they projected in the first place. Third, the victorious great powers prioritized geopolitical concerns at the expense of both sociospatial realities and their own (seemingly) idealistic discourses.

Compared with the other two, the first challenge was more structural; that is, it had less to do with how the architects of the post–World War I settlements implemented the principle of self-determination than with the self-determination principle itself. The Wilsonian assumption was that once the European map was redrawn so that the new borders "matched" the geographical distributions of the "peoples" (however they were to be defined and categorized), a major source of interstate instability and conflict would cease to exist. In this geographical imagery, the European landscape constituted a territorial "puzzle," the solution of which depended on figuring out the "correct" borders that would ensure self-determination for all. Nonetheless, the European landscape, which the great powers hoped to reorganize according to the monolithic ideal, had been host to numerous complexities that defied monolithic territoriality. As Andreas Osiander points out, "There would certainly have been problems in any case: ethnic groups were often entangled, and perfect solutions based on the separation of ethnic groups were therefore impossible."[163] In such a landscape, short of radical population transfers, it was impossible even to approximate the ideal of monolithic territoriality.

---

[161] Fromkin 1989, 383–462, 493–539. Of course, both France and Britain were concerned with imperial expansion and containing Germany.
[162] Tooze 2015, 259.
[163] Osiander 1994, 289.

204 How Wars Affect Territorial Ideas

In the words of Robert Lansing, US secretary of state at the time of the Paris Peace Conference, "The phrase [self-determination] is simply loaded with dynamite. It will raise hopes which can never be realized."[164] Most notably, legal scholar Sir Ivor Jennings identified a major problem with the concept of self-determination: "People cannot decide [their fates] until someone decides who are the people."[165] In reality, it was the great powers who did much of the deciding.[166] Furthermore, the settlements of 1919 reterritorialized Europe, but this transformation was not merely limited to the location of borders. Imperial territorial arrangements in Europe were destroyed, and the Continent was reimagined as a collection of nation-states. In this sense, "the year 1919 saw . . . a rearrangement of boundaries in Europe" as "established hierarchies of politics, culture, and ethnicity were overturned"[167] in a rapid and somewhat superimposed fashion.

The second problem that bedeviled the postwar settlements had to do with how the architects of settlements handled the aforementioned territorial transformation. As Osiander highlights, while a perfect territorial reordering of the European landscape established around the idea(l) of monolithic orders was an impossible task, "There could have been more acceptable solutions" than the ones produced.[168] Overall, there was insufficient attention to "details" that involved sociospatial dynamics at the regional and local levels. Therein lay the paradox. In a landscape dominated by mosaic territoriality, "details" over where to draw boundaries and the extent, as well as the depth, of reterritorialization efforts mattered less. By contrast, adherence to monolithic territoriality as the ideational gold standard raised the stakes over even "small" (territorial) details.[169] This is hardly surprising. Nationalistic discourses usually anthropomorphize both the putative nation and state space, pushing forward narratives where "loss of territory is inevitably comparable to bodily mutilations."[170] As A. J. P. Taylor recognized, "A hereditary monarch [can] lose provinces; a people cannot do so easily abandon its national territory."[171]

However, Wilson was willing to tolerate "minor injustices of frontier" and hoped that the League of Nations would be able to help different factions sort out their differences.[172] Wilson "believed that the main task of the statesmen at the Conference would be to lay down the general principles that were to

---

[164] Quoted in Philpott 1995.
[165] Jennings 1956, 55–56. Also see Whelan 1994.
[166] Whelan 1994.
[167] Tooze 2015, 285.
[168] Osiander 1994, 289.
[169] Greenfeld 1992, 9; Taylor 1994, 155. Also see Wimmer 2012, 117; Fearon 1995.
[170] Dijkink 2005, 120.
[171] Taylor 1957, 211. Also see Malešević 2010, 324.
[172] Seymour 1965, 194. Also see Murray 2009, 226.

govern the settlement, and then leave the detailed application of these principles to the experts."[173] This was a problematic approach, especially because the instructions provided to the expert committees were lacking in precision.[174] Simply put, the conference made poor use of the experts and committees.[175] For example, the Central Territorial Committee, created by the Council of Ten (which was comprised of the heads of governments and foreign ministers of the United States, Britain, France and Italy, and two representatives from Japan) prepared numerous reports on the contested regions, but only two were brought before the Council.[176] Overall, by designating monolithic territoriality as the ideational gold standard, post–World War I arrangements amplified the importance of even the smallest territorial details but, at the same time, failed to pay sufficient attention to the same details. This paradox eventually left numerous states and nonstate actors (who sought their own state) dissatisfied, paving the way for territorial revanchism and irredentism.

The third factor that rendered the postwar settlements problematic was the contradiction between the idealistic discourses that Wilson promoted and the geopolitical priorities of the victorious great powers. Most notably, World War I led to the destruction of Russian, Austria-Hungarian, and Ottoman empires and the emergence of new independent states in Europe. Finland, Lithuania, Estonia, Latvia, Poland, and Iceland became independent either in the final stages of the war or right afterward. Czechoslovakia and Yugoslavia, in turn, were conceived as, if paradoxically, multiethnic nation-states. Not surprisingly, some of these states were founded on territories that had been governed by other states. For example, the Polish Republic "had to be assembled out of the territories of three defunct empires—German, Austrian and Russian."[177]

There were two challenges associated with incorporating these new states into the European landscape. First, the new states, more often than not, hosted "radically different political traditions and wildly mixed populations,"[178] a factor that made it difficult to establish even a modicum of monolithic territoriality. Second, the victorious great powers simultaneously promoted and violated the principle of self-determination (and monolithic territoriality). As British diplomat Harold Nicolson identified, ideally, "Peoples and provinces . . . shall not be battered about from sovereignty to sovereignty as if they were but chattels or pawns in a game."[179] The reality, however, contradicted

---

[173] Marston 1978, 111. On the role of experts during postwar negotiations, see Goettlich 2019.
[174] Marston 1978, 116.
[175] Marston 1978, 233.
[176] Marston 1978, 119–124. The two reports were on Belgian-Danish and German-Polish borders.
[177] Tooze 2015, 284.
[178] Tooze 2015, 284.
[179] Nicolson 1933, 31.

the ideal, and "peoples and provinces" were often treated as if they were easily transferable (or substitutable) items. Again, in a landscape that elevated monolithic territoriality to the status of the aspirational gold standard, the result was persistent territorial revanchism, widespread discontent, and irredentism.

The case of Germany is telling. Most notably, Woodrow Wilson's references to his Fourteen Points, which included self-determination for all nations, played a role in convincing (or even "luring")[180] German leaders to accept the armistice and come to the negotiation table.[181] German leadership hoped that the principle of self-determination would (or could) apply to Germany. In practice, the great powers' geopolitical priorities trumped both idealistic sensibilities and, with hindsight, common sense, and Germany faced humiliating territorial punishment. On the one hand, especially considering that the majority of the Austrians demanded unification with Germany, complete adherence to the self-determination principle would in fact "reward Germany for the war,"[182] an outcome not acceptable, especially for France and Britain. The victorious powers—again, especially France and Britain—sought to keep Germany (militarily) weak. They also aimed to empower newly created states such as Poland and Czechoslovakia so that these new states could help the victorious great powers balance against future military threats that could emanate from Germany.

Regardless of the great powers' motives, the treatment of Germany entailed a direct violation of the self-determination principle. For instance, Britain's rejection of Austria-German unification "against Austria's express wishes" was "perhaps the most flagrant violation . . . of the principle of self-determination."[183] Furthermore, about eleven million Germans were "ethnically cleansed from the contested borderlands in the East."[184] The fate of areas such as Silesia, given the number of German-speaking inhabitants, invoked upheaval in Germany, leading to crises in the long run. Furthermore, in order to secure Polish access to the sea, the victorious powers established what would be known as the "Polish Corridor," which included Danzig, an area inhabited by a significant number of Germans. Similarly, while the industrially advanced and strategically important Sudetenland was home to many Germans, the great powers found it expedient for the region to be included in the newly established Czechoslovakia.[185] In addition, Wilson promised

---

[180] Bailey 1944, 297.
[181] Also see Osiander 1994, 277. On war termination, see Stevenson 2005.
[182] Osiander 1994, 314.
[183] Osiander 1994, 287.
[184] Tooze 2015, 175.
[185] Murray 2009, 233.

Brenner Pass to Italy, a decision wildly contested by the German leadership, since about two hundred thousand Austrian-Germans lived in the area.[186]

It was not only the location of new borders that offended German sensibilities; areas that were left out of the core German state space, if occasionally, also became subject to reterritorialization efforts. For instance, in Saarland, which was placed under the French mandate, the French government promoted French in schools, presumably with the intention of transforming the sociospatial organization within the area.[187] As also highlighted in Chapter 4, the violation of the German homeland fueled territorial revanchism in Germany, where the lost provinces were not forgotten but instead ingrained in the national geographical memory. For example, as Guntram Herb pointed out, maps that emphasized the "lost" provinces were widely circulated, reminding German citizens that the indivisibility of their putative homeland was violated by the victorious great powers.[188]

Overall, World War I and the Paris Peace Conference rendered monolithic territoriality the ultimate aspirational principle in Europe but did not deal with the complexities and problems that would follow. The League of Nations, especially given that the United States ended up not joining the organization, also failed to manage the tensions that emanated from postwar settlements. Harold Nicolson's self-reflective comments summarize the sentiment in the aftermath of the peace negotiations: "[We] arrived determined that a Peace of justice and wisdom should be negotiated: [we] left it, conscious that the Treaties imposed upon [our] enemies were neither just nor wise."[189]

In IR literature (as well as the Western historiography of World War I), World War I is often portrayed as a war "fought in Europe between European nation-states."[190] Everything else, in this reading, was a "side-show."[191] However, as Gerwarth and Manela highlighted, "Thinking about the Great War as a conflict of nation-states is a case of reading history backward. The world before 1914 was at least as much a world of empires as it was a world of nations even within Europe, not to mention in vast expanses of Asia and Africa."[192] In 1914, "Much of the landmass of the inhibited world was divided into formal empires or economically dependent territories."[193] Therefore, World War I is best seen not solely as a war between European nation-states

---

[186] Bailey 1944, 252.
[187] Osiander 1994, 286.
[188] Herb 2002.
[189] Nicolson 1933, 187.
[190] Gerwarth and Manela 2014, 787.
[191] Gerwarth and Manela 2014, 787.
[192] Gerwarth and Manela 2014, 791.
[193] Gerwarth and Manela 2014, 787.

but also, and perhaps primarily, as a war of "supranational, multi-ethnic, global empires."[194]

In addition, postwar settlements did not mark the end of empires. The immediate aftermath of World War I represented "a world of sharp contradictions," where "empires both disintegrated and expanded, and while violence ended on the Western front and in some other theaters, it continued unabated and sometimes even intensified elsewhere."[195] Most notably, the victorious great powers, such as Britain and France, attempted to expand their imperial reach across the globe. In contrast with the idealistic pretensions at the discursive level, victorious European great powers aimed to establish an "imperial peace."[196] In so many ways, the post–World War I era was the time for acute territorial hypocrisy. It follows that the impacts of World War I on non-Western geographies need to be examined in the context of the territorial hierarchy between the Global North and Global South.

The question then becomes: How did World War I affect territorial ideas in the Global South? Put differently, how did World War I contribute to the rise of monolithic territoriality as the aspirational principle in the Global South? Compared with previous systemic wars, World War I had a much more profound impact on the non-Western world. Paradoxically, World War I temporarily disturbed the territorial hierarchy in geographies such as China and India, but the postwar arrangements also extended the same Western-dominated hierarchy to new locations like the Middle East. More specifically, World War I set the monolithic order as the new gold standard through the principle of self-determination and other Wilsonian principles, but did so only selectively: non-European societies were excluded. Regardless, establishing monolithic territorial orders emerged as the key objective for many elites and political entrepreneurs in the non-Western world, which revolved around the idea of an independent nation-state. In some cases like Turkey and Siam (Thailand), the political elites were able to invoke the monolithic order to establish independence and later recognition at the interstate level, without being directly colonized in the first place.[197] In such cases, state elites, following the monolithic ideal, strove for homogenizing space-society association through nationalistic indoctrination, assimilation of ethnic minorities, and, in some cases, population exchanges. However, in many other cases, the colonial or quasi-colonial arrangements remained in place, in sharp contradiction with the self-determination principle.

---

[194] Gerwarth and Manela 2014, 793.
[195] Gerwarth and Manela 2014, 791.
[196] Andelman 2009, 13.
[197] Özkan 2012; Winichakul 1994.

Put differently, the self-determination principle—as imperfect as it was in practice—became the new ideational gold standard, a "new master principle."[198] Paradoxically, monolithic territoriality was enshrined as the territorial gold standard, but it was denied, selectively, to certain geographies. This "territorial hypocrisy" was most evident in the concept of "liberation of subject peoples," which was, on paper, a common liberalist aim. In reality, this liberation took place only in geographies that used to be ruled by defeated imperial powers. The victorious great powers not only refrained from liberating subject peoples within their imperial domains, but also categorically refused to admit to ruling over subject peoples themselves.[199] Furthermore, the imperial powers were usually oblivious of their own biased and racist inclinations. For example, speaking at the Imperial Conference of 1921, Lloyd George referred to the British Empire as an aspiring "democratic empire" that was built on the consent of "all the races that [were] inside it."[200] This, of course, was only two years after the infamous Jallianwala Bagh Massacre of 1919, where the British troops opened fire on a large group of protestors in Punjab and kept firing until they ran out of ammunition, killing hundreds of civilians. At the time, arguably, the British government could think of a similar act only in "inferior" British territories, not in "superior" locations such as London or Birmingham.

The League of Nations, in turn, only institutionalized the aforementioned territorial double standard. The concept of "nationhood" was portrayed as the core criterion for being admitted to the "club" of sovereign states, but it was also employed by the Western powers to legitimize the exclusive nature of the territorial hypocrisy embedded in global politics. More specifically, the victorious great powers portrayed numerous geographies as immature and deficient, implying that the associated societies did not constitute nations yet. The relevant arguments were based on a certain assumption or argument: societies in the "backward territories"[201] had not yet matured into full-blown nationhood; therefore they needed the guidance and assistance of the so-called advanced nations. This assumption was also engrained in the Article 22 of the League of Nations Covenant.[202] In other words, while "nationhood" was conceived as the master criterion for becoming a sovereign member of the so-called society (or league) of states, Western states exploited the same criterion to exclude countless societies and geographies from the same society.

[198] Osiander 1994, 255.
[199] Smith 2016, 5.
[200] Gerwarth and Manela 2014, 792.
[201] Jackson 1993, 70.
[202] Gerwarth and Manela 2014, 73.

The territorial double standard was not limited to colonized geographies, and it extended to countries such as China, which at the time "existed in a state of semicolonial subjugation."[203] Post–World War I settlements denied the right of self-determination and ignored Chinese claims about the inviolability of what the Chinese perceived to be their homeland. Most notably, the Paris Peace Conference agreed to Japanese demands over Shantung Province. The Chinese representatives were "acutely unhappy,"[204] especially considering that a region of forty million Chinese was to be ruled by Japan, whose population at the time was perhaps sixty million.[205] Regardless, the victorious powers chose to accommodate the demands of a rising, if non-European, great power at the expense of the Chinese claims.

Overall, World War I did not immediately transform how the ruling elites in imperial powers such as Britain and France saw and portrayed the colonized (or colonizable) geographies. The colonial ideology—where "Colonial peoples were conceived as civilizationally distinct from the people of colonizing powers"[206]—remained intact. Consequently, the colonized geographies were portrayed as territorially distinct from the colonizing geographies. In this sense, the mandate (or later, trusteeship) system is best understood as a slight modification of existing colonial arrangements.[207] Broadly defined as International Territorial Administrations (ITAs), the relevant practices conceptualized "the relationship between the foreign actor and the territory and its people in a particular manner: the trustee/guardian state is controlling the beneficiary/ward territory, acting on the behalf of the latter entity—the 'sacred trust of civilization' or the 'civilizing manner.' "[208]

The fate of ITAs, in turn, was to be decided according to the great powers' assessments about the "maturity" of the relevant geographies. Most notably, the mandates were classified into three categories. Category A, which included Palestine and Iraq, referred to geographies that could become independent relatively soon. Category B implied regions (mostly in Africa) that needed "unspecified period of European economic and political guidance."[209] Category C was reserved for the "most primitive peoples" that would require European rule indefinitely, "probably forever."[210] In practice, the mandate system also entailed "cutting" the target areas—for instance,

---

[203] Manela 2006, 1329.
[204] Bailey 1944, 282.
[205] Bailey 1944, 283.
[206] Wilde 2010, 305.
[207] Wilde 2010, 306.
[208] Wilde 2010, 318.
[209] Philpott 2001, 157.
[210] Philpott 2001, 157.

Asia Minor—into bits as if they were a "cake" to be divided.[211] The League of Nations, in this context, "simply became a depository for decisions taken elsewhere," rather than a vessel that would help transition toward decolonization and self-government.[212] In the end, Western powers, once again, were simultaneously portraying their schemes in idealistic terms and professing geographical racism: some territories were more equal than others, and it was the right and responsibility of those who live in the superior territories to decide which territories in the Global South deserved an equality of some sorts.

When expanding their imperial reach in the aftermath of World War I, the colonial powers not only divided up spheres of influence, but also engaged in considerable reterritorialization efforts. For example, the so-called Peace Handbooks, prepared by the British Foreign Office right after the war, occasionally "invented" new geographies and attributed sociospatial characteristics to them. For example, "Syria" was established as both an old (ancient) and a new geography, while in reality, the term was not based on any preexisting political dynamic.[213] Similarly, the British reinvented an ancient concept, Palestine, and the Peace Handbook bluntly "observed" that "the people west of the Jordan [River] are not Arabs, but only Arab-speaking. This observation portrayed the Arabic-speaking inhabitants of these lands as not "Arabs," but 'Palestinians.'"[214] Overall, as the European empires expanded, they continued to try to reshape the sociospatial ideas as well as the realities in target areas, with long-lasting impacts.

In sum, the territorial implications of postwar settlements, best encapsulated with the self-determination principle and the League of Nations, differed largely in the Global North and the Global South. In such a setting, it is possible to argue that "self-determination had virtually no impact on the colonial empires of the victorious powers."[215] However, as Manela pointed out, such a perspective would be misleading, since post–World War I settlements had dramatic impacts on the colonial world, marking 1919 as one of the most crucial turning points in twentieth-century international history.[216]

In particular, World War I and the postwar settlements affected the territorial ideas and practices in the Global South through two interrelated mechanisms. First, the war efforts weakened the grip of the imperial powers over subject peoples. During the war, the (colonialist) great powers such as

---

[211] Andelman 2009, 2.
[212] Andelman 2009, 10.
[213] Smith 2016, 9.
[214] Smith 2016.
[215] Brilmayer 1991, 180.
[216] Manela 2007, 224–225.

212 How Wars Affect Territorial Ideas

France and Britain paid a steep price in blood and taxes. War-weariness also made it difficult for colonizing powers to tighten their grip in their colonies after 1918.[217] In relation, World War I triggered economic, social, and political crises in colonial geographies, further instigating anticolonial sentiments. The colonial powers' attempts to "recruit men and agricultural and industrial resources for the war effort created in the colonial territories a greater common territorial consciousness," which itself was fueled by "a sense of exploitation, and intensified by shortages of basic commodities."[218] For instance, in India, the economic distress instigated by the British war efforts led to protesting crowds in the tens of thousands in 1916; in 1919, the anti-British movement "ran into the millions."[219] By 1922, the British were able to keep the anticolonial movement at bay. Even though the British Empire was able to survive the crisis, its "victory" in India was a "hollow" one.[220] In sum, World War I made it possible for countries like Britain and France to expand their colonial reach in the short run. However, over the long run, it also "hastened a process of imperial decline that would eventually lead to the collapse of a global order based on territorial empires and replace it by one predicated on the nation-state as the only internationally legitimate form of political organization."[221]

The second mechanism through which World War I contributed to the rise of monolithic territoriality in the non-Western world involves the ideational struggle (or interaction) between Global North and Global South. The impacts of World War I on territorial ideas in the Global South can be examined in terms of two interrelated dimensions: international (or global) and domestic. At the international level, the so-called Wilsonian moment encouraged numerous political entrepreneurs across the globe to make their case for independence in Paris. As Gerwarth and Manela put it, "all national movements" in the aftermath of the war "took inspiration from US President Woodrow Wilson's promise."[222] Accordingly, hundreds of representatives from the Global South—from Indochina to the Levante—were present in Paris during the peace negotiations, seeking sympathy and support for their demands for self-governance.[223] The Western powers neglected these voices in Paris, but the struggle for "sovereignty, equality, and dignity as independent actors in international society continued"[224] in the Global South.

---

[217] Kennedy 1987.
[218] Hutchinson 2017, 101.
[219] Tooze 2015, 382.
[220] Tooze 2015, 390.
[221] Gerwarth and Manela 2014, 790.
[222] Gerwarth and Manela 2014, 793.
[223] Bailey 1944, 134; Andelman 2009, 5.
[224] Manela 2007, 225.

More specifically, as discriminatory as it was, the Wilsonian moment created a "common political language with which to make claims" over independence and self-governance.[225] The practice of self-determination might have been denied to countless non-Western geographies in the immediate aftermath of the conference. However, as a normative theory that stipulated how the global landscape should be ordered, the principle encouraged decolonization movements to "formulate their claims for self-government in language that resonated with a wider, international discourse of legitimacy."[226] The international discourse of legitimacy, in turn, was defined in terms of the principle of nationalism in general, the nation-state in particular, which was becoming the "sole legitimate entity" in world politics."[227] In this context, the settlements of 1919 suggested that "across the world, the imperial state as a form of territorial governance was under attack and in retreat, while the nation-state was on the rise."[228]

In other words, from a territorial perspective, the Paris Peace Conference christened monolithic order as the dominant aspirational model, not only in the Global North, but also in the Global South. Of course, the subject peoples were denied their own putative homelands, but the so-called international community, shorthand for the Global North at the time, had formally set the standard for territorial self-governance: nationhood. In this sense, World War I and postwar settlements provided an ideational platform for decolonization movements across the globe to legitimize their claims. If they were to be successful, their claims for self-governance would have to be based on claims about nationhood and therefore monolithic territoriality, regardless of whether or not nationalism was a robust and widely shared sentiment among the local populations in the colonial geographies.

Beyond the international domain, but not independent from it, post–World War I arrangements also provided the blueprints for domestic social and political mobilization for indigenous political entrepreneurs. Note that while the relevant debates in mainstream IR about "decolonization" usually consider the colonial episode and the postcolonial era in terms of a mutually exclusive dichotomy, the territorial orders framework suggests that the association was neither mutually exclusive nor dichotomous. Put differently, at least in theory, decolonization did not necessarily (have to) entail a binary choice between imperial territorial arrangements imposed by the European colonialists and the nation-state ideal (or monolithic territoriality), yet another European

---

[225] Tooze 2015, 374.
[226] Manela 2007, 217.
[227] Manela 2007, 61.
[228] Gerwarth and Manela 2014, 800.

construct. For example, at least in theory, decolonization processes could involve demands for "returning" to the precolonial and traditional sociospatial arrangements, none of which entailed nationalism, at least in the sense we have come to understand the term in the present day.

The internationally acknowledged legitimacy attributed to nationhood, however defined, also empowered indigenous political movements that adhered to nationalism as a mobilizing ideology to "unite disparate peoples."[229] The international legitimacy attributed to the nation-state form put political entrepreneurs who portrayed the nation-state as the ultimate goal in an advantageous position. Consequently, in practice, decolonization processes did not entail reverting to the precolonial territorial arrangements but instead implied convergence on a relatively novel one, monolithic territoriality. Ergo, the settlements of 1919 created a discursive and normative benchmark where the nation-state ideal constituted the only territorial model that would (or could) pave the way for self-governance. In such a landscape, alternative political ideologies and territorial models offered little potential for gaining legitimacy at the international level and unifying the masses living inside the colonial administrative boundaries. Accordingly, nationalism and its territorial underpinnings became the dominant reference points through which indigenous political entrepreneurs could hope to frame their claims over self-governance successfully.

In such a setting, nationalism did not spread to the Global South "with the same ease as football," as Buzan and Lawson argue.[230] Buzan and Lawson are right that nationalism eventually became a "naturalized discourse that plays a central role in defining the terms of political identity and legitimacy around the world."[231] However, the process itself was more nuanced and nonlinear than usually assumed. As Manela argued, "Nationalism, as an ideology and as a form of political practice, evolved conceptually and historically within an international context, and it cannot be fully understood outside that context."[232] In this sense, the spread of nationalism in the Global South hardly entailed a spontaneous process. In the aftermath of World War I, the nation-state idea(l) and its territorial underpinnings were construed as the only viable path to self-governance in the Global South. Therefore, claims for self-governance needed to be framed around nationalism and demands for an independent nation-state, with its own putative homeland. On theoretical and normative grounds, monolithic territoriality had already undermined its mosaic and

---

[229] Anderson 1996, 3.
[230] Buzan and Lawson 2015, 118.
[231] Buzan and Lawson 2015.
[232] Manela 2007, 8.

amorphous alternatives, but it would take yet another global conflict for the monolithic order to supplant them.

In the end, establishing monolithic territoriality as the dominant aspirational principle did not rid Europe and the world of large-scale interstate war. In fact, strict adherence to monolithic orders exacerbated internal instability and irredentist claims in numerous cases. While World War II was not caused solely by the tensions between monolithic ideals and mosaic realities or the contradicting claims about the location of (national) state spaces, these dynamics still played a role, especially in driving Germany's irredentist claims in Austria, Czechoslovakia, and beyond. Beyond Europe, World War I weakened imperial powers' grip in their colonies and set the stage for monolithic order as the dominant aspirational model, around which to formulate claims about self-governance.

World War II

Similar to World War I, the causes, conduct, and consequences of World War II have attracted considerable attention in IR, with good reason. World War II remains the last systemic "hot" war, and it categorically shaped present-day world politics. Overall, World War II triggered a process that eventually sanctified the primacy of monolithic territoriality as a key component of the global territorial arrangement(s). At this juncture, three dynamics need to be addressed. First, obviously, World War II neither invented nor created monolithic territoriality; instead, it tilted the balance in favor of monolithic orders at the expense of other alternatives, and, unlike World War I, it did so decisively. Second, the monolithic order was enshrined as the sole legitimate territorial model in global politics, but the transition from imperial arrangements to monolithic territoriality (as an aspirational model) took some decades in many cases. Most notably, countries like France, Belgium, and Britain kept some of their overseas colonies under control until the 1960s, and the decolonization process was categorically complete only by the 1970s, when Portugal finally agreed to independence for its former colonial possessions in Africa.[233]

Third, the territorial underpinnings of the nation-state ideal, associated with monolithic territoriality, proved extremely difficult to establish in numerous geographies: in most cases, it wasn't the inhabitants of the existing or new states who decided the location of the borders. Furthermore, the relevant geographies had been governed through heterogeneous arrangements

---

[233] On contemporary exceptions to this rule, see Sharman 2013.

for centuries. In this reading, the territorial disputes and intrastate conflicts in the post–World War II era had to do with not only where borders were drawn, but also the contradictions between the monolithic ideal and the entrenched and complex sociospatial realities on the ground.

The ambitions of Germany and Japan, driven by their expansionist geopolitical visions, played an essential role in the outbreak and severity of the war. Nazi Germany sought to expand into Europe and Eurasia, with the intention of reterritorializing the target areas in radical terms. Japan, in turn, aimed to control much of Asia under the banner of the "sphere of co-prosperity."[234] As far as the conduct of the war was concerned, the level of mass mobilization overshadowed World War I; consequently, military casualties and civilian victimization reached unprecedented levels. Overall, the destruction that the war brought was unparalleled, a dynamic that prompted the victorious great powers to reorder the global territorial arrangements in order to prevent the recurrence of a similar global catastrophe. Furthermore, the advent of nuclear weapons provided further incentives to prevent interstate war over territory, which could now escalate into a full-blown nuclear Armageddon.[235] As they did at the Congress of Vienna and the Paris Peace Conference, victorious great powers played the most critical roles in (re)designing the new global order. In the words of Marc Trachtenberg, the great powers "might talk a lot about the rights of small nations, [but] they certainly understood that in the final analysis the interests of countries like Panama, Egypt, and Turkey were of minor importance."[236]

From a territorial point of view, the architects of the post–World War II arrangements were concerned about territorial irredentism and expansionism that had led to interstate crises and conflict in the past. The challenge was then to establish a new global order that could curb irredentism and expansionist policies, at least to the extent that territorial issues would not spark another catastrophic war. In order to address this challenge, the architects of the post–World War II settlements aimed to "freeze" borders by establishing the so-called border fixity norm, while also emphasizing the inviolability of the self-determination principle.[237] In so many ways, these efforts enshrined monolithic territoriality as the ultimate aspirational model in world politics.[238]

---

[234] On the Japanese strategy, see Paine 2017.

[235] On this point, see Jervis 1989.

[236] Trachtenberg 1999, 19.

[237] Atzili 2012.

[238] Note that the border fixity norm was recognized and empowered not only by the Western powers, but also by the Soviet Union. As Katz (1993, 374) highlighted, "Although Moscow did seek to change governmental policy or change the government itself in many states, the Soviets for the most part did not support demands for altering borders or secession."

In addition, United Nations was established as an organization that would facilitate and oversee both the transition from decolonization to a global system of (putative) nation-states and the "freezing" of borders old and new.

Overall, post–World War II arrangements differed from those established after World War I in two domains. First, while the architects of the post–World War I arrangements made an effort, if discriminatory and imperfect, to "figure out" the sociospatial distribution of the "peoples" of Europe through plebiscites and similar measures, post–World War II peace negotiations took a more pragmatic turn. Overall, the Western policymakers "by and large understood that Wilsonian principles could not be applied dogmatically."[239] Accordingly, political and geopolitical concerns played an even more critical role in transforming the European landscape than they did after World War I. The second difference entailed the "enforcement" mechanisms that would keep the desired "order" in place. As is well known, the League of Nations remained a relatively ineffective organization. The UN, in turn, was conceived as a more robust and inclusive organization, backed by both superpowers of the time, the United States and the Soviet Union.

The impacts of World War II on the Global North has been examined in great detail by IR scholars, and there is little reason to rehearse the associated narratives here. Overall, from the perspective of the territorial orders framework, postwar arrangements entailed radical reterritorialization efforts in some geographies, ossifying the monolithic ideal, even if it meant population transfers. For instance, between 1945 and 1948, the entire German population in Silesia, which numbered 3 million, was "violently expelled," with 100,000 confirmed dead, and 630,000 recorded as missing.[240] German state space itself was divided into two, and the notion of "national state space" was reimagined and reconstituted in different ways in West and East Germany.[241] Similar, if not always as radical, processes took place in the Global North, usually at the expense of defeated powers.

How World War II affected the territorial ideas and practices in the Global South have attracted much less attention in mainstream IR. Broadly speaking, World War II undermined the West-imposed territorial hierarchy in many parts of the world, if temporarily: European countries proved unable to fully sustain their colonial rule due to war efforts and Japanese or German occupation. Furthermore, the creation of the UN and the border fixity norm established the idea that monolithic orders should be the only legitimate

---

[239] Trachtenberg 1999, 15.
[240] Tooze 2015.
[241] Herb 2004.

aspirational territorial model. Local elites in the non-Western world mobilized domestic support by invoking the idea that self-determination was their right too, and drew upon the rhetoric of nationhood to gain international recognition. As highlighted above, while colonialism as an idea was condemned in the aftermath of World War II, the practice persisted, as many European states rushed to their colonies in order to re-establish hegemony. The practice of colonialism eventually faded away, mostly thanks to the struggles of indigenous populations.[242] Nevertheless, the territorial hierarchy still shaped the evolution of the territorial orders in the non-Western world. Most notably, in numerous former colonies, the self-determination principle was applied to existing administrative units, not "nations" per se. The so-called border fixity norm, and its postcolonial extension, the principle of *uti possidetis*, eventually limited the risk of wars of conquest, but did not prevent—and might have even contributed to—the outbreak and persistence of intrastate territorial conflicts.

In the words of political geographer Liam O'Dowd, the settlements of 1945 "[replaced] the imperial ideal with the ideological hegemony of the nation-state ideal on a global basis."[243] From the perspective of the territorial orders framework, World War II and postwar settlements had a decisive impact on the rise of monolithic territoriality as the ultimate aspirational model across the globe. Colonialism persisted as a practice, but at the ideational level, the colonial powers had little normative ground left to legitimize their imperial grip across the globe, for two reasons. First, the racist and social Darwinist ideas that were closely associated with European colonialism revealed their extreme forms during the reign of the Nazi Party in Germany, a common enemy for the Western powers and the Soviet Union. The Nazi ideology took social Darwinism to its logical conclusion, portraying numerous social groups as "lesser" beings who inhabited geographies that they did not deserve to govern. During and after the war, the Allied powers relentlessly demonized the Nazi ideology and its social Darwinist underpinnings. Such demonization then made it increasingly difficult for pro-empire elites across Europe to legitimize colonial rule through discourses that directly and explicitly invoked social Darwinism (e.g., "lesser peoples require Europeans' guidance for the foreseeable future").[244]

The second factor that doomed the fate of the colonial enterprise at the ideational level was the rise of the Soviet Union (and, later, China as well) in

---

[242] Barkawi 2018.
[243] O'Dowd 2010, 1043.
[244] See Chapter 5 for a broader discussion.

particular and the Cold War in general. World War II diminished European states' primacy in global politics and established the Soviet Union as a superpower with global reach and influence. Unlike numerous European countries with a legacy of colonialism (where downplaying or whitewashing imperialism had long been a common practice), the Soviet Union openly acknowledged and harshly criticized the central role of imperialism in world politics. Most notably, Lenin, the founding father of the Soviet Union, suggested that at the heart of the economic, social, and political troubles in the Global South lay imperialism, the "highest stage of capitalism," which itself depended on exploiting the subjugated geographies.[245] In this reading, the main culprits of poverty and repression in the Global South were Western capitalists and their willing local partners (or compradors). From a strategic communications perspective,[246] the Soviets' message about imperialism directly undermined the legitimacy of colonial rule.[247] Under these circumstances, it became difficult for the colonial powers to preserve their overseas possessions and dependencies indefinitely, especially given that the Soviet Union possessed both a potent message and the material capabilities of a superpower.[248]

Furthermore, the global ideological competition between the United States and the Soviet Union put the former in a precarious position: American decision-makers, who branded the United States as the champion of liberal democracy across the globe, were stuck between their colonialist allies and an opponent whose ideology not only openly criticized colonialism but also offered a solution (or an alternative) in the form of socialist emancipation. In such a setting, the political elites in the colonized geographies could (and did) play one superpower against the other to further their quest for self-governance. The United States might occasionally turn a blind eye to its European allies' colonial ambitions (at the cost of contradicting its own position over decolonization) but could not easily defend colonialism at the ideational level. Put simply, colonialism persisted as a practice for a couple of decades after World War II, but the global transformation triggered by the war rendered colonialism (which came with an understanding of amorphous territoriality) an indefensible idea. In addition, as IR scholars Kathleen Cunningham and Katherine Sawyer have recently documented,

---

[245] Lenin [1916] 1999.

[246] On strategic communications, see Dew et al. 2019.

[247] On Soviet strategy, see Zubok 2008.

[248] It is no coincidence that numerous independence movements across the globe framed their struggle for decolonization in terms of Marxist-Leninist ideology, as the Soviet Union could offer both ideological and material support. Also note that the Soviet Union ignored and violated the right to self-determination in numerous cases, both in its own state space and in its satellites in Central and Eastern Europe. On the territorial contradictions of the Soviet Union, see Suny 1993.

claims to self-determination proved to be "contagious" and spread across the colonial geographies.[249] The sole path out of colonization, in turn, entailed reimagining the global landscape as a collection of independent nation-states, each with its own (national) homeland, each built on the notion of monolithic territoriality.

The UN, in this context, acted as both a platform and a medium for decolonization. Most notably, Articles 1(2) and 55 of the UN Charter defined the self-determination of peoples as a critical goal for the organization. The UN finally formalized its stand over decolonization with General Assembly Resolution 1514 of 1960, which stipulated the following: "The subjection of peoples to alien subjugation, domination and exploitation constitutes a denial of fundamental human rights, is contrary to the Charter of the United Nations and is an impediment to the promotion of world peace and co-operation. All peoples have the right to self-determination; by virtue of that right they freely determine their political status and freely pursue their economic, social and cultural development."[250]

While decolonization finally became a formalized feature of global politics by 1960, in the immediate aftermath of World War II, the great powers did not necessarily agree on how to move forward with the process. Most notably, the United States preferred a "revolutionary" approach to decolonization, which would entail swift and immediate reterritorialization efforts on a global scale; Britain, in turn, supported an "evolutionary" approach where decolonization would take a gradual path.[251] In fact, beyond the colonial powers' "evolutionary" approach to decolonization lay incentives to preserve their colonial possessions and spheres of influence. Britain, France, the Netherlands, Belgium, and Portugal all hoped to reassert colonial rule right after 1945.[252] Put differently, these colonial powers made an effort to openly profess dual territoriality, adhering to monolithic territoriality at home, but professing amorphous (or mosaic, if rigid colonial borders were established) territoriality in their colonies. These states were initially successful in preventing the immediate collapse of colonial rule across the globe. Most notably, while the UN Charter established the right to self-determination as a principal goal, Article 73 of the same chapter also recognized the potential role of "trusteeship" as an interim arrangement.[253]

---

[249] Cunningham and Sawyer 2017.
[250] Quoted in Brilmayer 1991, 182.
[251] Jackson 1993, 88.
[252] Spruyt 2000, 65; Jackson 1993, 84.
[253] Jackson 1993, 74.

Put bluntly, the territorial hypocrisy that dominated the age of Western colonialism was still in place: colonial powers "freely acknowledged that the principle of sovereign territoriality formed a constitutive rule of international relations," but "they denied that this implied decolonization."[254] Regardless, as highlighted above, the ideational tide had already turned against colonialism. For example, in the Atlantic Charter of 1941, where the United States and Britain specified their vision for the postwar global order, Winston Churchill had praised all peoples' rights to self-government, but "interpreted this pledge as applying only to peoples living under Nazi occupation."[255] From 1945 onward, this imperialist vision could no longer be easily defended on its own terms, a dynamic exemplified by the British decision to recognize the independence of colonial India only a couple of years after the war.

While Indian independence signaled the coming of a future without colonial rule across the globe, the transition was hardly a smooth process. The principle of self-determination and monolithic territoriality had already achieved supremacy at the ideational level. However, the global transformation from colonial rule to a system of nation-states was still hampered by the reluctance of the colonizers in particular and by the politics of the Cold War in general. The case of Vietnam is telling.[256] Vietnam, along with much of Indochina, was colonized by the French for almost a century and later occupied by Japan during World War II. After the war, France attempted to reclaim its former colony. The French attempts were backed, and eventually financed, by the United States, a putative champion of decolonization. The initial US decision was partially driven by concerns about France's support and cooperation in Europe against the Soviet Union.[257] While the principle of self-determination gained much more traction after World War II, it was still being filtered through great power politics. In this sense, for the great powers of the Global North, some geographies were still more "important" (or, alternatively, more "expendable") than others, a dynamic that pointed toward the persistence of the territorial hierarchy and hypocrisy.

Regardless, World War II rendered the idea(l) of self-determination, which would reveal itself in terms of monolithic territoriality, the ultimate aspirational model in the Global South through two mechanisms. First, the war efforts severely disrupted the European powers' grip on their overseas colonies. A key factor was the German military onslaught in Europe: Germany not only occupied almost all of Western Europe (which effectively undermined the

---

[254] Spruyt 2000, 73.
[255] Barkawi and Laffey 2006, 339.
[256] On the relevant conflicts, see Joes 2010.
[257] On US priorities and geopolitical vision during the Cold War, see Gaddis 2005.

power projection capabilities of colonizing European powers), but also forced the British Empire to focus on the defense of home islands, sometimes at the expense of British colonial possessions and dependencies. Another important dynamic involved Japan, which took advantage of the turmoil in Europe and occupied numerous European colonies in geographies such as Indochina and the Dutch East Indies.[258] Japan immediately launched efforts to radically reterritorialize these former colonial territories, with an intention to reconfigure the sociospatial arrangements in a way that would fit its interests. The Japanese rule, more precisely, effectively upended the colonial administrative and political legacies, making it extremely difficult for the colonial powers to reassert their dominance after the war. In Asian and South Asian colonies that were not directly occupied by Japan, the European powers' attempts to extract resources and manpower in order to support their war efforts also empowered anticolonial sentiments.[259] As mentioned above, the rise of the Soviet Union (and, later, Maoist China) after World War II also exacerbated the difficulties and challenges European powers faced in their colonies.

The second mechanism that contributed to the transformation of the colonial spaces involved the ideational struggle between the Global North and Global South after World War II. Broadly speaking, there are two alternative perspectives about how the self-determination principle emerged as an indispensable norm in world politics. The first suggests that the normative change took place primarily in the Global North, and self-determination was eventually granted to subject geographies by the great powers in 1960.[260] The second perspective, in turn, prioritizes the struggles of the subject peoples in the relevant processes.[261] As far as territorial ideas were concerned, the story was rather interactive. Similar to the post–World War I era, but much more forcefully so, indigenous elites drew upon the nation-state ideal to legitimize their claims to self-governance in the international arena. The same ideal also helped indigenous political entrepreneurs mobilize and unify the masses living within the associated colonial state spaces. Hendrik Spruyt identifies this dynamic succinctly: "Nationalist leaders adopted the system of sovereign territorial rule from the West,"[262] and "The periphery rather than the metropoles invoked the normative arguments for decolonization, and did so by turning Western principles against their rulers."[263]

---

[258] On the relationship between the war in Europe and the Pacific, see Weinberg 1995, 205–216.
[259] For example, Barkawi 2017.
[260] For example, Philpott 2001.
[261] For instance, Barkawi 2018, 325.
[262] Spruyt 2000, 78.
[263] Spruyt 2000, 80.

Even more than was the case after World War I, the emphasis placed on nationhood "empowered,"[264] or selected out, political elites who drew upon nationalistic discourses (and the notion of an inviolable homeland) over elites and political entrepreneurs who championed alternative political and territorial models. The nationalist elites, in turn, were also quite selective themselves, especially when it came to defining the geographical scope and (national) characteristics of the putative "nation." Portraying nationhood as the ultimate principle around which to legitimize their claims, the nationalist elites, more often than not, denied similar demands (for self-governance or indigenous rights) voiced by minority groups living within the same state space they claimed. In this sense, "Appropriation of the Western script was selective."[265] Nationalist (or nationalizing) elites championed the idea of the nation-state and monolithic territoriality, but they denied, ignored, or downplayed the claims of other indigenous groups who disagreed with the geographical scope and particular characteristics (such as ethnicity or "national" language) of the putative nation. Instead, many nationalist elites reverted to assimilation or repression of minority groups. This was in fact the dark side of some independence movements. The claim for independence were portrayed through the prism of nationhood (and monolithic territoriality); when independence finally came, the nationalizing elites turned to the task of homogenizing the sociospatial arrangements within their respective countries, sometimes through brutal measures.

Therein lay the paradox: while many nationalist elites justified their claims to self-governance and political authority by invoking arguments about nationhood and inviolable homeland, they also violated the very principle, self-determination, that lay at the heart of the same arguments. In return, minority groups defined their political claims by invoking the same principle, with varying degrees of success. For instance, Pakistan was initially founded as a nation-state in 1947, comprising two noncontiguous territorial units, West and East Pakistan. The political elites in West Pakistan attempted to impose the dominant language within their domain, Urdu, on East Pakistan, where the majority spoke Bengali, while also denying the Bengalese equal (or equitable) political representation. From a territorial perspective, this was an attempt to impose sociospatial homogeneity in both West and East Pakistan. The crisis eventually led to open conflict between West and East Pakistan and culminated with the secession of East Pakistan, which emerged as a new nation-state, Bangladesh, in 1971.[266]

---

[264] Spruyt 2000, 80.
[265] Spruyt 2000, 79.
[266] On this conflict, Johnson 2005, 117–162.

224 How Wars Affect Territorial Ideas

In sum, World War II exerted a decisive impact on territorial ideas about state space, eventually leading to a global landscape where the earth's landmass came to be conceived (or imagined) as a collection of nation-states, each of which was geographically organized around the ideal of monolithic territoriality. However, the transformation took place under the shadow of the territorial hierarchy that for centuries defined the relationship between the Global North and the Global South. Of all the dynamics and cases that can be examined in order to highlight this hierarchy, the doctrine of *uti possidetis* stands out as a paradigmatic example. According to legal scholar Joshua Castellino, *uti possidetis* is "perhaps the single greatest influence on the shaping of the map of the world today" and "the most important factor in the creation and maintenance of modern postcolonial identities."[267] Historically speaking, the application of the doctrine to interstate borders can be traced to the early nineteenth century, or the decolonization process in Latin America. The doctrine was eventually canonized in international law in 1960, with UN Assembly Resolution 1514, which also finally formalized colonial geographies' right to self-governance. The resolution, in particular, stipulated that "any attempt aimed at the partial or total disruption of the national unity and territorial integrity of a country is incompatible with the purposes and principles of the Charter of the United Nations,"[268] ossifying the border fixity norm while also institutionalizing the doctrine of *uti possidetis*.

The doctrine of *uti possidetis* was later reaffirmed in numerous platforms. For example, in 1963, the Organization of African Unity declared that its members embraced the doctrine, which, according to Mbembe, only emboldened the "dogma" of the intangibility of the colonial boundaries.[269] In addition, the centrality of the doctrine for the post–World War II global political order was reiterated in the Helsinki Final Act of 1975, and later reemphasized with the Charter of Paris (1990) in order to ensure its continued prominence in the post–Cold War era.[270]

From a territorial perspective, the doctrine can be seen as a direct extension of the border fixity norm, which itself aimed to freeze the existing borders in order to prevent wars of territorial conquest. As applied to colonial geographies, the doctrine stipulated that "boundaries left behind by colonial rulers, whether sanctified by treaties or not, remain untouched by the succession of the state by independent non-colonial rulers."[271] In this sense, *uti possidetis*

---

[267] Castellino 1999, 527.
[268] Mahmud 2010, 64.
[269] Mbembe and Rendall 2000, 261–262.
[270] Holsti 2016, 53.
[271] Castellino 1999, 529.

"upgraded" colonial administrative boundaries to the status of interstate borders.[272] In practice, *uti possidetis* not only upgraded the legal status of the existing colonial borders, but also "froze" them—presumably, for posterity— by way of foreclosing debates (and claims) over their location.[273]

The doctrine's impacts on (post)colonial geographies can hardly be interpreted in terms of a dichotomy that differentiates between "success" and "failure." On the one hand, the application of the *uti possidetis* to international boundaries could be seen as an attempt on the part of the UN to "maximize the viability of the new states, rather than ethnic or tribal ties."[274] *Uti possidetis* aimed to negate (or limit) the potential risks that could follow from the immediate withdrawal of colonial powers, such as political (and territorial) fragmentation and wars of territorial conquest as well as rampant irredentism, which could potentially "defeat the fruits of independence."[275] In other words, the application of *uti possidetis* to colonial geographies sought to freeze the administrative boundaries right where they were in order to prevent, or at least limit, the extent and scope of territorial conflict in the postcolonial environment.[276]

On the other hand, the doctrine, as it was applied to colonial geographies, was problematic at least in two ways. First, the doctrine of *uti possidetis* was built on the implicit assumption that new states would be based on monolithic territoriality, identified with clearly demarcated borders—which were to be emboldened and guaranteed by the so-called border fixity norm—and sociospatial homogeneity. In many, if not all, cases decolonization implied not the self-determination of peoples (or nations), but the self-determination of the existing colonial territorial units. In fact, the *uti possidetis* doctrine inverted the territorial logic of the original self-determination principle. In theory, the principle of self-determination, as it was conceived (or imagined) after World War I, had a simple, if impractical, logic: the global (or more specifically, European) landscape was imagined as a territorial "puzzle" waiting to be solved, and the solution would entail "figuring out" correct the sociospatial distribution of the "peoples" and matching them with proper borders. Put differently, this vision aimed (or hoped) to take the identities of numerous peoples as givens and define borders to establish sociospatial homogeneity in terms of such identities. By contrast, the doctrine of *uti possidetis* took the existing colonial borders as givens and defined the sociospatial identities

---

[272] Mahmud 2010, 61.
[273] Castellino 1999, 524.
[274] Barkin and Cronin 1994, 125.
[275] Castellino 1999, 529.
[276] Mahmud 2010, 65.

in terms of the same borders, with the assumption that the result would (or could) entail a modicum of sociospatial homogeneity. Simply put, the doctrine neglected "all the other criteria of identity" in favor of preexisting colonial boundaries.[277]

The second problem associated with the doctrine is that it was both a product and enabler of what legal scholar Gerry Simpson referred to as "legalized hegemony."[278] A closer inspection of the concept of *uti possidetis* in the context of its original use and function in Roman law can provide insights into this observation. In Roman law, the doctrine was conceived as an "interim" measure to be applied in cases where the title ownership was contested.[279] Modern international law, by contrast, "conveniently" elided this nuance and interpreted the doctrine as the final and permanent arbitrator of postcolonial borders.[280] In this reading, *uti possidetis*—as it was applied to colonial geographies—legitimized and perpetuated the "spatial history of colonialism"[281] by transferring sovereignty not to peoples, but to preexisting colonial administrative units, and then rendering their borders inviolable and permanent. Freezing the existing colonial borders and defining these administrative units as sociospatially homogeneous nation-states, in turn, "presented a challenge to postcolonial formations to imagine and manage a 'nation' and 'national identity' in the heterogeneity contained within inherited boundaries."[282] As mentioned above, in theory, *uti possidetis* aimed to limit the risk of wars of territorial conquest in postcolonial geographies. In practice, in some cases, this attempt also led to "genocide and/or fracturing of the state."[283]

Of course, not all cases in the Global South (or non-Western world) were directly influenced by the doctrine of *uti possidetis*. Regardless, in many parts of the non-Western world, the contrast between the ethnic, linguistic, and religious facts on the ground and the ideal of sociospatial homogeneity was stark. Numerous governments possessed neither sufficient time nor the infrastructural power to effectively construct a unifying identity that would live up to the ideal of the monolithic order. In this context, the problems associated with what Robert Jackson referred to as "quasi-states"[284] can be read through the territorial orders framework: the challenges did not solely derive from the

---

[277] Castellino 1999, 530.
[278] Simpson 2004.
[279] Mahmud 2010, 65.
[280] Mahmud 2010, 65.
[281] Mahmud 2010, 60.
[282] Mahmud 2010, 60.
[283] Mahmud 2010, 60. Also see Atzili 2012 and Katz 1993, 371.
[284] Jackson 1993.

so-called artificial borders or state weakness, but also had a lot to do with the contrast between monolithic ideal and mosaic (or amorphous) realities. In sum, World War II and postwar settlements alleviated the risk of interstate war, but also set in motion a process that failed to prevent, and in some cases set the stage for, intrastate territorial conflict and instability.

Conclusion

This chapter made the case that just as territorial ideas can affect how states and societies approach war, wars themselves, especially systemic wars, can exert a significant impact on territorial ideas. As highlighted in Chapter 3, systemic wars are not the sole drivers of the transformation of territorial ideas in general, or territorial orders in general. However, historically speaking, these systemic wars acted as powerful catalysts that shaped the nature, direction, and pace of the aforementioned transformation. The effects of these wars on territorial ideas and associated practices, in turn, were hardly linear. Instead, these wars and postwar settlements had nonlinear and multifaceted effects across the globe, pointing toward a simple observation: territorial ideas and practices have rarely, if ever, been uniform on a global scale.

This observation may initially appear redundant, and rightfully so. That being said, more often than not, mainstream IR tends to bypass this observation and does not deal in great detail with the variation in territorial ideas and practices across time and space. The literature on "systemic wars," which also inspired this chapter, also adheres to this tendency. Scholars like Robert Gilpin and John Ikenberry, among many others, go to great lengths to examine how these wars shaped and reshaped the very fabric of international system. New distributions of power, new institutional rules and systems, new sorts of interstate relations, new social norms emerge as a result of systemic wars, but "territory" remains, at best, a mute canvas on which these transformations take place. This chapter made the case that territory, as far as systemic wars are concerned, has been far more than a passive, mute, and blank canvas. How power (as a relational concept) is conceived is usually a function of how we think of territory. Postwar settlements may not be only about territorial ideas, but all rules and institutions that emerge after systemic wars have a territorial component; they actually change or modify how states and societies approach territories. Similarly, "new" patterns of interstate interactions, not to mention societal norms, that emerge after systemic wars also have a sociospatial component.

Perhaps even more importantly, this chapter makes two specific interventions in the existing literature on systemic wars, both revolving around the "canvas" metaphor highlighted above. First, for the existing studies, territory-as-canvas in fact goes through significant changes after systemic wars, best encapsulated by the ways in which borders are redrawn, that is, how these wars erase old "lines" on said canvas and redraw new ones. This chapter suggested that systemic wars do not merely change the location of the territories or change the locations of the lines on the canvas; they repaint the canvas, that is, they reterritorialize the relevant regions in radical ways.

The second intervention involves the specific geographical scope, or at least emphasis, that usually lies at the heart of these studies. In the conventional wisdom, systemic wars take place primarily among "great powers," which usually happen to be the members of the Global North, one way or another. In other words, the existing studies tend to focus mostly on the Western (great) powers and their territories; even when non-Western geographies are mentioned, they are usually invoked with reference to such powers' interests, trials, and tribulations. Non-Western geographies and societies are usually absent from the relevant narratives. In other words, the territorial focus of these studies, the specific canvas they examine, is usually the Global North; this focus, then, is masked under the concepts of international system and/ or great power politics, which we are typically asked to take as "universal" concepts. In contrast to this perspective, this chapter explicitly pushed forward the idea that we need to expand our empirical canvases and pay much closer attention to the implications of these systemic wars for non-Western geographies, or the Global South, for a simple reason: examining the relationship between wars and territorial ideas from a macrohistorical and global perspective that incorporates non-Western experiences can not only shed light on the past, but also inform our assessments of both the present and the future of world politics.

8
Conclusion

Territory and Territoriality in the Twenty-First Century

> What has changed in the post-colonial era is not the alleged unimportance of space but the illegitimacy of territorial conquest. In fact, space is now more important than ever before as it is institutionalized and taken for granted.
>
> —Siniša Malešević[1]

Shifting Grounds aims to establish two central claims. First, different territorial ideas affect how states and societies approach organized violence in different ways. Second, wars can also transform territorial ideas, sometimes in radical ways. To develop these arguments at the conceptual and analytical levels, *Shifting Grounds* builds on what I refer to as a territorial orders framework. Said framework draws upon insights from political geography, taking one of the simplest (social constructivist) definitions of territory as its starting point: territories emerge when physical space is demarcated and organized for political and social purposes. Broadly speaking, territorial orders are aspirational models that aim to regulate the demarcation and sociospatial organization within state spaces. For the sake of simplicity, the territorial orders framework identifies both demarcation and sociospatial organization principles in dichotomous terms. Demarcation principles can be thought in terms of either rigid and clearly defined borders or fluid and "hazy" frontiers. Sociospatial organization, in turn, can be conceived in terms of heterogeneity or homogeneity. This two-dimensional framework reveals four different aspirational territorial models, or ideal types: mosaic, monolithic, amorphous, and virulent. Chapter 3 established the conceptual and theoretical foundations of the relevant arguments, making a case for an interdisciplinary approach that brings together insights from IR and political geography.

---

[1] Malešević 2010, 323.

Shifting Grounds. Burak Kadercan, Oxford University Press. © Oxford University Press 2023.
DOI: 10.1093/oso/9780197686690.003.0008

230 Shifting Grounds

From the lenses of the territorial orders framework, the first claim can be summarized as follows: different territorial orders are associated with different approaches to war over territory. Chapter 4, in this context, compared and contrasted two territorial orders—mosaic and monolithic—that are usually (and mistakenly) collapsed under the so-called Westphalian territoriality, with an emphasis on the French and Prussian/German experiences before and after the rise of nationalism. Chapters 5 and 6 dealt with two territorial orders (amorphous and virulent) that envision the demarcation of the state space in terms of fluid frontiers, a characteristic that has been shared by countless polities across time and space. Chapter 5 scrutinized two distinct paradigmatic cases associated with amorphous orders: the Ottoman Empire and the British experience in South Asia, especially during the nineteenth century. Chapter 6, in turn, examined the association between virulent territoriality and armed conflict by focusing on two distinct cases: revolutionary and Napoleonic France and ISIS.

Different from the preceding empirical chapters, Chapter 7 dealt with the ways in which wars can transform territorial orders, with an emphasis on systemic wars. The analysis suggests that transformations took different paths in the "West" and the "Rest," and the rise of the dominant territorial vision of the present day, encapsulated in monolithic territoriality, has more to do with World War I and World War II than the Peace of Westphalia.

This study aimed to offer insights about the association between territorial ideas and armed conflict in the past (with the exception of the case of ISIS). The arguments offered in the preceding chapters also have far-reaching implications for IR theories and the present and future of world politics. In the remainder of this chapter, I address four broader topics: interdisciplinary dialogues between IR and political geography, the association between territory and organized violence in the twenty-first century, the Russo-Ukrainian War, and the colonial and racist origins of the modern state system and mainstream IR theories.

A Case for Common Grounds between IR and Political Geography

Interdisciplinary research is a popular catchphrase, but—unless the disciplines in question already share certain epistemological and methodological elements (such as political science and economics)—it is rarely taken up due to two inhibiting factors. First, interdisciplinary research is rarely rewarding (and rewarded), since it carries the risk of leaving all relevant disciplines in discontent. The second obstacle to interdisciplinary research is the "overhead costs" of crossing the interdisciplinary barriers: scholars who aim to crossover may need to learn a new (academic) "language" and practice considerable open-mindedness about research questions as well as research designs that are usually antithetical to their own training.

The first obstacle is partially inescapable. For example, some IR scholars may argue that this study is not (social) scientific enough, and some political geographers may find the conceptualization of specific terms relatively "thin" when it comes to multilayered debates revolving around concepts such as land, place, and scale. Of course, just because a study makes claims about interdisciplinarity does not absolve it from its flaws and shortcomings. Still, we can appreciate the fact that for truly interdisciplinary research to flourish, it is expedient for scholars hailing from one discipline or the other to approach the attempt with open minds. In that, *Shifting Grounds* aimed to establish a "middle ground" between the two disciplines, which makes it counterproductive to adopt a position that would be too esoteric on behalf of—or at the expense of—one field or the other.

As far as the second challenge is concerned, to my best knowledge, *Shifting Grounds* is the first dedicated monograph-length attempt to construct a basic conceptual and analytical vocabulary—the territorial orders framework in particular—that can speak to both IR scholars and political geographers. The arguments offered in this book may or may not convince its respective audiences in these fields, but hopefully they will be accessible by the aforementioned audiences. Note that I am not making claims about reinventing the wheel with this statement: as highlighted in Chapter 2, critical IR scholars and political geographers have interacted with each other for decades.[2] My goal has been slightly more ambitious: constructing a conceptual and analytical common ground that will make it possible for the adherents of the mainstream approaches in both disciplines (especially in IR) to be able to relate to and digest the core ideas and claims.

As far as IR scholars are concerned, I tried to offer a conceptual toolbox and a series of narratives that, ideally, would not require much of a background in political geography, that is, prior to this study. So if some IR scholars end up asking, "Where is political geography in all of this?" it means, paradoxically, that I have accomplished what I originally intended: building on and synthesizing countless insights from political geography, while also framing the discussions in a certain way so that the political geography-oriented insights remain almost invisible yet omnipresent.

---

[2] Power and Campbell 2010, 343.

232   Shifting Grounds

Of course, some might still argue that drawing upon political geography for insights is a redundant practice, since IR constructivism already possesses the necessary analytical tools. However, while constructivist research in political geography is inherently compatible with IR constructivism (which has come to be associated with the works of scholars such as Alexander Wendt, Ted Hopf, and Peter Katzenstein, among many others),[3] at the moment, they are not synonyms. Most prominent IR constructivists do not deal with the concepts of territory and territoriality in detail, emphasizing the social interactions between agents, which presumably occur within or between "preexisting" territorial units. Assuming that such interactions—either between states or individuals—take place in a spatial vacuum, however, rules out the possibility that territories are also shaped by, and in turn shape, the same social interactions. Paradoxically, this approach leaves out a crucial component of the constructivist research program in IR, that is, its emphasis on the ways in which social interactions take place in a "structure of meaning."[4] As political geographers have long pointed out, such structures cannot easily be examined and scrutinized if their sociospatial components are ignored.[5] In sum, IR constructivism can serve as a bridge between the two disciplines, but it would most certainly benefit from the constructivist research in political geography.

As far as political geographers are concerned, my intention was to further expose the relevant scholarship to some of the key debates, approaches, and narratives in IR. John Agnew's territorial trap intervention remains one of the core "bridges" between political geographers and IR scholarship. Still, Agnew's original article was published in 1994, a time when IR scholarship looked very different from its current form. It is true that mainstream IR has yet to fully engage the territorial trap even today, but IR scholarship today is, arguably, more diverse and vibrant in terms of accommodating different approaches and methodologies; long gone are the days when IR literature was dominated by the so-called paradigm wars between realists, liberals, and constructivists (as had been the case during the 1990s). If the intent is not to merely discount "IR research" wholesale but to move beyond the territorial trap, a mutual rapprochement between the two disciplines is not only useful, but imperative. IR constructivism, in this context, can serve as an analytical beachhead for political geographers to engage the greater debates in IR.

---

[3] On IR constructivism, see Adler 2013. Most notably, Alexander Wendt (1999) engages numerous aspects of mainstream IR theories, but does not fully engage IR's geographical assumptions.

[4] Wiener and Puetter 2009.

[5] Paasi 1996.

In sum, this study attempted to overcome the aforementioned dual obstacles and make a contribution to our understanding of the relationship between territory and world politics from an interdisciplinary perspective. In Chapter 2, I highlighted two specific issues that need to be addressed for such an interdisciplinary perspective to flourish. The first is IR scholars' inattention to the task of explicitly defining the terms "territory" and "territoriality." At face value, this is not a real challenge; all that IR scholars would need to do is simply define these concepts in explicit terms. It is utterly irrelevant whether IR researchers use the specific definitions offered in this study or not. From an analytical perspective, there is also nothing wrong with adhering to the categorically materialistic interpretations of territory, which are discussed in Chapter 2. The key point is that IR scholars who work on territory should provide *a* definition, even if their intent is not to engage the relevant (constructivist) research in political geography. Defining territory as a social and political construct, in this context, would come with the additional benefit of taking advantage of the existing insights on the other side of the disciplinary fences.

The second challenge is overcoming, or escaping from, the territorial trap. A key question in terms of interdisciplinary dialogues is the following: Is the territorial trap more of a molehill or a mountain that stands between IR and political geography?[6] This is in fact a fair question: it's been almost three decades since Agnew's influential piece on IR's geographical assumptions was published, but the article's influence has yet to penetrate mainstream IR scholarship. So a claim might be made that the territorial trap is an insurmountable mountain. I disagree. It is not an insurmountable (analytical) mountain; in fact, it is not even a molehill. The main reason why IR scholars do not usually try to "escape" from the territorial trap is not because it is an analytical mountain. It is not the case that IR scholarship tried to move beyond the territorial trap but failed in the face of overwhelming challenges. Instead, mainstream IR scholarship simply has *not* engaged the trap; in fact, it would not be far-fetched to suggest that many IR scholars are not even fully aware of the decades-long debates in political geography about their own (or IR's) geographical assumptions.

In the end, the aforementioned trap is essentially socially constructed; it is neither a real trap nor an insurmountable obstacle. Accordingly, social constructivist approaches, not only in IR but also in the greater social sciences and humanities, offer a relatively easy way out of the territorial trap: all that it would take is to acknowledge that "territory" is not a synonym for physical

---

[6] I'd like to thank an anonymous reviewer for this analogy.

234 Shifting Grounds

space or a "mute" and passive object, but a social construct with countless different interpretations. In fact, the territorial trap is like robust wall paint that covers over the complexity and richness of structures by imposing a single color on them. All that IR scholars need to do is to scratch off this paint, revealing how varied these structures are—by which I mean the complex, contingent, and ever-shifting nature of territorial ideas and practices. In the end, the territorial trap is not about a "real" problem in IR; it is about the geographical assumptions of IR. Once we relax and/or problematize these assumptions, it becomes easier to see the past and present of world politics in a much more "colorful" way.

A final question to address is the following: So, where do we go from here? Put differently, how do the interdisciplinary insights offered in the preceding chapters help us better understand the trends and developments that go beyond the empirical scope of this study? In the next three sections, I briefly comment on a number of topics where the aforementioned insights can contribute to our understanding of territories' place in world politics.

Territory, Territoriality, and Organized Violence in the Twenty-First Century

The preceding chapters did not directly address numerous topics that involve territory and territoriality, such as civil wars and secessionist movements, the so-called nation-building campaigns, and "new" methods for expanding territorial influence (if not direct control). Dealing with the relevant cases and research questions in great detail is beyond the scope of this study, which already covered a wide variety of cases from different geographies and time periods. That being said, the territorial orders framework can still offer insights about these topics, which can guide future research.

Most notably, from 1945 onward, interstate wars over territory in general, wars of territorial conquest in particular, have become rare events, but intrastate conflicts (over territory) and secessionist movements persist.[7] Put differently, war over territory has become an intrastate, rather than interstate, affair, when compared with the pre-1945 period. In this context, *Shifting Grounds* has direct implications for the debates over the so-called artificial borders, or the idea that numerous borders across the globe, especially in the former colonies, have been drawn with little attention to the geographical distribution of "peoples," broadly defined. This artificiality, so the argument

---

[7] On civil wars, see Fearon and Laitin 2003.

goes, has contributed to the emergence of numerous problems including, but not limited to, chronic state weakness, irredentism, and intrastate disputes and conflicts.[8] As highlighted in Chapter 7, the dominance of the European/ Western powers during the course of the nineteenth and twentieth centuries in global politics eventually made the "rigid delineations observed in Europe"[9] an aspirational master model to be employed by local actors. In many parts of the globe, in this reading, the process of establishing hard borders was "rushed," with adverse effects on peace and stability. In particular, as Boaz Atzili argues, the emergence of the border fixity norm, by way of hardening borders "from the outside," led to chronic instability in regions ranging from the Middle East to Africa.[10]

The relevant trends, which usually come with an intent to "freeze" the existing borders, reflect an overwhelming emphasis on demarcation principles. The dominant, if implicit, assumption in present-day world politics is that the global landscape should be conceived in terms of monolithic territoriality. However, monolithic orders require a modicum of societal homogeneity to function properly. In many parts of the world, monolithic ideals are in direct contrast with mosaic realities, a dynamic that triggered intrastate conflicts and even genocide in the past, as well as the present. The underlying cause of these conflicts and crises is not merely "artificial borders"; attempts to impose the principle of sociospatial homogeneity on parts of the world that had been governed through heterogeneous arrangements for a very long time have also contributed to such tensions. If that is the case, "redrawing borders" does not necessarily constitute an adequate solution to the problems associated with territorial disputes and conflicts across the globe. As political geographer Alexander Murphy pointed out, "The rigid territorial structure of the modern state system is poorly suited to deal with a world of complexly intertwined peoples with differing political and cultural identities and aspirations"; therefore, "No amount of . . . boundary redrawing can address this fundamental problem."[11]

The second, and related, insight that follows from the preceding chapters entails the paradoxical relationship between the primacy of monolithic territoriality as an aspirational model and intrastate disputes over territory as well as secessionist movements: the monolithic ideal not only tends to "harden" the existing borders, but also creates incentives for numerous social groups (usually minorities) to redraw the same borders. More specifically, intrastate

---

[8] Jackson 1993.
[9] Horowitz 2004, 478.
[10] Atzili 2012.
[11] Murphy 2013, 1222.

236 Shifting Grounds

territorial conflicts and secessionist movements do not take place in a (historical) vacuum; instead, they play out in a global landscape that has long been dominated by monolithic territoriality as an aspirational principle.

Note that ideas about demarcating state spaces and organizing the space-society association have never been globally uniform or static. For example, so-called Westphalian territoriality, however it is defined, rose to prominence in Europe in the seventeenth century. However, as argued in Chapter 5, the European states adhered to extra-Westphalian ideas and practices while colonizing non-European geographies. More specifically, in Europe, states fought over territory during the eighteenth and twentieth centuries; but why and how they fought displayed considerable variation, thanks in part to the impacts of nationalism on how states and societies conceived of territory in general, state spaces in particular. Similarly, European states long considered many parts of the non-Western geographies to be "open" and "backward" territories, ripe for Western intervention, a geographical assumption that has become much less prevalent, if not completely extinct.

The post–World War II period, however, is distinct from the previous eras in one crucial dimension: *at the aspirational level*, dominant territorial ideas have converged on the monolithic ideal, enshrined in the nation-state model. Therein lies the paradox: in countless cases, there has long existed a gap between the monolithic ideal and the fluid sociospatial facts on the ground. For example, in many cases, borders do not simply separate one nation, supposedly a sociospatially homogeneous entity, from others, but sometimes also separate groups who perceive themselves to be a nation. As a result, establishing even a modicum of sociospatial homogeneity within their domains has proven a challenging task for many states. Regardless, the discourse and practice of international politics are still built on a particular assumption: the global landscape is (or should be) ordered in terms of discrete pieces of clearly demarcated territories, each hosting a sociospatially homogeneous population. Put differently, as in previous eras, the present-day global landscape is best defined in terms of diversity, not uniformity. Again, the main difference from previous eras is that the conventional and dominant geographical imageries tend to downplay this diversity.

At the aspirational level, monolithic orders, which emphasize rigid borders and sociospatial homogenization, are reproduced and reified continuously by both international and domestic dynamics. At the international level, as examined in Chapter 7, the border fixity norm (which has been hardened by its postcolonial extension, the doctrine of *uti possidetis*) renders existing borders extremely rigid, if not impregnable. Domestically, as argued in Chapter 4, the notion of "inviolable homeland," which lies at the heart of nationalistic discourses, creates strong incentives for state élites to prioritize the preservation of the state space per se, reifying the existing borders. Similarly, the legitimacy attributed to "nationhood" at the international level motivates governments across the globe to define their populations in terms of sociospatial homogeneity, even when the sociospatial facts on the ground do not align with such definitions. Domestic political factors further ossify this dynamic: in many cases, state elites legitimize their claims to authority by invoking their (supposed) role as the protector of both the putative nation (which is imagined as a sociospatially homogeneous entity) and the homeland (which is imagined to be inviolable).

These dynamics have direct implications for the study of secessionist movements and intrastate conflicts in the recent past and present. Note that secessionist movements (which can sometimes trigger and fuel civil wars over territory) do not challenge the dominant territorial model of present-day global politics, that is, monolithic territoriality. On the contrary, much like the independence movements of the early twentieth century, such movements acknowledge monolithic territoriality as an aspiration.[12] Put differently, secessionist movements do not contest, but in fact embrace, the nation-state ideal and its territorial underpinnings, claiming an inviolable homeland of their own, which would act as a "cultural container" for their own sociospatially homogeneous group. As Ariel Ahram put it, secessionist or irredentist movements "reject particular states but embrace the model of statehood," and even "those orphaned by twentieth century Wilsonianism still cling to its core values in the new millennium."[13]

So, what does the territorial orders framework tell us about secessionist movements and associated intrastate conflicts? *Shifting Grounds* points toward a pessimistic vision about the future of intrastate territorial disputes and secessionism. The hegemony of monolithic territoriality, as an aspirational model, traps both state elites and their domestic (territorial) contenders in a Catch-22. Social groups that do not feel that they belong to the putative "nation," as it is defined and reified by state institutions and indoctrination, are incentivized to frame their claims in terms of territorial autonomy or independence, the latter usually defined in terms of monolithic territoriality.[14] Paradoxically, the primacy of monolithic territoriality as an aspirational ordering principle also makes it extremely difficult for state elites to give up pieces of what the majority of their constituents deem their inviolable

[12] Murphy 2013.
[13] Ahram 2018, 326.
[14] See Chapter 7 for a similar mechanism in the context of post–World War I and post–World War II settlements.

238   Shifting Grounds

homeland. Furthermore, as highlighted in previous chapters, all by itself, redrawing borders guarantees neither the emergence of sociospatially homogeneous geographical units nor stability and peace. Especially in geographies that used to be governed through heterogeneous sociospatial arrangements, new borders can lead to further waves of instability, abuses of minority rights, and irredentist claims.

Again, these observations paint a rather pessimistic picture about the future of secessionist movements and associated intrastate conflicts: as long as monolithic territoriality remains the aspirational hegemon, secessionism and irredentism, not to mention the risk of intrastate conflicts over territory, will likely persist. Conversely, the territorial orders framework also points toward the possibility of a more optimistic vision in the long run, attached to a rather radical solution to the relevant tensions: if, or when, the dominant territorial ideas move away from monolithic territoriality and become more tolerant of heterogeneous sociospatial arrangements, most intrastate disputes and conflicts over territory will become easier to manage, if not disappear entirely.

Of course, that is a big "if." Both international and domestic dynamics reify the primacy of monolithic territoriality. Put simply, such primacy cannot be easily wished away. However, if this study has one insight to offer about territory and territoriality, it is the following: territorial ideas have shown significant variation across time and space. The primacy of monolithic territoriality in world politics, which is hardened by the territorial trap, is neither a "natural" artifact nor the "end of history" as far as territorial ideas are concerned; instead, monolithic territoriality's conceptual, legal, and normative hegemony is based on historical contingencies and (institutionalized and internalized) discourses. As R. B. J. Walker put it, mainstream IR theories reify a "discourse of eternity," which emphasizes the permanent dynamics of interstate politics.[15] However, territorial ideas and practices are anything but constant. Thinking beyond the territorial trap and considering alternative sociospatial arrangements may be insufficient all by themselves to prompt a peace-inducing transformation in territorial ideas. However, such measures can also act as the first step in questioning, and perhaps improving upon, present-day global territorial arrangements. In such a setting, a more constructive, as well as social constructivist, path forward might be to move beyond the territorial trap and explore measures that could realign sociospatial ideals with sociospatial realities.

Another relevant implication that follows from the arguments provided above concerns foreign-imposed regime change and so-called nation-building

---

[15] Walker 1995, 306. Also see Albert 1998, 55.

or state-building campaigns.[16] As John Owen has shown, foreign-imposed regime change is not a new phenomenon in world politics, and, in Europe, it can be traced at least to the sixteenth century.[17] In the post–Cold War era, and especially in the immediate aftermath of the September 11, 2001, attacks, however, foreign-imposed regime change took a turn toward "nation-building" campaigns. While a popular idea two decades ago among certain circles, nation-building (that would follow a foreign intervention) has proven ineffective and even counterproductive. Iraq and Afghanistan stand out as two examples that undermine the logic behind imposed nation-building: almost two decades after the US-led interventions, and despite trillions of dollars spent and tens of thousands of lives lost, both countries are still troubled by civil strife and chronic instability. The territorial orders framework offers not only insights about the origins of the initial optimism of those who cheered for nation-building in the Middle East and why their efforts failed, but also policy advice for Western governments that may consider similar campaigns in the future.

So, how can a territorial perspective help explain the initial optimism that led to the foreign-imposed nation-building campaigns in Iraq and Afghanistan? Simply put, optimism was fueled by the territorial trap, which reifies the primacy of monolithic orders at the aspirational level. In that reading, Iraq is both a spatially enclosed geographical entity and a nation-state. Iraqis, in turn, are a sociospatially homogeneous group. Once policymakers internalize these assumptions, it becomes easier to impose regime change and nation-building: all that the intervening foreign powers need to do is to topple the existing regime and help the "people" to march through the transition process. Leading up to the invasion of Iraq, these assumptions were backed by "success" stories of the past, especially the cases of Japan and Germany after World War II.[18] Once combined, the relevant (territorial) assumptions and success stories render forceful regime change (to be followed by a nation-building campaign) a seemingly feasible policy option, paving the way for "nation-building optimism."

The territorial orders framework can also help explain why the imposed attempts at nation-building in Iraq and Afghanistan failed. As mentioned in this and previous chapters, the dominant territorial assumptions, especially in the post–World War II era, take monolithic orders as givens, even when sociospatial facts on the ground contradict the monolithic ideal. Destabilizing

---

[16] For a broader discussion on the topic, see Downes and O'Rourke 2016.
[17] Owen 2010.
[18] For the relevant debates, see Edelstein 2004 and Dower 1999.

240 Shifting Grounds

and toppling the target regimes, in turn, appears to be a viable option, even when it is not. Selectively invoking past successes ossifies the faulty nature of territorial assumptions. For example, for historical reasons, both Germany and Japan are two (rare) cases where the sociospatial facts were in relatively close alignment with the monolithic ideal. In this sense, post-1945 reconstruction efforts in these two countries did not amount to "nation-building," as a sense of geographically defined national identity was already robust in Japan and Germany well before 1945.

Unlike Japan and Germany, neither Iraq nor Afghanistan has enjoyed geographically defined sociospatial homogeneity. The borders of Iraq, to a large extent, were a product of the negotiations between France and Britain during and following World War I. The territory we now refer to as Iraq had been affiliated with amorphous territoriality for centuries. Furthermore, like their counterparts in numerous Arab-majority geographies, Iraqi citizens were locked in a paradox. On the one hand, ethnicity and language alone did not confirm the existence of a unique Iraqi nation; to the contrary, the dominant ethnicity and language pointed toward a sense of shared heritage with Arab populations and geographies beyond Iraqi borders, a dynamic that also fueled pan-Arab movements in the Middle East, ranging from Nasserism to Baathism.[19] On the other hand, beyond ethnicity and language, the citizens of Iraq differed from each other in terms of religious and confessional affiliations. In addition, the existence of Kurdish populations in northern Iraq complicated the task of establishing even a modicum of sociospatial homogeneity within Iraqi borders. Afghanistan, in turn, has a different historical trajectory, but can hardly be conceived in terms of sociospatial homogeneity and clearly defined (and enforced) borders. As Mark Bayly put it, Afghanistan has long been more of a geographical expression than a nation-state.[20] Under these circumstances, destabilizing existing regimes with the intention of launching a nation-building campaign is a costly and potentially counterproductive option. As can be seen in the example of Iraq, once the existing regimes collapse, sociospatial affiliations also tend to disintegrate, and mosaic realities, or the mosaic of local and subnational territorial loyalties, rise to surface.

If this analysis has merit, what policy advice follows? Simply put, Western governments, especially the United States, should approach nation-building with extreme caution. Transforming political institutions alone, especially in the wake of forceful and foreign-imposed regime change, does not guarantee the emergence of a sociospatially homogeneous "nation." On the contrary, a

---

[19] On nationalism in Arab-majority countries, see Barnett 1995.
[20] Bayly 2014.

radical restructuring of the political landscape can fragment sociospatial identities and loyalties. Note that this policy advice may resemble those offered by scholars such as John Mearsheimer.[21] Mearsheimer opposes the idea that the United States and its allies should, or could, "spread" democracy through the use of armed force and regime change, to be followed by a nation-building campaign. For Mearsheimer, one obstacle that impedes the relevant efforts is the resilience and salience of nationalism in target geographies. The territorial orders framework agrees with the idea that foreign-imposed nation-building is usually counterproductive, but offers a categorically different rationale for it: Foreign-imposed nation-building is usually a futile, or at least extraordinarily difficult, undertaking *not because (territorial) nationalism is robust in target geographies, but because it is weak.* The weakness of a shared sense of sociospatial homogeneity renders foreign-imposed nation-building campaigns extremely costly and potentially counterproductive.

It is true that, as highlighted in Chapter 5, empires of the past encouraged heterogeneous sociospatial arrangements, partially to rule on the cheap, partially for the fear that unified, organized, and motivated local groups could undermine imperial authority. In fact, imperial governance usually aimed to "divide and rule" target areas, usually by empowering some local actors at the expense of others, a practice that not only exploited local grievances, but also exacerbated them. The relevant tactics might have worked for imperial governance, at least for a while, but they would be utterly counterproductive if the intention involves nation-building or, at the very least, establishing social and political stability.

This observation about the shifting nature of territorial ideas, which becomes more visible when examined through the lenses of a macrohistorical and global perspective, also has implications for the ways in which we think about the future of world politics. One insight that follows from the analysis provided in the previous chapters, especially Chapter 7, is that the dominant territorial ideas across the globe have never been truly static, and the relevant transformations have rarely followed a linear trajectory. This dynamic has two implications for the future of world politics. First, while the territorial trap makes it challenging to conceive of the state-society-space nexus in ways that go beyond monolithic territoriality, there is no reason to think that the dominance of monolithic orders as the aspirational model will remain intact for the foreseeable future. In other words, the malleable nature of territorial ideas does not guarantee a regional or even global "great transformation" in the same ideas, but such transformation cannot be considered an improbable development. The increasing

---

[21] Mearsheimer 2018.

242 Shifting Grounds

relevance of cyberspace for everyday and international politics, yet another catastrophic war, an environmental crisis, or a global pandemic can act as a catalyst for transformation. If the past is any guide, a great transformation in territorial ideas would likely take a nonlinear path, and its impacts as well as internalization across the globe would be far from uniform.

Another implication that follows from this study involves "new" forms of territorial expansion. Numerous countries, from Russia (in Georgia, Chechnya, and Ukraine) to Iran (in Syria and Lebanon), to China (in the South China Sea) to Turkey (in Syria), among many others, are pursuing policies to expand their territorial reach. The territorial orders framework suggests that while these measures may appear to be novelties, from a macrohistorical perspective, they are hardly so. Just as most Western states did throughout the nineteenth and early twentieth centuries in non-Western geographies, Russia, Iran, and Turkey, among others, are pursuing a dual approach to territoriality: these states adhere to monolithic ideals within their borders but profess an amorphous approach beyond them, using unconventional methods and strategies to expand their spheres of influence. Iran, for example, projects influence and power into countries like Lebanon and Syria, while Turkey is actively controlling and governing large swaths of territory in northern Syria. In this sense, the methods that countries like Iran and Turkey are adopting to expand their spheres of influence can hardly be categorized as new. China, in turn, has been involved in the creation of artificial islands in the South China Sea, an act that defies conventional understandings of territorial waters. China's policies resemble acts of symbolic reterritorialization, which are carried out through the establishment of certain landmarks. This practice is hardly a novelty. For example, the Netherlands in the seventeenth century undertook similar measures in order to create new spaces, which would pave the way for long-term economic and geopolitical benefits.

The relevant research questions deserve dedicated scholarly attention, which, again, is beyond the scope of this study. Still, especially over questions about the relationship between territoriality and organized violence, *Shifting Grounds* makes the case for two arguments. First, moving beyond the territorial trap is an essential step, of course, if we intend to make better sense of the territory-related challenges of the twenty-first century. Second, once we move beyond the territorial trap and recognize the wide range of possible territorial arrangements, the past reveals itself as an invaluable source from which we can extract insights about the present as well as future of world politics.[22]

---

[22] Similarly, the territorial orders framework suggests that the European Union professes a form of territoriality akin to neither a post-territorial entity nor a giant nation-state, but the early Westphalian state of

Conclusion **243**

Territory Strikes Back: The Russo-Ukrainian War

In February 2022, Russia launched what Vladimir Putin framed as a "special military operation" in Ukraine, with a dual purpose: capture territory and impose regime change in Kyiv. Russia's incursion was not an isolated incident, but the culmination of a thirty-year crisis that first revealed itself with the dissolution of the Soviet Union. This crisis reached new heights in 2014, when the Maidan Revolution led to the removal of Ukraine's pro-Russia president, Viktor Yanukovych. The Maidan Revolution paved the way for two crucial developments. First, in direct violation of the so-called border fixity norm, Russia occupied Crimea,[23] and after an internationally condemned referendum in the occupied territory, annexed the peninsula. Second, the revolution set the stage for an unconventional, "frozen," territorial conflict between Ukraine and Russian proxies (as well as some Russian military personnel presumably under cover) in eastern and southern Ukraine, especially in Donetsk and Luhansk provinces, which, as of 2018, might have claimed as many as ten thousand lives.[24] While Russia denied direct involvement, from the analytical lenses offered in this study, the Russian state was waging "hybrid warfare" in eastern and southern Ukraine, in ways that were not all that different from the imperial practices of the past. In so many ways, the Russian practices, guided by amorphous territoriality, did not respect the international borders between Ukraine and Russia and aimed to create spheres of direct influence and indirect control, a hallmark of countless empires from the Ottomans to the British.[25]

The crisis and the slow-burning territorial conflict in eastern and southern Ukraine eventually led to the Russian invasion of Ukraine in February 2022. The Russo-Ukrainian War is of crucial importance for three reasons. First, it is the first large-scale interstate conflict in Europe since the end of World War II. Second, the war is about territory. The territorial dimensions of the conflict reveal themselves in terms of the origins of the conflict, its conduct, and even discussions about its termination. The territorial nature of the war, in turn, upends the "end of territory" thesis, which posits that, in the face of globalization and changing patterns of (economic) production, territory is no longer

---

the eighteenth century: the EU's *external* borders are as rigid as any functioning nation-state, and the EU project has been built on the ideal of sociospatial heterogeneity (which would undermine the sociospatial homogeneity encompassed in the nationalism). In this sense, the EU might be better described as a "rebundling" of territorialities than an "un-bundling" (Longo 2017a, 760; also see Ansell 2004).

[23] On the Crimean crisis of 2014, see Wilson 2014.
[24] Sasse and Lackner 2018, 139.
[25] See Chapter 5.

244 Shifting Grounds

as salient a concern in world politics. The third relevant dynamic—which surprised many, if not all, spectators—was the resilience of the Ukrainians in the face of overwhelming odds. As of late 2022, no one would question the Ukrainians' determination to preserve the territorial integrity of their country. However, when hostilities began in February 2022, few predicted that the Ukrainians would be able to resist the Russian onslaught.

In sum, not only is the Russo-Ukrainian War the first large-scale interstate war in Europe since 1945, it is also a territorial conflict par excellence; furthermore, the Ukrainian resilience in the face of Russian incursions highlights that the notion of (inviolable) homeland is still alive and kicking. These dynamics collectively render the war of direct relevance to this study. At this juncture, two disclaimers are in order. First, the overwhelming majority of this book was completed before the Russo-Ukrainian War broke out in February 2022. In other words, while this study will meet with its audiences more than a year after the war started, it was not written as a response to the war. Second, the analysis to be offered below is from late 2022. At the time of writing, the war is still raging, and the tempo and direction of the military operations remain extremely fluid and uncertain. That being said, *Shifting Grounds* has insights to offer about the origins, conduct, and potential consequences of the war.

In terms of the origins of the conflict, there exist two main perspectives. On the one hand, there are those who make the case that the war was triggered by the Western countries' ill-advised attempts to bring Ukraine into the fold through membership in the EU and NATO. This perspective, which constitutes the minority view at the moment, is usually associated with realist IR scholars such as John Mearsheimer.[26] The relevant logic is usually portrayed as a timeless fact of international politics: great powers tend to be jealous of their own region, and they perceive incursions into it as threats to their security and status as a great power. In this reading, the Western countries' attempts to pull Ukraine to their side inadvertently incentivized Russia to respond harshly. Not surprisingly, Putin and his establishment make a similar case, putting the blame for the war on the Western countries and their "expansionist" ambitions. On the other hand, there are those who put the entire blame on Russia: Putin is an insatiable aggressor, he had long planned to conquer Ukraine, and if he succeeds, he will make similar attempts to acquire more territory elsewhere. Unlike the realist perspective, this position does not limit analysis to the "West versus Russia" narrative; Ukraine, a sovereign country with its own people and territory, also has an agency and rights of its own.

---

[26] Chotiner 2022.

So what do the preceding chapters have to say about the origins of the Russo-Ukrainian War? First, a "territorial" interpretation of the origins of the conflict suggests that the realist perspective is not only painfully incomplete but also misleading. Above all, the realist approach is incapable of putting the "territorial" component of the conflict into perspective, in two ways. Most notably, for some realists, Ukraine does not even amount to a territory, that is, a sociospatial arrangement with its own people and borders. Instead, Ukraine is seen as an "object" that is stuck between the Western bloc and Russia. Ukraine, in this reading, is also an "unfortunate" object, whose fate is to be determined by its proximity to Russia. Furthermore, the realist approach, not all that different from other (mainstream) IR paradigms, ignores the role that territorial ideas play in this conflict. In so many ways, incompatible territorial ideas lie at the heart of the war. Russian state elites have long seen Ukraine through the lens of amorphous territoriality, and the Ukrainians have long sought to solidify monolithic territoriality within their borders. These two visions are inherently incompatible, and, as Alexander Motyl put it, "No amount of goodwill can force [them] to coexist."[27] This incompatibility is largely a function of the Russia's dualistic approach to territory and territoriality. Russia's approach not only to Ukraine, but also to geographies such as Abkhazia, South Ossetia, and Transnistria, reflects a crude demonstration of dual territoriality.

Especially in the last two decades, Russia has witnessed the rise (or comeback) of an explicitly imperial understanding of territoriality.[28] Just as was the case for numerous European states during the course of late nineteenth and early twentieth centuries, Putin's Russia effectively combines nationalistic and imperialistic discourses. In fact, Russian nationalism has become a reflection of Russian imperial imageries (and vice versa):[29] in simple terms, it is Russia's imperial legacy that makes Russia great. According to the dominant geopolitical vision in Russia, the Russian territory is inviolable and belongs solely to Russians. The territories of some of its neighbors, almost all of which were part of either the Russian Empire or the Soviet bloc or both, are, or should be, open to Russian influence and partial control. In that, with respect to some of its neighbors, Russian political elites profess an understanding that can be summarized as "What's ours is only ours, and what's yours is yours to the extent that [we] allow it to be." In other words, monolithic territoriality is the gold standard within Russia's sovereign borders; beyond it, Russia can or should follow the dictates of amorphous territoriality, where state borders are

---

[27] Motyl 2010, 61. Also see Brubaker 1996 and Harris 2020, 610.
[28] On Russia's imperial/colonial leanings, see Surzhko Harned 2022; Knott 2022; Aridici 2019.
[29] Laruelle 2019; Knott 2022.

246 Shifting Grounds

not supposed to stop the Russian influence and control. In this reading, Russia does not necessarily aim to expand its sovereign territory at the expense of its neighbors. Instead, according to this territorial vision, Kremlin has the right and responsibility to project influence and even control into the territories of its neighbors, and reserves the option to intervene in these territories. The question of Russian minorities in numerous former Soviet republics, in turn, is usually invoked to justify the relevant Russian rights and responsibilities.

Russia specialists usually refer to this phenomenon as the "Russian World," or *Russkii Mir*, idea.[30] This geopolitical vision is both new and old. It is new in the sense that its current version came to dominance in Russia during Vladimir Putin's reign. The Russkii Mir Foundation was launched by Putin himself in 2007.[31] In 2008, at the NATO summit, Putin went to lengths to make the case that Ukraine was not a "real state" and owed much of its territorial existence (and population) to Russia; according to Putin, "The Russian nation [is] greater than its borders."[32] In 2009, during his speech at the newly reopened Russian Geographical Society, Putin also "explicitly linked the greatness of Russia as a state and as a culture to the size of its territory," and suggested that Russia's destiny was linked to its "geographical scope."[33] In a similar vein, in 2011, Putin announced his intention to establish a "Eurasian Union," whose objective "would not be to rebuild a unified state, but to institute a few supranational mechanisms in specific domains that would guarantee Moscow a right to oversee the evolution of some of its neighbors."[34]

The *Russkii Mir* idea offers an eclectic understanding of the relationship between Russia and territoriality, formulated around the questions of "what and where was Russia" and "what and where is Russia *now*." Russia's imperial past, its leadership during the Soviet era, and its Orthodox-Christian identity are all mixed together in order to make the case that it is not only Russia's right, but also moral and historical responsibility, to project power and influence well beyond its sovereign borders. As Ernest Renan most famously argued in 1882, becoming a nation involves selective remembering (and selective forgetting).[35] The *Russkii Mir* idea is, arguably, an attempt to construct a new Russian (national) identity for the twenty-first century by forgetting some facts, selectively remembering some others, while also fabricating some details as needed.[36] This idea, in fact, is not entirely new; it is an updated and

[30] On this concept, see Kuzio 2015. For the similar concept of "New Russia," *Novorossiya*, see Harris 2020, 603–604.
[31] Harris 2022, 603–604; Aridici 2019.
[32] Harris 2022, 600.
[33] Laruelle 2019, 37.
[34] Laruelle 2019, 40.
[35] Renan 2018.
[36] Harris 2020, 602–603.

augmented version of the concept of *Blizhneye Zarubezhye*, better known in the Western world as the "near abroad," which came to prominence during the rule of Boris Yeltsin in the 1990s.[37]

For the idea of *Russkii Mir* to appear natural and old, as opposed to consciously formulated and novel, it needs to selectively draw upon the Russian past.[38] Accordingly, whenever it serves the narrative, the *Russkii Mir* idea invokes the (supposedly) glorious imperial past of the prerevolution Russia. This move has a certain benefit: Russia, as a state, as a territory, and as an idea becomes "timeless"; the *Russkii Mir* idea then becomes not a postmodern fabrication, but the reawakening of the great Russian legacy, the roots of which go back in history by more than a millennium. Even though Russia's imperial past should contradict the anti-imperialistic discourses of the Soviet Union, the *Russkii Mir* idea usurps the historical record to make it possible to eat the cake and have it too: it was none other than the Russians who initiated and then guided the Russian Revolution, and therefore they should be credited for the accomplishments of the Soviet Union (but, presumably, none of its failings). Also note that this narrative dovetails with the idea that while the Soviet Union defined itself as opposed to "imperialism," it was, in the end, an empire where Russians sat at the top.[39] On top of this discursive cocktail comes the religious dimension, which, in theory, should contradict the openly atheist nature of the Soviet regime: God is on Russia's side, just as Russia is God's chief servant on earth.[40] The result is a set of territorial ideas that fuel Russia's imperial posture toward some of its neighbors.

Of course, the key question for our purposes is the following: Where does Ukraine stand in this geopolitics vision? Simply put, the Ukrainians are portrayed as "inferior" people and Ukraine as an inferior place; in fact, Ukraine is an inferior place mostly because it is inhabited, or governed, by inferior people. Obviously, the war itself will eventually have a drastic impact on where Ukrainians will stand in the relevant narratives. Still, prior to the war, this geopolitical vision, if implicitly, tended to portray the Ukrainians as "little Russians":[41] Ukrainians were in fact Russians (who suffered from a collective confusion about their real identity), but even then, they were "little," of course, when compared with the real and "great" Russians. This perspective cannot be divorced from its territorial underpinnings: since Ukrainians were

---

[37] For a detailed discussion, see Toal 2017.
[38] Surzhko Harned 2022, 2.
[39] On this point, see Suny 1993.
[40] Surzhko Harned 2022; Aridici 2019; Marson 2009.
[41] This vision is not specific to Putin's Russia, but can be traced to both the Soviet Union and imperial Russia. See Harris 2020, 606.

248   Shifting Grounds

little Russians, their territory technically belonged to the great Russians. At the very least, the Ukrainian territory was for "little Russians" to claim only to the extent that the real owners, the great Russians, allowed them to.

Leading up to the war, Putin became increasingly vocal about this vision. In 2021 Putin made the case that for Ukraine to enjoy "true sovereignty," it needed to partner up with Russia,[42] paradoxically arguing that Ukrainian sovereignty was in fact contingent on Russian consent and patronage. In his speeches during the same year, Putin continuously emphasized the "historical unity of Russians and Ukrainians,"[43] while also highlighting that Russians sat at the top of this particular unity. Only three days before Russia launched its military into Ukraine, on February 21, 2022, Putin referred to Ukraine as an "inalienable part of [Russian's own] history, culture, and spiritual space."[44] The messages behind these discourses are clear: Ukraine is not a real sovereign territory, but merely a "place";[45] it exists at the whim of the "great" Russia,[46] and therefore remains a most natural part of Russia's sphere of influence.[47] If the "little Russians" misbehave or "betray" the perennially Russian territory they inhabit, Russia has not only a natural right, but also a responsibility, to intervene.

Note that, in the context of this master narrative, it is possible to make the case that the realist perspective gets something right, but for the wrong reasons. The realist perspective correctly identifies the ways in which the Western countries' affiliation with Ukraine is portrayed as a threat in Russia, at least by the leadership.[48] However, the "perceived" threat is not a function of timeless principles best captured by IR realism; it is a direct function of the imperialistic territorial ideas that have come to guide Russian discourses and behavior in foreign politics.[49] In this sense, by portraying the Russian sensitivity toward Ukraine as a natural result of the logic of great power politics, the realist perspective is effectively whitewashing Russian imperialistic designs over Ukraine.[50] This line of thinking also masks the basic fact that Russian leadership does not consider Ukraine to be a sovereign territorial unit. Put bluntly, the Russian perception of threat is a result of a sense of "territorial entitlement" over Ukraine that Putin-led Russia has been nourishing for quite

---

[42] Knott 2022.
[43] Surzhko Harned 2022, 5.
[44] Surzhko Harned 2022, 1.
[45] Motyl 2013.
[46] Knott 2022.
[47] Knott 2022.
[48] Knott 2022.
[49] Laruelle 2019.
[50] Realists do not have a well-defined understanding of "empire" and collapse the term under the category of "great powers."

some time, not a natural byproduct of a "timeless" logic of great power politics that realists discovered few decades ago.

The *Russkii Mir* idea is also built on a specific interpretation of the dominant territorial ideas in Ukraine: as little Russians, the Ukrainians did not, or could not, profess monolithic territoriality in a robust fashion. This interpretation made it possible for the Russian leadership to act on the idea that Ukrainian territory was ripe for the taking, if it came to that. More precisely, the Russian leadership acted under the impression that, since they did not amount to a "real" nation, the Ukrainians would not put up much resistance to preserve the territorial integrity of their country. From the perspective of the territorial orders framework, Russian leadership was convinced that while Ukraine (as a state) "appeared" to profess monolithic territoriality, the dominant territorial ideas among the Ukrainians resembled (at best) mosaic territoriality, or a fragmented mosaic of local and subnational territorial loyalties, a hallmark of European/Westphalian states before the rise of nationalism.

Arguably, two underlying assumptions sustained this interpretation. First, the evolution of nationalism in Ukraine has followed a particular path that partially prevented the Ukrainians from formulating and sustaining a distinct, territorially defined national identity until the end of the Cold War. In fact, as Mark Von Hagen put it, even the concept of "Ukrainian [national] history" remained underdeveloped until the end of the Cold War.[51] In this sense, both Ukrainian historiography and Ukrainian nationalism had long been victims of the imperial policies that dominated the broader region for centuries. As a geographical entity (or expression), Ukraine was "stuck" between Russian and (to a lesser extent) German as well as Habsburg imperial, cultural, and intellectual traditions.[52] Ukraine for centuries was seen by the imperial powers as a chaotic borderland, its "chaos" defined in terms of ethnic, linguistic, and religious diversity and fluidity.[53] This very sociospatial heterogeneity—which has been the norm, not the exception, in global history—was in fact a "direct consequence" of centuries of imperial policies;[54] paradoxically, the Russian Empire and later the Soviet Union used this sociospatial heterogeneity to justify "further imperial hegemony."[55]

Beyond sociospatial arrangements, the boundaries (and, later, borders) of Ukraine were also a byproduct of (Russian/Soviet) imperial policies.[56]

---

[51] Von Hagen 1995.
[52] Von Hagen 1995, 660.
[53] Knott 2022.
[54] Von Hagen 1995, 661.
[55] Von Hagen 1995, 661.
[56] Von Hagen 1995, 671.

The modern borders of Ukraine date back to 1954 for Crimea and 1939 (or 1945) for Western Europe.[57] Therefore, "Today's Ukraine is a very modern creation, with little firmly established precedent in the national past."[58] In such a landscape, the notion of an independent and distinct Ukrainian nationalism hardly found fertile intellectual and political ground in which to flourish. Even Ukrainian historiography was dominated by Russia-centric or Soviet-centric narratives, where Ukraine was relegated to the status of a periphery that perpetually needed Russian/Soviet "overlordship."[59]

The end of the Cold War created new opportunities for Ukrainian nationalism to rise to prominence. In the post-Soviet era, this "new national identity"[60] had to overcome centuries of Russian hegemony and seventy years of Soviet domination and indoctrination, especially in eastern and southern Ukraine, where Russian cultural and political influence had been more robust. Regardless, an all-Ukrainian sense of unity (and historiography) and a growing sense of civic nationhood eventually began to dominate "the educational system and intellectual discourse."[61] In such a setting, the Ukrainian borders (and therefore territory) became salient for the resurgence of Ukrainian national identity. Arguably, considering the ethnic, linguistic, and religious diversity of the Ukrainian population, a civic understanding of Ukrainian nationalism was increasingly defined in terms of territory, or the inviolable Ukrainian homeland.[62] Long story short, the *Russkii Mir* idea drew upon the (wrong) assumption that Ukrainians were failing to formulate and rally around a robust sense of territorially defined nationalism, and that they would be unable to do so for the foreseeable future.

The second assumption that most likely guided Putin's hand in February 2022 involved the annexation of Crimea in 2014: the Ukrainians did not (or could not) defend or recapture Crimea in 2014. Putin might have taken this episode as direct evidence for the accuracy of the existing Russian biases about the weakness of territorially defined nationalism among the Ukrainians.

As of late 2022, it is clear that the unadulterated optimism prevalent among Russian policymakers prompted them to misunderstand three key dynamics. First, territorial ideas are not static; they can change, especially when the risk of territorial conflict is real. That the real-life reflections and demonstrations of territorially defined nationalism were not very robust in Ukraine some

---

[57] Von Hagen 1995, 667.
[58] Von Hagen 1995, 667.
[59] Motyl 2010, 59.
[60] Harris 2020, 607.
[61] Kuzio 2006, 423.
[62] On how borders may end up sustaining distinct national identities, see Sahlins 1989.

thirty years ago does not necessarily mean that this is the case for the foreseeable future. Second, monolithic territoriality is still the aspirational model in world politics. While the idea of the territorial state has been challenged by the rise of globalization in the post–Cold War era, as John Agnew put it succinctly, this idea still has considerable mileage in it.[63] As an aspirational model, monolithic territoriality (and the notion of an inviolable homeland) remains a robust focal point in both domestic political discourses and interstate politics. Therefore, it should come as surprise to no one that, for Ukraine-as-government and the Ukrainians, the idea of a territorially defined nationalism proved to be a unifying theme in the past decades, during which Ukraine had to deal with numerous political crises and a persistent Russian threat.

Third, while the annexation of Crimea might have verified Putin's biases about Ukraine, it most likely had the paradoxical consequence of strengthening territorially defined nationalism among Ukrainians. This is what exactly this study would expect to happen: just as territorial ideas affect the nature of territorial conflicts, territorial conflicts can and do shape the dominant territorial ideas in a given geography. From such a perspective, the loss of Crimea and the subsequent hybrid war (over territory) that took place in eastern and southern Ukraine ended up emboldening the notion of monolithic territoriality in the country. With the benefit of hindsight, we can perhaps compare Ukraine's loss of Crimea in 2014 to France's loss of Alsace-Lorraine to Germany in 1871. The French loss did not "break" the notion of territorially defined nationalism in France; to the contrary, the loss of Alsace-Lorraine galvanized and crystalized French nationalism. As highlighted in Chapter 4, referring to Alsace-Lorraine, the French politician Leon Gambetta famously said, "Think of [it] always; speak of [it] never."[64] As the Ukrainian president Volodymyr Zelensky's statements from fall 2022 onward about the intention to recover Crimea suggest,[65] the Ukrainians may not have spoken all that much of Crimea in the past decade, but they most certainly have been thinking about it. Furthermore, the Crimean episode crystalized the idea that Ukraine should explicitly distance itself from Russia in both political and cultural terms, and that the Ukrainians should unify around a distinct sense of nationhood.[66]

[63] Agnew 2009.
[64] Quoted in Morgenthau 1949, 118.
[65] Schonfeld 2022.
[66] Cheskin 2017; Kulyk 2016; Samokhvalov 2015; Berezhnaya 2015. Berezhnaya (2015, 66–67) argues that this tendency can also partially explain the general tendency especially among the Western Ukrainians to "turn to" Europe.

252   Shifting Grounds

So, what about the conduct of war? As a first cut, the war is becoming a contest between two nation-states with their own understanding of national homeland. As already argued in Chapter 4, this kind of conflict can be exceptionally severe; as of late 2022, the casualties of the war are measured in the tens of thousands and the war is becoming intractable. Regardless, as mentioned above, in the very opening stages of the war, many expected a swift victory for Russia, perhaps akin to Russia's war with Georgia in 2008. This expectation followed from two assumptions. First, the West will most likely stay out of the conflict, as it did in Georgia and Crimea (or Chechnya). Second, Russia possesses a formidable and competent military. As of late 2022, both assumptions have proven to be at least partially wrong: the Western countries have been providing considerable diplomatic, economic, and material support to sustain the Ukrainian war efforts, and the Russian military performance has so far failed to impress even the staunchest supporters of Russia and its leader. In retrospect, it is safe to argue that if not for yet another, territory-related, factor, neither Western support nor poor Russian military performance would have led to an outcome where Ukraine could actually stand firm in the face of the Russian juggernaut: Ukrainians' will and determination to defend the territorial integrity of their homeland. Without such determination, the Russian military would not have much of a difficulty in defeating the Ukrainian army in the opening stages of the war, which then would have upended the Western support before it began to have a visible impact on the battlefield.

The conduct of the war is arguably affecting the dominant territorial ideas in Russia as well. Increasingly so, the Russian narratives portray the war in existential terms, where what is at stake is the greater "Russian territories" that now extend to the four Ukrainian oblasts (Donetsk, Kherson, Luhansk, and Zaporizhzhia) that Putin annexed in September 2022, in addition to Crimea. Of course, it is very difficult to offer concrete analyses about an ongoing war with an uncertain future, especially at a time when the risk of global nuclear war is on the table.[67] That being said, as of late 2022, the Russian leadership has already come to terms with the fact that the "special military operation" proved to be ineffective, in terms of securing the original Russian policy objectives. As things stand, Russia seems to be responding to this development in two ways. First, as of late September 2022, Russia initiated partial mobilization, raising the stakes on the battlefield. Second, as Russia is elevating its war efforts, it also seems to be lowering its expectations, defined in terms of war aims: while the original military campaign appeared to entail maximalist

---

[67] Bollfrass and Herzog 2022.

policy objectives (which included regime change in Ukraine), Putin, as of late 2022, seems more and more interested in holding onto the areas occupied during the opening stages of the war, especially the four oblasts that Putin annexed in September 2022, even though, at the time, Russia does not have complete control over these oblasts.

If this turns out to be the case, what does the territorial orders framework have to say about it? In simple terms, the difficulties that Russia faced on the battlefield are forcing Putin to reframe the territorial nature of the conflict. As mentioned above, Russia's approach to Ukraine was guided by amorphous territoriality (and the assumption that mosaic, not monolithic, territoriality was dominant in Ukraine). In the face of the difficulties Russia has faced on the battlefield, Putin will likely draw more and more on monolithic territoriality. One likely scenario is that Putin will be tempted to make the case that the areas that Russia captured in eastern and southern Ukraine, where separatism was stronger, are not merely within Russia's natural and historical sphere of influence, but in fact indivisible parts of the Russian homeland.[68] On the one hand, this would be a defeat of some sorts for Putin, since Russia would be conceding its claims over its right to exert influence and indirect control in the rest of the Ukrainian territory. On the other hand, this scenario will also pave the way for an intractable territorial dispute between Ukraine and Russia even after hostilities end, as both countries will now have claimed the aforementioned territories as parts of their inviolable homeland.

As far as the consequences of the Russo-Ukrainian War are concerned, this study can hardly make strong claims, simply because the hostilities continue at the time of writing. Still, one potential consequence is almost guaranteed: monolithic territoriality, as an aspirational model, will become increasingly robust and visible in Ukraine and possibly beyond. In terms of territorial ideas, the war will have solidified monolithic territoriality as the indisputable gold standard among the overwhelming majority of Ukrainians, *even if Ukraine ends up losing territory*. Writing in 1995, Von Hagen argued that "Ukrainian history is a veritable laboratory for viewing several processes of state and nation building and for comparative history generally."[69] After almost three decades, Von Hagen's observation still holds, with a twist: war over territory has become a crucial part of Ukraine's state- and nation-building efforts. The Ukrainian case is now an acute demonstration of the ways in which wars, state-building, and nation-building processes interact. At the very heart of this interaction lie territorial ideas and associated practices. The

[68] Schreck 2022.
[69] Von Hagen 1995, 673.

254   Shifting Grounds

Russo-Ukrainian War, in this context, is a potent, if painful, reminder that we should take the association between the socially constructed nature of territories and conflict much more seriously than we have in the past.

Ethnocentrism and Racism in World Politics and IR Theories

Since the end of World War II, most IR scholars have imagined their field of study to be a social scientific enterprise in search of value-free and "objective" theories and observations. In recent years, numerous scholars have challenged this approach, exploring the colonial and racist origins of both the so-called modern state system and IR. The relevant research is not merely retrospective; it aims not only to uncover the past, but also to expose the legacies of this past with respect to the ways in which we think and talk about international politics today. A common theme runs through this research: while IR, as a discipline, systematically voices an interest in world history, it does a poor job of engaging its own history. Instead, IR scholars have long professed what Sankaran Krishna referred to as a "willful amnesia," especially on the question of race.[70] As Freeman, Kim, and Lake recently pointed out, "The invisibility of race in IR was not accidental but designed."[71] In other words, only by (consciously) ignoring IR's colonial and racist origins (and IR's status and function before 1945) can most IR scholars claim that IR is a social scientific enterprise in search of value-free and objective theories and observations.

The emerging literature on the subject is robust and does not require an extended rehearsal here. It is now widely accepted that, during the late nineteenth and early twentieth centuries, IR emerged as an independent field of study partially (or mostly) to serve and inform colonial administrations.[72] Scholars such as Robert Vitalis have also made the case (or simply reminded us) that, during the same time, IR openly reflected, fed off, and fed the rampant racist biases of the time.[73] For instance, the first American academic journal of international relations, established in 1910, was named *Journal of Race Development*. More strikingly, as of 1922, *Journal of Race Development* was eventually rebranded as *Foreign Affairs*, which has long been one of the most influential IR journals in the world. Upon reflection, as Kelebogile

---

[70] Krishna 2001. Debra Thompson (2013) refers to this dynamic as "racial aphasia." Also see Anievas et al. 2014.

[71] Freeman et al. 2022, 177.

[72] Gani and Marshall 2022, 9.

[73] Vitalis 2016. Also see Hobson 2012; Keal 2003; DuBois 1925; and Henderson 2017.

Zvobgo and Meredith Loken aptly put it, "Race is not a perspective on international relations, it is a central organizing feature of world politics."[74] Kerem Nişancıoğlu, in a similar vein, argues that even the term "sovereignty," which many IR scholars take to be a value-free concept, should be examined in terms of its association with race relations.[75] Freeman, Kim, and Lake, in turn, suggest that the existing hierarchies in the modern state system are closely linked with the legacies of the colonial and racist (recent) past, and that "race is hidden behind international law and principle of sovereign equality."[76]

It is true that, after World War II, both the practice and the scholarly study of international politics have moved away from blatant racism. In terms of the practice of international politics, as Zoltan Buzas highlights, the diplomatic discourses of the post-1945 era have gone to lengths to render openly racist policies and statements unacceptable.[77] In IR, in turn, building on openly racist discourses has become inadmissible; long gone are the times when IR scholars could effortlessly justify certain imperial and racist policies by merely pointing out that the lesser races "deserved" whatever they were suffering at the hands of their colonial and racial overlords.

These being said, at least two analytical problems (with real-life consequences) persist. First, while adopting a politically correct posture over the question of race is a necessary step when addressing racist biases, IR also needs to acknowledge and explore the racist and colonial origins of present-day global politics. John Hobson succinctly emphasizes yet another problem: the concept of racial hierarchy has been taken out of IR, but it was replaced by an "equally distorted conception of 'cultural hierarchy.'"[78] This "subliminal Eurocentrism," according to Hobson, merely recycles some of the old themes of the colonial-racist past but does so without invoking race. In this new-but-old narrative, "Decolonization becomes reimagined as a result of the 'triumph of the moral ideas of the West,' specifically the principles of national self-determination and social justice."[79] This new master narrative is part of a "happy story," as Hobson put it, "in which the West diffused its 'rational' civilizational institutions and practices outwards so that the East too could come to enjoy the benefits of residing within civilized international society."[80]

---

[74] Zvobgo and Loken 2020, 11.
[75] Nişancıoğlu 2020, 40. Also see Mbembe 2001.
[76] Freeman et al. 2022, 182.
[77] Buzas 2021.
[78] Hobson 2014, 82.
[79] Hobson 2014, 86.
[80] Hobson 2014, 86.

256 Shifting Grounds

This study contributes to the ongoing debate in two ways. First, it helps expose the long-term impacts of the modern state system's colonial-racist origins on the ways in which we think about international politics. Second, it offers paths forward to reform the ways in which IR scholarship considers the relationship between colonialism, racism, and the modern state system not only in the distant past, but also in the present. In terms of further exposing the colonial-racist origins of the modern state system, this study offers two key insights. First, in world politics, racism is geographical. Second, the territorial trap lies at heart of what Hobson referred to as subliminal Eurocentrism.

Especially Chapters 5 and 7 point toward a certain dynamic: racism has been a core component of world politics, and in international politics it has revealed itself in terms of geography. Put differently, in international politics, racism is geographical and plays itself out in terms of discourses about "backward," "lazy," and "savage" geographies. We may be tempted to believe that this "geographical racism" is a thing of the past, but as political geographers have long recognized, this is far from the case. Many politicians and scholars continue to draw upon similar tropes to make their case, if without explicitly invoking the race component. For instance, on October 13, 2022, the high representative of the European Union for Foreign Affairs and Security Policy, Josep Borrell, referred to Europe as a "garden," which stood for "the best combination of political freedom, economic prosperity and social cohesion that the humankind has been able to build."[81] Borrell proceeded to refer to the non-Western world as "a jungle," warning the young EU diplomats whom he was addressing that "the jungle could invade the garden." Borrell did not stop there; he likened the young diplomats to "gardeners" tasked with cultivating the "jungle" so that the jungle would not "invade" the "garden." Borrell's remarks neither are the first to "territorialize" what Hobson referred to as subliminal Eurocentrism (a direct descendant of nineteenth-century racism), nor will they be the last. However, the fact that this geographical perspective is being openly voiced by the EU's top diplomat *in 2022* speaks volumes about the persistence of geographical racism in world politics.

The second, and related, problem that this study exposes involves the relationship between IR's geographical assumptions (or the territorial trap) and subliminal Eurocentrism. Put bluntly, the territorial trap does not merely follow from an innocent, analytical mistake; the territorial trap is a direct reflection—or demonstration—of subliminal Eurocentrism. As highlighted in the previous chapters, an ethnocentric and presentist understanding of the past and present of world politics lies at the heart of the territorial trap.[82] The

---

[81] Stevis-Gridneff 2022.
[82] For a similar argument, also see Ringmar 2012.

Conclusion **257**

territorial trap prioritizes the nation-state ideal, or monolithic territoriality, as it is usually conceived in the Global North. The territorial trap obfuscates the racist and imperialist origins and legacies of the so-called modern state system by perpetuating a global geographical vision that privileges clearly demarcated sovereign pieces of territory as the ultimate—and superior— units of analysis.

Without a demonstration of some sorts, the real-life consequences of this tendency are bound to remain abstract. A hypothetical illustration can help drive the point home. Imagine a hypothetical scenario where, during the early nineteenth century, a number of European colonial powers subjugated a region in the Global South that they perceived to be a collection of "empty" or "lesser" territories filled with inferior (or uncivilized) societies. The political and ideational currents of the day easily justified (that is, in the eyes of many Europeans) the European attempts to colonize distant geographies: the inhabitants of these "lesser" territories were solely responsible for their own "inferior" status. Not only did these territories "deserve" to be cultivated by the advanced Europeans, but it was also Europeans' responsibility to "fix" these lesser territories.

Just like most geographies at the time, the aforementioned region was home to amorphous territoriality, professed by a multitude of local political and social actors in various ways. The boundaries were fluid and flexible, and none of the political players in the region sought, or even considered, sociospatial homogeneity. The arrival of the Europeans, of course, upended the traditional territorial ideas and practices. To begin with, these European powers, partially to manage the relations among each other, partially for administrative reasons, drew "borders" on their maps, creating brand-new administrative-colonial (territorial) units. Of course, the European empire-builders did not bother with details such as linguistic, ethnic, and religious affiliations, not to mention the "old" (that is, indigenous) traditions and institutions. Naturally, the Europeans named the very territorial units they had just created on their maps. One such territorial unit, let's assume, was named *Ceres* by its colonial owners.[83] Obviously, Ceres did not exist as a territorial unit prior to its "creation." The name may perhaps be traced to a historical reference point selectively cultivated by the European colonizers; regardless, prior to the Europeans' systematic reterritorialization efforts, Ceres simply did not exist, at least with the borders it now had, with the population it now hosted.

The colonial overlords ruled Ceres not only with an iron fist, but also through numerous methods that pitted some social groups against others (so

---

[83] The inspiration for the choice of "Ceres" for the hypothetical example comes from Corey 2011.

258   Shifting Grounds

that the colonial masters could rule on the cheap through local proxies) while preventing the diverse population of Ceres from forming a unified, collective identity defined in terms of the territory of Ceres. The inhabitants of Ceres occasionally rose up against their colonial overlords and eventually made their case for independence to the "international" audiences of the Paris Conference of 1919, where they hoped that the principle of "self-determination" would apply to them. The international audiences, dominated by European/Western politicians, barely felt the need to hide their racist inclinations, simply telling the representatives from Ceres that Ceres was not yet "mature enough" a territorial unit to qualify as an independent state. If the Ceresians only waited a little longer for their European overlords to complete their civilizing mission, transforming the inferior territory of Ceres so that it fits the standards of the civilized world, perhaps Ceres might be granted the right to exist as an independent (nation-)state.

Due to the anticolonial struggles and the impacts of World War II (not to mention the increasing costs of maintaining overseas empires for European powers), the particular European powers that colonized Ceres for a century and a half finally granted independence to Ceres during the 1960s, allowing the Ceresians to enter the sovereign club as a legitimate member of the United Nations. Of course, the anticolonial struggles of the inhabitants of Ceres were territorially limited to the colonial-administrative borders that had been drawn during the early nineteenth century. The inhabitants of Ceres could not easily ask for a bigger Ceres that would go beyond the borders that the European colonial officers drew so carelessly more than a century ago. They were even discouraged from establishing multiple (nation-)states in Ceres's territory, which might have paved the way for the emergence of more coherent territorial units, coherence defined in terms of sociospatial homogeneity and the match between territorial identities and borders. So the inhabitants of Ceres had to contend with the borders that were imposed on them more than a century ago, regardless of the sociospatial facts on the ground. Nonetheless, the outcome was a success for the inhabitants of Ceres, as they finally freed themselves from the colonial yoke after more than a century of humiliation and subjugation at the hands of the Europeans.

Once the initial euphoria washed away, the Ceresians now realized that while being a nation-state required a modicum of sociospatial homogeneity and a "match" between their borders and the Ceresian nation, not only did Ceres lack experience with monolithic territoriality in the precolonial era, it also had been ruled through colonial arrangements that empowered (and twisted) amorphous territoriality. The absence of even a modicum of sociospatial homogeneity, when combined with the expectation that Ceresian territory should be organized in terms of such homogeneity, led to a paradox: while a number of ideological, ethnic, religious, and linguistic groups competed with each other to make the case it was they who were the "true" Ceresians (so they should be in charge), other groups argued that their territories should not be a part of Ceres since they were not Ceresians in the first place. Under such circumstances, "capturing the Ceresian state" and "taking territory from the Ceresian state in order to establish yet another nation-state" became two dominant motives that shaped Ceresian political life, paving the way for chronic instability and even civil strife. This is where the notion of "artificial borders" came into play: Ceres's neighbor, Eros, another colonial territorial construct turned nation-state, began to interfere with the affairs of Ceres, partially to protect Eros's "ethnic/religious kin" in Ceresian territory, partially to take advantage of the ongoing instability in Ceres. For Ceres, the result was further instability, corruption (usually fueled by ethnic and/or religious nepotism), chronic poverty, and violence.

In the present day, few would question the colonial and racist origins of this "past," yet few would accept that the echoes of this colonial episode persist to this day, under different discursive and institutional configurations. Recall that the European colonizers once deemed Western territories "superior" places, and "other" geographies were seen as inferior; the locals, in this thinking, were held responsible for their territorial-political "shortcomings." In present-day politics, the territorial trap sets the context for a similar approach, where the impacts and ever-vibrant echoes of the racist and colonial origins of the so-called modern state system, or sovereign territorial order as some call it, are systematically forgotten and whitewashed. The present-day status of the hypothetical case of Ceres would directly speak to this dynamic.

Ceres is now seen as a "problematic" country in the Western eyes, which, to a large extent, determine where the "international opinion" will land. In so many ways, Ceres is now being judged by the criteria associated with monolithic territoriality, defined in terms of clearly defined (and enforced) borders and a modicum of sociospatial homogeneity. The more "generous" interpretations of Ceres, especially in the Western world, will portray Ceres as a "failed state," as if Ceres failed to pass a fair test that countless Western states have long been acing with flying colors. Political scientists and economists, for example, wrapped up in their version of the territorial trap, will then focus on dissecting numerous (quantifiable) "variables" ranging from the strength of institutions to topography to explain why Ceres failed where many Western countries "succeeded." Doing so, these analysts will often bypass the centuries-long divergence in the evolution of territorial ideas and practices across different cases. In the end, almost all states in the present day are, by definition,

260 Shifting Grounds

modern nation-states, and the notion of a racism- and colonialism-infused "territorial divergence" may not be an easy angle to study.

Much less generous interpretations of Ceres will follow, most likely dominating the debate in the public sphere, and even among policymakers in the Global North. These interpretations will merely recycle the very racist and imperialistic tropes that Ceres's former colonial overlords used to justify their deeds for more than a century, with two twists. First, these much less generous (and self-righteous) comments will not frame their "assessments" in terms of biological race; that is no longer acceptable. Second, while the colonial overlords of the past centuries openly embraced imperialism as a legitimizing principle, those who weigh in on Ceres today will likely have "forgotten" the legacies of the colonial and racist past, putting the blame for Ceres's problems on something that is wrong with Ceres. Some commentators will implicitly draw upon the "linear" narrative that portrays the Western path to monolithic territoriality as the universal and normatively superior one. Through such lenses, Ceres will once again appear to be a "backward" territorial unit, still on its way toward catching up with contemporary civilizational standards, which will be framed in terms of political development, modernity, and the like.

Some commentators will go even further, suggesting that if only the broader region where Ceres is located were to experience what Europe experienced in the past, for example its own Thirty Years' War, Ceres might finally emerge as a proper and functional nation-state. Of course, this interpretation does not engage two facts. First, the history of the modern state system cannot be boiled down to a master narrative where the territorial state is born in Europe, in isolation from the rest of the world; on the contrary, not only was this "system" born in the age of imperialism and racism, it also became what it is today because of imperialism and racism. Second, in relation, the colonial and racist origins of the same system explicitly denied the inhabitants of Ceres the kind of territorial path that played out in Europe over centuries.

Even harsher comments will systematically put the entire blame on Ceres. Some prominent IR scholars, policy wonks, or "area specialists," for example, will weigh in on the subject with their hard-earned expertise. Leading "policy relevant" journals will publish numerous articles with titles such as "What's *Really* Wrong with Ceres: Ancient Hatreds Strike Back." When the efforts of the international community fail to "fix" Ceres, the same experts will call on the Ceresians to take responsibility for their own country, rather than wait for the international community to fix their country for them. Similarly, when a Western attempt to "export democracy" (or "bring order") to Ceres fails, the main culprit will be neither colonial legacies nor Westerners' inability to comprehend the sociospatial complexity of Ceres; the ill-fated attempt will be whitewashed by claims that Ceres is not ready for democracy yet, implying that some territories, for some reason, are less receptive to democracy than others.

Of course, Ceres is not a real country, merely a hypothetical one. That being said, Ceres is more than just one country, as some of its characteristics are shared by numerous countries in the Global South. In so many ways, the story above is an acute demonstration of what Hobson refers to as subliminal Eurocentrism. More importantly for the purposes of this study, this subliminal Eurocentrism is directly associated with the territorial trap, which effectively erases the past and whitewashes the present, rendering inherent biases about world politics invisible.

Shifting Grounds points toward three research venues that can be explored further in the future. The first involves the "reflective" origins of present-day world politics in general, the global territorial arrangements in particular. As highlighted by numerous scholars, such as economic historian Kenneth Pomeranz,[84] the "West" did not endogenously emerge and evolve in a vacuum that expanded to include the rest of the world. Instead, Western geographies were in almost constant contact with the "Rest." Consequently, Western ideas and identities were formulated (and evolved) not merely in the presence of, but also due to interaction with the "others."[85] Once we move beyond the territorial trap, or more precisely, once we see the association between this analytical trap and the colonial-racist origins of the present-day global territorial arrangements, we can hardly unsee it. Such awareness renders the task of further exposing the "mutual constitution of [Western] and non-[Western] world and their joint role in making history"[86] from a territorial perspective not only much easier, but also an intellectual responsibility of some sorts. The relevant research can then shed light on some of the core debates in IR theory, such as the anarchy-hierarchy dualism,[87] as well as more recent contentions, for example, the so-called rules-based liberal international order.[88]

Second, *Shifting Grounds* is also an attempt to address a question recently raised by Tarak Barkawi: "What if the study of war lets go of the Eurocentric paradigms that have governed it? What will we learn about war and wars?"[89] Revisiting IR's geographical assumptions in order to move beyond the

---

[84] Pomeranz 2000.
[85] For a similar argument, see Lopez 2016.
[86] Barkawi and Laffey 2006, 330. Also see Acharya and Buzan 2017 and 2019.
[87] On this debate, see Lake 2011. Also see Adelman and Aron 1999, 815.
[88] For example, Porter 2020.
[89] Barkawi 2016, 213.

262 Shifting Grounds

territorial trap is not the only way to address Barkawi's question, but it can still be seen as a step toward taking up the challenge that he posed in the first place.

Third, in terms of facing IR's own colonial and racist origins, IR scholarship can also benefit from further engaging political geographers, for a simple reason: modern political geography emerged as a reaction to the ways in which the discipline of geography served the interests of imperialist policies and whitewashed racism in the pre-1945 era. In other words, the very fabric of modern political geography is a direct response to the imperialist and racist leanings of the discipline of geography in the pre-1945 period.[90] As IR is coming to terms with its own past before 1945 and its subsequent collective, self-chosen amnesia, it has a lot to learn from political geographers, especially with respect to the role of territory and territoriality in world politics. More precisely, the topic of "geographical racism" constitutes yet another potentially fertile intellectual ground for IR scholars and political geographers to explore from an interdisciplinary perspective.

Conclusion

In conventional wisdom, territory is typically portrayed as a "passive stage"[91] that exerts little influence on world politics. This study aimed to establish the conceptual, theoretical, and historical foundations of an observation that challenges the conventional wisdom: territory is what states and societies make of it. That is, territory is best conceived not as a mute and static object, but as a social and political construct. Territorial behavior, in turn, is not driven solely by materialistic considerations or innate evolutionary instincts, but is in fact also shaped by ideas about territory. John Ruggie famously wrote that, for the students of international politics, neglecting territory and territoriality is not all that different from "never looking at the ground that one is walking on."[92] A closer look on the proverbial grounds, this study argued, can help us better grasp the relationship between organized violence and the shifting nature of territories.

Admittedly, this study covers considerable conceptual, theoretical, and historical ground, while also leaving out numerous aspects involved with territory and territoriality in world politics. For example, it does not deal with the political economy of the ways in which territories are constructed and

---

[90] For an overview, see Kadercan 2015.
[91] Murphy 2002, 208; see also Agnew 2010, 780; Kadercan 2015.
[92] Ruggie 1993, 174.

reconstructed. Similarly, *Shifting Grounds* limits its understanding of territories to "state spaces," and deals neither with other kinds of territories, nor with different spatial arrangements (such as "places" or "regions").[93] Furthermore, the four territorial orders examined in the preceding chapters do not capture all the subtleties and nuances associated with the wide variety of territorial ideas across time and space. This study also does not offer "hard" and conclusive arguments about the causes and consequences of territorial conflict; it merely presents a complimentary, and territorial, perspective to the existing explanations.[94]

That being said, there is something this study does forcefully: draw attention to the role that territorial ideas play in world politics. Territorial ideas may be constructs of the mind, but they have real impacts. We may or may not be able to quantify or measure these ideas, but if our intention is to advance our understanding of the past and present of global politics, we will be better off taking the socially constructed nature of territories and territoriality more seriously.

In an intellectual and academic landscape where the territorial trap has long been the invisible yet omnipresent guiding principle, this is not an easy task. In Turkish, there is an old saying: *bir elin nesi var, iki elin sesi var*. A liberal translation would be, "A single hand is silent, but two hands can make a lot of sound." When it comes to the relationship between territory and world politics, if IR scholars and political geographers actually do engage each other's research, they can make a lot of intellectual sound, contributing to our understanding of the aforementioned relationship.

Sun Tzu, the famous ancient Chinese general and strategic thinker, wrote that "the musical notes are only five in number but their melodies are so numerous that one cannot hear them all."[95] When it comes to the study of the relationship between territory and world politics, we do not necessarily need more musical notes, or never-heard-before insights and ideas. What we need to do is to move beyond using the same musical notes in the same sequence to perform the same melodies—or narratives, approaches, and methodologies— over and over again. To carry the metaphor to its logical conclusion, this book does not intend to invent brand-new musical notes. Instead, *Shifting Grounds* seeks to draw upon existing musical notes, or ideas and insights, in both IR and political geography in order to synthesize a new melody, or a new approach to the study of territory and territoriality.

---

[93] I'd like to thank John Agnew for bringing these two issues to my attention.

[94] See Kadercan 2011 for a detailed examination of these alternative explanations.

[95] Sun Tzu 2005, 137. Note that Sun Tzu was most likely referring to the pentatonic scale commonly used in China at the time. In Western music, by contrast, there are typically seven notes in a given musical key.

This new melody may not appeal to all spectators, but that's beside the point. The point is that, to better understand the role of territory and territoriality in world politics, we need to move beyond our own disciplinary territories, which are usually guarded by strict epistemological and methodological borders. Admittedly, our own disciplinary territories provide us with great comfort, since they usually come with epistemological and methodological certainties, as learned and artificial as these certainties may be. As Erich Fromm alluded to, creativity requires the faith, or the courage, to let go of certainties.[96] In the end, *Shifting Grounds* is such an attempt.

[96] Fromm 1959, 54.

References

Abramson, Scott F. 2017. The Economic Origins of the Territorial State. *International Organization* 71 (1): 97–130.

Abramson, Scott F., and David B. Carter. 2016. The Historical Origins of Territorial Disputes. *American Political Science Review* 110 (4): 675–698.

Acemoglu, Daron, Davide Cantoni, Simon Johnson, and James A. Robinson. 2011. The Consequences of Radical Reform: The French Revolution. *American Economic Review* 101 (7): 3286–3307.

Acharya, Amitav, and Barry Buzan. 2017. Why Is There No Non-Western International Relations Theory? *International Relations of the Asia-Pacific* 17 (3): 341–370.

Acharya, Amitav, and Barry Buzan. 2019. *The Making of Global International Relations*. Cambridge: Cambridge University Press.

Addington, Larry H. 1984. *The Patterns of War since the Eighteen Century*. Bloomington: Indiana University Press.

Adelman, Jeremy, and Stephen Aron. 1999. From Borderlands to Borders: Empires, Nation-States, and the Peoples in between in North American History. *American Historical Review* 104 (3): 814–841.

Adler, Emanuel. 2013. Constructivism in International Relations: Sources, Contributions, and Debates. In *Handbook of International Relations* 2, edited by Walter Carlsnaes, Thomas Risse, and Beth A. Simmons, 85–118. London: Sage.

Agamben, Giorgio. 1998. *Homo Sacer: Sovereign Power and Bare Life*. Translated by Daniel Heller-Roazen. Stanford, CA: Stanford University Press.

Agamben, Giorgio. 2005. *State of Exception*. Translated by Kevin Attell. Chicago: University of Chicago Press

Agnew, John. 1994. The Territorial Trap: The Geographical Assumptions of International Relations Theory. *Review of International Political Economy* 1 (1): 53–80.

Agnew, John. 2008. Borders on the Mind: Re-framing Border Thinking. *Ethics & Global Politics* 1 (4): 175–191.

Agnew, John. 2009. *Globalization and Sovereignty*. Lanham, MD: Rowman & Littlefield.

Agnew, John. 2010. Still Trapped in Territory? *Geopolitics* 15 (4): 779–784.

Agnew, John. 2015. Revisiting the Territorial Trap. *Nordia Geographical Publications* 44 (4): 43–48.

Agnew, John. 2017. *Globalization and Sovereignty: Beyond the Territorial Trap*. Lanham, MD: Rowman & Littlefield.

Agoston, Gabor. 2007. Information, Ideology, and Limits of Imperial Policy: Ottoman Grand Strategy in the Context of Ottoman-Habsburg Rivalry. In *The Early Modern Ottomans: Remapping the Empire*, edited by Virginia Aksan and Daniel Goffman, 75–103. New York: Cambridge University Press.

Ahmad, Aziz. 1976. The Shrinking Frontiers of Islam. *International Journal of Middle East Studies* 7 (2): 145–159.

Ahmed, Akbar. 2002. Ibn Khaldun's Understanding of Civilizations and the Dilemmas of Islam and the West Today. *Middle East Journal* 50 (1): 20–45.

Ahram, Ariel I. 2018. On the Making and Unmaking of Arab States. *International Journal of Middle East Studies* 50 (2): 323–327.

266 References

Ahram, Ariel I. 2019. *Break All the Borders: Separatism and the Reshaping of the Middle East.* Kindle ed. New York: Oxford University Press.

Al-Qattan, N. 2007. Inside the Ottoman Courthouse: Territorial Law at the Intersection of State and Religion. In *The Early Modern Ottomans: Remapping the Empire*, edited by Virginia Aksan and Daniel Goffman, 201–212. New York: Cambridge University Press.

Al-Tamimi, A. Jawad. 2014. The Dawn of the Islamic State of Iraq and ash-Sham. *Current Trends in Islamist Ideology* 16 (5): 5–15.

Albert, Mathias. 1998. On Boundaries, Territory and Postmodernity: An International Relations Perspective. *Geopolitics* 3 (1): 53–68.

Albert, Mathias, David Jacobson, and Yosef Lapid. 2001. *Identities, Borders, Orders: Rethinking International Relations Theory.* Minneapolis: University of Minnesota Press.

Almohammad, Asaad. 2018. *ISIS Child Soldiers in Syria: The Structural and Predatory Recruitment, Enlistment, Pre-training Indoctrination, Training, and Deployment.* The Hague: International Centre for Counter-Terrorism.

Andelman, David A. 2009. *A Shattered Peace: Versailles 1919 and the Price We Pay Today.* Hoboken, NJ: John Wiley & Sons.

Anderson, Benedict. 1983. *Imagined Communities: Reflections on the Origin and Spread of Nationalism.* London: Verso.

Anderson, James, and Liam O'Dowd. 1999. Borders, Border Regions and Territoriality: Contradictory Meanings, Changing Significance. *Regional Studies* 33 (7): 593–604.

Anderson, Malcolm. 1996. *Frontiers, Territory and State Formation in the Modern World.* Cambridge: Polity.

Angell, Norman. 1910. *The Great Illusion: The Relation of Military Power to National Advantage.* London: William Heinemann.

Angelov, Dimiter, Yota Batsaki, and Sahar Bazzaz. 2013. Introduction. In *Imperial Geographies in Byzantine and Ottoman Space*, edited by Sahar Bazzaz, Yota Batsaki, and Dimiter Angelov, 1–22. Cambridge, MA: Harvard University Press.

Anghie, Antony. 2007. *Imperialism, Sovereignty and the Making of International Law.* Cambridge: Cambridge University Press.

Anievas, Alexander, Nivi Manchanda, and Robbie Shilliam. 2014. *Race and Racism in International Relations: Confronting the Global Colour Line.* London: Routledge.

Ansell, Christopher. 2004. Restructuring Authority and Territoriality. In *Restructuring Territoriality: Europe and the United States Compared*, edited by Christopher K. Ansell, 3–18. Cambridge: Cambridge University Press.

Antonsich, Marco. 2009. On Territory, the Nation-State and the Crisis of the Hyphen. *Progress in Human Geography* 33 (6): 789–806.

Antonsich, Marco. 2011. Rethinking Territory. *Progress in Human Geography* 35 (3): 422–425.

Antonsich, Marco. 2015. Territory and Territoriality. In *International Encyclopedia of Geography: People, the Earth, Environment and Technology*, edited by Douglas Richardson, Noel Castree, Michael F. Goodchild, Audrey Kobayashi, Weidong Liu, and Richard A. Marston, 1–9. Chichester: Wiley.

Ardrey, Robert. 1969. *The Territorial Imperative: A Personal Inquiry into the Animal Origins of Property and Nations.* New York: Atheneum.

Arı, Bülent. 2004. Early Ottoman Diplomacy: Ad Hoc Period. In *Ottoman Diplomacy: Conventional or Unconventional?*, edited by A. Nuri Yurdusev, 36–65. Basingstoke: Palgrave Macmillan.

Aridici, Nuray. 2019. The Power of Civilizational Nationalism in Russian Foreign Policy Making. *International Politics* 56 (5): 605–621.

Ashley, Richard K. 1987. The Geopolitics of Geopolitical Space: Toward a Critical Social Theory of International Politics. *Alternatives* 12 (4): 403–434.

References 267

Ashworth, Lucian M. 2011. Realism and the Spirit of 1919: Halford Mackinder, Geopolitics and the Reality of the League of Nations. *European Journal of International Relations* 17 (2): 279–301.

Atzili, Boaz. 2012. *Good Fences, Bad Neighbors: Border Fixity and International Conflict.* Chicago: University of Chicago Press.

Atzili, Boaz, and Burak Kadercan. 2017. Territorial Designs and International Politics: The Diverging Constitution of Space and Boundaries. *Territory, Politics, Governance* 5 (2): 115–130.

Atzili, Boaz, and Burak Kadercan. 2018. *Territorial Designs and International Politics: Inside-Out and Outside-In.* London: Routledge.

Bahgat, Karim, and Richard M. Medina. 2013. An Overview of Geographical Perspectives and Approaches in Terrorism Research. *Perspectives on Terrorism* 7 (1): 38–72.

Bailey, Thomas Andrew. 1944. *Woodrow Wilson and the Lost Peace.* New York: Macmillan.

Banai, Ayelet, Margaret Moore, David Miller, Cara Nine, and Frank Dietrich. 2014. Symposium: Theories of Territory beyond Westphalia. *International Theory* 6 (1): 98–104.

Barkawi, Tarak. 2004. On the Pedagogy of "Small Wars." *International Affairs* 80 (1): 19–37.

Barkawi, Tarak. 2016. Decolonising War. *European Journal of International Security* 1 (2): 199–214.

Barkawi, Tarak. 2017. *Soldiers of Empire.* Kindle ed. New York: Cambridge University Press.

Barkawi, Tarak. 2018. From Law to History: The Politics of War and Empire. *Global Constitutionalism* 7 (3): 315–329.

Barkawi, Tarak, and Mark Laffey. 2002. Retrieving the Imperial: Empire and International Relations. *Millennium* 31 (1): 109–127.

Barkawi, Tarak, and Mark Laffey. 2006. The Postcolonial Moment in Security Studies. *Review of International Studies* 32 (2): 329–352.

Barkey, Karen. 1991. Rebellious Alliances: The State and Peasant Unrest in Early Seventeenth-Century France and the Ottoman Empire. *American Sociological Review* 56 (6): 699–715.

Barkey, Karen. 2005. Islam and Toleration: Studying the Ottoman Imperial Model. *International Journal of Politics, Culture, and Society* 19 (1–2): 5–19.

Barkey, Karen. 2008. *Empire of Difference: The Ottomans in Comparative Perspective.* Cambridge: Cambridge University Press.

Barkey, Karen. 2014. Political Legitimacy and Islam in the Ottoman Empire: Lessons Learned. *Philosophy & Social Criticism* 40 (4–5): 469–477.

Barkey, Karen, and George Gavrilis. 2016. The Ottoman Millet System: Non-territorial Autonomy and Its Contemporary Legacy. *Ethnopolitics* 15 (1): 24–42.

Barkey, Karen, and Frederic C. Godart. 2013. Empires, Federated Arrangements, and Kingdoms: Using Political Models of Governance to Understand Firms' Creative Performance. *Organization Studies* 34 (1): 79–104.

Barkin, J. Samuel, and Bruce Cronin. 1994. The State and the Nation: Changing Norms and the Rules of Sovereignty in International Relations. *International Organization* 48 (1): 107–130.

Barnett, Michael N. 1995. Sovereignty, Nationalism, and Regional Order in the Arab States System. *International Organization* 49 (3): 479–510.

Barua, Pradeep. 2005. *The State at War in South Asia.* Lincoln: University of Nebraska Press.

Bates, Robert H., Avner Greif, Margaret Levi, Jean-Laurent Rosenthal, and Barry Weingast. 1998. *Analytic Narratives.* Princeton, NJ: Princeton University Press.

Bayly, Christopher A. 2007. Distorted Development: The Ottoman Empire and British India, circa 1780–1916. *Comparative Studies of South Asia, Africa and the Middle East* 27 (2): 332–344.

Bayly, Martin J. 2014. The "Re-turn" to Empire in IR: Colonial Knowledge Communities and the Construction of the Idea of the Afghan Polity, 1809–38. *Review of International Studies* 40 (3): 443–464.

268 References

Beccaro, Andrea. 2018. Modern Irregular Warfare: The ISIS Case Study. *Small Wars & Insurgencies* 29 (2): 207–228.

Berezhnaya, Liliya. 2015. A View from the Edge: Borderland Studies and Ukraine, 1991–2013. *Harvard Ukrainian Studies* 34 (1/4): 53–78.

Best, Geoffrey. 1982. *War and Society in Revolutionary Europe, 1770–1870.* Bungay, UK: Fontana.

Betts, Raymond F. 1975. *The False Dawn: European Imperialism in the Nineteenth Century.* Minneapolis: University of Minnesota Press.

Biggs, Michael. 1999. Putting the State on the Map: Cartography, Territory, and European State Formation. *Comparative Studies in Society and History* 41 (2): 374–405.

Billig, Michael. 1995. *Banal Nationalism.* London: Sage.

Bjork, James E. 2008. *Neither German Nor Pole: Catholicism and National Indifference in a Central European Borderland.* Ann Arbor: University of Michigan Press.

Black, Jeremy. 1987. *The Origins of War in Early Modern Europe.* Edinburgh: J. Donald.

Black, Jeremy. 1990. *The Rise of the European Powers: 1679–1793.* New York: Routledge.

Black, Jeremy. 1994. *European Warfare, 1660–1815.* New Haven, CT: Yale University Press.

Black, Jeremy. 2001. *Western Warfare, 1775–1882.* Bloomington: Indiana University Press.

Black, Jeremy. 2002a. *Warfare in the Western World, 1882–1975.* Bloomington: Indiana University Press.

Black, Jeremy. 2002b. *European Warfare, 1494–1660.* London: Routledge.

Black, Jeremy. 2010. *A History of Diplomacy.* London: Reaktion.

Blanning, Timothy C. M. 1986. *The Origins of the French Revolutionary Wars.* London: Longman's.

Blanning, Timothy C. M. 1996. *The French Revolutionary Wars, 1787–1802.* London: Arnold.

Bollfrass, Alexander K., and Stephen Herzog. 2022. The War in Ukraine and Global Nuclear Order. *Survival* 64 (4): 7–32.

Bonney, Richard. 1991. *The European Dynastic States, 1494–1660.* Oxford: Oxford University Press.

Branch, Jordan. 2014. *The Cartographic State: Maps, Territory and the Origins of Sovereignty.* Cambridge: Cambridge University Press.

Brauer, Ralph W. 1995. Boundaries and Frontiers in Medieval Muslim Geography. *Transactions of the American Philosophical Society* 85 (6): 1–69.

Braumoeller, Bear F. 2019. *Only the Dead: The Persistence of War in the Modern Age.* Kindle ed. New York: Oxford University Press.

Brecke, Peter. 1999. *Violent Conflicts 1400 AD to the Present in Different Regions of the World.* Ann Arbor, MI: Meeting of the Peace Science Society.

Brenner, Neil, Bob Jessop, Martin Jones, and Gordon Macleod. 2003. *State/Space: A Reader.* Oxford: Blackwell.

Breuilly, John. 1994. *Nationalism and the State.* Chicago: University of Chicago Press.

Bridge, Francis Roy, and Roger Bullen. 1980. *The Great Powers and the European States System, 1815–1914.* London: Longman.

Brilmayer, Lea. 1991. Secession and Self-Determination: A Territorial Interpretation. *Yale Journal of International Law* 16: 177–202.

Broers, Michael. 2014. *Europe under Napoleon.* New London: I.B. Tauris.

Brooks, Stephen G. 1999. The Globalization of Production and the Changing Benefits of Conquest. *Journal of Conflict Resolution* 43 (5): 646–670.

Brooks, Stephen G. 2011. *Producing Security: Multinational Corporations, Globalization, and the Changing Calculus of Conflict.* Princeton, NJ: Princeton University Press.

Brown, Kate. 2001. Gridded Lives: Why Kazakhstan and Montana Are Nearly the Same Place. *American Historical Review* 106 (1): 17–48.

Brubaker, Rogers. 1996. Nationalizing States in the Old "New Europe"—and the New. *Ethnic and Racial Studies* 19 (2): 411–437.

Brummett, Palmira. 2015. *Mapping the Ottomans*. New York: Cambridge University Press.

Bueno de Mesquita, Bruce, Alastair Smith, Randolph M. Siverson, and James D. Morrow. 2005. *The Logic of Political Survival*. Cambridge, MA: MIT Press.

Bukovansky, Mlada. 2009. *Legitimacy and Power Politics*. Princeton, NJ: Princeton University Press.

Bull, Hedley. 1977. *The Anarchical Society: A Study of Order in World Politics*. New York: Columbia University Press.

Bunzel, Cole. 2016. *From Paper State to Caliphate: The Ideology of the Islamic State*. Washington, DC: Brookings Institution.

Büthe, Tim. 2002. Taking Temporality Seriously: Modeling History and the Use of Narratives as Evidence. *American Political Science Review* 96 (3): 481–493.

Butt, Ahsan I. 2013. Anarchy and Hierarchy in International Relations: Examining South America's War-Prone Decade, 1932–41. *International Organization* 67 (3): 575–607.

Buzan, Barry. 2010. *From International to World Society? English School Theory and the Social Structure of Globalisation*. Cambridge: Cambridge University Press.

Buzan, Barry, and George Lawson. 2015. *The Global Transformation: History, Modernity and the Making of International Relations*. New York: Cambridge University Press.

Búzás, Zoltán I. 2021. Racism and Antiracism in the Liberal International Order. *International Organization* 75 (2): 440–463.

Byman, Daniel. 2015. *Al-Qaeda, the Islamic State, and the Global Jihadist Movement: What Everyone Needs to Know*. New York: Oxford University Press.

Byman, Daniel. 2016. Understanding the Islamic State: A Review Essay. *International Security* 40 (4): 127–165.

Calvert, Peter. 1984. *Revolutions and International Politics*. New York: Pinter.

Campion, Kristy. 2017. Blast through the Past: Terrorist Attacks on Art and Antiquities as a Reconquest of the Modern Jihadi Identity. *Perspectives on Terrorism* 11 (1): 26–39.

Can, Serra. 2017. Making Sense of ISIS' Geopolitical Imagination. MA thesis, Sakarya University Middle East Institute.

Caporaso, James A. 2000. Changes in the Westphalian Order: Territory, Public Authority, and Sovereignty. *International Studies Review* 2 (2): 1–28.

Carpenter, Daniel. 2000. Commentary: What is the Marginal Value of Analytic Narratives?." *Social Science History* 24 (4): 653–667.

Carter, David B. 2010. The Strategy of Territorial Conflict. *American Journal of Political Science* 54 (4): 969–987.

Carter, David B., and Hein Goemans. 2011. The Making of the Territorial Order: New Borders and the Emergence of Interstate Conflict. *International Organization* 65 (2): 275–309.

Carter, Paul. 1988. *The Road to Botany Bay: An Exploration of Landscape and History*. New York: Knopf.

Castellino, Joshua. 1999. Territory and Identity in International Law: The Struggle for Self-Determination in the Western Sahara. *Millennium* 28 (3): 523–551.

Cederman, Lars-Erik, T. Camber Warren, and Didier Sornette. 2011. Testing Clausewitz: Nationalism, Mass Mobilization, and the Severity of War. *International Organization* 65 (4): 605–638.

Celso, Anthony N. 2016. Jihadist Failure, Resilience, and Never-Ending Warfare. *Terrorism and Political Violence* 28 (4): 813–822.

Cengiz, Mahmut, Kutluer Karademir, and Huseyin Cinoglu. 2022. The ISIS Model and Its Influence over Global Terrorism. *European Scientific Journal* 18 (7): 14–35.

Centeno, Miguel A. 2002. *Blood and Debt: War and the Nation-State in Latin America*. University Park: Pennsylvania State University Press.

270 References

Chatterjee, Partha. 1993. *The Nation and Its Fragments: Colonial and Postcolonial Histories.* Princeton, NJ: Princeton University Press.

Cheskin, Ammon. 2017. Russian Soft Power in Ukraine: A Structural Perspective. *Communist and Post-Communist Studies* 50 (4): 277–287.

Chickering, Roger. 1998. *Imperial Germany and the Great War, 1914–1918.* Cambridge: Cambridge University Press.

Chotiner, Isaac. 2022. Why John Mearsheimer Blames the U.S. for the Crisis in Ukraine. New Yorker, March 1. https://www.newyorker.com/news/q-and-a/why-john-mearsheimer-blames-the-us-for-the-crisis-in-ukraine.

Clark, Christopher. 2012. *The Sleepwalkers: How Europe Went to War in 1914.* London: Penguin.

Clauset, Aaron. 2018. Trends and Fluctuations in the Severity of Interstate Wars. *Science Advances* 4 (2): 1–9.

Clausewitz, Carl von. [1832] 1976. *On War.* Edited and translated by Michael Howard and Peter Paret. Princeton, NJ: Princeton University Press.

Clement, Vincent. 2019. Beyond the Sham of the Emancipatory Enlightenment: Rethinking the Relationship of Indigenous Epistemologies, Knowledges, and Geography through Decolonizing Paths. *Progress in Human Geography* 43 (2): 276–294.

Clodfelter, Michael. 2002. *Warfare and Armed Conflicts: A Statistical Reference to Casualty and Other Figures, 1618–1991.* Jefferson, NC: McFarland.

Coakley, John. 2018. "Primordialism" in Nationalism Studies: Theory or Ideology? *Nations and Nationalism* 24 (2): 327–347.

Cockburn, Patrick. 2015. *The Rise of Islamic State: ISIS and the New Sunni Revolution.* London: Verso.

Cockburn, Patrick. 2020. *War in the Age of Trump: The Defeat of ISIS, the Fall of the Kurds, the Conflict with Iran.* London: Verso.

Colás, Alejandro. 2007. *Empire.* Cambridge: Polity.

Collins, James B. 1997. State Building in Early-Modern Europe: The Case of France. *Modern Asian Studies* 31 (3): 603–633.

Collins, Randall. 1999. *Macrohistory: Essays in Sociology of the Long Run.* Stanford, CA: Stanford University Press.

Comaroff, John L. 2001. Colonialism, Culture, and the Law: A Foreword. *Law & Social Inquiry* 26 (2): 305–314.

Confino, Alon. 1997. *The Nation as a Local Metaphor: Württemberg, Imperial Germany, and National Memory, 1871–1918.* Chapel Hill: University of North Carolina Press.

Connelly, Owen. 1965. *Napoleon's Satellite Kingdoms.* New York: Free Press.

Cooper, Frederick. 2004. Empire Multiplied. *Comparative Studies in Society and History* 46 (2): 247–272.

Cooper, Randolf G. S. 2005. Culture, Combat, and Colonialism in Eighteenth- and Nineteenth-Century India. *International History Review* 27 (3): 534–549.

Copeland, Dale C. 2000. *The Origins of Major War.* Ithaca, NY: Cornell University Press.

Corey, James S. A. 2011. *Leviathan Wakes.* New York: Orbit.

Crankshaw, Edward. 1981. *Bismarck.* New York: Viking Press.

Croxton, Derek, and Geoffrey Parker. 2009. A Swift and Sure Peace: The Congress of Westphalia 1643–1648. In *The Making of Peace: Rulers, States, and the Aftermath of War,* edited by Williamson Murray and Jim Lacey, 71–100. New York: Cambridge University Press.

Culcasi, Karen. 2016. Images and Imaginings of Palestine: Territory and Everyday Geopolitics for Palestinian Jordanians. *Geopolitics* 21 (1): 69–91.

Cunningham, Kathleen Gallagher, and Katherine Sawyer. 2017. Is Self-Determination Contagious? A Spatial Analysis of the Spread of Self-Determination Claims. *International Organization* 71 (3): 585–604.

References 271

Çolak, Hasan. 2015. Tekfur, Fasiliyus, and Kayser: Disdain, Negligence and Appropriation of Byzantine Imperial Titulature in the Ottoman World. In *Frontiers of the Ottoman Imagination*, edited by Marios Hadjianastasis, 5–28. Boston: Brill.

Dakin, Douglas. 1973. *The Greek Struggle for Independence, 1821–1833*. London: B.T. Batsford.

Dalby, Simon. 2010. Recontextualizing Violence, Power and Nature: The Next Twenty Years of Critical Geopolitics? *Political Geography* 29 (5): 380–288.

Dale, Stephen F. 2010. *The Muslim Empires of the Ottomans, Safavids, and Mughals*. New York: Cambridge University Press.

Daly, Gavin. 2016. War and the French Revolution. *Agora* 51 (1): 13–19.

Darden, Keith. 2014. *Resisting Occupation: Mass Schooling and the Creation of Durable National Loyalties*. New York: Cambridge University Press.

Darling, Linda T. 2000. Contested Territory: Ottoman Holy War in Comparative Context. *Studia Islamica* 91: 133–163.

Darwin, John. 1997. Imperialism and the Victorians: The Dynamics of Territorial Expansion. *English Historical Review* 112 (447): 614–642.

Delaney, David. 2005. *Territory: A Short Introduction*. Oxford. UK: Blackwell.

Delaney, David, and Helga Leitner. 1997. The Political Construction of Scale. *Political Geography* 16 (2): 93–97.

Desan, Suzanne. 2013. Foreigners, Cosmopolitanism, and French Revolutionary Universalism. In *The French Revolution in Global Perspective*, edited by Suzanne Desan, Lynn Hunt, and William Max Nelson, 86–100. Ithaca, NY: Cornell University Press.

Dew, Andrea J., Marc A. Genest, and Sarah C. M. Paine, eds. 2019. *From Quills to Tweets: How America Communicates about War and Revolution*. Washington, DC: Georgetown University Press.

Dhondt, Frederik. 2011. From Contract to Treaty: The Legal Transformation of the Spanish Succession 1659–1713. *Journal of the History of International Law / Revue d'histoire du droit international* 13 (2): 347–375.

Diehl, Paul F., and Gary Goertz. 1988. Territorial Changes and Militarized Conflict. *Journal of Conflict Resolution* 32 (1): 103–122.

Diehl, Paul F., and Gary Goertz. 2002. *Territorial Changes and International Conflict*. London: Routledge.

Dijkink, G. J. W. 2005. Soldiers and Nationalism: The Glory and Transience of a Hard-Won Territorial Identity. In *The Geography of War and Peace: From Death Camps to Diplomats*, edited by Colin Flint, 113–132. Oxford: Oxford University Press.

Dobbins, James, and Seth G. Jones. 2017. The End of a Caliphate. *Survival* 59 (3): 55–72.

Doboš, Bohumil. 2016. Shapeshifter of Somalia: Evolution of the Political Territoriality of Al-Shabaab. *Small Wars & Insurgencies* 27 (5): 937–957.

Dodds, Klaus, and David Atkinson. 2000. Preface. In *Geopolitical Traditions: A Century of Geopolitical Thought*, edited by Klaus Dodds and David Atkinson, xiv–xvi. London: Routledge.

Donnelly, Jack. 2012. The Elements of the Structures of International Systems. *International Organization* 66 (4): 609–643.

Dostal, Jörg Michael. 2017. The Crisis of German Social Democracy Revisited. *Political Quarterly* 88 (2): 230–240.

Doumanis, Nicholas. 2013. *Before the Nation: Muslim-Christian Coexistence and Its Destruction in Late-Ottoman Anatolia*. Oxford: Oxford University Press.

Dower, John W. 1999. *Embracing Defeat: Japan in the Wake of World War II*. New York: Norton.

Downes, Alexander B., and Lindsey A. O'Rourke. 2016. You Can't Always Get What You Want: Why Foreign-Imposed Regime Change Seldom Improves Interstate Relations. *International Security* 41 (2): 43–89.

Downing, Brian M. 2000. Economic Analysis in Historical Perspective. *History and Theory* 39 (1): 88–97.

272 References

Doyle, Michael W. 1986. *Empires*. Ithaca, NY: Cornell University Press.

Doyle, William. 1988. *Origins of the French Revolution*. Oxford: Oxford University Press.

DuBois, William Edward Burghardt. 1925. Worlds of Color. *Foreign Affairs* 3 (3): 423–444.

Duffy, Christopher. 1985a. *Frederick the Great: A Military Life*. London: Routledge & Kegan Paul.

Duffy, Christopher. 1985b. *The Fortress in the Age of Vauban and Frederick the Great, 1660–1789*. London: Routledge & Kegan Paul.

Dunn, David J. 2018. *The First Fifty Years of Peace Research: A Survey and Interpretation*. London: Routledge.

Dwyer, Philip G. 2014. *The Rise of Prussia, 1700–1830*. Kindle ed. London: Routledge.

Dzurek, Daniel J. 2005. What Makes Territory Important: Tangible and Intangible Dimensions. *GeoJournal* 64 (4): 263–274.

Eckstein, Harry. 1975. Case Studies and Theory in Political Science. In *Handbook of Political Science*, vol. 7, edited by Fred Greenstein and Nelson Polsby, 79–138. Reading, MA: Addison-Wesley.

Edelstein, David M. 2004. Occupational Hazards: Why Military Occupations Succeed or Fail. *International Security* 29 (1): 49–91.

Edney, Matthew H. 2009. *Mapping an Empire: The Geographical Construction of British India, 1765–1843*. Chicago: University of Chicago Press.

Ekberg, Carl J. 1974. From Dutch to European War: Louis XIV and Louvois Are Tested. *French Historical Studies* 8 (3): 393–408.

Elden, Stuart. 2005. Missing the Point: Globalization, Deterritorialization and the Space of the World. *Transactions of the Institute of British Geographers* 30 (1): 8–19.

Elden, Stuart. 2009. *Terror and Territory: The Spatial Extent of Sovereignty*. Minneapolis: University of Minnesota Press.

Elden, Stuart. 2010. Land, Terrain, Territory. *Progress in Human Geography* 34 (6): 799–817.

Elden, Stuart. 2013. *The Birth of Territory*. Chicago: University of Chicago Press.

Eley, Geoff. 1991. *Reshaping the German Right: Radical Nationalism and Political Change after Bismarck*. Ann Arbor: University of Michigan Press.

Elster, Jon. 2000. Rational Choice History: A Case of Excessive Ambition. *American Political Science Review* 94 (3): 685–695.

Emiralioglu, Pınar. 2012. Relocating the Center of the Universe: China and the Ottoman Imperial Project in the Sixteenth Century. *Osmanlı Araştırmaları* 39: 160–187.

Emiralioğlu, Pinar. 2014. *Geographical Knowledge and Imperial Culture in the Early Modern Ottoman Empire*. Surrey: Ashgate.

Etherington, John. 2010. Nationalism, Territoriality and National Territorial Belonging. *Papers: Revista de Sociologia* 95 (2): 321–339.

Etherington, Norman. 1982. Reconsidering Theories of Imperialism. *History and Theory* 21 (1): 1–36.

Eyck, Erich. 1970. *A History of the Weimar Republic*. New York: Atheneum.

Fall, Juliet J. 2010. Artificial States? On the Enduring Geographical Myth of Natural Borders. *Political Geography* 29 (3): 140–147.

Fawaz, Gerges A. 2016. *ISIS: A History*. Princeton, NJ: Princeton University Press.

Fazal, Tanisha M. 2007. *State Death: The Politics and Geography of Conquest, Occupation, and Annexation*. Princeton, NJ: Princeton University Press.

Fearon, James D. 1995. Rationalist Explanations for War. *International Organization* 49 (3): 379–411.

Fearon, James D., and David D. Laitin. 2003. Ethnicity, Insurgency, and Civil War. *American Political Science Review* 97 (1): 75–90.

Fehér, Ferenc. 1990. *The French Revolution and the Birth of Modernity*. Berkeley: University of California Press.

References   273

Findlay, Ronald, and Mats Lundahl. 2017. *The Economics of the Frontier*. London: Palgrave Macmillan.

Fischer-Fabian, S. 1981. *Prussia's Glory: The Rise of a Military State*. New York: Macmillan.

Fishman, Brian H. 2016. *The Master Plan: ISIS, al-Qaeda, and the Jihadi Strategy for Final Victory*. New Haven, CT: Yale University Press.

Flint, Colin. 2003. Terrorism and Counterterrorism: Geographic Research Questions and Agendas. *Professional Geographer* 55 (2): 161–169.

Flint, Colin. 2005. *The Geography of War and Peace: From Death Camps to Diplomats*. Oxford: Oxford University Press.

Flint, Colin. 2006. *Introduction to Geopolitics*. London: Routledge.

Flint, Colin, Paul Diehl, Juergen Scheffran, John Vasquez, and Sang-hyun Chia. 2009. Conceptualizing ConflictSpace: Toward a Geography of Relational Power and Embeddedness in the Analysis of Interstate Conflict. *Annals of the Association of American Geographers* 99 (5): 827–835.

Flint, Colin, and Steven M. Radil. 2009. Terrorism and Counter-terrorism: Situating al-Qaeda and the Global War on Terror within Geopolitical Trends and Structures. *Eurasian Geography and Economics* 50 (2): 150–171.

Flyvbjerg, Bent. 2001. *Making Social Science Matter: Why Social Inquiry Fails and How It Can Succeed Again*. Cambridge: Cambridge University Press.

Flyvbjerg, Bent. 2006. Five Misunderstandings about Case-Study Research. *Qualitative Inquiry* 12 (2): 219–245.

Foeken, Dick. 1995. On the Causes of the Partition of Central Africa, 1875–1885. *Political Geography* 14 (1): 80–100.

Foucault, Michel. 1977. *Discipline and Punish: The Birth of the Prison*. Translated by Alan Sheridan. London: Allen Lane.

Foucault, Michel. 1986. Space, Knowledge, Power. In *The Foucault Reader*, edited by Paul Rabinow, 239–256. New York: Penguin.

Franke, Ulrich, and Ralph Weber. 2012. At the Papini Hotel: On Pragmatism in the Study of International Relations. *European Journal of International Relations* 18 (4): 669–691.

Frederick, Bryan A., Paul R. Hensel, and Christopher Macaulay. 2017. The Issue Correlates of War Territorial Claims Data, 1816–2011. *Journal of Peace Research* 54 (1): 99–108.

Freeman, Bianca, D. G. Kim, and David A. Lake. 2022. Race in International Relations: Beyond the "Norm against Noticing." *Annual Review of Political Science* 25: 175–196.

Friedman, Thomas L. 2007. *The World Is Flat: A Brief History of the Twenty-First Century*. New York: Picador.

Friedman, Thomas L. 2000. *The Lexus and the Olive Tree: Understanding Globalization*. New York: Picador.

Friedrichs, Jörg, and Friedrich Kratochwil. 2009. On Acting and Knowing: How Pragmatism Can Advance International Relations Research and Methodology. *International Organization* 63 (4): 701–731.

Fromkin, David. 1989. *A Peace to End All Peace*. New York: Henry Holt.

Fromm, Erich. 1959. The Creative Attitude. In *Creativity and Its Cultivation: Addresses Presented at the Interdisciplinary Symposia on Creativity, Michigan State University*, edited by Harold H. Anderson, 44–54. New York: Harper & Row.

Fromson, James, and Steven Simon. 2015. ISIS: The Dubious Paradise of Apocalypse Now. *Survival* 57 (3): 7–56.

Fukuyama, Francis. 1992. *The End of History and the Last Man*. London: Penguin.

Gaddis, John L. 2005. *Strategies of Containment: A Critical Appraisal of American National Security Policy during the Cold War*. New York: Oxford University Press.

Gagliardo, John G. 1991. *Germany under the Old Regime, 1600–1790*. London: Longman.

274 References

Galbraith, John S. 1960. The "Turbulent Frontier" as a Factor in British Expansion. *Comparative Studies in Society and History* 2 (2): 150–168.

Gani, Jasmine K., and Jenna Marshall. 2022. The Impact of Colonialism on Policy and Knowledge Production in International Relations. *International Affairs* 98 (1): 5–22.

Gates, Scott, and Sukanya Podder. 2015. Social Media, Recruitment, Allegiance and the Islamic State. *Perspectives on Terrorism* 9 (4): 107–116.

Gedikli, Yusuf. 2021. Osmanlı Devletini Kuran Osman Bey'in Adı Sorunu. *Türk Dünyası Araştırmaları* 129 (255): 449–480.

Gellner, Ernest. 1983. *Nations and Nationalism*. Ithaca, NY: Cornell University Press.

Gerwarth, Robert, and Erez Manela. 2014. The Great War as a Global War: Imperial Conflict and the Reconfiguration of World Order, 1911–1923. *Diplomatic History* 38 (4): 786–800.

Geyer, Michael. 1985. The Dynamics of Military Revisionism in the Interwar Years: Military Politics between Rearmament and Diplomacy. In *The German Military in the Age of Total War*, edited by Wilhelm Deist and Paul Kennedy, 101–150. Warwickshire, UK: Berg.

Geyer, Michael. 1992. The Stigma of Violence, Nationalism, and War in Twentieth-Century Germany. *German Studies Review* 15: 75–110.

Giddens, Anthony. 1985. *The Nation-State and Violence*. Cambridge: Polity.

Giddens, Anthony. 1986. The Nation-State and Violence. *Capital & Class* 10 (2): 216–220.

Giesey, Ralph E. 1983. State-Building in Early Modern France: The Role of Royal Officialdom. *Journal of Modern History* 55 (2): 191–207.

Gilpin, Robert. 1981. *War and Change in World Politics*. Cambridge: Cambridge University Press.

Gleditsch, Kristian. 2004. A Revised List of Wars between and within Independent States, 1816–2002. *International Interactions* 30 (3): 231–262.

Göçek, Fatma M. 2013. Parameters of a Postcolonial Sociology of the Ottoman Empire. *Political Power and Social Theory* 25: 73–104.

Goddard, Stacie E. 2009. *Indivisible Territory and the Politics of Legitimacy: Jerusalem and Northern Ireland*. Cambridge: Cambridge University Press.

Goemans, Hein E. 1975. The Evolution of the Concept of Territory. *Information (International Social Science Council)* 14 (3): 29–47.

Goemans, Hein E. 2000. *War and Punishment*. Princeton, NJ: Princeton University Press.

Goemans, Hein E. 2006. Bounded Communities: Territoriality, Territorial Attachment, and Conflict. In *Territoriality and Conflict in an Era of Globalization*, edited by Miles Kahler and Barbara F. Walter, 25–61. Cambridge: Cambridge University Press.

Goemans, Hein E., and Kenneth A. Schultz. 2017. The Politics of Territorial Claims: A Geospatial Approach Applied to Africa. *International Organization* 71 (1): 31–64.

Goettlich, Kerry. 2019. The Rise of Linear Borders in World Politics. *European Journal of International Relations* 25 (1): 203–228.

Gottmann, Jean. 1973. *The Significance of Territory*. Charlottesville: University Press of Virginia.

Graham, Stephen. 1998. The End of Geography or the Explosion of Place? Conceptualizing Space, Place and Information Technology. *Progress in Human Geography* 22 (2): 165–185.

Graham, Stephen. 2011. *Cities under Siege: The New Military Urbanism*. London: Verso.

Gray, Colin S. 1991. Geography and Grand Strategy. *Comparative Strategy* 10 (4): 311–329.

Greenfeld, Liah. 1992. *Nationalism: Five Roads to Modernity*. Cambridge, MA: Harvard University Press.

Greig, Michael J. 2002. The End of Geography? Globalization, Communications, and Culture in the International System. *Journal of Conflict Resolution* 46 (2): 225–243.

Griffiths, Ryan D. 2018. The Waltzian Ordering Principle and International Change: A Two-Dimensional Model. *European Journal of International Relations* 24 (1): 130–152.

Gross, Leo. 1948. The Peace of Westphalia, 1648–1948. *American Journal of International Law* 42 (1): 20–41.

References 275

Grygiel, Jakub J. 2006. *Great Powers and Geopolitical Change.* Baltimore: Johns Hopkins University Press.

Grygiel, Jakub J. 2013. The Primacy of Premodern History. *Security Studies* 22 (1): 1–32.

Guilmartin, John F. 1988. Ideology and Conflict: The Wars of the Ottoman Empire, 1453–1606. *Journal of Interdisciplinary History* 18 (4): 721–747.

Gulick, Edward V. 1955. *Europe's Classical Balance of Power: A Case History of the Theory and Practice of One of the Great Concepts of European Statecraft.* New York: Norton.

Gürkan, Emrah S. 2013. *Batı Akdeniz'de Osmanlı Korsanlığı Ve Gaza Meselesi. Kebikeç: Insan Bilimleri Için Kaynak Araştırmaları Dergisi* 33: 173–204.

Haas, Ernst B. 1986. What Is Nationalism and Why Should We Study It? *International Organization* 40 (3): 707–744.

Häkli, Jouni. 1994. *Territoriality and the Rise of Modern State.* Helsinki: Geographical Society of Finland.

Häkli, Jouni. 2001. In the Territory of Knowledge: State-Centred Discourses and the Construction of Society. *Progress in Human Geography* 25 (3): 403–422.

Hall, John A., and Siniša Malešević. 2013. Introduction: Wars and Nationalism. In *Nationalism and War*, edited by Jahn A. Hall and Siniša Malešević, 1–28. Cambridge: Cambridge University Press.

Hall, Rodney B. 1999. *National Collective Identity: Social Constructs and International Systems.* New York: Columbia University Press.

Halliday, Fred. 1999. *Revolution and World Politics: The Rise and Fall of the Sixth Great Power.* Basingstoke: Macmillan.

Hamdan, Ali N. 2016. Breaker of Barriers? Notes on the Geopolitics of the Islamic State in Iraq and Sham. *Geopolitics* 21 (3): 605–627.

Harris, Erika. 2020. What Is the Role of Nationalism and Ethnicity in the Russia-Ukraine Crisis? *Europe-Asia Studies* 72 (4): 593–613.

Hassner, Ron E. 2009. *War on Sacred Grounds.* Ithaca, NY: Cornell University Press.

Haug, Robert. 2011. Frontiers and the State in Early Islamic History: Jihad between Caliphs and Volunteers. *History Compass* 9 (8): 634–643.

Healy, Maureen. 2004. *Vienna and the Fall of the Habsburg Empire: Total War and Everyday Life in World War I.* Cambridge: Cambridge University Press.

Hechter, Michael. 2000. *Containing Nationalism.* Oxford: Oxford University Press.

Henderson, Errol A. 2017. The Revolution Will Not Be Theorised: Du Bois, Locke, and the Howard School's Challenge to White Supremacist IR Theory. *Millennium* 45 (3): 492–510.

Hensel, Paul R., and Sara McLaughlin Mitchell. 2005. Issue Indivisibility and Territorial Claims. *GeoJournal* 64 (4): 275–285.

Herb, Guntram H. 1999. National Identity and Territory. In *Nested Identities: Nationalism, Territory, and Scale*, edited by Guntram H. Herb and David H. Kaplan, 9–30. Lanham, MD: Rowman & Littlefield.

Herb, Guntram H. 2002. *Under the Map of Germany: Nationalism and Propaganda, 1918–1945.* London: Routledge.

Herb, Guntram H. 2004. Double Vision: Territorial Strategies in the Construction of National Identities in Germany, 1949–1979. *Annals of the Association of American Geographers* 94 (1): 140–164.

Herbst, Jeffrey. 2000. *States and Power in Africa.* Princeton, NJ: Princeton University Press.

Herz, John H. 1950. Idealist Internationalism and the Security Dilemma. *World Politics* 2 (2): 157–180.

Herz, John H. 1957. Rise and Demise of the Territorial State. *World Politics* 9(4): 473–493.

Hewitson, Mark. 2000. Germany and France before the First World War: A Reassessment of Wilhelmine Foreign Policy. *English Historical Review* 115 (462): 570–606.

Hibbert, Christopher. 1980. *The Days of the French Revolution.* New York: Morrow.

276 References

Hillgruber, Andreas.1981. *Germany and the Two World Wars*. Cambridge, MA: Harvard University Press.

Hirst, Paul Q. 2005. *Space and Power: Politics, War, and Architecture*. Cambridge: Polity.

Hobbs, Joseph J. 2005. The Geographical Dimensions of al-Qaida Rhetoric. *Geographical Review* 95 (3): 301–327.

Hobsbawm, Eric J. 1962. *Age of Revolution: 1789-1848*. London: Weidenfeld and Nicolson.

Hobsbawm, Eric J. 1991. *Nations and Nationalism*. Cambridge: Cambridge University Press.

Hobson, John M. 2012. *The Eurocentric Conception of World Politics: Western International Theory, 1760-2010*. Cambridge: Cambridge University Press.

Hobson, John M. 2014. Re-embedding the Global Colour Line within Post-1945 International Theory. In *Race and Racism in International Relations*, edited by Alexander Anievas, Nivi Manchanda, and Robbie Shilliam, 81–97. London: Routledge.

Hochedlinger, Michael. 2003. *Austria's Wars of Emergence: War, State and Society in the Habsburg Monarchy, 1683-1797*. Harlow: Longman.

Hoffman, Bruce. 2015. A First Draft of the History of America's Ongoing Wars on Terrorism. *Studies in Conflict and Terrorism*, 38 (1): 75–83.

Holborn, Hajo. 1964. *A History of Modern Germany: 1840-1945*. Vol. 3. New York: Alfred A. Knopf.

Holsti, Kalevi J. 1991. *Peace and War: Armed Conflicts and International Order, 1648-1989*. Cambridge: Cambridge University Press.

Holsti, Kalevi J. 2016: *Major Texts on War, the State, Peace, and International Order*. New York: Springer.

Holtman, Robert B. 1950. *Napoleonic Propaganda*. Baton Rouge: Louisiana State University Press.

Hooson, David J. M. 1993. *Geography and National Identity*. Oxford: Blackwell.

Horowitz, Richard S. 2004. International Law and State Transformation in China, Siam, and the Ottoman Empire during the Nineteenth Century. *Journal of World History* 15 (4): 445–486.

Howard, Michael. 1976. *War in European History*. London: Oxford University Press.

Howard, Michael. 1981. *The Franco-Prussian War: The German Invasion of France, 1870–1871*. London: Methuen.

Howard, Michael. 1983. *The Causes of War and Other Essays*. London: Temple Smith.

Howard, Michael. 2002. *The First World War*. Oxford: Oxford University Press.

Hudson, B. 1977. The New Geography and the New Imperialism: 1870–1918. *Antipode* 9: 12–19.

Hughes, Judith M. 1971. *To the Maginot Line: The Politics of French Military Preparation in the 1920's*. Cambridge, MA: Harvard University Press.

Hull, Isabel V. 2005. *Absolute Destruction: Military Culture and the Practices of War in Imperial Germany*. Ithaca, NY: Cornell University Press.

Hunt, Lynn. 1984. *Politics, Culture and Class during the French Revolution*. Berkeley: University of California Press.

Huntington, Ellsworth. 1915. *Civilization and Climate*. New Haven, CT: Yale University Press.

Huntington, Samuel P. 1993. The Clash of Civilizations? *Foreign Affairs* 72 (3): 22–49.

Hutchins, Francis G. 2015. *The Illusion of Permanence: British Imperialism in India*. Princeton, NJ: Princeton University Press.

Hutchinson, John. 1987. *Dynamics of Cultural Nationalism: The Gaelic Revival and the Creation of the Irish Nation State*. London: Allen and Unwin.

Hutchinson, John. 2017. *Nationalism and War*. Oxford: Oxford University Press.

Huth, Paul K., and Todd L. Allee. 2003. *The Democratic Peace and Territorial Conflict in the Twentieth Century*. Cambridge: Cambridge University Press.

Huth, Paul K. 1996. *Standing Your Ground: Territorial Disputes and International Conflict*. Ann Arbor: University of Michigan Press.

References 277

Ikenberry, G. John. 2001. *After Victory: Institutions, Strategic Restraint, and the Rebuilding of Order after Major Wars*. Princeton, NJ: Princeton University Press.

İnalcık, Halil. 1954. Ottoman Methods of Conquest. *Studia Islamica* 2: 103–129.

İnalcık, Halil. 1973. *The Ottoman Empire: The Classical Age, 1300–1600*. New York: Praeger.

Ingrao, Charles W. 1994. *The Habsburg Monarchy, 1618–1815*. Cambridge: Cambridge University Press.

Isaac, Benjamin H. 1990. *The Limits of Empire: The Roman Army in the East*. Oxford: Clarendon Press.

Iyigun, Murat. 2015. *War, Peace, and Prosperity in the Name of God: The Ottoman Role in Europe's Socioeconomic Evolution*. Chicago: University of Chicago Press.

Jabareen, Yosef. 2015. The Emerging Islamic State: Terror, Territoriality, and the Agenda of Social Transformation. *Geoforum* (58): 51–55.

Jackson, Robert H. 1993. *Quasi-States: Sovereignty, International Relations and the Third World*. Cambridge: Cambridge University Press.

Jaques, Tony. 2007. *Dictionary of Battles and Sieges*. Westport, CT: Greenwood Publishing Group.

Jennings, Ivor. 1956. *The Approach to Self-Government*. Cambridge: Cambridge University Press.

Jervis, Robert. 1978. Cooperation under the Security Dilemma. *World Politics* 30 (2): 167–214.

Jervis, Robert. 1989. *The Meaning of the Nuclear Revolution: Statecraft and the Prospect of Armageddon*. Ithaca, NY: Cornell University Press.

Joes, Anthony J. 2010. *Victorious Insurgencies: Four Rebellions That Changed the World*. Lexington: University of Kentucky Press.

Joffé, George. 2016. Global Jihad and Foreign Fighters. *Small Wars & Insurgencies* 27 (5): 800–816.

Johnson, Dominic D. P., and Monica Duffy Toft. 2014. Grounds for War: The Evolution of Territorial Conflict. *International Security* 38 (3): 7–38.

Johnson, Rob. 2005. *A Region in Turmoil: South Asian Conflicts since 1947*. London: Reaktion Books.

Johnston, Ron J. 1995. Territoriality and the State. In *Geography, History and Social Sciences*, edited by Georges B. Benko and Ulf Strohmayer, 213–225. Dordrecht: Kluwer.

Jones, Rhys. 2008. Relocating Nationalism: On the Geographies of Reproducing Nations. *Transactions of the Institute of British Geographers* 33 (3): 319–334.

Jordheim, Helge, and Iver B. Neumann. 2011. Empire, Imperialism and Conceptual History. *Journal of International Relations and Development* 14 (2): 153–185.

Kadercan, Burak. 2011. Politics of Survival, Nationalism, and War for Territory. PhD dissertation, University of Chicago.

Kadercan, Burak. 2012. Military Competition and the Emergence of Nationalism: Putting the Logic of Political Survival into Historical Context. *International Studies Review* 14 (3): 401–428.

Kadercan, Burak. 2013. Making Sense of Survival: Refining the Treatment of State Preferences in Neorealist Theory. *Review of International Studies* 39 (4): 1015–1037.

Kadercan, Burak. 2014. Strong Armies, Slow Adaptation: Civil-Military Relations and the Diffusion of Military Power. *International Security* 38 (3): 117–152.

Kadercan, Burak. 2015. Triangulating Territory: A Case for Pragmatic Interaction between Political Science, Political Geography, and Critical IR. *International Theory* 7 (1): 125–161.

Kadercan, Burak. 2017. Territorial Design and Grand Strategy in the Ottoman Empire. *Territory, Politics, Governance* 5(2): 158–176.

Kadercan, Burak. 2018. Nationalism and War for Territory: From "Divisible" Territories to Inviolable Homelands. *Cambridge Review of International Affairs* 30 (4): 368–393.

Kadercan, Burak. 2019. Territorial Logic of the Islamic State: An Interdisciplinary Approach. *Territory, Politics, Governance* 9 (1): 94–110.

278 References

Kafadar, Cemal. 1995. *Between Two Worlds: The Construction of the Ottoman State*. Berkeley: University of California Press.

Kahler, Miles. 2006. Territoriality and Conflict in an Era of Globalization. In *Territoriality and Conflict in an Era of Globalization*, edited by Miles Kahler and Barbara Walters, 1–21. Cambridge: Cambridge University Press.

Kahler, Miles, and Barbara F. Walter. 2006. *Territoriality and Conflict in an Era of Globalization*. Cambridge: Cambridge University Press.

Kaldor, Mary. 1999. *Old and New Wars: Organized Violence in a Global Era*. Stanford, CA: Stanford University Press.

Kalyvas, Stathis N. 2015. Is ISIS a Revolutionary Group and If Yes, What Are the Implications? *Perspectives on Terrorism* 9 (4): 42–47.

Kaplan, David. 1999. Territorial Identities and Geographic Scale. In *Nested Identities: Nationalism, Territory and Scale*, edited by Herb Guntram and David Kaplan, 31–49. Lanham, MD: Rowman & Littlefield.

Kaplan, Robert. 2012. *The Revenge of Geography: What the Map Tells Us about Coming Conflicts and the Battle against Fate*. New York: Random House.

Karpat, Kemal. 1977a. Introduction. In *The Ottoman State and Its Place in World History*, edited by Kemal Karpat, 1–14. Leiden: E. J. Brill.

Karpat, Kemal. 1977b. The Stages of Ottoman History: A Structural Comparative Approach. In *The Ottoman State and Its Place in World History*, edited by Kemal Karpat, 79–98. Leiden: E. J. Brill.

Katz, Mark N. 1993. The Legacy of Empire in International Relations. *Comparative Strategy* 12 (4): 365–383.

Kayaoğlu, Turan. 2010. *Legal Imperialism: Sovereignty and Extraterritoriality in Japan, the Ottoman Empire, and China*. New York: Cambridge University Press.

Keal, Paul. 2003. *European Conquest and the Rights of Indigenous Peoples: The Moral Backwardness of International Society*. Cambridge: Cambridge University Press.

Kearns, Gerry. 2004. The Political Pivot of Geography. *Geographical Journal* 170 (4): 337–346.

Kearns, Gerry. 2009. *Geopolitics and Empire: The Legacy of Halford Mackinder*. Oxford: Oxford University Press.

Kearns, Gerry. 2010. Geography, Geopolitics, and Empire. *Transactions of the Institute of British Geographers* 35 (2): 187–203.

Keegan, John. 1994. *A History of Warfare*. London: Pimlico.

Keegan, John. 1998. *The First World War*. London: Hutchinson.

Keene, Edward. 2002. *Beyond the Anarchical Society: Grotius, Colonialism and Order in World Politics*. Cambridge: Cambridge University Press.

Keitner, Chimène I. 2000. National Self-Determination in Historical Perspective: The Legacy of the French Revolution for Today's Debates. *International Studies Review* 2 (3): 3–26.

Kennedy, David. 1997. International Law and the Nineteenth Century: History of an Illusion. *Quinnipiac Law Review* 17: 99.

Kennedy, Hugh. 2007. *The Great Arab Conquests: How the Spread of Islam Changed the World We Live in*. London: Phoenix.

Kennedy, Paul. 1987. *The Rise and Fall of the Great Powers: Economic Change and Military Conflict from 1500 to 2000*. New York: Random House.

Keohane, Robert O. 1984. *After Hegemony*. Princeton, NJ: Princeton University Press.

Keyder, Caglar. 1997. The Ottoman Empire. In *After Empire: Multiethnic Societies and Nation-Building: The Soviet Union and the Russian, Ottoman, and Habsburg Empires*, edited by Karen Barkey and Mark V. Hagen, 30–44. Boulder, CO: Westview Press.

Kfir, Isaac. 2015. Social Identity Group and Human (In)Security: The Case of Islamic State in Iraq and the Levant (ISIL). *Studies in Conflict & Terrorism* 38 (4): 233–252.

Khadduri, Majid. 1955. *War and Peace in the Law of Islam*. Baltimore: Johns Hopkins Press.

References 279

Kiernan, Victor G. 1969. *The Lords of Human Kind: European Attitudes to Other Cultures in the Imperial Age*. London: Zed Books.

Kiernan, Victor G. 1998. *Colonial Empires and Armies, 1815–1960*. Montreal: McGill-Queen's University Press.

King, Gary, Robert O. Keohane, and Sidney Verba. 1994. *Designing Social Inquiry: Scientific Inference in Qualitative Research*. Princeton, NJ: Princeton University Press.

Knight, David B. 1982. Identity and Territory: Geographical Perspectives on Nationalism and Regionalism. *Annals of the Association of American Geographers* 72 (4): 514–531.

Knott, Eleanor. 2022. Existential Nationalism: Russia's War against Ukraine. *Nations and Nationalism* 29 (1)45–52.

Koch, Hannsjoachim W. 1978. *A History of Prussia*. London: Longman.

Koch, Natalie. 2015. "Spatial Socialization": Understanding the State Effect Geographically. *Nordia Geographical Publications* 44 (4): 29–35.

Kolsky, Elizabeth. 2015. The Colonial Rule of Law and the Legal Regime of Exception: Frontier "Fanaticism" and State Violence in British India. *American Historical Review* 120 (4): 1218–1246.

Koopman, Sara. 2016. Beware: Your Research May Be Weaponized. *Annals of the American Association of Geographers* 106 (3): 530–535.

Korzybski, Alfred. 1933. A Non-Aristotelian System and Its Necessity for Rigour in Mathematics and Physics. In *Science and Sanity*, edited by Alfred Korzybski, 747–761. New York: Institute of General Semantics.

Krasner, Stephen D. 1999. *Sovereignty: Organized Hypocrisy*. Princeton, NJ: Princeton University Press.

Kratochwil, Friedrich. 1986. Of Systems, Boundaries, and Territoriality: An Inquiry into the Formation of the State System. *World Politics* 39 (1): 27–52.

Krieg, Andreas, and Jean-Marc Rickli. 2019. *Surrogate Warfare: The Transformation of War in the Twenty-First Century*. Washington, DC: Georgetown University Press.

Krishna, Sankaran. 2001. Race, Amnesia, and the Education of International Relations. *Alternatives* 26 (4): 401–424.

Kulyk, Volodymyr. 2016. National Identity in Ukraine: Impact of Euromaidan and the War. *Europe-Asia Studies* 68 (4): 588–608.

Kumar, Krishan. 2010. Nation-States as Empires, Empires as Nation-States: Two Principles, One Practice? *Theory and Society* 39 (2): 119–143.

Kunt, Metin. 1995. State and Sultan up to the Age of Suleyman: Frontier Principality to World Empire. In *Süleyman the Magnificent and His Age: The Ottoman Empire in the Early Modern World*, edited by Metin Kunt and Christine Woodhead, 3–29. London: Longman, 1995.

Kurzman, Charles. 2013. Death Tolls of the Iran-Iraq War. Available at https://kurzman.unc.edu/death-tolls-of-the-iran-iraq-war/. Accessed September 21, 2022.

Kuzio, Taras. 2006. National Identity and History Writing in Ukraine. *Nationalities Papers* 34 (4): 407–427.

Kuzio, Taras. 2015. Competing Nationalisms, Euromaidan, and the Russian-Ukrainian Conflict. *Studies in Ethnicity and Nationalism* 15 (1): 157–169.

Lacina, Bethany, and Nils Petter Gleditsch. 2005. Monitoring Trends in Global Combat: A New Dataset of Battle Deaths. *European Journal of Population/Revue Européenne de Démographie* 21 (2): 145–166.

Lake, David. 2011. *Hierarchy in International Relations*. Ithaca, NY: Cornell University Press.

Lake, David A., and Angela O'Mahony. 2004. The Incredible Shrinking State: Explaining Change in the Territorial Size of Countries. *Journal of Conflict Resolution* 48 (5): 699–722.

Larkins, Jeremy. 2010. *From Hierarchy to Anarchy: Territory and Politics before Westphalia*. New York: Palgrave Macmillan.

280 References

Larsson, Gustav. 2017. The Caliphate and the Aiding Sword: A Content Analysis of "Islamic State" Propaganda. Unpublished manuscript, Stockholm University.

Laruelle, Marlene. 2019. *Russian Nationalism: Imaginaries, Doctrines, and Political Battlefields.* London: Taylor & Francis.

Lawrence, James. 1997. *Raj: The Making and Unmaking of British India.* New York: St. Martin's.

Lawson, George. 2006. The Promise of Historical Sociology in International Relations. *International Studies Review* 8 (3): 397–423.

Lawson, George. 2019. *Anatomies of Revolution.* Kindle ed. Cambridge: Cambridge University Press.

Le Billon, Philippe. 2001. The Political Ecology of War: Natural Resources and Armed Conflicts. *Political Geography* 20 (5): 561–584.

Lefebvre, Henri, and Donald Nicholson-Smith. 1991. *The Production of Space.* Oxford: Blackwell.

Lenin, Vladimir Il'ich. [1916] 1999. *Imperialism: The Highest Stage of Capitalism.* Broadways, Australia: Resistance Books.

Lepsius, M. Rainer, and Jean A. Campbell. 1985. The Nation and Nationalism in Germany. *Social Research* 52: 43–64.

Levi, Margaret. 1997. *Consent, Dissent, and Patriotism.* New York: Cambridge University Press.

Levy, Jack S. 1983. *War in the Great Power System, 1495–1975.* Lexington: University Press of Kentucky.

Levy, Jack S. 1997. Prospect Theory, Rational Choice, and International Relations. *International Studies Quarterly* 41 (1): 87–112.

Levy, Jack S. 2008. Case Studies: Types, Designs, and Logics of Inference. *Conflict Management and Peace Science* 25 (1): 1–18.

Levy, Jack S., and William R. Thompson. 2011. *The Arc of War: Origins, Escalation, and Transformation.* Chicago: University of Chicago Press.

Lia, Brynjar. 2015. Understanding Jihadi Proto-States. *Perspectives on Terrorism* 9 (4): 31–41.

Lindley, Mark Frank. 1926. *The Acquisition and Government of Backward Territory in International Law: Being a Treatise on the Law and Practice Relating to Colonial Expansion.* London: Longmans, Green.

Lister, Charles. 2015. A Long Way from Success: Assessing the War on the Islamic State. *Perspectives on Terrorism* 9 (4): 3–13.

Little, Daniel. 1991. *Varieties of Social Explanation: An Introduction to the Philosophy of Social Science.* Boulder, CO: Westview.

Lockyer, Roger. 1974. *Habsburg and Bourbon Europe, 1470–1720.* London: Longman.

Long, Mark. 2009. *Ribat,* al-Qa'ida, and the Challenge for US Foreign Policy. *Middle East Journal* 63 (1): 31–47.

Longo, Matthew. 2017a. From Sovereignty to Imperium: Borders, Frontiers and the Specter of Neo-imperialism. *Geopolitics* 22 (4): 757–771.

Longo, Matthew. 2017b. *The Politics of Borders: Sovereignty, Security, and the Citizen after 9/11.* Cambridge: Cambridge University Press.

Lopez, Anthony C. 2016. The Evolution of War: Theory and Controversy. *International Theory* 8 (1): 97–139.

Lopez, Julia Costa. 2016. Beyond Eurocentrism and Orientalism: Revisiting the Othering of Jews and Muslims through Medieval Canon Law. *Review of International Studies* 42 (3): 450–470.

Luard, Evan. 1987. *War in International Society.* New Haven, CT: Yale University Press.

Lustick, Ian S. 1993. *Unsettled States, Disputed Lands: Britain and Ireland, France and Algeria, Israel and the West Bank–Gaza.* Ithaca, NY: Cornell University Press.

Luttwak, Edward N. 1976. *The Grand Strategy of the Roman Empire: From the First Century A.D. to the Third.* Baltimore: Johns Hopkins University Press.

References 281

Lynn, John A. 1999. *The Wars of Louis XIV: 1667–1714*. London: Longman.

Lynn, John A. 2003. *Battle: A History of Combat and Culture*. Boulder, CO: Westview.

Lyons, Martyn. 1994. *Napoleon Bonaparte and the Legacy of the French Revolution*. London: Macmillan.

Mabon, Simon. 2017. Nationalist Jāhiliyyah and the Flag of the Two Crusaders, or: ISIS, Sovereignty, and the "Owl of Minerva." *Studies in Conflict & Terrorism* 40 (11): 1–20.

Mackinder, Harold J. 1904. The Geographical Pivot of History. *Geographical Journal* 23 (4): 421–437.

Mackinder, Harold J. 1943. Round World and the Winning of the Peace. *Foreign Affairs* 21 (4): 595–605.

Mahan, Alfred. T. 1890. *The Influence of Sea Power upon History, 1660–1783*. Boston: Little, Brown.

Mahmud, Tayyab. 2010. Colonial Cartographies, Postcolonial Borders, and Enduring Failures of International Law: The Unending Wars along the Afghanistan-Pakistan Frontier. *Brooklyn Journal of International Law* 36: 1–74.

Maier, Charles S. 2016. *Once within Borders*. Cambridge, MA: Harvard University Press.

Makdisi, Ussama. 2002. Ottoman Orientalism. *American Historical Review* 107 (3): 768–796.

Malešević, Siniša. 2010. *The Sociology of War and Violence*. Cambridge: Cambridge University Press.

Malešević, Siniša. 2012. Did Wars Make Nation-States in the Balkans? Nationalisms, Wars and States in the 19th and Early 20th Century South East Europe. *Journal of Historical Sociology* 25 (3): 299–330.

Malešević, Siniša. 2013. *Nation-States and Nationalisms: Organization, Ideology and Solidarity*. Oxford: Polity.

Malešević, Siniša. 2017a. *The Rise of Organised Brutality*. Kindle ed. Cambridge: Cambridge University Press.

Malešević, Siniša. 2017b. The Foundations of Statehood: Empires and Nation-States in the Longue Durée. *Thesis Eleven* 139 (1): 145–161.

Mamadouh, Virginie. 1999. Reclaiming Geopolitics: Geographers Strike Back. *Geopolitics* 4 (1): 118–138.

Manela, Erez. 2006. Imagining Woodrow Wilson in Asia: Dreams of East-West Harmony and the Revolt against Empire in 1919. *American Historical Review* 111 (5): 1327–1351.

Manela, Erez. 2007. *The Wilsonian Moment: Self-Determination and the International Origins of Anticolonial Nationalism*. Oxford: Oxford University Press.

Mann, Michael. 1986. *The Sources of Social Power*. Cambridge: Cambridge University Press.

Mann, Michael. 1995. A Political Theory of Nationalism and Its Excesses. In *Notions of Nationalism*, edited by Sukumar Periwal, 44–64. Budapest: Central European University Press.

Mann, Michael. 2013. The Role of Nationalism in the Two World Wars. In *Nationalism and War*, edited by John A. Hall and Siniša Malešević, 172–196. Cambridge: Cambridge University Press.

Mann, Michael. 2018. Have Wars and Violence Declined? *Theory and Society* 47 (1): 37–60.

March, James G., and Johan P. Olsen. 2006. The Logic of Appropriateness. In *The Oxford Handbook of Public Policy*, edited by Robert E. Goodin, Michael Moran, and Martin Rein, 698–708. Oxford: Oxford University Press.

Marriott, John A. R., and Charles G. Robertson.1915. *The Evolution of Prussia: The Making of an Empire*. Oxford: Clarendon Press.

Marson, James. 2009. Putin to the West: Hands off Ukraine. *Time*, May 25. http://content.time.com/time/world/article/0,8599,1900838,00.html.

Marston, Frank S. 1978. *The Peace Conference of 1919: Organization and Procedure*. New York: AMS Press.

282 References

Marx, Anthony. 2003. *Faith in Nation: Exclusionary Origins of Nationalism*. New York: Oxford University Press.

May, Arthur J. 1933. *The Age of Metternich, 1814–1848*. New York: H. Holt.

Mayall, James. 1990. *Nationalism and International Society*. Cambridge: Cambridge University Press.

Mayer, Arno J. 2000. *The Furies: Violence and Terror in the French and Russian Revolutions*. Princeton, NJ: Princeton University Press.

Mbembe, Achille. 2001. *On the Postcolony*. Berkeley: University of California Press.

Mbembé, J.-A., and Steven Rendall. 2000. At the Edge of the World: Boundaries, Territoriality, and Sovereignty in Africa. *Public Culture* 12 (1): 259–284.

McCants, William. 2015. *The ISIS Apocalypse: The History, Strategy, and Doomsday Vision of the Islamic State*. New York: Picador.

McKay, Derek, and Hamish M. Scott. 1983. *The Rise of the Great Powers, 1648–1815*. London: Pearson.

Meadwell, Hudson. 1999. Republics, Nations and Transitions to Modernity. *Nations and Nationalism* 5 (1): 19–51.

Meadwell, Hudson. 2001. The Long Nineteenth Century in Europe. *Review of International Studies* 27 (5): 165–189.

Mearsheimer, John J. 2001. *The Tragedy of Great Power Politics*. New York: Norton.

Mearsheimer, John J. 2018. *Great Delusion: Liberal Dreams and International Realities*. New Haven, CT: Yale University Press.

Mee, Charles L. 1980. *The End of Order: Versailles, 1919*. New York: EP Dutton.

Megoran, Nick. 2010. Neoclassical Geopolitics. *Political Geography* 4 (29): 187–189.

Meyer, John W., John Boli, George M. Thomas, and Francisco O. Ramirez. 1997. World Society and the Nation-State. *American Journal of Sociology* 103 (1): 144–181.

Michael, Bernardo. 2017. States and Territories: The Anglo-Gorkha War as a Diagnostic Event. *European Bulletin of Himalayan Research* 50–51: 34–57.

Mikhail, Alan, and Christine M. Philliou. 2012. The Ottoman Empire and the Imperial Turn. *Comparative Studies in Society and History* 54 (4): 721–745.

Miller, Benjamin. 2007. *States, Nations, and the Great Powers: The Sources of Regional War and Peace*. Cambridge: Cambridge University Press.

Miller, Charles, and K. Shuvo Bakar. 2022. Conflict Events Worldwide since 1468BC: Introducing the Historical Conflict Event Dataset. *Journal of Conflict Resolution* 67 (2–3): 522–554.

Miller, David. 2012. Territorial Rights: Concept and Justification. *Political Studies* 60 (2): 252–268.

Milner, Thomas. 1876. *The Turkish Empire: The Sultans, the Territory, and the People*. New ed. London: Religious Tract Society.

Min, Eric. 2021. Interstate War Battle Dataset (1823–2003). *Journal of Peace Research* 58 (2): 294–303.

Minca, Claudio, Jeremy W. Crampton, Joe Bryan, Juliet J. Fall, Alex B. Murphy, and Anssi Paasi. 2015. Reading Stuart Elden's *The Birth of Territory*. *Political Geography* 46 (9): 93–101.

Minkov, Anton. 2004. *Conversion to Islam in the Balkans: Kisve Bahas Petitions and Ottoman Social Life, 1670–1730*. Boston: Brill.

Mishra, Sandip Kumar. 2016. The Colonial Origins of Territorial Disputes in South Asia. *Journal of Territorial and Maritime Studies* 3 (1): 5–23.

Misra, Sanghamitra. 2005. Changing Frontiers and Spaces: The Colonial State in Nineteenth-Century Goalpara. *Studies in History* 21 (2): 213–246.

Moore, Adam. 2013. *Peacebuilding in Practice*. Ithaca, NY: Cornell University Press.

Moore, Adam. 2019. *Empire's Labor: The Global Army That Supports US Wars*. Ithaca, NY: Cornell University Press.

Moore, Gregory. 2009. *Fichte: Addresses to the German Nation*. Cambridge: Cambridge University Press.

Morgenthau, Hans J. 1949. *Politics among Nations: The Struggle for Power and Peace*. New York: Alfred A. Knopf.

Motyl, Alexander J. 2010. Can Ukraine Have a History? *Problems of Post-Communism* 57 (3): 55–61.

Motyl, Alexander J. 2013. Deconstructing Putin on Ukraine. *Kyiv Post*. http://www.kyivpost.com/article/opinion/op-ed/motyl-deconstructing-putin-on-ukraine-329347.html. Accessed November 9, 2022.

Mountz, Alison. 2013. Political Geography I: Reconfiguring Geographies of Sovereignty. *Progress in Human Geography* 37 (6): 829–841.

Mowat, Robert B. 1924. *The Diplomacy of Napoleon*. London: Longmans, Green.

Mueller, John. 1989. *Retreat from Doomsday: The Obsolescence of Major War*. New York: Basic.

Mukerji, Chandra. 1997. *Territorial Ambitions and the Gardens of Versailles*. Cambridge: Cambridge University Press.

Mukerji, Chandra. 2011. Jurisdiction, Inscription, and State Formation: Administrative Modernism and Knowledge Regimes. *Theory and Society* 40 (3): 223–245.

Münkler, Herfried. 2007. *Empires: The Logic of World Domination from Ancient Rome to the United States*. Oxford: Polity.

Murphy, Alexander B. 1990. Historical Justifications for Territorial Claims. *Annals of the Association of American Geographers* 80 (4): 531–548.

Murphy, Alexander B. 2002. National Claims to Territory in the Modern State System: Geographical Considerations. *Geopolitics* 7.2 (2002): 193–214.

Murphy, Alexander B. 2005. Territorial Ideology and Interstate Conflict: Comparative Considerations. In *The Geography of War and Peace: From Death Camps to Diplomats*, edited by Colin Flint, 280–296. Oxford: Oxford University Press.

Murphy, Alexander B. 2010. Identity and Territory. *Geopolitics* 15 (4): 769–772.

Murphy, Alexander B. 2013. Territory's Continuing Allure. *Annals of the Association of American Geographers* 103 (5): 1212–1226.

Murray, Williamson. 2009. Versailles: The Peace without a Chance. In *The Making of Peace: Rulers, States, and the Aftermath of War*, edited by Murray Williamson and Jim Lacey, 209–239. Cambridge: Cambridge University Press.

Murray, Williamson, and Peter R. Mansoor. 2012. *Hybrid Warfare: Fighting Complex Opponents from the Ancient World to the Present*. Cambridge: Cambridge University Press.

Mylonas, Harris. 2012. *The Politics of Nation-Building: Making Co-nationals, Refugees, and Minorities*. New York: Cambridge University Press.

Mylonas, Harris, and Nadav G. Shelef. 2014. Which Land Is Our Land? Domestic Politics and Change in the Territorial Claims of Stateless Nationalist Movements. *Security Studies* 23 (4): 754–786.

Naumkin, Vitaly. 2014. ISIS' Blitzkrieg across Iraq. *Al-Monitor*, June 23. https://www.al-monitor.com/pulse/originals/2014/06/iraq-isis-mosul-russia-obama-kurds-turkmen-violence.html.

Neal, Larry. 1977. Interpreting Power and Profit in Economic History: A Case Study of the Seven Years War. *Journal of Economic History* 37 (1): 20–35.

Neep, Daniel. 2017. State-Space beyond Territory: Wormholes, Gravitational Fields, and Entanglement. *Journal of Historical Sociology* 30 (3): 466–495.

Neumann, Iver B., and Jennifer M. Welsh. 1991. The Other in European Self-Definition: An Addendum to the Literature on International Society. *Review of International Studies* 17 (4): 327–348.

Newbury, Colin. 2000. Patrons, Clients, and Empire: The Subordination of Indigenous Hierarchies in Asia and Africa. *Journal of World History* 11 (2): 227–263.

284 References

Newman, David. 2006a. The Resilience of Territorial Conflict in an Era of Globalization. In *Territoriality and Conflict in an Era of Globalization*, edited by Miles Kahler and Barbara F. Walter, 85–110. New York: Cambridge University Press.

Newman, David. 2006b. The Lines That Continue to Separate Us: Borders in Our "Borderless" World. *Progress in Human Geography* 30 (2): 143–161.

Newman, David. 2010. Territory, Compartments and Borders: Avoiding the Trap of the Territorial Trap. *Geopolitics* 15 (4): 773–778.

Newman, David. 2015. Revisiting Good Fences and Neighbors in a Postmodern World after Twenty Years: Theoretical Reflections on the State of Contemporary Border Studies. *Nordia Geographical Publications* 44 (4): 13–19.

Newman, David, and Anssi Paasi. 1998. Fences and Neighbors in the Postmodern World: Boundary Narratives in Political Geography. *Progress in Human Geography* 22 (2): 186–207.

Newman, Saul. 2004. Terror, Sovereignty and Law: On the Politics of Violence. *German Law Journal* 5 (5): 569–584.

Nexon, Daniel H. 2009. *The Struggle for Power in Early Modern Europe: Religious Conflict, Dynastic Empires, and International Change*. Princeton, NJ: Princeton University Press.

Nexon, Daniel H., and Thomas Wright. 2007. What's at Stake in the American Empire Debate. *American Political Science Review* 101 (2): 253–271.

Nicolson, Harold. 1933. *Peacemaking 1919*. Boston: Houghton Mifflin.

Nine, Cara. 2008. A Lockean Theory of Territory. *Political Studies* 56 (1): 148–165.

Nişancıoğlu, Kerem. 2014. The Ottoman Origins of Capitalism: Uneven and Combined Development and Eurocentrism. *Review of International Studies* 40 (2): 325–347.

Nişancıoğlu, Kerem. 2020. Racial Sovereignty. *European Journal of International Relations* 26 (1): 39–63.

Nolan, Michael E. 2005. *The Inverted Mirror: Mythologizing the Enemy in France and Germany, 1898–1914*. Vol. 2. New York: Berghahn Books.

Novak, Paolo. 2011. The Flexible Territoriality of Borders. *Geopolitics* 16 (4): 741–767.

Noyes John K. 1992. *Colonial Space. Spatiality in the discourse of German South West Africa, 1884–1914*. Chur, Reading: Harwood.

O'Dowd, Liam. 2010. From a "Borderless World" to a "World of Borders": "Bringing History Back In." *Environment and Planning D: Society and Space* 28 (6): 1031–1050.

O'Lear, Shannon, Paul F. Diehl, Derrick V. Frazier, and Todd L. Allee. 2005. Dimensions of Territorial Conflict and Resolution: Tangible and Intangible Values of Territory. *GeoJournal* 64 (4): 259–261.

Ohmae, Kenichi. 1999. *Borderless World: Power and Strategy in the Interlinked Economy*. Rev. ed. New York: HarperCollins.

Onnekink, David. 2009. *The Last War of Religion? The Dutch and the Nine Years War*. London: Routledge.

Onorato, Massimiliano Gaetano, Kenneth Scheve, and David Stasavage. 2014. Technology and the Era of the Mass Army. *Journal of Economic History* 74 (2): 449–481.

Onuf, Peter S. 2004. Nations, Revolutions, and the End of History. In *Revolutionary Currents: Nation Building in the Transatlantic World*, edited by Michael A. Morrison and Melinda S. Zook, 173–188. Lanham, MD: Rowman & Littlefield.

Opello, Walter C., and Stephen J. Rosow. 1999. *The Nation-State and Global Order: A Historical Introduction to Contemporary Politics*. Boulder, CO: Lynne Rienner.

Osiander, Andreas. 1994. *The States System of Europe, 1640–1990: Peacemaking and the Conditions of International Stability*. Oxford: Clarendon Press.

Osiander, Andreas. 2001. Sovereignty, International Relations, and the Westphalian Myth. *International Organization* 55 (2): 251–287.

Osiander, Andreas. 2007. *Before the State: Systemic Political Change in the West from the Greeks to the French Revolution*. Oxford: Oxford University Press.

References   285

Outram, Dorinda. 1995. *The Enlightenment*. New York: Cambridge University Press.

Overy, Richard J. 1998. *Russia's War*. New York: Penguin.

Owen, John M., IV 2010. *The Clash of Ideas in World Politics: Transnational Networks, States, and Regime Change, 1510–2010*. Princeton, NJ: Princeton University Press.

Özkan, Behlül. 2012. *From the Abode of Islam to the Turkish Vatan: The Making of a National Homeland in Turkey*. New Haven, CT: Yale University Press.

Özkan, Behlül. 2014. Turkey, Davutoglu and the Idea of Pan-Islamism. *Survival* 56 (4): 119–140.

Paasi, Anssi. 1996. *Territories, Boundaries, and Consciousness: The Changing Geographies of the Finnish-Russian Boundary*. Chichester: Wiley.

Paasi, Anssi. 1998. Boundaries as Social Processes: Territoriality in the World of Flows. *Geopolitics* 3 (1): 69–88.

Paasi, Anssi. 1999. Nationalizing Everyday Life: Individual and Collective Identities as Practice and Discourse. *Geography Research Forum* 19 (1): 4–21.

Paasi, Anssi. 2003. Territory. In *A Companion to Political Geography*, edited by John Agnew, Katharyne Mitchell, and Gerard Toal, 109–122. Oxford: Blackwell.

Paasi, Anssi. 2005. The Changing Discourses on Political Boundaries: Mapping the Backgrounds, Contexts and Contents. In *Bordering the World*, edited by Henk van Houtum, Olivier Kramsch, and Wolfgang Zierhofer, 17–31. London: Ashgate.

Paasi, Anssi. 2009. Bounded Spaces in a "Borderless World": Border Studies, Power and the Anatomy of Territory. *Journal of Power* 2 (2): 213–234.

Paavola, Sami. 2004. Abduction as a Logic and Methodology of Discovery: The Importance of Strategies. *Foundations of Science* 9 (3): 267–283.

Paine, Sarah C. M. 2017. *The Japanese Empire: Grand Strategy from the Meiji Restoration to the Pacific War*. Cambridge: Cambridge University Press.

Palmer, Robert R. 1986. Frederick the Great, Guibert, Bulow: From Dynastic to National War. In *The Makers of Modern Strategy: From Machiavelli to the Nuclear Age*, edited by Peter Paret, 95–99. Princeton, NJ: Princeton University Press.

Panaite, Viorel. 2000. *The Ottoman Law of War and Peace: The Ottoman Empire and Tribute Payers*. New York: Columbia University Press.

Parikh, Sunita. 2000. Commentary: The Strategic Value of "Analytic Narratives." *Social Science History* 24 (4): 677–684.

Parker, Geoffrey. [1982] 2006. *The Thirty Years' War*. London: Routledge.

Parker, Geoffrey. 1998. *Geopolitics: Past, Present and Future*. London: Pinter.

Parker, Noel. 2010. Empire as a Geopolitical Figure. *Geopolitics* 15 (1): 109–132.

Parvin, Manoucher, and Maurie Sommer. 1980. *Dar al-Islam*: The Evolution of Muslim Territoriality and Its Implications for Conflict Resolution in the Middle East. *International Journal of Middle East Studies* 11 (1): 1–21.

Pedriana, Nicholas. 2005. Rational Choice, Structural Context, and Increasing Returns: A Strategy for Analytic Narrative in Historical Sociology. *Sociological Methods & Research* 33 (3): 349–382.

Penrose, Jan. 2002. Nations, States and Homelands: Territory and Territoriality in Nationalist Thought. *Nations and Nationalism* 8 (3): 277–229.

Pérouse de Montclos, Marc-Antoine. 2016. A Sectarian Jihad in Nigeria: The Case of Boko Haram. *Small Wars & Insurgencies* 27 (5): 878–895.

Pflanze, Otto. 1990. *Bismarck and the Development of Germany*. Princeton, NJ: Princeton University Press.

Philpott, Daniel. 1995. In Defense of Self-Determination. *Ethics* 105 (2): 352–385.

Philpott, Daniel. 2001. *Revolutions in Sovereignty: How Ideas Shaped Modern International Relations*. Princeton, NJ: Princeton University Press.

Polasky, Janet L. 2015. *Revolutions without Borders: The Call to Liberty in the Atlantic World*. New Haven, CT: Yale University Press.

286 References

Polisensky, Josef V., and Frederick Snider. 1978. *War and Society in Europe, 1618–1648.* Cambridge: Cambridge University Press.

Pomeranz, Kenneth. 2000. *The Great Divergence: China, Europe and the Making of the Modern World Economy.* Princeton, NJ: Princeton University Press.

Porter, Patrick. 2015. *The Global Village Myth: Distance, War, and the Limits of Power.* Washington, DC: Georgetown University Press.

Porter, Patrick. 2020. *The False Promise of Liberal Order: Nostalgia, Delusion and the Rise of Trump.* Hoboken, NJ: John Wiley & Sons.

Posen, Barry. 1993. Nationalism, the Mass Army, and Military Power. *International Security* 18 (2): 80–124.

Powell, Robert. 1991. Absolute and Relative Gains in International Relations Theory. *American Political Science Review* 85 (4): 1303–1320.

Power, Marcus, and David Campbell. 2010. The State of Critical Geopolitics. *Political Geography* 29 (5): 243–246.

Pratt, Sisson C. 1914. *Saarbrück to Paris, 1870: A Strategical Sketch.* London: G. Allen & Unwin.

Psathas, George. 2005. The Ideal Type in Weber and Schutz. In *Explorations of the Life-World,* edited by George Psathas, Martin Endress, and Hisashi Nasu, 143–169. Dordrecht: Springer.

Ratzel, Friedrich. 1899. *Anthropogeographie.* 2nd ed. Stuttgart: J. Engelhorn.

Reiter, Dan. 2003. Exploring the Bargaining Model of War. *Perspectives on Politics* 11 (1): 27–43.

Renan, Ernest. 2018. *What Is a Nation? and Other Political Writings.* New York: Columbia University Press.

Reus-Smit, Christian. 2013. *Individual Rights and the Making of the International System.* Cambridge: Cambridge University Press.

Rieber, Alfred J. 2014. *The Struggle for the Eurasian Borderlands.* New York: Cambridge University Press.

Rieber, Alfred J. 2015. Struggle over the Borderlands. *Kritika: Explorations in Russian and Eurasian History* 16 (4): 951–959.

Ringmar, Erik. 2012. Performing International Systems: Two East-Asian Alternatives to the Westphalian Order. *International Organization* 66 (1): 1–25.

Robinson, Linda. 2008. *Tell Me How This Ends: General David Petraeus and the Search for a Way out of Iraq.* New York: Public Affairs.

Ronart, Stephan. 1937. *Bugünkü Türkiye.* Ankara: Müdafaa-i Hukuk Yayinlari.

Roosen, Williams J. 1976. *The Age of Louis XIV: The Rise of Modern Diplomacy.* Cambridge, MA: Schenkman.

Ropes, Arthur R. 1889. The Causes of the Seven Years' War. *Transactions of the Royal Historical Society* 4: 143–170.

Rosecrance, Richard. 1986. *The Rise of the Trading State: Commerce and Conquest in the Modern World.* New York: Basic Books.

Rosecrance, Richard. 1999. *The Rise of the Virtual State: Wealth and Power in the Coming State.* New York: Basic Books.

Rosenberg, Arthur. 1970. *Imperial Germany: The Birth of the German Republic, 1871–1918.* New York: Oxford University Press.

Ross, Graham. 1983. *The Great Powers and the Decline of the European States System, 1914–1945.* London: Longman.

Roy, Kaushik. 2015. *War and Society in Afghanistan: From the Mughals to the Americans, 1500–2013.* New York: Oxford University Press.

Ruggie, John G. 1983. Continuity and Transformation in the World Polity: Toward a Neorealist Synthesis. *World Politics* 5 (2): 261–285.

Ruggie, John G. 1993. Territoriality and Beyond: Problematizing Modernity in International Relations. *International Organization* 47 (1): 139–174.

References 287

Sack, Robert D. 1986. *Human Territoriality: Its Theory and History*. Cambridge: Cambridge University Press.

Sahlins, Peter. 1989. *Boundaries: The Making of France and Spain in the Pyrenees*. Berkeley: University of California Press.

Sahlins, Peter. 1990. Natural Frontiers Revisited: France's Boundaries since the Seventeenth Century. *American Historical Review* 95 (5): 1423–1451.

Said, Edward, 1994. *Culture and Imperialism*. New York: Vintage.

Samokhvalov, Vsevolod. 2015. Ukraine between Russia and the European Union: Triangle Revisited. *Europe-Asia Studies* 67 (9): 1371–1393.

Sartori, Andrew. 2006. The British Empire and Its Liberal Mission. *Journal of Modern History* 78 (3): 623–642.

Sasse, Gwendolyn, and Alice Lackner. 2018. War and Identity: The Case of the Donbas in Ukraine. *Post-Soviet Affairs* 34 (2–3): 139–157.

Sassen, Saskia. 1996. *Losing Control? Sovereignty in an Age of Globalization*. New York: Columbia University Press.

Sassen, Saskia. 1998. *Globalization and Its Discontents*. New York: New Press.

Sassen, Saskia. 2008. *Territory, Authority, Rights: From Medieval to Global Assemblages*. Princeton, NJ: Princeton University Press.

Schama, Simon. 1990. *Citizens: A Chronicle of the French Revolution*. New York: Vintage.

Schelling, Thomas C. 1966. *Arms and Influence*. New Haven, CT: Yale University Press.

Schelling, Thomas C. 1978. *Micromotives and Macrobehavior*. New York: Norton.

Schieder, Theodor, H. R. Scott, and Sabina Krause. [2000] 2016. *Frederick the Great*. Harlow, UK: Addison-Wesley Longman.

Schmidt, Sebastian. 2011. To Order the Minds of Scholars: The Discourse of the Peace of Westphalia in International Relations Literature. *International Studies Quarterly* 55 (3): 601–623.

Schonfeld, Zach. 2022. Zelensky: "We Will Definitely Liberate Crimea." *The Hill*, October 25. https://thehill.com/policy/international/3704092-zelensky-we-will-definitely-liberate-crimea/.

Schreck, Adam. 2022. Putin Finalizes Annexation of Ukrainian Regions as Russian Forces Struggle to Maintain Control. *PBS News Hour*, October 5. https://www.pbs.org/newshour/world/putin-finalizes-annexation-of-ukrainian-regions-as-russian-forces-struggle-to-maintain-control.

Schroeder, Paul W. 1994. *The Transformation of European Politics, 1763–1848*. New York: Oxford University Press.

Schultz, Kenneth A. 2017. Mapping Interstate Territorial Conflict: A New Data Set and Applications. *Journal of Conflict Resolution* 61 (7): 1565–1590.

Schulze, Hagen. 1991. *The Course of German Nationalism: From Frederick the Great to Bismarck, 1763–1867*. Cambridge: Cambridge University Press.

Scott, Hamish. 2011. The Seven Years War and Europe's Ancien Régime. *War in History* 18 (4): 419–455.

Scott, James C. 1998. *Seeing Like a State: How Certain Schemes to Improve the Human Condition Have Failed*. New Haven, CT: Yale University Press.

Semple, Ellen Churchill. [1911] 1968. *Influences of Geographic Environment, on the Basis of Ratzel's System of Anthropo-geography*. New York: Russell and Russell.

Sewell, William H., Jr. 1985. Ideologies and Social Revolutions: Reflections on the French Case. *Journal of Modern History* 57 (1): 57–85.

Sewell, William H., Jr. 1990. Collective Violence and Collective Loyalties in France: Why the French Revolution Made a Difference. *Politics & Society* 18 (4): 527–552.

Sewell, William H., Jr. 1996. Historical Events as Transformations of Structures: Inventing Revolution at the Bastille. *Theory and Society* 25 (6): 841–881.

288 References

Seymour, Charles. 1965. *Letters from the Paris Peace Conference*. New Haven. CT: Yale University Press.

Sharman, Jason C. 2013. International Hierarchies and Contemporary Imperial Governance: A Tale of Three Kingdoms. *European Journal of International Relations* 19 (2): 189–207.

Shatz, Howard J., and Erin-Elizabeth Johnson. 2015. *The Islamic State We Knew: Insights before the Resurgence and Their Implications*. Santa Monica, CA: Rand Corporation.

Shaw, Malcolm N. 1996. The Heritage of States: The Principle of Uti Possidetis Juris Today. *British Year Book of International Law* 67: 109.

Shaw, Stanford J., and Ezel K. Shaw. 1976. *History of the Ottoman Empire and Modern Turkey*. vol. 1, *Empire of the Gazis: The Rise and Decline of the Ottoman Empire, 1280–1808*. Cambridge: Cambridge University Press.

Sheehan, James J. 2006. The Problem of Sovereignty in European History. *American Historical Review* 111 (1): 1–15.

Shelef, Nadav. G. 2016. Unequal Ground: Homelands and Conflict. *International Organization*, 70 (1): 33–63.

Sheridan, Eugene R. 1994. The Recall of Edmond Charles Genet: A Study in Transatlantic Politics and Diplomacy. *Diplomatic History* 18 (4): 463–488.

Shields, Rob. 2013. *Places on the Margin: Alternative Geographies of Modernity*. London: Routledge.

Showalter, Dennis E. 1996. *The Wars of Frederick the Great*. London: Longman.

Sil, Rudra, and Peter J. Katzenstein. 2010. Analytic Eclecticism in the Study of World Politics: Reconfiguring Problems and Mechanisms across Research Traditions. *Perspectives on Politics* 8 (2): 411–431.

Simmons, A. John. 2001. On the Territorial Rights of States. *Philosophical Issues* 11 (1): 300–326.

Simmons, Beth A. 2005a. Rules over Real Estate: Trade, Territorial Conflict, and International Borders as Institution. *Journal of Conflict Resolution* 49 (6): 823–848.

Simmons, Beth A. 2005b. Forward Looking Dispute Resolution: Ecuador, Peru and the Border Issue. In *Peace v. Justice*, edited by I. W. Zartman and G. O. Faure, 283–308. New York: Rowan Littlefield.

Simmons, Beth A., and Hein E. Goemans. 2021. Built on Borders: Tensions with the Institution Liberalism (Thought It) Left Behind. *International Organization* 75 (2): 387–410.

Simpson, Gerry. 2004. *Great Powers and Outlaw States: Unequal Sovereigns in the International Legal Order*. New York: Cambridge University Press.

Singer, Joel David, and Melvin Small. 1972. *The Wages of War, 1816–1965: A Statistical Handbook*. Hoboken, NJ: John Wiley & Sons.

Sinnreich, Richard Hart. 2009. In Search of Military Repose: The Congress of Vienna and the Making of Peace. In *The Making of Peace: Rulers, States, and the Aftermath of War*, edited by Murray Williamson and Jim Lacey, 131–159. Cambridge: Cambridge University Press.

Skocpol, Theda. 1979. *States and Social Revolutions: A Comparative Analysis of France, Russia, and China*. New York: Cambridge University Press.

Skocpol, Theda. 1985. Cultural Idioms and Political Ideologies in the Revolutionary Reconstruction of State Power: A Rejoinder to Sewell. *Journal of Modern History* 57 (1): 86–96.

Skocpol, Theda. 2000. Commentary: Theory Tackles History. *Social Science History* 24 (4): 669–676.

Skurski, Julie. 1996. The Ambiguities of Authenticity and National Ideology in Latin America. In *Becoming National: A Reader*, edited by Geoff Eley and Ronald G. Suny, 371–402. New York: Oxford University Press.

Smith, Anthony D. 1981. States and Homelands: The Social and Geopolitical Implications of National Territory. *Millennium* 10 (3): 187–202.

References 289

Smith, Helmut Walser. 2020. *Germany: A Nation in Its Time: Before, during, and after Nationalism, 1500–2000*. New York: Liveright Publishing.

Smith, Leonard. 2016. Drawing Borders in the Middle East after the Great War: Political Geography and "Subject Peoples." *First World War Studies* 7 (1): 5–21.

Smith, Monica L. 2005. Networks, Territories, and the Cartography of Ancient States. *Annals of the Association of American Geographers* 95 (4): 832–849.

Snidal, Duncan. 1991. International Cooperation among Relative Gains Maximizers. *International Studies Quarterly* 35 (4): 387–402.

Snyder, Jack. 1991. *Myths of Empire: Domestic Politics and International Ambition*. Ithaca, NY: Cornell University Press.

Soja, Edward W. 1971. *The Political Organization of Space*. Washington, DC: Association of American Geographers, Commission on College Geography.

Solomon, Ty, and Brent J. Steele. 2017. Micro-moves in International Relations Theory. *European Journal of International Relations* 23 (2): 267–291.

Spruyt, Hendrik. 1994. *The Sovereign State and Its Competitors*. Princeton, NJ: Princeton University Press.

Spruyt, Hendrik. 2000. The End of Empire and the Extension of the Westphalian System: The Normative Basis of the Modern State Order. *International Studies Review* 2 (2): 65–92.

Spruyt, Hendrik. 2002. The Origins, Development, and Possible Decline of the Modern State. *Annual Review of Political Science* 5 (1): 127–149.

Starr, Harvey. 2005. Territory, Proximity, and Spatiality: The Geography of International Conflict. *International Studies Review* 7 (3): 387–406.

Starr, Harvey. 2013. On Geopolitics: Spaces and Places. *International Studies Quarterly* 57 (3): 433–439.

Steinmetz, George. 2005. Return to Empire: The New US Imperialism in Comparative Historical Perspective. *Sociological Theory* 23 (4): 339–367.

Stern, Jessica. 2016. ISIL and the Goal of Organizational Survival. In *Beyond Governance: World without Order*, edited by Hilary Matfess and Michael Miklaucic, 193–211.Washington, DC: National Defense University.

Stern, Jessica, and J. M. Berger. 2015. *ISIS: The State of Terror*. London: William Collins.

Stevenson, David. 2004. *Cataclysm: The First World War as Political Tragedy*. New York: Basic.

Stevenson, David. 2005. 1918 Revisited. *Journal of Strategic Studies* 28 (1): 107–139.

Stevis-Gridneff, Matina. 2022. Crude Comments from Europe's Top Diplomat Point to Bigger Problems. *New York Times*, October 17. https://www.nytimes.com/2022/10/17/world/eur ope/eu-ukraine-josep-borrell-fontelles.html.

Stilz, Anna. 2009. Why Do States Have Territorial Rights? *International Theory* 1 (2): 185–213.

Stirk, Peter M. R. 2016. *History of Military Occupation from 1792 to 1914*. Edinburgh: Edinburgh University Press.

Stone, Bailey. 2002. *Reinterpreting the French Revolution: A Global-Historical Perspective*. Cambridge: Cambridge University Press.

Stone, Lawrence. 1981. *The Past and the Present*. London: Routledge.

Storey, David. 2012. *Territories: The Claiming of Space*. London: Routledge.

Strachan, Hew. 2001. *The First World War*. Oxford: Oxford University Press.

Strandsbjerg, Jeppe. 2008. The Cartographic Production of Territorial Space: Mapping and State Formation in Early Modern Denmark. *Geopolitics* 13 (2): 335–358.

Strandsbjerg, Jeppe. 2010. *Territory, Globalization and International Relations: The Cartographic Reality of Space*. Basingstoke: Palgrave Macmillan.

Strange, Susan. 1998. *States and Markets*. London: Continuum.

Sugar, Peter F. 1977. *Southeastern Europe under Ottoman Rule, 1354–1804*. Seattle: University of Washington Press.

290 References

Sun Tzu. 2005. *The Illustrated Art of War*. Translated by Samuel B. Griffith. New York: Oxford University Press.

Suny, Ronald. 1993. *The Revenge of the Past: Nationalism, Revolution, and the Collapse of the Soviet Union*. Stanford, CA: Stanford University Press.

Suny, Ronald. 2017. *"They Can Live in the Desert but Nowhere Else": A History of the Armenian Genocide*. Princeton, NJ: Princeton University Press, 2017.

Surzhko Harned, Lena. 2022. Russian World and Ukrainian Autocephaly: Religious Narratives in Anti-colonial Nationalism of Ukraine. *Religions* 13 (4) 349. https://doi.org/10.3390/rel1 3040349.

Swedberg, Richard. 1998. *Max Weber and the Idea of Economic Sociology*. Princeton, NJ: Princeton University Press.

Tallett, Frank. 1992. *War and Society in Early Modern Europe: 1495–1715*. London: Routledge.

Talmadge, Caitlin. 2013. The Puzzle of Personalist Performance: Iraqi Battlefield Effectiveness in the Iran-Iraq War. *Security Studies* 22 (2): 180–221.

Taylor, Alan J. P. 1957. *The Struggle for Mastery in Europe, 1848–1918*. Oxford: Clarendon Press.

Taylor, Peter J. 1994. The State as Container: Territoriality in the Modern World-System. *Progress in Human Geography* 18 (2): 151–162.

Taylor, Peter J. 2002. Geopolitics, Political Geography and Social Science. In *Geopolitical Traditions*, edited by Klaus Dodds and Davod Atkinson, 391–395. London: Routledge.

Teschke, Benno. 1998. Geopolitical Relations in the European Middle Ages: History and Theory. *International Organization* 52 (2): 325–358.

Teschke, Benno. 2003. *The Myth of 1648: Class, Geopolitics, and the Making of Modern International Relations*. London: Verso.

Thomas, Gary. 2011. A Typology for the Case Study in Social Science Following a Review of Definition, Discourse, and Structure. *Qualitative inquiry* 17 (6) 511–521.

Thompson, Debra. 2013. Through, against and beyond the Racial State: The Transnational Stratum of Race. *Cambridge Review of International Affairs* 26 (1): 133–151.

Thomson, Mark A. 1954. Louis XIV and the Origins of the War of the Spanish Succession. *Transactions of the Royal Historical Society* 4: 111–134.

Tilly, Charles. 1975. Reflections on the History of European State-Making. In *Formation of National States in Western Europe*, edited by Charles Tilly, 601–686. Princeton, NJ: Princeton University Press.

Tilly, Charles. 1984. *Big Structures, Large Processes, Huge Comparisons*. New York: Russell Sage Foundation.

Tilly, Charles. 1990. *Coercion, Capital, and European States, AD 990–1990*. Cambridge, MA: Blackwell.

Tilly, Charles. 1993. Social Movements as Historically Specific Clusters of Political Performances. *Berkeley Journal of Sociology* 38: 1–30.

Tilly, Charles. 1994. States and Nationalism in Europe 1492–1992. *Theory and Society* 23 (1): 131–146.

Tilly, Charles. 1995. The Sovereign State and Its Competitors: An Analysis of Systems Change by Hendrik Spruyt. *American Political Science Review* 89 (3): 811–812.

Tilly, Charles, and Gabriel Ardant. 1975. *The Formation of National States in Western Europe*. Princeton, NJ: Princeton University Press.

Tingley, Dustin H., and Barbara Walter. 2011. Reputation Building in International Relations. *International Organization* 65 (2): 343–365.

Tir, Jaroslav. 2010. Territorial Diversion: Diversionary Theory of War and Territorial Conflict. *Journal of Politics* 72 (2): 413–425.

Toal, Gerard. 1996. *Critical Geopolitics: The Politics of Writing Global Space*. Minneapolis: University of Minnesota Press.

Toal, Gerard. 2017. *Near Abroad: Putin, the West, and the Contest over Ukraine and the Caucasus*. Oxford: Oxford University Press.

Toal, Gerard, and John Agnew. 1992. Geopolitics and Discourse: Practical Geopolitical Reasoning in American Foreign Policy. *Political Geography* 11 (2): 190–204.

Toft, Monica D. 2003. *The Geography of Ethnic Violence: Identity, Interests, and the Indivisibility of Territory*. Princeton, NJ: Princeton University Press.

Toft, Monica D. 2007. Getting Religion? The Puzzling Case of Islam and Civil War. *International Security* 31 (4): 97–131.

Toft, Monica D. 2014. Territory and War. *Journal of Peace Research* 51 (2): 185–198.

Tooze, Adam. 2015. *The Deluge: The Great War, America and the Remaking of the Global Order, 1916–1931*. New York: Penguin.

Trachtenberg, Marc. *A Constructed Peace: The Making of the European Settlement, 1945–1963*. Princeton, NJ: Princeton University Press, 1999.

Treitschke, Heinrich von. 1915. *The Confessions of Frederick the Great, and the Life of Frederick the Great*. New York: Putnam.

Tuchman, Barbara W. 1962. *The Guns of August*. New York: Macmillan.

Turner, Leonard C. F. 1970. *Origins of the First World War*. New York: Norton.

Tuttle, Herbert. 1883. *History of Prussia*. Vol. 2. Boston: Houghton, Mifflin.

Uberman, Matan, and Shaul Shay. 2016. Hijrah According to the Islamic State: An Analysis of *Dabiq. Counter Terrorist Trends and Analysis* 8 (9): 16–20.

Usher, Mark. 2020. Territory Incognita. *Progress in Human Geography* 44 (6): 1019–1046.

Van Evera, Stephen. 1994. Hypotheses on Nationalism and War. *International Security* 18 (4): 5–39.

Van Houtum, Henk. 2005. The Geopolitics of Borders and Boundaries. *Geopolitics* 10 (4): 672–679.

Vasquez, John A. 1993. *The War Puzzle*. Cambridge: Cambridge University Press.

Vasquez, John A., and Marie T. Henehan. 2001a. Territorial Disputes and the Probability of War, 1816–1992. *Journal of Peace Research* 38 (2): 123–138.

Vasquez, John A., and Marie T. Henehan. 2001b. Peace, Globalization, and Territoriality. In *Territory, War, and Peace*, edited by John Vasquez and Marie T. Henehan, 195–205. London: Routledge.

Vaughan-Williams, Nick. 2009. *Border Politics: The Limits of Sovereign Power*. Edinburgh: Edinburgh University Press.

Veinstein, Gilles. 2013. The Great Turk and Europe. In *Europe and the Islamic World: A History*, edited by John Tolan, Henry Laurens, and Gilles Veinstein, 111–253. Princeton, NJ: Princeton University Press.

Vitalis, Robert. 2016. *White World Order, Black Power Politics*. Ithaca, NY: Cornell University Press.

Vollaard, Hans. 2009. The Logic of Political Territoriality. *Geopolitics* 14 (4): 687–706.

Von Hagen, Mark. 1995. Does Ukraine Have a History? *Slavic Review* 54 (3): 658–673.

Walker, R. B. J. 1995. International Relations and the Possibility of the Political. In *International Political Theory Today*, edited by Ken Booth and Steve Smith, 306–327. Cambridge: Polity Press.

Walt, Stephen M. 1996. *Revolution and War*. Ithaca, NY: Cornell University Press.

Walt, Stephen, M. 2015. ISIS as Revolutionary State. *Foreign Affairs* 94 (6): 42–51.

Walter, Barbara F. 2006. Conclusion. In *Territoriality and Conflict in an Era of Globalization*, edited by Miles Kahler and Barbara F. Walter, 288–296. New York: Cambridge University Press.

Walter, Barbara F. 2009. Bargaining Failures and Civil War. *Annual Review of Political Science* 12: 243–261.

Waltz, Kenneth N. 1979. *Theory of International Politics*. Reading, MA: Addison-Wesley.

Warrick, Joby. 2015. *Black Flags: The Rise of ISIS*. New York: Anchor.

292 References

Wawro, Geoffrey. 2003. *The Franco-Prussian War: The German Conquest of France in 1870–1871*. Cambridge: Cambridge University Press.

Weber, Eugen. 1976. *Peasants into Frenchmen: The Modernization of Rural France, 1870–1914*. Stanford, CA: Stanford University Press.

Weinberg, Gerhard L. 1995, *World War II: Essays in Modern German and World History*. New York: Cambridge University Press, 1995.

Weiss, Michael, and Hassan, Hassan. 2015. *ISIS: Inside the Army of Terror*. New York: Regan Arts.

Wendt, Alexander. 1999. *Social Theory of International Politics*. Cambridge: Cambridge University Press.

Whelan, Anthony. 1994. Wilsonian Self-Determination and the Versailles Settlement. *International & Comparative Law Quarterly* 43 (1): 99–115.

White, George W. 2000. *Nationalism and Territory: Constructing Group Identity in Southeastern Europe*. Lanham, MD: Rowman & Littlefield.

Whiteside, Craig. 2014a. War, Interrupted, Part I: The Roots of the Jihadist Resurgence in Iraq. *War on the Rocks*, November 5. https://warontherocks.com/2014/11/war-interrupted-part-i-the-roots-of-the-jihadist-resurgence-in-iraq/.

Whiteside, Craig. 2014b. War, Interrupted, Part II: From Prisoners to Rulers. *War on the Rocks*, November 6. https://warontherocks.com/2014/11/war-interrupted-part-ii-from-prisoners-to-rulers/.

Whiteside, Craig. 2016. The Islamic State and the Return of Revolutionary Warfare. *Small Wars & Insurgencies* 27 (5), 743–776.

Whiteside, Craig. 2017. A Pedigree of Terror: The Myth of the Ba'athist Influence in the Islamic State Movement. *Perspectives on Terrorism* 11 (3): 2–17.

Wiener, Antje, and Uwe Puetter. 2009. The Quality of Norms Is What Actors Make of It: Critical-Constructivist Research on Norms. *Journal of International Law and International Relations* 5 (1): 1–16.

Wilde, Ralph. 2010. *International Territorial Administration: How Trusteeship and the Civilizing Mission Never Went Away*. Oxford: Oxford University Press.

Williams, John. 2006. *The Ethics of Territorial Borders: Drawing Lines in the Shifting Sand*. New York: Springer.

Williams, Colin, and Anthony D. Smith. 1983. The National Construction of Social Space. *Progress in Geography* 7 (4): 502–518.

Wilson, Andrew. 2014. *Ukraine Crisis: What It Means for the West*. New Haven, CT: Yale University Press.

Wilson, Peter H. 1998. *German Armies: War and German Politics, 1648–1806*. London: UCL.

Wilson, Peter H. 1999. Warfare in the Old Regime 1648–1789. In *European Warfare, 1453–1815*, edited by Jeremy Black, 69–95. London: Palgrave, London, 1999.

Wilson, Peter H. 2011. *The Thirty Years War: Europe's Tragedy*. Cambridge, MA: Harvard University Press.

Wimmer, Andreas. 2008. The Making and Unmaking of Ethnic Boundaries: A Multilevel Process Theory. *American Journal of Sociology* 113 (4): 970–1022.

Wimmer, Andreas. 2012. *Waves of War: Nationalism, State Formation, and Ethnic Exclusion in the Modern World*. New York: Cambridge University Press.

Winichakul, Thongchai. 1994. *Siam Mapped: A History of the Geo-body of a Nation*. Honolulu: University of Hawaii Press.

Wolf, John B. 1951. *The Emergence of the Great Powers, 1685–1715*. New York: Harper and Brothers.

Wolf, John B. 1968. *Louis XIV*. New York: Norton.

Wood, Anthony. [1964] 1984. *Europe, 1815–1960*. Boston: Addison-Wesley Longman.

Wood, Graeme. 2016. *The Way of the Strangers: Encounters with the Islamic State*. New York: Random House.

Woodward, Ernest L. 1963. *War and Peace in Europe 1815–1870*. East Sussex, UK: Psychology Press.

Woody, Christopher. 2017. US Special Operations Command Chief Claims "60,000 to 70,000" ISIS Fighters Have Been Killed. *Insider*, July 24. https://www.businessinsider.com/gen-raym ond-thomas-socom-60000-to-70000-isis-fighters-killed-2017-7.

Wright, Thorin M., and Paul F. Diehl. 2016. Unpacking Territorial Disputes: Domestic Political Influences and War. *Journal of Conflict Resolution* 60 (4): 645–669.

Yiftachel, Oren. 2002. Territory as the Kernel of the Nation: Space, Time and Nationalism in Israel/Palestine. *Geopolitics* 7 (2): 215–248.

Yılmaz, Samet. 2018. Human Territoriality: A Spatial Control Strategy. *Alternatif Politika* 10 (2): 131–155.

Yurdusev, A. Nuri. 2004. Introduction. In *Ottoman Diplomacy: Conventional or Unconventional*, edited by A. Nuri Yurdusev, 5–35. New York: Palgrave Macmillan.

Zacher, Mark W. 2001. The Territorial Integrity Norm: International Boundaries and the Use of Force. *International Organization* 55 (2): 215–250.

Zarakol, Ayse. 2017. Theorising Hierarchies: An Introduction. In *Hierarchies in World Politics*, edited by Ayse Zarakol, 1–14. Cambridge: Cambridge University Press.

Zelin, Aaron Y. 2016. The Islamic State's Territorial Methodology. *Washington Institute for Near East Policy Research Notes* 29: 1–24.

Zhang, Yongjin. 2001. System, Empire and State in Chinese International Relations. *Review of International Studies* 27 (5): 43–63.

Ziblatt, Daniel. 2006. *Structuring the State: The Formation of Italy and Germany and the Puzzle of Federalism*. Princeton, NJ: Princeton University Press.

Zubaida, Sami. 2002. The Fragments Imagine the Nation: The Case of Iraq. *International Journal of Middle East Studies* 34 (2): 205–215.

Zubok, Vladislav M. 2008. *A Failed Empire: The Soviet Union in the Cold War from Stalin to Gorbachev*. Chapel Hill: University of North Carolina Press.

Zvobgo, Kelebogile, and Meredith Loken. 2020. Why Race Matters in International Relations. *Foreign Policy* 237: 11–13.

Index

For the benefit of digital users, indexed terms that span two pages (e.g., 52–53) may, on occasion, appear on only one of those pages.

abduction, 38–39
Adalet ve Kalkınma Partisi (AKP), 18–19
Adolphus, Gustavus, 186
Afghanistan, 130, 239
Agamben, Giorgio, 137
Agnew, John, 36, 40–41, 232, 233, 250–51
Ahram, Ariel, 237
al-Awlaki, Anwar, 119–20
al-Baghdadi, Abu Bakr, 161, 165
Allied powers, 9, 15–16, 60–61, 218
al-Qaeda, 164
Al Qaeda in Iraq (AQI), 160–61
Alsace-Lorraine, 101, 102–3
Alternative für Deutschland (AfD), 10
al-Zarqawi, Abu Musab, 160–61
amorphous territorial orders
    defined, 14
    demarcation and, 126
    introduction to, 108–10
    Ottoman Empire, 109–10, 114–25
    overview of, 110–13
    sociospatial organization and, 109, 113, 127–34
    summary of, 139, 230
    territorial trap and, 39–40
    war and, 52, 56–57
Anderson, Malcolm, 24–25
Anthropomorphization 96, 204
asabiyyah, 165, 169
Ashley, Richard, 31
Asia Minor, 11–13, 15–16, 114, 115, 116, 123, 210–11
aspirational territorial models, 8, 14, 63–64, 175–76, 179, 217–18, 229
asylum seekers, 1–2
Ataturk, Mustafa Kemal, 1, 15, 16
Atzili, Boaz, 31–32
Austria-German unification, 206–7

Awakening campaign, 167

Bakar, Shuvo, 71–72
banal nationalism, 59–60, 98
Bangladesh, 223
Barkawi, Tarak, 36–37, 134, 261–62
Barkey, Karen, 117
Battle of Leipzig (1813), 5–6
Battle of Sedan (1870), 101–2
Battle of Verdun (1916), 104
Battle of Warsaw (1656), 87–88
bayah (pledge of allegiance), 169
Bayly, Christopher, 132
Bentham, Jeremy, 108
Billig, Michael, 59–60
Bismarck, Otto von, 101
Black, Jeremy, 75
Blizhneye Zarubezhye (near abroad), 246–47
Bohemian Revolt (1618), 185
Bolívar, Simón, 197–98
Bonaparte, Napoleon, 79, 155–58. *See also* Napoleonic Wars
border fixity, 31–32, 106, 216–18, 224–26, 234–35, 236–37, 243
Borrell, Josep, 256
Branch, Jordan, 31–32, 59, 190
Brecke, Peter, 71–73
Brissot, Jacques Pierre, 150
British colonialism, 109–10, 125–38, 218
British Foreign Office, 211
British imperialism, 128–29
Buzan, Barry, 38, 111–12, 127, 128, 143–44, 214–15
Buzas, Zoltan, 255

Calvinism, 185
Carter, David, 30
Castellino, Joshua, 224
Cataclysm (Stevenson), 103

296 Index

Catholic Church, 180, 181–86
Cederman, Lars-Erik, 71–72
Central Asia, 12, 115
Central Territorial Committee, 204–5
Ceres, 257–61
Charter of Paris (1990), 224
China, 111–12, 210
Christianity, 4, 12–13. *See also*
    Catholic Church
Churchill, Winston, 221
civilian victimization, 7, 53–54, 55, 57, 71,
    109, 216
Clausewitz, Carl von, 76, 149, 191
Cold War, 9–10, 23–24, 26–27, 57, 219–20,
    221, 224, 238–39, 249–51
collective reterritorialization, 61
colonial hegemony, 177–78
confessional absolutism, 185
Confino, Alon, 99
Congress of Angostura, 197
Congress of Vienna (1814-15), 191, 202, 216
Congress System, 195
constructivist approach to territorial conflict,
    26–27, 31–33, 34–35, 41, 42, 62, 232–34
Cooper, Randolf, 135
Correlates of War (COW), 70, 71–73
Crimea, 243, 249–50, 251
Crimean War (1854-56), 195
critical geopolitics, 33
critical International Relations (IR), 31, 33
Cunningham, Kathleen, 219–20

dar al-harb, 163–64
dar al-Islam, 118–19
dar al-sulh, 121, 165
Darwin, John, 126, 134–35
Declaration of Rights of Man and
    Citizen, 147–48
decolonization, 215–27
demarcation
    amorphous territoriality, 126
    defined, 45–47, 50–52
    fluid frontiers and, 111–12, 140–41, 145–
        46, 162–63
    monolithic orders and, 59–60, 96–97, 106–
        7, 138–39, 235
    mosaic territoriality and, 180–81
    postwar settlement efforts and, 58
    religion-based sociospatial
        homogenization, 187
    reterritorialization and, 44–46, 166

self-determination and, 105
sociospatial organization and, 115–18,
    127–34, 146–49, 152, 155–56, 163–
    65, 183
systemic wars and, 25–26
territorial orders and, 30, 31, 32–33,
    64, 229–30
twenty-first century territoriality, 229
virulent territorial orders, 163–65
Dhondt, Frederick, 84–85
Diehl, Paul, 30
dual territoriality, 53, 125, 127, 220, 245
Durand Line, 130–31
Dutch War (1672-78), 78, 80–81
Dwyer, Philip G., 86–87

East India Company, 126–27, 131, 135–36
Eckstein, Harry, 39
Edict of Fraternity (1792), 153
Edict of Restitution (1629), 185–86
Elden, Stuart, 35
Eley, Geoff, 99
end of territory thesis, 243–44
endogenous territorialization, 45
Erdoğan, Recep Tayyip, 18, 19–20
ethnocentrism, 128–29, 177, 254–62
Eurocentrism, 10–11, 37, 48–49, 261–62
European state system, 93–100
European Union (EU) 2, 45, 256
exogenous territorialization, 44

Fazal, Tanisha, 31–32
Federal Republic of Germany (FRG), 9–10
Fichte, Johann Gottlieb, 151–52
First Silesian War (1740-42), 90
fixed borders, 6, 51–52, 53, 112, 127–28,
    144–46
Flint, Colin, 175
fluid frontiers
    demarcation and, 111–12, 140–41, 145–
        46, 162–63
    Ottoman Empire and, 119–20
    virulent territorial orders and, 109, 140–
        42, 149, 162
    war and, 50, 52–53
Flyvbjerg, Bent, 39
Foucault, Michael, 59–60
France, 78–86, 101–6
Franco-Prussian War (1870-71), 6, 101–2
Frederick II (Frederick the Great), 87, 88–92
Frederick the Great, 5

Free Syrian Army, 168–69
French Revolution (1789)
  introduction to, 5
  mosaic territoriality and, 67–86
  nationalism and, 94–96, 99
  rigid borders and, 67–86
  as systemic war, 190–98
  virulent territorial orders and, 145–58

Gallipoli Campaign (1915-16), 16
Gambetta, Leon, 102
geographical cleansing, 169
geographical racism, 210–11, 256, 262
geopolitics of jihad, 118–19, 121, 129, 164–65
geopolitik, 8, 60–61, 143
George, Lloyd, 209
German Democratic Republic, 9
German Empire, 6–8
Germany
  actions during World War II, 1–2
  Austria-German unification, 206–7
  Christianity and, 4
  Heimat tradition, 100
  monolithic territoriality, 6, 7–8, 101–6
  nationalism and, 5–6, 99–100, 207
  nation-building, 6
  Nazi Germany, 1–2, 8–9, 52–53, 106, 140–41, 149
  reterritorialization, 60–61
  territorial orders, 1–11
  territorial structure of, 3–5
  World War II and, 1–2, 8–9, 215–27
  Gerwarth, Robert, 207–8, 212
Geyer, Michael, 143
ghaza (ghazi warfare), 122–23
Giddens, Anthony, 59–60
Gilpin, Robert, 227
Global North, 177, 211, 224
Global South, 177, 208, 211, 214–15, 217–18, 224, 257
globalization, 6–7, 23–24, 67–69, 243–44, 250–51
Goddard, Stacie, 31–32
Goemans, Hein, 30
Goethe, Johann Wolfgang von, 1, 5
Goettlich, Kerry, 31–32
Grand Duchy of Warsaw, 156
gray zones (ISIS), 119, 121
Great Wall of China, 111–12
Greenfeld, Liah, 94
Gross, Leo, 179

Hakli, Jouni, 97
Hassner, Ron, 31–32
hegira, 119–20, 168–69
Heimat tradition, 100
Helsinki Final Act (1975), 224
Herb, Guntram, 100, 143
Herero Wars (1904-8), 8
Hitler, Adolf, 8, 105
Hobsbawm, Eric, 150, 156–57
Hobson, John, 255–56
Hohenzollern, Albert von, 86
Holsti, Kalevi, 144–45
Holy Roman Empire, 52–53, 86, 143, 179–98
House of Hohenzollern, 73, 86
House of Osman, 12–13
Howard, Michael, 102, 104
Hughes, Judith, 76–77
Hull, Isabel, 134
human territoriality, 27–28
Hutchinson, John, 38
Huth, Paul, 30
hybrid warfare, 53, 109, 123, 243

Ikenberry, John, 227
Imperial Conference (1921), 209
İnalcık, Halil, 122–23
India (colonial), 126–27
indivisible territory, 31–32
institutionalized racism, 177–78
international relations (IR), 20, 23, 229–34. *See also* territorial conflict in international relations
International Territorial Administrations (ITAs), 210–11
interstate conflict, 30, 31–32, 138, 243–44
intrastate conflict, 31–32, 138, 216, 234–35, 237–38
inviolable homeland, 7, 51–52, 56, 91, 98, 103, 105–6, 223, 236–37, 244, 250–51, 253
Iran-Iraq War, 160
Iraq, 239
Islamic empire, 12, 14, 16–17, 116, 162–63
Islamic State (ISIS), 20, 23–24, 39–40, 141–42, 158–70

Jackson, Robert, 226–27
Jacques, Tony, 71–72
Jallianwala Bagh Massacre (1919), 209
Jama'at at-Tawhid wa Jihad, 160–61

298 Index

Japan, 216
Jennings, Ivor, 204
Journal of Race Development, 254–55
jus sanguinis, 10
jus soli, 10

Kafadar, Cemal, 115
Kagan, Donald, 103
kanun (traditional law), 117
Keene, Edward, 129, 189
Keiger, John, 102
Khomeini, Ayatollah, 140
Kolsky, Elizabeth, 136
Korzybski, Alfred, 108
Krasner, Stephen, 67–68
Kratochwil, Friedrich, 25n.14, 31, 32
Krishna, Sankaran, 254
Kurdish Workers' Party (PKK), 17–18

Lake, David, 62
Lakins, Jeremy, 31–32
Lansing, Robert, 204
Latin America, 196–98
lawfare, 138
Lawson, George, 30–31, 38, 111–12, 127, 128, 143–44, 214–15
League of Nations, 201, 209, 217
League of Nations Covenant, 209
legalized hegemony, 226
Levy, Jack, 70–71, 72–73, 149
Loken, Meredith, 254–55
Longo, Matthew, 111–12
longue durée perspective, 37, 38, 40–41, 58–59, 178
Louis XIV, King, 78–86
Luard, Evan, 76
Lustick, Ian, 31–32
Luther, Martin, 4
Luxemburg, Rosa, 128–29
Lynn, John, 78–79

Macaulay, Thomas, 108
Maginot Line, 76–77
Maji Maji Rebellion (1905-7), 8
Malešević, Siniša, 128–29, 200, 229
Manela, Erez, 207–8, 212, 214–15
Mann, Michael, 59–60
Marx, Anthony, 94
materialistic perspective on territory, 29–31
Mayall, James, 96
Mayer, Arno, 147–48, 152

Mazarin, Jules, 78
Mearsheimer, John, 240–41, 244
Merkel, Angela, 1, 10
Metternich, Klemens von, 194
Michael, Bernardo, 131–32
Mill, John Stuart, 108
Miller, Charles, 71–72
mission civilisatrice, 108
Monaco, 62
monolithic territorial order
    defined, 6–8, 175–76
    demarcation and, 59–60, 96–97, 106–7, 138–39, 235
    France, 101–6
    Germany, 6, 7–8, 101–6
    nationalism and, 67–94, 201–2
    self-determination principle, 208–9
    summary of, 106–7
    war and, 51–52, 54–55, 56, 59–60, 230
Morocco, 62
mosaic territorial order
    defined, 4–5
    demarcation and, 180–81
    French Revolution, 67–86
    nationalism and, 67–94
    Prussia and, 5–6, 86–94
    summary of, 106–7
    war and, 51–52, 54–56, 67–94
Motyl, Alexander, 245
Mueller, John, 58–59
Murphy, Alexander, 96–97, 235
Muslim Brotherhood, 19–20
Muslim territoriality, 119–20, 168
Mutiny of 1857-58, 133
mythmoetour, 60–61

Napoleonic Code, 157
Napoleonic Wars (1792-1815), 5, 40, 145–58, 190–98
national identity, 6, 112, 226, 239–40, 246–47, 249, 250
nationalism
    amorphous territorial orders, 128
    banal nationalism, 59–60, 98
    defined, 214–15
    French Revolution and, 94–96, 99
    Germany and, 5–6, 99–100, 207
    independence movements, 197
    monolithic territorial order, 67–94, 201–2
    mosaic territorial order, 67–94

Ottoman Empire and, 14–15
populist nationalism, 199–200
prenationalism, 68–69, 97, 143–44, 145–46
Prussia and, 5–6, 199–200
radical movements and, 192
rise of, 93–100, 127, 140
territorial conflict in international relations, 27–28
World War I and, 199–215
nation-building, 6, 125–26, 239, 240–41
nationhood, 10, 151–52, 209, 213, 214, 217–18, 223, 236–37, 250, 251
Nazi Germany, 1–2, 8–9, 52–53, 106, 140–41, 149
Neal, Larry, 85–86
Nicolson, Harold, 205–6
Nine Years War (1688-97), 78, 82–83

O'Dowd, Liam, 97, 218
Organization of African Unity, 224
organized violence, 37, 48, 234–42
Osiander, Andreas, 67–68, 194, 203, 204
Ottoman Empire
    amorphous territorial orders, 109–10, 114–25, 230
    geopolitics of jihad, 118–19, 121, 129, 164–65
    ghaza (ghazi warfare), 122–23
    nationalism and, 14–15
    territorial expansion, 14–15
    Turkey and, 11–14, 17
Owen, John, 238–39

Paasi, Anssi, 188
Pakistan, 138, 223
pan-Arab movements, 198
Paris Peace Conference, 202–3, 207, 216
Peace of Augsburg, 183–84, 188
Peace of Nygemen, 81–82
Peace of Ryswick, 83
Peace of Utrecht (1713-15), 84–85, 176
Peace of Westphalia (1648), 4, 58–59, 68–69, 77–78, 145, 178, 179–90, 230
Penrose, Jan, 45–46
people's wars, 4, 191
Philpott, Daniel, 180
physical geography, 2–3, 28–29
Pitt's India Act (1784), 126–27
plausibility probes, 39
Polasky, Janet, 147–48

political authority, 25, 44, 49–50, 52, 58–59, 67, 101–2, 117, 124, 126–27, 183, 185, 187, 191, 193–94, 223
political geography, 25, 230–34
Pomeranz, Kenneth, 261
populist nationalism, 199–200
prenationalism, 68–69, 97, 143–44, 145–46
Protestantism, 180, 182, 185, 186–87
Prussia
    Franco-Prussian War, 6, 101–2
    mosaic territoriality and, 5–6, 86–94
    nationalism and, 5–6, 99, 199–200
    rigid borders and, 86–94
punctuated equilibrium, 63
Putin, Vladimir, 243, 246, 248, 251, 253

racism, 16–17, 20, 42, 177, 211, 254–62
radical homogenization, 8–9
radical reterritorialization, 53–54, 56, 109, 114–15, 154, 185, 186, 191, 217
redrawing borders, 233–34, 235
Reformation, 4, 58–59
Reign of Terror (1793-94), 147
religious toleration, 187
Renan, Ernest, 246–47
republicanism, 5, 146–47, 150–51, 193
Republic of Turkey, 16
resource generator, 29–30
reterritorialization
    collective reterritorialization, 61
    defined, 44–45
    demarcation and, 44–46, 166
    Germany, 60–61
    radical reterritorialization, 53–54, 56, 109, 114–15, 154, 185, 186, 191, 217
    of sociospatial organization, 45–46, 53–54
    Soviet Union, 60–61
    territorial orders and, 43–46, 49, 53–54, 56–57, 60–62
    war and, 60–62
Rieber, Alfred, 178
rigid borders
    French Revolution, 67–86
    introduction to, 67–86
    Prussia and, 86–94
    war and, 52, 59–60
    Westphalian territoriality, 67–69
Ringmar, Erik, 108–9
Ruggie, John Gerard, 23, 31, 32, 262
Russia, 103–4, 243–53
Russian Geographical Society, 246

300 Index

Russkii Mir idea, 246–49
Russo-Ukrainian War, 20, 23–24, 243–54

Sack, Robert, 44
Said, Edward, 43
Salafism, 169
Sawyer, Katherine, 219–20
Schiller, Friedrich, 1
Schmidt, Sebastian, 67–68
Schulz, Kenneth, 30
Scott, James, 59–60
seccesionist movements, 235–36, 237
Second Northern War (1655-60), 87–88
Second Silesian War (1744-45), 90
security dilemma, 56, 149–50
self-determination principle, 201–2, 203,
    206–7, 208–9, 211–13, 216–18, 222,
    225–26, 255
Seljuk dynasty (1037-1194), 12–13
Seven Years' War (1756-63), 85–86, 90–91, 176
Sewell, William, 141, 146–47, 148
Sharia rule, 168
Silesia, 89
Simmons, Beth, 30
Simpson, Gerry, 226
small wars, 48–49, 126
Snyder, Jack, 147
social Darwinism, 8, 129, 130, 218
societal heterogeneity, 13–14, 110–11
sociospatial heterogeneity, 4, 131, 132–33,
    138, 249
sociospatial homogenization, 4, 97–98, 113,
    132, 149, 153, 155, 157, 183–84, 185,
    187, 188, 192, 199, 236–37
sociospatial organization
    amorphous territorial orders, 109,
        113, 127–34
    demarcation and, 115–18, 127–34, 146–
        49, 152, 155–56, 163–65, 183
    reterritorialization of, 45–46, 53–54
    systemic wars and, 181
    twenty-first century territoriality, 229
    virulent territorial orders, 109, 146–
        49, 163–65
    war and, 59–60
Sornette, Didier, 71–72
Soviet Union 218–19, 243
Soviet Union reterritorialization, 60–61
space-society-politics nexus, 2–3, 36, 109,
    124–25, 190
spatial portability, 115

spatial specificity, 163–64
Spruyt, Hendrik, 63, 222
Stevenson, David, 103
subliminal Eurocentrism, 255–57, 261
Sunni Muslims, 116, 169–70
Sun Tzu, 263
Sykes-Picot borders, 163–64
Syrian Civil War, 23–24
systemic wars
    defined, 58, 60
    demarcation and, 25–26
    French Revolution, 190–98
    impact on, 26
    introduction to, 175–78
    Napoleonic Wars, 190–98
    self-determination principle, 201–2,
        203, 206–7, 208–9, 211, 216–18,
        222, 225–26
    sociospatial organization and, 181
    territorial orders and, 58, 60, 63–64
    Thirty Years' War (1618-48), 179–90
    World War I, 199–215
    World War II, 215–27

Taliban, 164
Tallett, Frank, 78–79
Tanzimat Fermani (1839), 124–25, 126
Taylor, A. J. P., 204–5
Taylor, Peter, 96
terra nullius, 129–30
territorial abnormalities, 155–56, 158
territorial administration, 148–49, 210
territorial asymmetry, 62
territorial balance, 84–85, 92–93, 191–92
territorial conflict in international relations
    constructivist approach to, 26–27, 31–33,
        34–35, 41, 42, 62, 232–34
    contributions to, 41–42
    interdisciplinary approach, 26–37
    introduction to, 23–26
    research methodology, 38–41
territorial conquest, 23–24, 29, 54–55, 80,
    90–91, 118–19, 126, 167, 182, 224–26,
    229, 234–35
territorial deterrence, 55, 56
territorial equilibrium, 62
territorial expansion, 14–15, 103,
    118, 142–45
territorial fear, 69, 101, 103
territorial hierarchy, 62, 63–64, 129, 177–78,
    208, 217–18, 221, 224

Index   301

territorial integrity, 31–32, 54–56, 76–77, 89–90, 106, 224, 243–44, 249, 252
territoriality, defined, 44
territorialization, defined, 44
territorial hypocrisy, 125–26, 127, 208, 209, 221
territorial opportunism, 56, 69, 82–83, 103–4
territorial orders. *See also* amorphous territorial orders; monolithic territorial order; mosaic territorial order; virulent territorial orders
    concepts of, 44–49
    defined, 25–26
    demarcation and, 30, 31, 32–33, 64, 229–30
    framework of, 49–53
    Germany and, 1–11
    origins of, 57–64
    reterritorialization and, 43–46, 49, 53–54, 56–57, 60–62
    summary of, 234–42
    systemic wars and, 58, 60, 63–64
    Turkey and, 11–20
    war and, 43–44, 53–57
territorial peace, 48–49
territorial revanchism, 101, 104–5, 204–6, 207
territorial sovereignty, 23, 50, 52, 57–58, 59, 67, 68–69, 180, 187
territorial trap, 35–37, 39–40, 234–42
territory-as-canvas, 228
Teschke, Benno, 67–68, 74–75
Third Punic War (143 BC), 44–45
Thirty Years' War (1618-48), 4, 60, 71, 179–90
Tilly, Charles, 75, 110–11, 113, 175
Toft, Monica, 31–32
Treaty of Aix-la-Chapelle (1668), 80
Treaty of Aix-la-Chapelle (1748), 90
Treaty of Pyrenees, 77–78
Treaty of Versailles, 202
Turkey, 11–20
Turkish War of Independence (1919-23), 15–16, 18
twenty-first century territoriality
    demarcation and, 229
    ethnocentrism and racism, 254–62
    introduction to, 229–30
    organized violence, 234–42
    political geography, 230–34

Ukraine, 20, 23–24, 243–54

UN Charter, 220
universalizing empires, 52–53, 143
uti possidetis, 196–97, 217–18, 224–27

Vasquez, John, 27, 30
Vauban, Marquis de, 76–77
Vietnam, 221
virulent territorial orders
    armed conflict and, 166–70
    defined, 8–9
    demarcation, 163–65
    fluid frontiers and, 109, 140–42, 149, 162
    French Revolution and, 145–58
    introduction to, 39–40, 108–10
    ISIS and, 158–70
    Napoleonic Wars and, 145–58
    overview of, 142–45
    sociospatial organization and, 109, 146–49, 163–65
    summary of, 170–71, 230
    war and, 52–53, 56–57
Vitalis, Robert, 254–55
Von Hagen, Mark, 249, 253–54

Waldseemüller, Martin, 3
Walker, R. B. J., 238
Walt, Stephen, 149–50
War of Devolution (1667-68), 78, 79–81
War of Spanish Succession (1701-14), 78, 83
War of the Austrian Succession (1740-48), 89
War of the Bavarian Succession (1778-79), 92
War of the First Coalition, 153–54
War of the Polish Succession (1733-35), 85–86
War of the Quadruple Alliance (1718-20), 85–86
War of the Reunions (1683-84), 78, 81–82
War of the Second Coalition, 154
War of Turkish Independence (1919-23), 60–61
The War Puzzle (Vasquez), 27
Warren, Camber, 71–72
Weber, Max, 46–47, 49–50
Western colonialism, 16–17, 221
Westphalian territoriality, 6–7, 54, 67–69, 108–9, 230, 236
William of Orange, 84
Wilson, Peter, 81
Wilson, Woodrow, 201–2, 204–5, 206
Wimmer, Andreas, 36–37, 140–41

302 Index

World War I
  Germany's actions during, 7
  monolithic territoriality, 230
  origins of, 103–4, 106
  Ottoman Empire and, 13, 15–16
  as systemic war, 199–215
  territorial expansion and, 103
  Turkey and, 15–16
World War II
  Germany and, 1–2, 8–9, 215–27
  monolithic territoriality, 230
  origins of, 104–6

  as systemic war, 215–27
Wright, Thorin, 30

Yanukovych, Viktor, 243
YPG (People's Protection Units), 160

Zacher, Mark, 31–32
Zelensky, Volodymyr, 251
Zelin, Aaron, 168
zones of exception, 137
zones of insecurity, 167, 169
Zvobgo, Kelebogile, 254–55